After D-Day

The Art of War

Series Editor, Col. David Zabecki

After D-Day

Operation Cobra and the Normandy Breakout

James Jay Carafano

LYNNE
RIENNER
PUBLISHERS

BOULDER
LONDON

Published in the United States of America in 2000 by
Lynne Rienner Publishers, Inc.
1800 30th Street, Boulder, Colorado 80301
www.rienner.com

and in the United Kingdom by
Lynne Rienner Publishers, Inc.
3 Henrietta Street, Covent Garden, London WC2E 8LU

ISBN 1-55587-885-7

Printed and bound in the United States of America

*For Charles Carafano, Frank Cervellera, and B. L. Schulz —
American veterans*

Contents

Figures

Think you these places would satisfy an Alexander, Caesar, or a Napoleon? Never! Towering genius disdains a beaten path. It seeks a region hitherto unexplored.

—*Abraham Lincoln*

Prologue:
The Beaten Path

I n July 1944 Allied and Axis forces were battling each other on six fronts that spanned three continents and two oceans. Newspapers in the United States tended to follow the front that showed the most success for the Allies, but whatever news came from Normandy immediately dominated the morning headlines.[1] What was going on there, and what was happening to America's sons, husbands, and fathers? The concern at home was not just because so many U.S. soldiers were fighting in France, it was that their slow progress seemed so out of synch with the rest of the war. Other places in the world it seemed that the Allies were making steady, certain advances. Despite the 1 million Allied soldiers plus more than 150,000 vehicles and a half-million tons of supplies pouring onto the shores of France, the gains in Normandy seemed agonizingly slow. After successfully storming the beaches on 6 June 1944, Allied forces were to be bogged down in 7 weeks of grueling attrition warfare that was often fought within sight of the Normandy coast.

Finally, during Operation Cobra six divisions of the U.S. VII Corps broke the stalemate on the Western Front. In the 6 dramatic days of 25–30 July, these divisions were to clear a path into occupied France, precipitating the collapse of the Nazi defenses in the west, the liberation of Paris, and the invasion of Germany.

Operation Cobra proved to be one of the most climactic operations of World War II; yet, ironically, it is also one of the least remembered. The Normandy D-Day invasion has assumed almost mythic proportions in U.S. military history, generating volume after volume of research and study, but Cobra has never been the dedicated subject of a major work.

The irony is even more curious, considering the continuing controversies over the performance of the U.S. Army in Normandy, at both the tactical and operational level. A half-century later, and the same questions are asked again and again. Could soldiers fight? Could generals lead? These questions are argued as passionately today as they were by GIs and

1

Germans in the foxholes of Normandy. Was the U.S. Army in World War II a clumsy, blunt instrument substituting brute force for tactical skill?

Questioning the skill of America's leaders and warriors raised a second irony as well. The legacy of World War I was to make commanders determined to avoid at all costs the grinding attrition warfare that decimated armies on the Western Front. General Omar N. Bradley, the senior U.S. officer in Normandy, spoke for all U.S. soldiers when he said, "I was determined that we must avoid at all costs those pitfalls that might bog down our advance and lead us into the trench warfare of World War I."[2] No one wanted to refight the last war, but that seemed to be exactly the fate of the Americans in Normandy.

On the other hand, World War II had showed that campaigns could be won by rapid, decisive battles. Germany's swift invasions overran Poland and Western Europe in 1939 and 1940. The British conducted a spectacularly successful offensive in North Africa in 1942, and the Russians were sweeping across the Eastern Front in 1944. Before Operation Cobra, however, the most powerful U.S. Army ever created scratched out meager gains at the cost of tremendous losses.

Then, in the greatest irony of all, that same U.S. Army during Operation Cobra was able to reach beyond the beaten path, the mindless battering against the enemy's Normandy defenses, and in less than a week unhinge the German's Western Front in a victory that all but preordained the liberation of France and the invasion of Germany. In this respect, the diminished place Cobra holds in the history of World War II and the lack of a dedicated study on the operation is even more remarkable.

Although there is a tremendous amount of scholarship on the Normandy campaign, surprisingly, no work has ever focused specifically on the Cobra breakthrough. For more than 30 years, Martin Blumenson's *Breakout and Pursuit* has been the standard work on this operation.[3] Blumenson's work considered Cobra as part of the U.S. maneuvers from shortly after D-Day through the drive into Brittany, to the liberation of Paris and onto Germany's front doorstep. Yet his book does not, could not tell the whole story of Operation Cobra.

Several concerns may have limited Blumenson's critique of Cobra, including avoiding controversy. Many senior World War II U.S. military leaders were still alive at the time of writing in the 1950s. Some were still on active service in very powerful positions.[4] In addition, at the time the British and the Americans were in the midst of a polite war over the legacy of the Normandy battles. Any criticisms of U.S. generalship would only favor the reputation of the British commander Field Marshal Bernard Law Montgomery. Montgomery had already gone to some lengths to paint his own command in Normandy as flawless. Any admission of errors on the part of senior U.S. commanders would only be another feather in the

British cap, an affirmation of Monty's claim that he had tutored the Americans through the whole campaign.

Now, over 50 years after the battles of Normandy, there is more than enough time and distance, as well as an abundance of evidence, to warrant a reconsideration of Operation Cobra. There is a vast amount of documentary evidence from both sides to draw on. At the end of the war, Americans confiscated official German army records and U.S. intelligence units interviewed many German officers, including most of the principal high-ranking commanders who fought during Operation Cobra. Many of the U.S. air and ground battle plans, intelligence reports, combat logs, and after-action reports were also preserved. Blumenson used much, but not all, of this material. In addition, veteran soldiers and airman have since added their personal contemporary letters and diaries and written articles and books about their experiences. There have been decades of scholarship and research on two continents since the publication of Blumenson's book to add to the reflections on the Normandy battles. I have drawn heavily on all this material.

The result of bringing together all these sources suggests we need a more critical judgment on the Americans' first major effort to move beyond the beaten path. No historian has gone back over all the ground covered by Blumenson and analyzed the operation step by step. As a result, over the years there have been many one-dimensional explanations offered for the American contribution to the victory in Normandy. Explanations tossed out by some historians, including the force of air power, special tactics, brute logistics, the inestimable heroism of citizen-soldiers, or the advantage of hedgerow-busting "rhino" tanks, are all simply myths. In fact, Operation Cobra reveals a mixed bag of ambiguous and complicated results. Cobra showed glimmers of genius and exhilarating achievement, but also marks of bumbling mediocrity, missed opportunities, and heartbreaking tragedy.

In detailing the credits and faults of the operation, my attention was particularly drawn to the relationship between the preponderance of power the Americans brought to the battlefield and their combat leadership. Despite the Allies' overwhelming superiority in Normandy, the U.S. Army had glaring shortcomings. At the same time, the army's unparalleled ability to protect and sustain itself gave leaders the chance to recover from their limitations and mistakes. With the advantages the Americans did have failures could be, and were, overcome by battlefield leadership. The U.S. commanders made the most of the opportunity, building "operational flexibility"—the ability to change the course of a campaign. This unique dimension of leadership is perhaps the most intriguing aspect of Operation Cobra.

Concerning the most senior U.S. commanders in the battle—the U.S. First Army commander, General Omar Bradley, the highly respected VII Corps commander, General "Lightning Joe" Collins, and General Clarence

Huebner, commander of the renowned "Big Red One" Infantry Division—a detailed critique of Operation Cobra reveals that the quality of their leadership was decidedly uneven. At the same time, careful study does much to reaffirm the steady performance of Generals Manton Eddy, Leland Hobbs, and Raymond Barton, whose infantry divisions spearheaded the breakthrough. Finally, this operation offers an opportunity to judge two of the army's premier trailblazing but untested armor commanders, Generals Edward Brooks and Leroy Watson.

The senior commanders in Operation Cobra showed flashes of brilliance, initiative, and determination, but also critical lapses in operational and tactical judgment that dulled the luster of an otherwise inspired plan. In particular, the planning for the tragic aerial carpet bombing that proceeded the attack and modifications to the Cobra plan made before and during the operation were seriously flawed. The cost of these mistakes can be fully measured in the results of the Cobra battles.

In addition, Cobra suggests that in the execution of the operation the most critical leaders on the battlefield were the combat command, regimental, and battalion commanders, the "field-grade" leaders. In comparison with the scholarship on generals and the soldiers who fought in World War II, the field-grade commanders are the forgotten leaders of the conflict. Yet they played a vital part in linking success at the operational level of war to victory in close-quarter tactical combat across Normandy's narrow tree-lined lanes and muddy foxholes.

Neglecting the role of field-grade leaders has skewed our understanding of the U.S. Army's performance in World War II. Their contributions has been overshadowed by the attention focused on senior leaders. The emphasis is misplaced. Army, corps, and division commanders were most important before the battle because they set the conditions of the engagement and allocated combat power for each attack, but once the fight was joined they largely faded into the background. In execution, it was the field-grade leaders—the combat command, regiment, and battalion commanders—who made the key, immediate decisions on how to use all the resources available. During the course of a day's engagement, they were the only commanders who had access to both the arms and the timely, relevant combat information needed to bring the army's weapons to bear at the critical time and place.

The field-grade commanders' pivotal role was essential to winning battles, though these men were certainly not the only important warriors on the battlefield. The primacy of field-grade leadership in battle did not diminish the importance of the contributions and sacrifices of junior leaders and soldiers. In combat, energetic and resourceful junior leaders—company commanders, lieutenants, sergeants, and even individual soldiers—often made a sudden and impossible gain of ground through skill and courage. But, without the coordinated support of the weapons and reserves controlled by combat command, regiment, and battalion commanders, there was no way individual units could exploit success or even hold what they had taken. Conversely, when a company failed to take its objective, it was the field-grade commanders who had the means to rapidly shift resources and change the course of combat.

The criticality of combat decisionmaking by field-grade leaders and their unique contribution to building operational flexibility emerges from the narrative that follows by tracing the critical points of Operation Cobra—the key actions and maneuvers that turned a war of attrition into a campaign of swift maneuver. These critical points are laid out in three parts. Part 1, The Universe of Battle, is a prerequisite for understanding Cobra. No battle occurs in a vacuum. There are factors that set the conditions for every fight, limiting what commanders could and could not do. The first chapters look at these factors. Chapter 1 sets the stage for the difficult operational task facing the First Army commander, Omar Bradley, while Chapter 2 outlines the strategic, operational, and tactical situation that placed Bradley in such difficult circumstances. Chapter 3 analyzes the tools he had to fight with, examining the available combat power, how the U.S. forces were organized, equipped, trained, protected, and sustained—with specific emphasis on the issues relevant to Cobra's successes and failures. Chapter 4 investigates the genesis of Bradley's scheme for putting all his combat power into action. In particular, this chapter looks at the critical tasks the key units in the operation had to accomplish. Together the chapters of Part 1 form the backdrop for the execution of Cobra.

Parts 2 and 3 follow chronologically the critical actions of the assault. Part 2, The Day of Infantry, covers the four crucial events of the operation's first day, the initial bombardment of the German lines, and the critical attacks by the three lead infantry divisions. Part 3, A Clash of Armor, analyzes the attacks of the three follow-on exploitation divisions that completed the assault. Proceeding systematically through the critical points of Cobra from the conception of the operation to the completion of the breakthrough demonstrates well the roots of the U.S. Army's operational flexibility.

Revisiting Normandy through the narrative of Operation Cobra is more than just a study in the execution of a major operation. It is also an opportunity to push back the tides of time. In 1994 we marked the 50th anniversary of the Normandy campaign. Many veterans of that most personal and terrible war returned to walk again over the ground on which they had fought. There are still plenty of them left, the brave and terrified young men who fought across Normandy. They are part of the almost 9 million living American World War II veterans. Their legacy is relevant to all of us, and the memory of what they did must not pass with them.

There is a particular danger of forgetting the combat leader's place in World War II. The recent emphasis on "new military history" has shifted the focus of historical research to many long-neglected issues such as race, gender, and institutional and social history. These subjects are important, but their study has tended to crowd out traditional research on battles and campaigns. This is unfortunate.[5] As valuable as these other subjects are, combat, the bloody, armed conflict between two determined enemies, remains the essential issue of warfare. The events of the post–Cold War world, where Americans have faced the decisions of putting U.S. soldiers deliberately in harm's way in the Persian Gulf, Haiti, Somalia, Bosnia, Korea, and Kosovo, are powerful reminders of how important it is to think long and deep about the responsibilities, burdens, and risks of armed combat. In this respect the World War II generation has many lessons to teach— and military history has the tools to make these lessons real and relevant to all of us.

July 1944 was a desperate time. Operation Cobra is the kind of story we need to reflect on when we consider the decisions that lead us to war. If this work demonstrates anything, it is to beware of those who offer simple answers to the question of why armies win and lose battles. Nothing is inevitable. Nothing is preordained.

This study of Operation Cobra would not have been possible without the mentoring, criticism, and insights of Ed Drea, Robert Doughty, Lewis Sorley, Jack English, Nigel De Lee, Michael Chilcott, John Shortal, William "Wild Bill" Odom, David Zabecki, Jack Mountcastle, Lee Baxter, John Dubia, Boyd Dastrup, Larry Kaplan, Dave Hogan, Pat Hollis, Dan Eades, Mark Sherry, Diane Schulz (my best friend), and Peter and Luke Carafano. Special thanks go to Darrell Green and Ed Stiles for their work on the maps and illustrations. Finally, I am indebted to the unmatched professionalism and expertise of the staffs of the several research libraries and archives I visited in the course of preparing this study.

Notes

1. A sample of front-page newspaper items illustrates what was being reported. On the India-Burma frontier the Japanese invasion of India had failed. The British counterattacked, and on 14 July the British forces under General Slim defeated the last organized enemy resistance. The remaining Japanese forces retreated back toward the Chindwin River. The *Baltimore Sun* estimated Japanese casualties at about 90,000. In the Southwest Pacific the Allies were also on the offensive. On 7 July General MacArthur's forces trapped 45,000 Nipponese in British New Guinea. That same day, in the Central Pacific theater 3,000 Japanese troops under Admiral Nagumo, hero of the attack on Pearl Harbor, hurled a banzai attack against U.S. Marines commanded by General "Howlin Mad" Smith. The attack failed. On the Eastern Front in Europe the Soviets launched a major offensive on 10 July: Marshal Zhukov's armies stormed toward Warsaw. The *New York Times* reported 7,000 Germans killed and 1,500 taken prisoner in a single day. By 18 July the Soviets stood only 80 miles from Rastenburg, Hitler's wartime forward head-

quarters. In Italy the Allied forces also made progress; a coalition of Allied armies continued to push north across the Italian peninsula, and the Allies streamed into liberated Rome. The papers showed pictures of the Fifth Army Commander, General Mark Clark, at the Coliseum and the Vatican.

2. Omar N. Bradley, *A Soldier's Story,* pp. 318–319.

3. *Breakout and Pursuit* was part of the U.S. Army's official history of World War II. These books, commonly called the "green books" because they were originally published with hardback green covers, were prepared under the direction of the Historical Division, War Department Special Staff (later renamed the U.S. Army's Center of Military History). Kent Roberts Greenfield, the army's chief historian, was the project's architect. Greenfield made an important contribution to World War II scholarship by setting high standards for the official histories. He insisted that the green book authors have complete academic freedom and open access to sources. Unlike with other government publications, the writers were also given authorship credit and assumed individual responsibility for their work. See Robert F. Coakley, "Reflections on Writing the Green Books," *Army History* (Summer 1993): 37–39. See also A. F. Clark Jr., "History Through a Thousand Eyes," *Army Information Digest* 6 (June 1947): 51–55; Stetson Conn, *Historical Work in the United States Army 1862–1954,* pp. 115–156.

4. General Bradley, the overall commander for Operation Cobra, for example, became the chairman of the Joint Chiefs of Staff, and General Collins, who led the breakthrough, became the army chief of staff.

5. Peter Paret, "The New Military History," *Parameters* (Autumn 1991): 10–18; Jay Luvaas, "Military History: Is It Still Practicable?" *Parameters* (Summer 1995): 82–97.

PART 1

The Universe of Battle: Summer 1944

1

The Darkening Sky

July 24, 1944, dawn.

A short drive by jeep on Normandy's narrow, rutted, country lanes separated General Omar N. Bradley's U.S. First Army headquarters at Haut Chemin and the U.S. front lines south of Pont-Hébert just a few miles away. It was not, however, an effortless trip. Ragged columns of marching soldiers and lines of trucks, tanks, howitzers, and antitank guns choked the roads, all getting ready for the biggest U.S. Army attack since D-Day. General Bradley planned to launch six divisions, about 70,000 men, 3,000 airplanes, over 600 hundred tanks, and 43 battalions of artillery, straight at the center of the Germans' Normandy defenses.

Amid the greatest single concentration of combat power in United States military history, Major Chester B. Hansen, General Bradley's personal aide-de-camp, a small entourage of generals, and staff officers from the U.S. First Army headquarters wended their way through the traffic heading for the front.[1] It was an anxious day for all of them, for the First Army, and for General Bradley. No one knew that better than Major Hansen. He had been with the general since the North African campaign over 2 years before. Hansen had watched Bradley become one of the most respected and dependable field commanders of the war, a master tactician, and a decisive leader. Bradley was called "the G.I.'s General," as competent and determined as the headline-grabbing General George S. Patton, but with a quiet and subdued style.

Wherever Bradley went, as he moved up from corps to army commander, he brought a select group of officers and enlisted aides. Hansen was part of a small, close, though sometimes fractious family. Of these loyal soldiers, none would stand by Bradley longer than this major. Counting the times during the war and after, Hansen served his general for 9 straight years. In all the days of faithful service, Major Hansen expected that 24 July 1944 would be one of the most unforgettable—and a great day for General Bradley. Hansen thought July 24 might well become remembered as the most important day of the Normandy campaign after U.S. forces had stormed Omaha and Utah Beaches.

At first, the Americans had believed that getting ashore would be the most difficult and harrowing moment of the Normandy campaign. With brutal Soviet offensives tying down the German army on the Eastern Front and British-U.S. forces holding the attention of more German troops in Italy, the promise of a swift advance in France seemed possible once the British, Canadian, and U.S. divisions reached the Norman coast. The enemy defenses in Normandy, however, had proved tougher than expected. The Canadians had tried to break them and failed, as had the British. Now, the Americans had an opportunity to fight and win the first great battle after the beachhead, a breakthrough on the Normandy battlefield—and it would be General Bradley's victory.

The U.S. forces were about to attempt something they had never done before: mass six divisions on a very small 5-mile front and head straight through the enemy lines to objectives well behind the German defenses, while three other U.S. corps conducted simultaneous supporting attacks. To clear the path for the initial advance, the Americans planned to lay down a massive barrage with artillery, fighters, and bombers, including the big planes used to level German cities. The entire firepower assault would take place in the space of a few hours within sight of the GIs waiting to jump off. General Bradley expected a lot from what he called the "big attack," predicting that the U.S. Army would demonstrate it had the skill and flexibility to change the course of the campaign.

Bradley's operation was not without risks. Saturation, or "carpet," bombing enemy positions in front of friendly troops had never worked satisfactorily before. The British had tried a similar effort, Operation Charnwood, just 3 weeks before: on 7 July 460 bombers savaged a little less than a 2.5-mile-wide strip outside Caen. This bombing was followed by a ground attack by a British corps of two British and one Canadian divisions backed by two armored brigades. The assault hardly dented the German lines.[2]

To make sure his operation succeeded, General Bradley planned to attack on a front about twice that of British General Bernard L. Montgomery's Charnwood attack, but with more than double the amount of ground troops, which would be backed by more than six times as many planes. In addition, he would bring the aerial attack in as close to the U.S. lines as he dared, about 1,200 yards—little more than one-sixth of the safety distance used in Charnwood. Bradley had good reason to push his troops up so close. The British had taken 6 hours to reach the front after their preparatory bombing. Bradley wanted his troops coming to grips with the enemy in a fraction of that time and exploiting the effects of the bombardment as quickly as possible.

Even if the carpet bombing worked to perfection and the ground forces broke through, success was not assured. Some of the attacking troops might well find themselves advancing with their flanks exposed and Germans behind them, facing the risk of being cut off and surrounded behind enemy lines. If the Americans did not break through, the divisions would stack up like frustrated commuters, grinding away at the front for days of brutal, head-to-head, attrition warfare.

There were risks to reputations as well. Several of the best known U.S. Army combat leaders would be at the head of the charge. Major General J. Lawton, "Lightning Joe," Collins commanded the VII U.S. Corps, the force that would have to carry the whole attack. The youthful-looking, energetic, and decisive Collins would have direct control over the divisions making the main effort. A veteran of the war in the Pacific at Guadalcanal and the liberator of Cherbourg, the first port the Allies had captured in France, General Collins was arguably the U.S. Army's best and most famous corps commander.

General Collins's command included the ground army's big punch, the massive 2d and 3d Armored Divisions. The 2d Armored Division under Major General Edward H. Brooks was a veteran outfit, while the 3d Armored commanded by Major General Leroy H. Watson was earning its first campaign ribbon. Each general was out to prove the potential of U.S. tank forces in armor's first big test in Normandy.

The other divisions fighting under the VII Corps were proven combat outfits. The 9th Infantry Division had its share of headlines from fighting in both France and North Africa. Its commander, Major General Manton Eddy, was regarded as a cautious but dependable leader. Also joining in the attack was the only division in the theater more famous than the 9th, the 1st Infantry Division—the "Big Red One." The Big Red One's untried commander, Major General Clarence Huebner, was still earning his reputation. He had been tapped to replace Major General Terry Allen, a controversial and flamboyant leader who had been relieved of command by Bradley. The other infantry divisions in the assault, the 30th and the 4th, also had fine combat records and well-respected commanders. The 30th was led by the fiery Major General Leland "Hollywood" Hobbs, and the 4th was commanded by the steady Major General Raymond O. Barton.

All together, the spearhead of the operation included some of the best troops and best respected commanders that could be mustered. Reputations, as well as the success of the campaign, would be on the line in this bold and risky venture.

No one's prestige was more at stake than that of General Bradley. As the head of the U.S. First Army and the senior U.S. field commander in Normandy, he was responsible overall for the operation. He had planned the attack, including the aerial assault proceeding the advance. It was his plan, and within a very few hours it would be known whether or not he had planned well.

While General Bradley headed off to meet with Collins at the VII

Corps headquarters for last-minute coordination, Bradley's aide Major Hansen joined the group of generals and staff going to the front. Hansen was going to get to see firsthand if the operation would become the big attack Bradley had hoped for.

The weather on 24 July 1944 hardly matched the historic nature of the day. A wet mist hugged the trees, while a drab, cloudy sky darkened the battlefield. Traveling on the roads, it was hard to gain an appreciation for the scale of the offensive. Where the mist and sky came together they formed a murky backdrop to the long lines of troops and trucks moving ahead and disappearing into a damp gray curtain. Even though he couldn't see them, Major Hansen knew that there were thousands of U.S. troops out there, waiting for the bombers to hit the enemy lines to signal the start of the operation.

Among the expectant was Lieutenant George Tuttle, the liaison officer from the 120th Infantry to a sister regiment in the division, the 119th Infantry. This morning Tuttle was back at the 120th's command post, coordinating for the upcoming operation. General Bradley had packed a lot of troops across a very narrow axis of advance, the largest corps ever assembled, moving into a gap of rugged Norman terrain only a few miles wide. The lieutenant's job was to help sort out his regiment's advance so that its soldiers would not be tripping over other units trying to reach the front. To the young lieutenant the scope of the operation seemed monumental, bigger than D-Day. It would be a hell of an attack, like nothing he had seen before.

High above the regimental command post, obscured by the blanket of clouds, the lead plane from a formation of B24s from the 846th Bomber Squadron, 9th Air Force, piloted by Lieutenant Ed Florcyk circled, waiting for the go-ahead. Spearheading a flight of bombers was a lot of responsibility for a young lieutenant who had once had a reputation as a "happy-go-lucky swinger." The war, however, had changed a lot of things. Days before shipping out to train for overseas duty, he had met and married a young woman at Mitchell Field, New York, and then left her behind to prepare for the war in Europe. Now he was over the Normandy front on his eleventh combat mission, part of a four-squadron maximum effort, forty-three aircraft, alongside the rest of the almost 1,500 bombers that composed half the aerial force.

Although the bomb run over Normandy was short in comparison with the time required for the targets deep in Germany, it still made for a draining, tense day that was not made any easier by the planes' constant noise and vibration. The crew was constantly on the lookout for enemy fighters, as well as warily eyeing nearby planes flying in their dense formation. (Collisions between friendly aircraft were not unheard of.) There were many ways to die flying 3 miles above the battlefield.

In addition, Lieutenant Florcyk knew that this run would be unusually difficult. The planes of his squadron would be bombing close to U.S.

troops, so the formation would have to fly low, 15,000 feet, and visually identify the aiming points. They would be going in after a wave of fighter-bombers flying even lower, striking even closer to the troops, and leaving a lot of smoke and fire below, which would make it harder to identify aiming points. The fighter-bombers, such as the American P-47, would also further crowd the skies over Normandy, making a tempting target for German anti-aircraft gunners below.

To make matters worse, when Florcyk's squadron reached the target area there was a complete undercast. The pilots called it "10/10th cloud." Florcyk could not see the ground through the white floor below him. When the formation did find a break, lines of tracers and billowing puffs of dark, flak-filled clouds from German antiaircraft fire raced to greet them. "Flak hitting the belly of the ship," a crewmember from one bomber recorded in his diary, "sounded like someone throwing gravel at us." The aircrews, however, knew what would happen if that "gravel" hit a vulnerable part of the plane, engine, hydraulics, or fuel line.

Below Florcyk's circling plane, not far from where Lieutenant Tuttle had reviewed the final plans for the big attack, Major Hansen and the rest of the First Army contingent reached the Americans' forward positions. They occupied a little stone house on a road heading southwest out of Pont-Hébert, a short distance behind the U.S. lines. In the modest building of white scrubbed fieldstone and weathered yellow brick, they found a suit-able spot to observe the bombing and then watch the first troops jump off; they could clearly see both the target area and the troops assembling for the attack. Scattered furniture, ripped curtains, and a gaping hole in the roof made the poor house a fitting setting to observe the devastation to come. Among the ruins the First Army staff watched and waited. The operation was set to kick off at 1 P.M. with the first fighter-bombers hitting their tar-gets about an hour before.

Shortly before noon, 6,000 feet above the battlefield, the first wave of fighter-bombers headed in the direction of Pont-Hébert, approaching in long column formations, flight after flight of aircraft. On order, the pilots dropped to the designated bomb release altitude of 2,000 feet and released their payloads. The operation was underway.

Major Hansen recorded the day's events in his war dairy. He had been near aerial bombardments before and understood the dangers of observing them close up. "Sighted any number of slit trenches and foxholes that we could occupy," he recalled. "I wanted to get away from the building and the danger of falling bricks."[3] His forethought proved to be a sound precaution. From the slit trench, he watched the first wave of fighter-bombers head for the road. "First four, then eight and they came along in sweeping fours until the sky was heavy with them. Peeled off in single file; sighted their targets and down they swooped in long glides."

Hansen could see the bombs falling from their racks and feel the shud-

der of the explosions. Suddenly, eight of the aircraft broke formation and
headed toward the U.S. lines. "One flight went off to the left of us," Hansen
recalled, "the other came straight for us and let their bombs go." He saw
one bomb hit an ammunition truck several hundred yards away, wounding
three soldiers. Fire and smoke all around them blurred the distinction
between enemy and friendly lines. For a few minutes the entire countryside
was an explosion of sound, shrapnel, and chaos.

Major Hansen was not the only American attacked by his own planes.
At 11:40 A.M. fighter-bombers struck the 197th Field Artillery near Les
Hauts-Vents. The 743d Tank Battalion was bombed in its rallying area
north of Hebecrevon, and bombs landed on the 30th Infantry Division
artillery headquarters, elements of the 230th Field Artillery Battalion, and
other units in the division area. Ten minutes later, a rain of bombs rolled
across two companies from the 120th Infantry Regiment. It was an unset-
tling and disturbing way to start the big attack. Many GIs had been standing out in the open, hoping to get a glimpse of the massive air strike, and
the bombing left a wake of casualties and confusion behind the U.S. lines.

The roar of the fighter-bombers was followed by silence. This first air
attack was only a prelude, designed to hit the enemy targets closest to the
U.S. positions. Soon the medium and heavy bombers would arrive to strike
the targets deeper in enemy territory. With the first phase of the bombing
over, there was nothing to do but wait for the bombers that according to the
predetermined schedule were 30 minutes out. In the meanwhile, the First
Army staff members found that the kitchen stove still worked and in short
order had brewed hot coffee to go with their K-ration lunch. They anxiously ate, sipped coffee, and checked their watches. Close by they could see
infantry moving toward the front. A short while later the sound of the
troops was gradually drowned out by the rising drone of bombers, and it
was time for the main event.

Overhead, the first bombers had already passed over the target without
finding a break in the clouds and turned back for the airfields in Great
Britain. Other formations circled the target area three times, searching for
an open spot of sky. Lieutenant Florcyk's formation dropped to 13,500 feet
before it located a gap in the cloud cover, and when the pilots finally found
a clear view of the rolling farmlands below, the space was quickly filled
with German antiaircraft fire. Flak struck Florcyk's plane, piercing the thin
aluminum skin covering the wing fuel cells above the bomb bays. The
plane immediately erupted in flames and then abruptly exploded. The blast
blew one crew member standing near an open bomb bay free of the aircraft,
and he managed to parachute safely—but Lieutenant Florcyk and the
remainder of his crew perished. This was one of three bombers shot down
during the attack. Fifty-six other planes were damaged by enemy flak.

Meanwhile, the cloud cover continued to disrupt the aerial bombardment. Three hundred fifty-two planes, making up far less than a third of the

number of heavy bombers planned for the attack, found a gap in the clouds and dropped their payloads. The last planes over the target area were still looking for open skies when they received a recall signal. Before the attack had been called off, however, the fleet had released 10,124 high-explosive bombs and 1,822 fragmentation bombs over the Normandy countryside.[4]

Of the bombs that were dropped, not all landed on the enemy. One bombardier startled by a packet of chaff striking the nose of the plane's turret accidentally hit the release switch and unloaded a devastating attack on a U.S. airstrip at Chippelle. Another bombardier inadvertently activated a stuck release mechanism and dropped part of his bomb load. A dozen planes, following the actions of the lead aircraft, dropped all their bombs. Some of the ordnance fell over 2,000 yards short of the target area, right on the forward U.S. positions.

At 12:40 P.M. a horrified Lieutenant Tuttle saw a wave of bombs land around his regimental command post. He watched as an exploding bomb cut down Lieutenant Tyron H. Cutter (a liaison officer from another regiment) standing only a few feet away. Amazingly, Tuttle escaped unhurt.

Between the attack on the command post and the two nearby infantry companies, the regiment reported 14 dead and 65 wounded. The adjacent 119th Infantry Regiment reported 5 killed and 28 injured. Total ground causalities from the short bombings in the division area and at the Chippelle airfield were 29 dead and 145 wounded GIs. In addition to the physical casualties, the combat effectiveness of the units hit by the "short" bombing seemed to disintegrate in an instant: some of the troops appeared stunned, unable to function, while others raced about putting out fires or tending and evacuating the wounded.

Making the scene around the 120th headquarters even more unreal, Lieutenant Tuttle observed regimental commander Colonel Hammond D. Birks conferring with Lieutenant General Lesley J. McNair. Tuttle knew that McNair had been the commander of the U.S. Army Ground Forces, the stateside headquarters responsible for training units for overseas duty. The young lieutenant hardly expected to find the three-star general standing at the front lines of Normandy in the middle of what was shaping up to be one of the biggest screwups of the campaign. It had been a remarkable day.

Meanwhile, not far away bombs continued to fall. Major Hansen felt that "the ground grunted and heaved as the first cascade of bombs came down, horrible noise and the shuddering thunder." A screaming whistle overshadowed the other noises. It was a sound he had heard before, in North Africa, and it was a sound he should not be hearing now—the sound of bombs falling close by. Everyone scattered for cover. Major Hansen saw "angry black spirals of dirt boil out of the ground," not 500 yards from where he had stood moments before. A few minutes later, ambulances were moving down the road and coming back filled with wounded. Something had gone terribly wrong. Before the first soldier had moved to attack,

Bradley's bold scheme to break through German defenses and hopes of changing the course of the campaign seemed to be in jeopardy.

Disaster in the opening moment of the most important operation that U.S. forces had conducted since D-Day was to culminate 7 frustrating, debilitating weeks of fighting in Normandy. Standing amid confusion and casualties, on the fragile edge of the U.S. forces' foothold in Europe, Major Hansen and the other survivors of the past few harrowing moments could reflect on the hardships, sacrifices, and difficult decisions that had brought them to the cusp of ending the difficulties of the Normandy campaign: only to face another setback before the big attack had even begun.

Notes

1. Among the senior commanders in Hansen's party were U.S. First Army deputy commander Lieutenant General Courtney Hodges, Major General Matthew Ridgway, and Major General Lewis Brereton.

2. Ian Gooderson, "Heavy and Medium Bombers: How Successful Were They in Tactical Close Air Support During World War II?" *The Journal of Strategic Studies* 15 (September 1992): 378.

3. The accounts of the bombing on 24 July are taken from Chester B. Hansen, War Diary, 24–25 July 1944, MHI; William C. Sylvan, War Diary, 24–25 July 1944, MHI; *History of the 120th Infantry Regiment,* pp. 34–35; *History of the 489th Bomber Group,* pp. 109–110; Roger A. Freeman, *The Mighty Eighth: Units, Men and Machines,* pp. 163–164; Headquarters, 30th Infantry Division, U.S. Army, After Action Report, 24 July 1944; Headquarters 30th Infantry Division Artillery, U.S. Army, After Action Report, 24 July 1944.

4. Accounts of the number of bombers that actually attacked vary. A report in the Strategic Bombing Survey puts the number at 317. See Walter E. Todd, Report of Investigation of Bombing July 24–25, Box 71, RG 243, NARA.

2

Living in Hell

It would be difficult to overstate the burden on General Bradley as the U.S. First Army Commander after long weeks of difficult campaigning. The frustrating, grueling pace of the war had dismayed the U.S. soldiers at the front. No matter how many men poured into the theater, there never seemed to be enough to overcome the German defenders. One conversation went like this:

"What the hell is holding us up?"

"A bunch of Krauts, you goon."

Somebody else said, "Not enough troops over here yet."

I said, "*S&S* [*Stars and Stripes* newspaper] says there are over a million now."

"Well, there you are. What are we waiting for?"

"Another million."[1]

For the troops who hoped for a swift campaign there was nothing but more frustration and disappointment. They seemed to be refighting the war of a previous generation. World War I soldiers had compared their life in the trenches to living in hell, and many GIs in Normandy had begun describe their existence in similar terms. The possibility that war could re-create the pace and tactics of the battlefields of 1917 was a fearsome and melancholy thought.

The attitude of the U.S. Army's most senior commander was not much more optimistic. When General Dwight Eisenhower, the Supreme Commander of the Allied Expeditionary Force (SCAEF), briefed reporters on the situation in Normandy, he warned them not to be too optimistic in their dispatches. "Fighting will be most strenuous and there will be heavy losses, he warned. The Allies will have to fight hard for every foot they gain."[2] Eisenhower cautioned the reporters against expecting dramatic breakthroughs from General Bradley's forces anytime soon. To the readers back home such talk could not have been more disheartening: Bradley seemed more like a general commanding soldiers in the trenches of World War I than this war's swiftly advancing liberator of Europe.

Senior army leaders, like General Bradley veterans of World War I, understood well the cost of winning battles through the meatgrinder of attrition warfare.[3] Bradley was not interested in refighting one blood-soaked engagement after another of the Great War. He wanted to conduct an operational war of fast-moving, dramatic campaigns and believed that the U.S. Army could be a flexible instrument. Rather than bludgeoning an opponent to death, U.S. forces, if used skillfully, could outmaneuver an enemy and change the course of a campaign. Despite his determination, however, it appeared that so far Bradley had condemned his young soldiers to fight on the battleground of their fathers.

Understanding the origins of General Bradley's plan to break through the German defenses begins with considering why two great armies came to fight at a specific point and time. Commanders never have complete freedom in picking the exact time, location, and conditions of battle. An order to charge the enemy lines stands last in a long line of decisions. In truth, Bradley had few options in selecting the moment or place for launching what he would come to call his "big attack." Why armies clash is determined by the interaction of the three levels of war—strategy, operations, and tactics. In concert the levels of war create the place in which all conflicts are fought. Overlaid one upon the other on the battlegrounds of Normandy, they formed the universe of battle, and where they touched became the genesis of Bradley's great offensive—his start point for planning how he would change the course of the Normandy campaign.

A Strategy for Victory

It all began with strategy, the highest level of war. Strategy comprises the ways, means, and ends that nations employ in the quest for victory. This is the realm of men and women who have the power to shatter continents—a country's civilian and military leaders—the ones who make the most basic decisions of when, where, how and why countries go to war.

The United States developed its strategy for World War II in concert with its British and Soviet allies. The great Allied war leaders—President Franklin Delano Roosevelt of the United States, Prime Minister Winston Churchill of Great Britain, and Chairman Josef Stalin of the Soviet Union—made the fundamental choices of how the Allies would achieve their strategic objectives. It was the task of political leaders to focus on the big picture, while their military chiefs of staff worked out the details of military strategy.

Although the Allies' strategic leaders had many differences, debates, and doubts, they did concur (at least in principle) on the central strategic decision governing the conduct of the war: "Defeat Germany first." [4] The leaders planned to first mass the coalition's forces against Germany and then turn and face Japan.

The Allies initially assigned priority to the defeat of Germany at the Arcadia Conference in Washington (22 December 1941 to 14 January 1942), but achieving this objective hardly followed a straight line. First, the Americans joined in the invasion of North Africa. At the Casablanca Conference (14–23 January 1943), the British and Americans decided to put off the assault on Western Europe. It was only at the Trident Conference in Washington (15–25 May 1943) that they agreed to a cross-Channel invasion in the spring of 1944. The strategy meandered, but in the end it committed the United States to fighting a major land battle at the gates of Western Europe. This decision started that nation on its course toward Bradley's big attack, the largest and boldest air-ground operation up to that point in the war.

Operations—The Key to the Campaign

The operational level of war provided the link between Allied strategy and battlefield tactics. At the operational level commanders planned and conducted campaigns, a series of maneuvers designed to achieve strategic objectives. These commanders were the high-ranking generals who put soldiers in harm's way. General Eisenhower as SCAEF, commander of the European invasion force, assumed overall responsibility for the planning and execution of operations.

The first step of Eisenhower's campaign was to get on the Continent. The invasion plan called for an amphibious assault securing a lodgement area in Normandy. Afterward, Eisenhower intended to build up his base of operations, bringing in additional forces and supplies. With a solid base of supply behind him, he would launch an offensive to destroy the enemy's forces, overrun Germany, and secure an unconditional surrender.

General Eisenhower's principal ground commander for the first phase of the campaign was General (later Field Marshal) Bernard L. "Monty" Montgomery, the 21st Army Group commander. General Montgomery controlled two field armies in Normandy (plus an additional division and five armored brigades under the Army Group control). In the east was the British Second Army with twelve combat divisions (divided into three British and one Canadian corps) under the command of Lieutenant General Sir Miles Dempsey. In the west, General Bradley commanded the U.S. First Army, consisting of thirteen U.S. combat divisions organized in four U.S. corps.

From the beginning the ground war was pretty much Monty's show.[5] General Eisenhower's headquarters and, except for brief visits, Eisenhower himself remained in England until well after the Normandy fighting ended. A great controversy still lingers over how well General Montgomery conducted the campaign, and this debate is important for understanding the origins of Bradley's offensive. The controversy centers on Montgomery's intentions for the city of Caen, which, everyone agreed, was the key to the whole operation because the city offered the best routes beyond the D-Day beachheads. Even today most of Normandy remains farmland; Norman farmers are not worried about getting anywhere fast, and the countryside wholly reflects their character. The land had not been sculptured for fast-moving motorized armies. Caen, however, was different. It was the central transportation hub of the entire road network in Normandy, surrounded by good ground that could support rapid cross-country movement by large armored forces. For heading into France in a hurry without bogging down in a slug-fest reminiscent of World War I, Caen was the way to go.

Montgomery's advocates argue that the general meant for the British and Canadian forces to tie down the preponderance of the German armored forces around Caen. This would mean less pressure on the Americans. While the British Second Army ground down the Germans in the east, General Montgomery planned for the Americans to push through the less formidable defenses in the west, clear the way to the vital Brittany ports, and peel back the German front like a giant door swinging open around Caen.

General Montgomery's critics insist that the general's preinvasion master plan is a fiction. In fact, General Montgomery envisioned quickly seizing the city of Caen with British and Canadian forces and then rapidly expanding the lodgement area. When that maneuver failed the Allied offensive bogged down. The rest of the campaign, critics argue, was a makeshift attempt to make up for Montgomery's failure to take Caen.

No one has found a historical "smoking gun" to resolve the debate to everyone's satisfaction, but the balance of historical argument seems to weigh against Montgomery. Eisenhower, for one, clearly expected a more aggressive advance. Before the invasion, he wrote to the Combined Chiefs of Staff that he had agreed with all of General Montgomery's requests for the operation, including increasing the number of divisions and expanding the frontage of the assault, since they were all essential for "the early capture of the important focal point of CAEN."[6] When that failed, Eisenhower also wrote that the plan to breakout of Normandy as *"evolved* [emphasis added] by Field Marshal Montgomery in his capacity of tactical commander, with my complete concurrence, was to strike hard with his left [British-Canadian zone] and then follow through promptly with a right hand blow [American zone]."[7] In other words, when rapid exploitation around Caen failed, the Allies pursued a modified course of action that required greater U.S. Army initiative to unhinge the Germans' defensive scheme.

The most cogent, recent studies of the Normandy campaign suggest that General Montgomery was as frustrated with the difficulties of expanding the lodgement area as any of the Allied leaders. Like any experienced combat commander, he never expected his operations to go exactly as planned and made the best of the situation at hand. Montgomery's flawless "plan" was more a product of his postwar musings than a deliberate blueprint for breaking through the German coastal defenses.

Controversies aside, the reality of Montgomery's campaign was that by July 1944 it had put the Allies in a difficult situation. When Caen finally fell, the Germans had surrounded the good ground with a defensive ring of armor. Caen became the Germans' anchor and the rest of their defenses stretched like a chain from the city all the way west to the coast. The great crusade was on hold. General Eisenhower told reporters that "there was nothing spectacular in the picture or future prospects."[8] He was equally cautious when he wrote to General George C. Marshall, the U.S. Army Chief of Staff. "The going is extremely tough," General Eisenhower concluded.[9] The enemy was holding fast in France.

The German decision on how to defend Normandy also shaped General Bradley's choices. Like the Allied decision of when and where to attack, the Germans' approach to the Normandy campaign also resulted from the interplay of strategic and operational judgment. At the strategic level the German command structure roughly paralleled that of the Allies. At the top sat Adolf Hitler, leader in the Axis coalition, German head of state, and Oberster Befehlshaber der Wehrmacht (commander of the armed forces). The Oberkommando der Wehrmacht or OKW (armed forces high command) helped him with setting strategic direction.[10] In the summer of 1944, with the Germans being attacked on every front, Hitler had few options. One choice he could make was how and where to defend against the anticipated invasion of France. In theory it was a simple choice. There are two basic defensive patterns: the area defense and the mobile defense. The area defense (also called the passive defense) emphasizes retaining terrain rather than maneuvering forces. The defender holds his position and relies on firepower to defeat the attacker. In contrast, a mobile defense (also called the active defense) relies on maneuver as the primary tool for defeating the enemy. The defender uses the depth of the battlefield to draw the enemy into a position where the opponent is vulnerable to counterattack. The story behind Hitler's choice of defense is another of the controversies of the campaign that helped set the Americans inexorably on the course toward Bradley's big attack.

At the operational level, Oberbefehlshaber West or OB West under Field Marshal Gerd von Rundstedt commanded the ground forces in France. OB West contained two army groups. The Normandy area fell under the jurisdiction of Heeresgruppe (Army Group) B commanded by Field Marshal Erwin Rommel. Rommel's forces defended the coast from the Loire River to the Netherlands. Both he and Rundstedt agreed that

Germany needed an Atlantic Wall, a defense network to prevent the Allies from seizing a major port where they could build up an invasion army and march into the Continent and on to the homeland.

What the two principal German commanders in the west disagreed about was on how to stop the Allies from gaining a foothold in Europe.[11] Marshal Rundstedt, OB West commander, preferred a mobile defense. Concerned that the Germans lacked the firepower to engage the Allies head-on, he wanted to keep a large reserve, let the Allies make their move, and then counterattack. Army Group B commander, Marshal Rommel, feared that Allied air power would crush mobile counterattacks and argued that the situation called for an area defense. The only hope, he maintained, was to prevent the enemy from gaining a foothold to begin with; he wanted to fight as far forward as possible and stop the Allies at the beaches.

Historians still debate which of the great generals may have been right, the only consensus seems to be that it was not Hitler, who muddied the choice by adopting an ambiguous middle ground. He ordered some units added to Rommel's beach defenses, but also decided to hold back the bulk of the armor forces as a central reserve, a compromise that failed to defeat the Normandy landings. Once the Allies had gotten ashore Hitler's commitment to retaining every inch of ground was unshakable. He ordered the troops to hold fast, proclaiming that in their hands was the "security of the nation and the existence and future of our people."[12] Germany would win or lose in France.

Hitler's decision to hold on, while fanatical, was not irrational. A sound purpose stood behind his thinking. He believed that his empire's only chance was to stand fast on all fronts—show no weakness and hope that German determination would eventually crack the solidarity of the Allied alliance. Hitler was betting that a protracted war of attrition would exhaust one or more of his opponents and force a compromise based on self-interest.

Germany's war leader made a profound miscalculation—the Allies' resolve turned out to be unshakable. Not only did the alliance stand, but it continued to support its senior military leaders even though there were obvious missteps and heavy losses in the opening weeks of the Normandy battles. The German commanders soon found to their dismay that the Allies were willing to take risks, endure casualties, and suffer operational setbacks. In defiance of Hitler's hopes, the resolve of the alliance would give General Bradley the confidence he needed to attempt his big attack. Hitler was facing a determined foe.

In fact the Allied pressure was relentless. Thus the German decision to hold fast in France was to commit Hitler's commanders to an area defense for the rest of the campaign. The fighting was hard on Marshal Rundstedt, the 68-year-old veteran of two wars: contemporary pictures show an austere, hollow-cheeked face reflecting his age and long years of military service. Exasperated as much by disagreements with Hitler and the OKW as with the enemy attacks, Rundstedt requested relief. On 2 July Hitler released him.[13]

Hitler summoned Field Marshal Günther von Kluge from the Eastern Front to assume command of OB West. Kluge's command style contrasted sharply with Rundstedt's. Marshal Rundstedt was distant and aristocratic, rarely visiting the front lines; Kluge could also seem cool and diffident but, unlike Rundstedt, he seemed to be everywhere at once. He was a forceful, hard-driving commander, and his passion to lead from the front made some subordinates uncomfortable. They complained that he mirrored Hitler's reputation for oversupervising, often bypassing commanders and giving detailed instructions directly to tactical units.

To his credit, when he interfered Marshal Kluge spoke from experience. He had successfully commanded an army during the 1940 invasion of France and had proven an innovative and determined commander of the Army Group Center on the Eastern Front. Kluge considered himself a master tactician and field commander, often referring to himself as another Marshal Ney, who was Napoleon's colorful, energetic cavalry commander.[14] Kluge's troops nicknamed him "clever Hans."

Kluge's temperament was too similar to that of the famous Marshal Rommel, Army Group B commander, for the two to have any closer relationship than Rommel and Rundstedt had endured. When Rommel met his new commander on 5 July Kluge was alleged to have declared, "Field Marshal Rommel you must obey unconditionally from now. It is good advice that I am giving you."[15] The suggestion provoked a bitter exchange between the two commanders, but a Rommel-Kluge feud never became an issue. On 17 July British planes caught Rommel's staff car in the open, and he was badly wounded and put out of action for the rest of the campaign. Kluge would have to be the savior of the Western Front alone.

With Rundstedt and Rommel both gone, and Normandy being the only fighting front in France, Hitler streamlined the western command. Marshal Kluge took over both OB West and Army Group B. This arrangement gave Kluge responsibility for both operational command and the administrative tasks of running the theater, and he assumed his mission with unbridled optimism. His enthusiasm, however, was quickly tempered after briefings from front-line commanders and staff members, who offered a steady stream of complaints, problems, and dour predictions. They left him, Kluge's subordinates claimed, "with a far different impression of conditions at the front than was told him by OKW."[16]

To hold off almost three dozen Allied divisions Kluge had only General Paul Hausser's Seventh Army with two corps consisting of nine badly understrength divisions and an assortment of *kampfgruppen* (battle groups) directly facing General Bradley's U.S. First Army. Meanwhile, nine divisions organized in four corps under General Heinrich Eberbach's Panzer Group West held off the British-Canadian advance.

Even though he was outnumbered, Marshal Kluge had promised to hold at any cost and that was what he was going to do. His plan was to check the Allies in an operational stalemate, and through the first 7 weeks of the Normandy campaign the Germans did manage to do exactly that. The reason for the success of their operational efforts was that these efforts dovetailed well with their tactical plans—a match that so far in the campaign had spelled heartbreak for General Bradley and the U.S. Army.

The Tactical Dilemma

Once operational commanders had determined where, when, and with what great armies they would fight, tactics—the business of fighting battles— were to take over. Unfortunately for the U.S. Army, the Germans' tactical defenses were well suited to the Normandy battlefields—and this had a significant and dramatic impact on Bradley's operations and future plans. In the end the tactical situation, more than any other factor, created the conditions reminiscent of the trench combat in World War I and generated the need for a decisive battle on the scale that Bradley envisioned.

That the Germans' fighting tactics proved so ideal in the battles of Normandy was one of World War II's odd twists of fate. German defense techniques were a witch's brew of doctrine from World War I, experiences on the Eastern Front in World War II, and the unique character of the Normandy countryside. Initially, World War I German defense doctrine was based on the principle of *Halten was zu halten ist* (Hold on to what can be held). This guidance guaranteed frequent battles and high casualties, with front-line troops being subjected to punishing barrages from enemy artillery. In 1917 the Germans revamped their doctrine.[17] In the new defensive pattern only a security belt of observation posts remained in the front-line trenches, and the bulk of the German forces were placed farther back in a main line of resistance beyond the range of enemy artillery. When the enemy attacked, its barrages would fall on empty trenches in the security zone, and the assaulting infantry would find itself charging into the Germans' unfazed main defense line.

However, when the Germans applied their defense methods on the Eastern Front in World War II, they discovered significant problems. Units did not have enough manpower to organize a cohesive main line of resistance across the vastness of the Russian steppes. Even if the men could be found, static defenses were no match for Soviet breakthrough attacks of massed armor, mobile artillery, and airplanes. Hitler's virulent order to retain ground, regardless of its tactical value, only exacerbated the difficulties.

Drawing on experiences from the Eastern Front the Germans once again modified their defensive tactics.[18] Their new doctrine retained the idea of area defense with a security zone and a main line of resistance. The main defensive belt, however, was built around a series of mutually supporting strongpoints. Positions were dug in and camouflaged, with all fire carefully oriented to destroy the enemy to the front and flanks.

The Germans brought their defensive doctrine to the battlefields of Normandy and used it to fight the Allies to a standstill. German defenses proved particularly effective because they were ideally suited for the local terrain.

For centuries Norman farmers had used built-up banks of earth, called hedgerows, to fence off fields, and the bushes and trees growing on top of the banks often extended the height of these natural fences upward by several feet. These hedgerows divided a good part of Normandy into small, impenetrable fields. So, building on this, the German defenders had preset mortar and artillery fire on the hedgerows in front of their strongpoints and laced the area with booby traps, mines, obstacles, early-warning devices, and snipers. Therefore, a U.S. Army infantryman rustling a leaf in the hot summer silence could bring sniper fire, the crack of artillery, or the rip of machine gun fire. Each patch of farmland became its own miniature universe of battle.[19]

Even if a GI could peer through the vegetation without being shot dead, there was little reward for the dangerous effort. German strongpoints were virtually invisible, often dug in on the reverse side of the hedgerows. These positions not only concealed the defenders from observation, but also protected them from mortar and artillery fire and air attacks. German machine gun emplacements were carefully set to cover as much of the front as possible, being positioned in the corners of the hedgerows, oriented to fire over the open fields, and greet every rush of attacking infantry with interlocking fire. Even when the GIs got to the other side of a hedgerow field the danger was not over. There were the ubiquitous small sunken lanes, covered by a thick summer canopy, that bounded the hedgerows. The lanes offered ideal ambush sites and excellent routes for quick counterattacks.

To make matters worse, U.S. Army tactics were ill suited for hedgerow fighting. Unlike the singular evolution of German infantry defensive tactics, U.S. Army offensive small-unit doctrine was firmly established long before the landings in Normandy, embodied in a scheme called fire and movement. As one U.S. Army field manual explained: "Every movement must be covered by fire delivered by part of the company, by company supporting weapons, or both, and so placed that it neutralizes that part of the enemy's infantry which could otherwise effectively fire on the individuals or elements that are moving."[20]

In other words, one part of the unit would suppress the enemy's weapons while others assaulted. Field manuals provided a neat diagram showing commanders how to integrate supporting heavy weapons including tanks, machine guns, mortars, and artillery. The manuals depicted a line for each weapons system extending out to its maximum effective range, illustrating how each system would thicken the base of fire for the infantry assault.[21]

After the Normandy landings General Bradley, providing his assessment as the senior U.S. field commander, declared confidently that "our tactics as taught at home are as sound as a dollar. We only need to apply the things we learned in training."[22] He could not have been more wrong. In practice, units on the ground could not duplicate the diagrams in the field manuals. The broken Normandy terrain compartmentalized forces and masked fields of fire. Attackers proved incapable of developing adequate supporting fire for the infantry assault against prepared enemy positions. The problem was simple: weapons could fire to the maximum ranges listed in the field manuals, but men could not see that far, and what they could not see they could not kill. Without fire support to destroy or suppress the enemy's fire the U.S. Army scheme for maneuvering through the hedgerows proved fruitless.

Even the U.S. tanks made little difference in the outcome of the battles. If armor could work past the broken countryside and reach a hedgerow, the tankers often found that they could not break through the thick undergrowth. When it was tried to drive over a hedgerow, the tanks would rise at a steep angle, preventing them from using their cannon or machine guns and exposing the weak underside armor to German antitank weapons. If the tanks did get through, the Germans would fall back to the next line of hedgerows, where they had prepared alternative positions, and the whole bloody business would start all over again.

Bradley's Dilemma

Instead of advancing steadily from the coast, the interplay of strategy and operations had brought the Americans to a time and place where unsuitable tactics and centuries-old terrain kept them from exploiting their advantages in mobility and firepower. The situation created by the three levels of war set the conditions for the battle of the hedgerows, leaving a difficult operational challenge for U.S. forces. While the considerations of strategy, operations, and tactics were not the only factors that influenced commanders in determining how, when, and where to fight, such considerations were the taproot for considering what to do next. The levels of war marked the possible paths for how U.S. forces could traverse the universe of battle, avoiding debilitating combat in the hedgerows and restoring maneuver to the campaign.

In retrospect, considering the combination of strategic and operational decisions that placed them in the hedgerows of Normandy, it is difficult to fault General Bradley for the situation in which he found himself. And, in fact, Bradley could be well justified in being reasonably pleased with what the U.S. forces had achieved so far in the campaign. Piercing the Atlantic Wall and putting at risk the lives of over a million soldiers on the thin rim of a continent, soldiers who were tethered to supply lines dependent on the fortunes of wind and water, was no simple task.

The choice of when and where to invade had been an impossible one. Each day that the Allies waited, the gap between their strength and the enemy widened, but conversely it gave the Germans one more day to prepare. As a result, there probably never was a time when invading Europe would have been easy. Unless Germany had collapsed completely, it is difficult to imagine a less risky alternative to how the Allies chose to crack the Atlantic defenses. The situation General Bradley faced in July 1944 was a fair outcome for all the years of planning and preparation.

On the other hand, shifting blame for the slowness of the campaign's progress to the British and Canadian failure to take Caen or the difficulties of hedgerow fighting seems disingenuous. Campaigns never go as planned, and the U.S. First Army had to consider the alternative that it would have to assume a larger share of the responsibility for fighting its own way out of Normandy. Planning for likely contingencies was a standard operational practice. The U.S. forces had participated in more than their share, both before and in the earliest stages of the Normandy campaign.[23]

General Bradley also knew from intelligence reports and terrain analysis the nature of the ground beyond the beachhead. Determining how the ground could be used to influence tactical engagements took no imagination; in fact, some of the training grounds used in Great Britain had similar features. If Bradley underestimated the capability of the Germans' use of the Norman terrain or discounted the threat because he hoped U.S. troops would be beyond the hedgerows in a matter of days, he had only himself to blame. The fact was that the operational requirements of the campaign had changed, and U.S. forces were slow to respond.

Could General Bradley and his army of young soldiers have done better? Moved faster? Cleared the Normandy hedgerows before being trapped between operational requirements and the tactical meat grinder of the summer battles? The answer is probably not. This conclusion is based on how the Americans chose to develop and employ their combat power during World War II. That is another important part of the universe of battle, and the subject of the next chapter.

Notes

1. Henry Giles, *The G.I. Journal of Sergeant Giles,* p. 50.
2. "Eisenhower Warns of Losses; Urges a Check on Optimism," *New York Times,* 11 July 1944, p. 1.
3. Today, it seems difficult to imagine that commanders like General Bradley glanced uncomfortably over their shoulders at the battlefields of the Great War, but these men knew well the history of their own time. Every one of the U.S. Army's thirty-four combat corps commanders had been on active service in World War I, twenty-three in the American Expeditionary Forces. See Robert H. Berlin, *U.S. World War II Corps Commanders: A Composite Biography,* p. 7. Even though Americans did not endure the years of trench warfare experienced on the Western Front by the Europeans, their lessons learned from the war focused on avoiding static warfare. See, for example, *Infantry in Battle.*
4. For concise statement of Allied strategy, see *Biennial Reports of the Chief of Staff of the United States Army to the Secretary of War, 1 July 1939–30 June 1945,* pp. 113–117. For an introduction to the historiographical debate over the complexities of Allied strategy, see Albert A. Nofi, ed., *The War Against Hitler: Military Strategy;* Kent Roberts Greenfield, *American Strategy in World War II: A Reconsideration.* For a recent assessment of Churchill's military leadership in relation to the Normandy campaign, see Richard Lamb, *Churchill as War Leader,* pp. 276–298; Tuvia Ben-Moshe, "Winston Churchill and the Second Front: A Reappraisal," *Journal of Modern History* 62 (September 1990): 503–537. Thomas Parrish, *Roosevelt and Churchill: Partners in Politics and War,* pp. 240–258, provides a useful account of the development of U.S. strategy. See also Robin Renwick, *Fighting with Allies: America and Britain in Peace and War;* Brian P. Farrell, "Grand Strategy and the 'Second Front' Debate," in *World War II in Europe, Africa and the Americas with General Sources: A Handbook for Literature and Research.*
5. For a summary of the Allied operational plan up to Operation Cobra, see *Strategy of the Campaign in Western Europe 1944–1945,* Report of the General Board, United States Forces, European Theater, Study No. 1, pp. 1–26. For a cogent introduction to the historiography over the debate on the campaign's conduct, see G. E. Patrick Murray, *Eisenhower Versus Montgomery: The Continuing Debate;* Stephen T. Powers, "The Battle of Normandy: The Lingering Controversy," *The Journal of Military History* 56 (July 1992): 455–471. See also Martin Blumenson, *The Battle of the Generals,* p. 78; Carlo D'Este, *Decision in Normandy,* pp. 337–339, and *Patton: A Genius for War,* p. 615; Russell F. Weigley, *Eisenhower's Lieutenants,* pp. 116–118; Max Hastings, *OVERLORD: D-Day and the Battle for Normandy,* pp. 249–250; Martin Blumenson, "Some Reflections on the Immediate Post-Assault Strategy," in *D-Day, The Normandy Invasion in Retrospect,* pp. 201–218. For those interested in General Eisenhower's role in the campaign, there is a wealth of studies addressing the subject. An excellent guide to these sources is Elizabeth R. Snoke, *Dwight David Eisenhower: A Centennial Biography.* For an interesting recent study on the relationship between Generals Eisenhower and Montgomery, see Norman Gelb, *Ike & Monty: Generals at War,* pp. 304–336. Readers will also want to consult David Eisenhower, *Eisenhower at War;* Stephen E. Ambrose, *Supreme Commander: War Years of General Dwight D. Eisenhower.* For a cogent defense of General Montgomery's conduct of the campaign in Normandy, particularly with respect to Carlo D'Este's critiques, see Alisaier Horne with David Montgomery, *Monty: The Lonely Leader, 1944–1945.* See also Richard Lamb, *Montgomery in Europe, 1943–1945: Success on Failure?;* Nigel Hamilton, *Master*

of the Battlefield: Monty's War Years, 1942–1944. For recent critiques on the Allied operational objectives in World War II, see Martin Blumenson, "A Deaf Ear to Clausewitz: Allied Operational Objectives in World War II," *Parameters,* XXIII (Summer 1993): 16–27; Russell Weigley, "From the Normandy Beaches to Falaise-Argentan Pocket: A Critique of Allied Operational Panning," *Military Review* 70 (September 1990): 45–64. For comments specifically on General Bradley's role, see also D. K. R. Crosswell, "Anglo-American Strategy and Command in Northwest Europe, 1944–45," in *World War II in Europe, Africa and the Americas with General Sources: A Handbook for Literature and Research,* p. 211.

6. SHAEF Diary, Book X, January 23, 1944, A-1007, File 2-3.7 CB 8, CMH.

7. Carl A. Spaatz, The Papers of Carl A. Spaatz, Supreme Commander's Dispatch for Operations in N.W. Europe to January 1945, Box 104, p. 105, LC.

8. "Eisenhower Warns of Losses," p. 1.

9. Joseph Patrick Hobbs, ed., *Dear General: Eisenhower's Wartime Letters to Marshall,* p. 185.

10. For a useful introduction to the structure of the German OKW, particularly with regard to the Normandy campaign, see Alan F. Wilt, *War from the Top: German and British Military Decision Making During World War II,* pp. 1–61, 255–271. See also Gerhard L. Weinberg, *Germany, Hitler and World War II,* pp. 254–286.

11. Gordon A. Harrison, *Cross-Channel Attack,* pp. 253–258. See also Dieter Ose, "Rommel and Rundstedt: The 1944 Panzer Controversy," *Military Affairs* 50 (January 1986): 7–11; Dieter Ose, *Entscheidung im Westen 1944: Der Oberbefehlshaber West die Abwehr der aliierte.* General Rommel also had serious disagreements with General Leo Freiherr Geyr von Schweppenburg, the commander of Panzer Group West. See Alan F. Wilt, *The Atlantic Wall: Hilter's Defense in the West, 1941–1944,* pp. 105–115. See also Samuel W. Mitcham, *The Desert Fox in Normandy: Rommel's Defense of Fortress Europe,* pp. 1–31; Geyr von Schweppenburg, "Reflections on the Invasion," 2 parts, *Military Review* 41 (February 1961): 2–11, (March 1961): 12–21.

12. Headquarters, 7th Armored Division, U.S. Army, "Translation of the Order of the Day by Hitler from a Copy Issued by the Operations Branch 277th Infantry Division," Division Intelligence Summary #40, July 1944, CARL.

13. For a recent biography on Rundstedt, see Charles Messenger, *The Last Prussian: A Biography of Field Marshal Gerd Von Rundstedt 1875–1953.*

14. Fritz Bayerlein, "An Interview with GENLT Fritz Bayerlein: Critique of Normandy Breakout Panzer Lehr Division from St. Lo to the Ruhr," ETHINT 67, pp. 13–14; and Guenther Blumentritt, "Three Marshals, National Character, and the 20 July Complex," MS B-344, pp. 89–92.

15. Hans Spiedel, *We Defended Normandy,* p. 121. The most recent works that looks at Rommel's contribution to the Normandy campaign are David Fraser, *Knight's Cross: A Life of Field Marshal Erwin Rommel,* pp. 452–513; and Mitcham, *The Desert Fox in Normandy: Rommel's Defense of Fortress Europe.* See also Speidel, *Invasion 1944: Rommel and the Normandy Campaign;* Friedrich Ruge, *Rommel in Normandy.*

16. The OKW's daily assessments of conditions in Normandy are recorded in *Kriegstagebuch des Oberkommandos der Wehrmacht. Band IV. 1. Januar 1944–22. Mai 1945.* See also Eugen Meindl, "II Parachute Corps," MS B-401, pp. 36–37; Max Joseph Pemsel, "Comments on the Study: Dealing with the Battle in Normandy," MS C-056, p. 3; Speidel, *We Defended Normandy,* p. 120. Speidel claims that merging Army Group B and the OB West was Marshal Kluge's initiative. See Speidel, *We Defended Normandy,* p. 130.

17. Timothy L. Lupfor, *The Dynamics of Doctrine: The Changes in German Tactical Doctrine During the First World War.*

18. Timothy A. Wray, *Standing Fast: German Defensive Doctrine on the Russian Front During World War II,* pp. 68–76; Department of the Army Pamphlet No. 20-233, *German Defensive Tactics Against Russian Breakthroughs,* pp. 27–40. See also Steven H. Newton, *German Battle Tactics on the Russian Front.*

19. Information on the German defenses was taken from Headquarters SHAEF, "Notes on German Booby Traps," letter dated October 1944, CARL; AGF Observation Board, ETO, Report No. 141, "German Defenses in the Hedgerow Terrain," CARL; AGF Observation Board, ETO, Report No. 138, "Notes on Hedgerow Warfare in the Normandy Beachhead," pp. 1–2, CARL; Günther Blumentritt, "Defense," MS B-299, CARL. See also Michael Doubler, *Closing with the Enemy,* pp. 41–45. The Americans were so impressed by their experiences with the German defenses in the hedgerows that, during the early years of the Cold War, they considered using the area as a last-ditch defensive line against a Soviet invasion. See General Staff, G-2, Terrain Estimate of Nantes-Caen Line as a General Line of Defense, Intelligence Research Project 6183, April 1951, MHI.

20. U.S. Forces, European Theater, *Report of the General Board: Organization, Equipment and Tactical Employment of the Infantry Division, Study, No. 15,* p. 7. For a study of the evolution of U.S. doctrine in the interwar years, see William O. Odom, *After the Trenches: The Transformation of U.S. Army Doctrine 1918–1939.*

21. FM 71-15, *Infantry Field Mannal, Heavy Weapons Company, Rifle Regiment,* p. 31.

22. Charles H. Coates, "Notes on Interviews with Various Infantry Commanders in Normandy, France, 6 June–8 July 1944," Report to War Department Observation Board (5 August 1944), p. 1, CARL.

23. Among the pre-Normandy contingency plans was Operation Rankin, a plan for invasion in the case of the collapse of Germany. See *Operation RANKIN: Revision of the Spheres of Responsibility,* Report by the JCS Planners, File 2025, MC. Early contingency plans in Normandy to push east into Normandy or south toward Brittany included Lucky Strike, Swordhilt, Beneficiary, and Hands Up. For discussions on contingency planning see Weigley, *Eisenhower's Lieutenants,* pp. 119–120; and D'Este, *Decision in Normandy,* pp. 345–346.

3

A Measure of Power

T wo months of constant fighting against the U.S. infantry had left some of General Bradley's opponents unimpressed. The II Parachute (*Fallschirmjäger*) Corps commander, General Eugen Meindl, whose men had been battling Bradley's since the campaign's start, listed a litany of shortfalls.[1] The Americans were too timid. They wouldn't fight at night. And their attacks lacked drive. Official U.S. after-action reports echoed the German general's criticisms. One American observer concluded that units did not acquire a bold and aggressive attitude "until long after their entry into combat and some never acquire it."[2] Perhaps Bradley's soldiers did not have the right stuff to handle the obstinate combination of French terrain and German defenders.

The levels of war established the bounds of the possible, but they were only part of what went into planning the U.S. First Army's next move. The greatest limits of warfare were not in the theories of strategy, operations, and tactics, but in the capabilities of the soldiers on the ground, what they had, and what they could do with it. Before Bradley committed his troops to a new major operation, he had to take a measure of their power and gauge his confidence in the army's ability to bring all that power into battle.

The armies of Normandy were complex organizations whose performance resulted from a combination of factors that included organization, equipment, protection, and sustainment. Understanding how these factors blended to create something soldiers call combat power is tricky. There are a number of studies that look at the performance of the U.S. Army during World War II.[3] Most suffer from two limitations. First, they tend to overgeneralize. There was no such thing as the "American combat experience." Fighting in the Pacific was not the same as fighting in Europe. Suffering in the Ardennes was different from the misery of Normandy. Although there were many constants and common threads, the unique manner in which the factors of war combined to influence each campaign make each worthy of separate study.

Second, and even more important, many of these studies fail to consider the crucial factors that went into determining the available combat power. Even such distinguished historians of the Normandy battles as John Keegan and Stephen Ambrose have failed to cover all the critical details and give them their proper weight. A full consideration of all the "measures of power" reveals that in Normandy, U.S. combat power reflected both significant weaknesses and great strengths—and it was this combination that was both the cause of the campaign's setbacks and the source of General Bradley's hopes for the future.

Long before the invasion of France, the U.S. Army had suffered from some serious shortcomings. To execute the previously mentioned tactics of fire and movement, and conduct the battles of World War II, the Americans started out with doctrine and organization based on the "rule of threes": three teams in a squad, three squads in a platoon, three platoons in a company, three companies in a battalion, three battalions in a regiment, and three regiments in a division. The U.S. Army believed that the "triangular" design provided the optimal mixture of mobility and firepower: one element to fix the enemy, a second to envelop the enemy's flank, and the third to act as a reserve and ready to exploit success. Unfortunately, in Normandy the "rule of threes" failed to rule the battle, for at the sharp edge of combat the Americans did not have the firepower needed to overwhelm the enemy. This failing can be directly traced to how General Bradley's troops had been organized, equipped, and trained.

Organizing for Combat

In considering how to crack the German defenses, General Bradley's biggest concern was the state of the three infantry divisions that would lead his big attack and have to break through the German line. However, starting with the most basic constituent of an infantry division, the squad, the U.S. Army division compared poorly with the enemy.[4] (See Figure 3.1 for a U.S. infantry division table of organization.) The German infantry section (the equivalent of the squad) had the advantage of the MG42 machine gun, which fired 1,200 rounds a minute of 7.92mm ammunition and had an effective range of 800 yards. The MG42 weighed less than 24 pounds and could be carried by one man. The German infantry section was built around this formidably agile and dependable weapon. The section leader assigned his best man to operate the gun and used the rest of the unit to protect the machine gunner and bring forward ammunition. The Germans also preplanned their engagement areas to take maximum advantage of the MG42's range and power, using *stellungswechsel* (shifting positions) tactics to affect maximum surprise on the advancing U.S. infantry. Shifting location frequently also made the German machine gun position difficult to pinpoint and outflank.

Figure 3.1   Table of Organization, U.S. Infantry Division

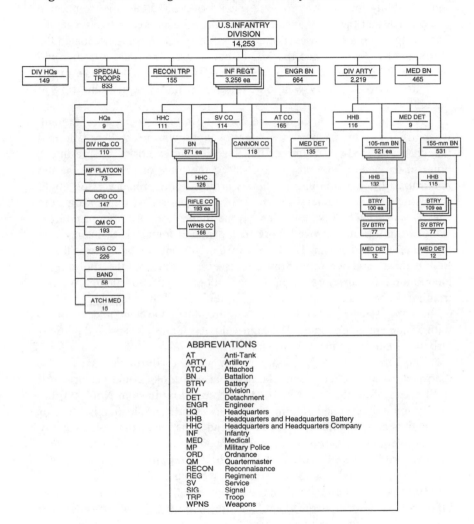

ABBREVIATIONS	
AT	Anti-Tank
ARTY	Artillery
ATCH	Attached
BN	Battalion
BTRY	Battery
DIV	Division
DET	Detachment
ENGR	Engineer
HQ	Headquarters
HHB	Headquarters and Headquarters Battery
HHC	Headquarters and Headquarters Company
INF	Infantry
MED	Medical
MP	Military Police
ORD	Ordnance
QM	Quartermaster
RECON	Reconnaisance
REG	Regiment
SV	Service
SIG	Signal
TRP	Troop
WPNS	Weapons

The U.S. infantry squad had nothing that could touch the MG42.

For squad firepower U.S. troops relied on the Browning automatic rifle (BAR), a weapon that was in essence an infantry heavy rifle. Like the MG42 the BAR was reliable and durable, and it even weighed 4 pounds less than the German machine gun. To increase their firepower infantry squads usually found a way to get a second BAR, and the practice became so common that the army eventually authorized each squad two weapons. Even with two BARs, however, the U.S. infantry squad could not match the Germans' firepower, since the MG42 had a greater effective range and twice the BAR's rate of fire. In fact, the MG42 alone could almost match the rate of fire of every weapon in a U.S. infantry squad shooting at once.

The German section could also count on a big advantage in antitank weapons. The primary infantry antitank weapon was a recoilless rifle that launched a shaped-charge projectile. Shaping the explosive charge into a point in the head of the projectile focused the force of the explosion and maximized the penetration of a tank's armor. The German version could penetrate 200 millimeters of armor at 150 meters. At close range the *raketenpanzerbuchse,* popularly called the *ofenrohr* (stovepipe) or *panzerschreck* (tank terror), proved more than a match for the U.S. main battle tank, the M4A1 Sherman. The German weapon's only drawback was that it took a lot of practice to employ effectively. Because of the shortage of ammunition, German infantry rarely had an opportunity to conduct live-fire training. In battle inexperienced troops often missed their targets. To thicken antitank defenses, the Germans supplemented the handheld weapons with 75mm and 88mm guns. The high-velocity 88mm guns proved particularly devastating against U.S. armor.

The U.S. infantry's antitank weapon was the "bazooka" that fired a 2.36-inch rocket. Its designers claimed that a bazooka could penetrate 50 millimeters of armor, but it had received mixed reviews in North Africa, Sicily, and Italy. At one point the U.S. Army stopped production because of complaints about malfunctions. In Normandy, the bazooka proved equally ineffective against German tanks, except at point-blank range. General Manton Eddy, the 9th Infantry Division commander, found that his infantrymen were reluctant to even use the weapon in battle.[5]

Exacerbating the ineffectiveness of squad antitank weaponry, the U.S. infantry lacked other adequate antitank fire. In each U.S. infantry regiment was an antitank company with towed 57mm antitank guns, but these guns lacked cross-country mobility, armor protection, and, most important, the ability to stop a German tank. GIs called the 57mm gun the "wonder weapon": the guns were so ineffective that it was a wonder the army ever had developed them. The American infantry also had tank destroyer units, armed with either the self-propelled M10 carrying a 3-inch gun or the towed M5 3-inch gun. The 3-inch guns were designed to defeat a Pzkw VI

[German] tank, but one report concluded that "while penetration of frontal armor has been effected at a range of 50 yards, it is believed in general the 3" gun is ineffective against the front armor of the Mark VI."[6] These guns could be effective against the German Pzkw IV and V tanks used in Normandy, but on the whole the U.S. infantry was a poor match for enemy armor. The inadequacy of the U.S. forces' antiarmor punch would be a serious problem during any attempted breakthrough because many of the key German front-line positions in Normandy consisted of strongpoints organized around one or more tanks.

At the platoon level U.S. units were also at a disadvantage. Both the Americans and Germans had three squads in a platoon and three rifle platoons in an infantry company, with each platoon commanded by a lieutenant. The German infantry company, commanded by a captain, continued to hold the edge. Its major advantage was firepower. The German company headquarters had its own machine gun, making for a total of thirteen machine guns at the company commander's disposal, versus two in a U.S. infantry company. The company's machine gun section carried a heavy version of the MG42, which included a tripod mount that extended the effective range to 2,500 yards. The U.S. company had a weapons platoon with three 60mm mortars and two Browning 1919 machine guns. The Brownings weighed 16 pounds more than the MG42 and had a far slower rate of fire.

It was only at the higher levels of organization that General Bradley's infantry divisions had a clear advantage. At the start of World War II a regular German infantry division was authorized 2,900 more soldiers than its U.S. counterpart, but by the time the Allies invaded Normandy all that had changed. As fighting drained available manpower, the Germans adopted a smaller division, the Infanterie Division Kreigestat 44, or the Infantry Division Type 1944. Each regiment was reduced to two battalions, and the battalions were also decreased in size, leaving the division 1,200 fewer authorized men than the U.S. infantry division.

In contrast, the U.S. infantry division had three infantry regiments, each commanded by a colonel, and each with three infantry battalions, plus headquarters, service, antitank, and artillery companies.[7] The regiment's infantry battalions, commanded by a lieutenant colonel, included a headquarters and a heavy-weapons company and three infantry companies. These companies were designated alphabetically—1st Battalion (Company A, B, C, D), 2d Battalion (Company E, F, G, H), and 3d Battalion (Company I, K, L, M).

As a whole the U.S. infantry divisions that would attempt the breakthrough were larger and more robust than their German counterparts, but the difficulties of the Normandy battlefields, at the sharp edge of battle, limited the Americans' ability to bring all of their division's firepower to bear on the enemy. At the front, it was the German infantry squad that held the decisive tactical advantage.

Preparing for the Fight

How General Bradley's army had been fielded and trained for war had exacerbated the disparities between adversaries at the front. In 1939 there were 190,000 men in the U.S. Army; by the end of the war there were over 8 million soldiers. An army of this size developed over a span of few years ensured that trained professional soldiers and National Guard and Reserve members would be a tiny minority in a citizen army of average Americans. Before Pearl Harbor most Americans had lived their lives untouched by military service; a 20-year-old private fighting in the Normandy hedgerows was born 6 years after the armistice of 1918. By 1943 these citizens had swelled the Army to its peak combat strength of 90 divisions, almost nine times the number that existed before the war. As a result of the rapid buildup and turbulence of absoring personnel, by D-Day the men of the old army had found themselves outnumbered more than forty to one. A typical division participating in the breakthrough in Normandy would have regular army regimental commanders and executive officers and an even mix of regular, Reserve, and National Guard battalion commanders. Two-thirds of the company-grade officers, captains and lieutenants, had come from Officer Candidate School. The other third had come from the National Guard, West Point, or the Reserve. The division's noncommissioned officers and soldiers were a mix of volunteers and draftees.[8]

The Army Ground Forces (AGF) had responsibility for training this "army turned upside down" before divisions were deployed overseas. Lieutenant General Lesley J. McNair (whom the luckless Lieutenant Tuttle had first seen on the afternoon of the disastrous bombing of 24 July 1944) as AGF commander was the driving force behind preparing the U.S. Army to fight World War II. To quickly ready units for wartime service General McNair had emphasized unit training: he wanted men assembled into teams as quickly as possible to learn to work and fight as one. Carrying out this training strategy was no easy task. Planners allowed only a year to turn basic-training graduates into combat-ready divisions, which would have to fight an enemy army with 4 years of extensive battle experience.[9]

The AGF training program was comprehensive: AGF guidance told divisions not only what tasks to train but how to train. One officer called it the "directive to end all training directives."[10] In no time commanders found themselves overwhelmed with information on how to prepare for combat. The number of publications tripled during the course of the war, with doctrine revised and updated every 9 months. It was impossible to keep up with all the changes.

To maintain standards General McNair directed innumerable training inspections. Commanders could expect a blitzkrieg of visits from corps and field army commanders at least once a month, and the AGF once every 3 months. Completing training before deployment seemed an insurmountable challenge. The crush to complete the program often led to results that fell far below AGF objectives. "Get it done!" one commander complained. "Never mind whether or not the troops learned anything."[11] With the pressure of getting divisions ready for deployment, training focused more on finishing the scheduled program than ensuring the proficiency of the soldiers.

The AGF tested each division before it was deployed overseas. For instance, all the infantry divisions spearheading the VII Corps's breakthrough had their skills evaluated in large-scale maneuvers in Louisiana or the Carolinas in 1941 and 1942. General McNair placed great stock in the exercises, calling them the "fairest test short of war itself."[12]

Despite McNair's expectations many soldiers found the exercises wanting. Small units gained little experience where fake battles featured "simulated artillery, flour-sack bombs, broomstick guns, and beer can mortar shells."[13] As one soldier recalled, "Mainly, we learned there is no limit to the hours an Army will expend on teaching its foot soldiers to walk and dig holes in which to hide, use as a latrine, or bury garbage."[14]

General McNair recognized the inefficiency of the maneuvers for training small units, yet he still believed the exercises were an important part of the overall training program. Even for the leaders, however, the benefits proved transient: after the maneuvers the AGF reorganized divisions or stripped them of cadre to train other units, and not even the senior leadership remained untouched. Of the twenty-seven division commanders that participated in the 1941 maneuvers, only seven commanded their units a year later. The rest were promoted or fired.[15]

General McNair believed that evaluating leaders was an important part of the training program. "The unit," he declared, "can be no better than the commander is able to make it."[16] In part, the tremendous officer turnover in the divisions was intentional. General McNair used the training exercises as part of his campaign to eliminate poor leaders and identify and promote the good ones. After reviewing the results of one maneuver, he declared that "leadership will be improved by the removal of weak officers."[17]

McNair was ruthless. Six of the eighteen National Guard division commanders were gone within a year.[18] Junior leaders were not spared either: one division removed 119 officers.[19] In all this toss and tumble there were many inequities, of course. Some outstanding leaders were shunted aside simply because they were too old or did not have a regular army commission, while, on the other hand, indifferent leaders slipped through the training program and found themselves commanding men in battle. All the same, McNair's shaking up of the officer corps made room for new leaders to move up and take on more responsibility, including a young general named Omar N. Bradley.

Without question, McNair's methods and training exercises were imperfect. But if the U.S. Army had started its training, doctrinal, organizational, and field-testing revolution earlier, no doubt many of the flaws might have been worked out and American soldiers would have been far better prepared for the battlefields of World War II. The U.S. Army, however, had started late in the race to get ready for battle and deploy 90 combat divisions. As a result, the instrument they gave General Bradley to fight the war was imperfect at best.

After deployment overseas the same problems persisted. The quality of training in Great Britain, where the Americans were staged for the D-Day invasion, proved a mixed bag. Some soldiers claimed the overseas training was useful; others were less enthusiastic. One officer, whose division did very poorly in the opening battles of Normandy, recalled: "Our tactical training in England was perfunctory. I do not remember ever hearing about hedgerows and their effects on tactics."[20] He had good reason for this assessment. There were other obstacles to effective training in Great Britain. First, units had to compete for scarce training areas and ranges on a small island packed with Allied troops. Second, some of the training was also not well thought out. For example, General Barton's 4th Infantry Division habitually trained with the 899th Tank Destroyer Battalion, but during most of the Normandy campaign the battalion was assigned to another division.[21] Third, there was the "fire-and-movement" problem, the limitations of which were recognized by U.S. Army commanders.[22]

In ensuing combat what most units tried to do, following the doctrine of fire and movement, as one officer remembered, was to "find a hole somewhere around the flank and go around the enemy position."[23] Against well-prepared defenses, however, this tactic rarely worked because the German security zone and interlocking fields of fire covered any gaps in the defenses. If gaps were found or forced, the defenders would fall back to the next line of defense or seal the breakthroughs with counterattacks. Bradley's soldiers quickly found that there was no simple solution for fighting through the Normandy countryside.

The changing nature of modern war further intensified the dilemma of fighting in the hedgerows of Normandy. The expanding range and power of weapons was making attacks in large formations suicidal. Attacking forces had to be dispersed into small groups, depriving men of a shared common knowledge of the situation and the physical comfort of adjacent soldiers. Individuals had to assume greater responsibility. Dispersion heightened stress, which in turn further deepened the fear and anxiety of isolation, particularly in the complex terrain the American soldiers found in Normandy.

This stress of modern war highlighted more than ever the importance of unit cohesion. As one soldier wrote: "One's values change when faced with the rigors of combat. The everyday living and sharing of hardships and danger with buddies result in a closeness and trust that would be difficult to duplicate anywhere else.[24] Cohesion sustained unit effectiveness and morale. The breakdown of cohesion through casualties, on the other hand, further intensified the fears and uncertainties confronting soldiers, further diminishing the unit's fighting power.

Army replacement procedures inadvertently worsened the problem of maintaining cohesion. The U.S. Army used a system of replacement by individuals that left soldiers virtually alone in the personnel pipeline until they reported to their new units, where they had little time to be integrated into their units before going into battle.

New troops were pushed so quickly to their units because the divisions were always desperate for new infantry soldiers. In the first week of July alone the U.S. First Army requested 20,000 additional replacement infantrymen—more than an entire infantry division. Despite the tide of replacements pouring into Normandy, as one division commander pointed out, "It is a fact that front line units fought under strength."[25] Casualties increased faster than replacements could arrive. When replacements came in, commanders had to balance the need for orientation training and integration into the new units with the desperate demand to fill the ranks as quickly as possible. It was a never ending Hobson's choice. All the infantry division commanders leading the breakthrough attack—Eddy, Barton, Huebner, and Hobbs—complained bitterly about the state of infantry replacements.

But, the combat performance of General Bradley's army was not just the sum of its shortfalls in replacing personnel and organizing, training, and equipping forces. Not all units reacted to the challenges of the battlefield in the same way. General Barton's 4th Division and General Hobbs's 30th Division, for example, were in their first campaigns and yet soon earned reputations as hard-fighting, dependable outfits. Meanwhile, others units failed miserably against trifling opposition.

Half the divisions that would fight under General Collins's VII Corps for the big attack had gained combat experience before the Normandy campaign, but even this fact was not an absolute discriminator in predicting performance. Physical losses, the degradation of unit cohesion, and frequent command changes could diminish the veteran character of a unit in no time.

How divisions performed depended, naturally, on what their own units did after they reached the battlefield. Regimental and battalion commanders, by and large, were to become more proficient at managing combat assets on the hedgerow battlefields—though this is not to say that all such commanders participating in the breakthrough had 7 weeks of continuous combat command. In fact, there was a fair amount of turnover among these leaders, mostly the result of promotions, injuries, or combat exhaustion. Still, even the officers who took command shortly before the breakthrough attack had gained valuable combat experience in the theater, watching and learning, observing how the U.S. Army was performing in real battles against a determined enemy.

The good leaders learned how to "read the battlefield," interpret the tactical situation from the combat information available, recognize the reports that held the key indicators of failure or success, and then unleash supporting arms and reinforcements to the right place, at the right time to influence the battle.

Commanders also created programs to integrate battlefield lessons learned, modify tactics and equipment, and incorporate replacements. As recent studies of American combat performance in Europe have documented, units that continued to train after they entered battle, innovated, and adjusted the fighting machine to overcome its inadequacies did well and continued to improve.[26]

With their combat experience leaders developed techniques to overcome the many obstacles to fighting in the hedgerows, carefully orchestrating the employment of artillery, engineers, infantry, and armor. The artillery was used to suppress the enemy machine guns and antitank fire; the engineers blew holes through the hedgerows with explosives; and the tanks flanked by the infantry advanced to the next hedgerow. This coordinated effort markedly improved combat performance, demonstrating that once leaders had improvised the means to overcome deficiencies in organization, training, and equipment, the American soldier would prove an equal match for his German counterpart. Even General Eugen Meindl, the II Parachute Corps commander, concluded that as the summer went on the Americans "got better."[27]

Still, even though some U.S. units were developing sophisticated techniques for hedgerow busting, their efforts were no solution for breaking out of Normandy. Michael Doubler's study of innovation in U.S. Army tactics, *Closing with the Enemy,* has done much to rehabilitate the reputation of the U.S. combat forces in Normandy, but the infantry innovations he describes had little effect on the outcome of the campaign and virtually nothing to do with success or failure of the breakout. The battles of the 2d and 29th Infantry Divisions fighting outside St-Lô were a case in point. One engagement Doubler cites to demonstrate the maturing of the U.S. small-unit operations is the successful 11 July assault on the key elevation called Hill 192. U.S. infantry from one battalion took the summit of the formidable objective in a single day, but even after all the practice, coordination, and massing of combat power that went into preparing for the attack, the effort was far from flawless. The infantry, for example, stored extra blasting material for blowing up hedgerows on the back of the assaulting tanks. German artillery fire detonated the explosives, destroying the American armor.

In addition, the attack on Hill 192 required over a week of planning, scouting, and rehearsal, as well as the combined effort of three divisions and the artillery and air support for an entire corps—all for an objective that turned out to be tactically insignificant. The infantry was improving, but the U.S. First Army could not afford the lives, time, and vast resources required to win the difficult battles of Normandy one hedgerow and one objective at a time.[28]

The Difference in Combat Power

While the U.S. infantry struggled to adapt to the trials of hedgerow fighting, three powerful pieces of modern combat power—artillery, armor, and aviation—helped keep the army in the fight. In particular, General Bradley had at his disposal the most powerful and flexible artillery in the world. What made the U.S. artillery unique was an innovation called the battalion fire direction center (FDC). In World War I, before FDC, each artillery battery had calculated and controlled its own fire. When a commander wanted to mass fire on an objective, all that meant was that the guns would fire somewhere on or around the target. Artillery could not concentrate fire precisely on single target with more than one battery's guns.

U.S. Army artillery began experimenting with new techniques in the mid-1930s, but the tradition-bound Artillery School at Fort Sill, Oklahoma, saw little reason for changes. In fact, the school expressly forbade teaching different fire control methods. Finally, in 1942, after a decade of debate, the Fort Sill school officially announced that it was both faster and more accurate for the battalion rather than the battery to control fire. The battalion FDC had radio and wire communications to link units quickly and could compute firing data for multiple batteries at one time. These capabilities gave commanders an unprecedented capability to quickly and accurately mass and shift artillery fire on the battlefield. Battalion-controlled fire quickly became standard practice.[29]

In another significant change, the fixed artillery brigade structure used in World War I was abandoned. Instead a division artillery headquarters controlling four artillery battalions was created. The remaining guns were kept by the field army in a central pool of artillery groups, which were assigned to individual corps for each operation. The corps could control the groups' artillery battalions through corps artillery headquarters or allocate them to reinforcing a division's artillery. Battalions could be detached from a group, or the whole group could be assigned in support. To further increase the breadth of control, the U.S. Army created a handful of field artillery brigade headquarters to assist the corps artillery in commanding the field artillery groups.[30]

The first battles fought by the United States in the Philippines and

North Africa confirmed the new responsiveness and flexibility of the U.S. artillery, which, for example, stopped the German attack after the U.S. Army's debacle at Kasserine Pass in Tunisia. Division and corps commanders, including men like Generals Bradley and Eddy, came away from the North African campaign impressed more than anything else by the ability to quickly mass artillery fire.[31] U.S. commanders learned the lesson well and carried it forward to Normandy. In fact, Bradley always assumed that massing the artillery's firepower would be important for the breakthrough attack.

In contrast, the impact of armor on the Normandy campaign proved more ambiguous. Since the appearance of the mechanization of armies in World War I, there had been predictions of a new age of armored mobile warfare. It never happened during the Great War, but the promise was not forgotten. The lightning German victories in the opening months of World War II rekindled the vision, and all modern armies of the world came to believe that motorized teams of armor, infantry, and artillery represented the force of the future.

How to organize and employ tanks had generated a great deal of controversy and discussion, particularly in the U.S. Army. The opening campaigns of World War II had only increased the intensity of the debate. The early German successes seemed to validate the need for armored commands capable of quickly striking deep into an enemy's defenses, and the emergence of the German armored force alarmed the U.S. military because its development of armor lagged behind the Europeans'. In 1940, influenced by German, British, and Soviet innovations, the U.S. Army organized an independent armored corps.[32] The history of this corps was brief: General McNair, the AGF commander, disapproved of the concept, believing that armor was best employed in combined-arms teams with infantry and artillery. Rather than concentrating tanks in independent commands, he organized separate armored battalions to support the infantry divisions and a handful of armored divisions.

The number of armored units had to be limited because they were expensive. An armored unit had fewer men than an equivalent infantry unit (about one-third less), but the support requirement to maintain an entire armored division on wheels and tracks was enormous. The logistical force assembled to support the U.S. armored units in the European theater eventually required 75,000 men to operate assembly plants, repair shops, salvage centers, and depots. Every tank that arrived in theater contained 500 items of equipment that had to be unpacked, cleaned, mounted, and checked before the tank was ready for the front. It took a minimum of 50 hours to get one tank ready for combat.[33]

The Americans tried very hard to get their investment right. The U.S. Army went through six organization modifications for armored forces during the course of the war looking for the optimal structure of an armored division. The 1942 organization, known as the "heavy" armored division, combined a lot of tanks with relatively little infantry (see Figure 3.2). But armored clashes between the British and Germans in North Africa had revealed the importance of infantry support for armored striking power, suggesting that the American 1942 organization was too tank heavy. Also, the shortage of Allied shipping argued against the heavy division, and so in 1943 the Americans reorganized again, settling on a "light" division with a more even balance of armor and infantry.

Major General Edward H. Brooks's 2d Armored Division and Major General Leroy H. Watson's 3d Armored Division (both scheduled to support Bradley's breakthrough offensive) were "heavy" divisions. By the time the 1943 round of modification came around, the two divisions had already been deployed to Britain and had begun preparing for the Normandy invasion. It seemed an inopportune time to stop and reorganize them. After some debate, Eisenhower made the decision to leave both divisions alone. As a result, a "light" armored division was authorized 10,937 men, 186 medium tanks, and 77 light tanks, but the "heavy" 2d and 3d Armored Divisions had almost 4,000 more men, 56 more medium tanks, and 82 more light tanks. Eisenhower's decision gave Bradley the two most powerful armored divisions on the Western Front for the big attack.

The "heavy" armored division consisted of three regiments, two tank regiments and one armored infantry regiment. Each tank regiment consisted of a headquarters, a reconnaissance company, and three armored battalions, two medium and one light. Each armored battalion contained three tank companies. The medium tank battalions were armed with 75mm-gun M4 Sherman tanks. The light battalion was equipped with 37mm-gun M5 light tanks. The companies of the regiment were labeled alphabetically from A to I ("Able" to "India").

The armored infantry regiment contained a headquarters and three battalions, each with three companies. The regiment differed from those of the infantry divisions because the units were equipped with armored halftracks to transport the soldiers; these infantry halftracks were not designed to fight alongside tanks. The halftracks were lightly armored and had no overhead cover, and their job was to get the infantry up to the fight.

The artillery of the armored division was also armored and mechanized.[34] The armored artillery consisted of three 105mm howitzer battalions. Armored artillery batteries contained six self-propelled guns, as opposed to the four in the towed-gun units supporting the infantry. The armored division artillery's guns were M7s, standard 105mm howitzers mounted on a Sherman tank chassis, and on the right front of each howitzer was a ring mount for a .50-caliber machine gun. The construction resembled a preacher's pulpit, earning the M7 howitzer the nickname "priest."

Another unique feature of the armored division was that it could be organized around two combat command headquarters designated Combat

Figure 3.2   Table of Organization, U.S. (Heavy) Armored Division

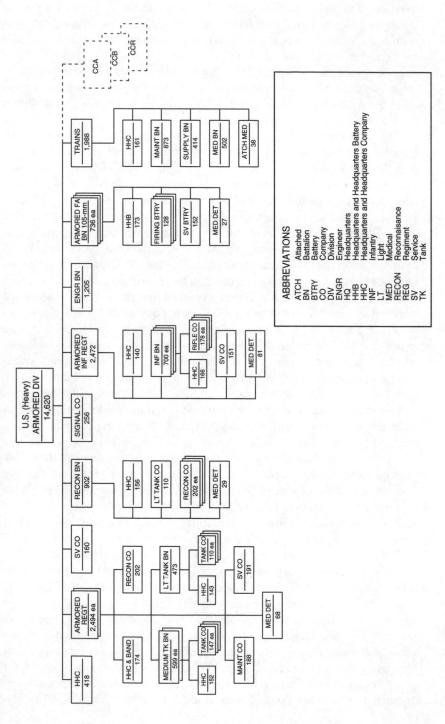

Command A (CCA) and Combat Command B (CCB). Each combat command consisted of a mix of tank and armored infantry battalions, at least one artillery battalion, and a collection of other support units, including an antiaircraft battery, an engineer company, a tank destroyer company, a medical company, and a maintenance company. The assistant division commander normally commanded CCA, and one of the tank regiment commanders commanded CCB. The remainder of the division, designated the division reserve and commanded by the armored infantry regimental commander, was referred to by the name of the commanding officer or simply called the division reserve or, more simply, CCR.

Within the combat commands, the battalions would further task organize into task forces, cross-attaching infantry and armored companies and platoons to form combined-arms company teams. Commanders designated the task forces by letters or numbers, such as "Task Force 1" or "Task Force X." As the war progressed, the teams were usually just named after the senior commander. The composition of the task force was determined by the mission. For example, if the division was going up against a firmly entrenched enemy, a task force would be infantry heavy and beefed up with a lot of artillery support. On the other hand, if the mission was to move fast through an area that was lightly defended, the column might be armor heavy with a minimum of supporting units. This ability to organize by task allowed commanders great flexibility, an important attribute for units conducting the fast-moving, flexible kind of war General Bradley wanted to fight.

There was one overwhelming problem with U.S. armor on the eve of the entry of the United States into the war. It was that no one was quite sure what the tanks were capable of achieving in battle. Doctrine for employing tanks and infantry together was sketchy. All the manuals had to say was that armor would probably make the rate of advance "faster."[35] Tank warfare in the Louisiana maneuvers and other exercises with their simulations, restrictions, and approximations offered only educated guesses about what tanks could really do in combat. In these maneuvers the rules of engagement were skewed against the tanks: according to the rules, for example, small-caliber-gun tank destroyers and even machine guns could knock out armor.[36]

While armored battles in North Africa and Italy had added to U.S. forces' brief armor expertise (particularly for General Brooks's 2d Armored Division), in Normandy the slow advance and poor terrain gave commanders few chances to try out their armored punch. The opportunities the commanders did have showed a serious problem: the constricted Normandy terrain required tanks and dismounted infantry to constantly work closely together. Breakdowns in coordination were not uncommon, even in the independent tank battalions that habitually supported the infantry divisions. General Eddy, the 9th Infantry Division commander, was so frustrated with the problem that he once threatened to court-martial tankers that withdrew, abandoning their infantry support.[37]

Part of the problem was that the U.S. Army had not foreseen the requirement for close infantry-armor coordination, and did not have radios that allowed small infantry units and individual tanks to communicate. In an infantry division, for example, only the infantry company commander had a radio to talk to the tanks. In a tank platoon, only platoon leaders' and platoon sergeants' radios could communicate with the infantry. As General Bradley well knew, tankers and infantry would have to work closely together to break through enemy lines, but they had not yet proved in Normandy that they could in large-scale operations.[38]

While armor had been used sparingly and indecisively so far in the campaign, U.S. aircraft were a common feature on the Normandy front: ground troops could receive close support from one of three U.S. Army Air Corps fighters.[39] The most frequently employed close-support aircraft was the P-47 Thunderbolt.[40] Designed as a high-altitude fighter, the Thunderbolt proved equally adept at supporting ground troops. It had an air-cooled radial engine that proved very survivable in close combat. Sometimes called "the jug," P-47s returned from battle with gaping holes and whole cylinders blown off the engine, but still flying. The Thunderbolt's major weakness was a high rate of fuel consumption, but to compensate the plane's range could be extended with externally mounted fuel tanks. As for weapons, P-47s in 80 percent of the sorties flew with a payload of two 500-pound bombs, while the rest carried fragmentation bombs or napalm. The P-47 was also armed with eight .50-caliber machine guns, each with 400 rounds. It was claimed that these planes could even take out an enemy tank by shooting at the road and bouncing bullets into the underbelly of the tank's armor (although it is more likely that the bullets were passing through such weak rear points of the tank as the exhaust system).

In Normandy, the greatest challenge to bringing the Thunderbolt's capabilities to bear on the battlefield was the lack of experience. The field manual governing ground-support operations was obsolete. In fact, official doctrine declared that close ground support was "difficult to control, expensive and, in general, the least effective . . . [useful] only at critical times." In North Africa, Bradley and other U.S. commanders had found their initial concept for ground support woefully inadequate. They had parceled out planes to everybody; this system lacked flexibility and denied ground commanders the means to take advantage of air power's greatest potential, the ability to concentrate firepower rapidly. And so, during the opening weeks of the Normandy campaign, ground commanders did not get their own personal slice of air assets. Tactical air support remained under the central control of the Ninth Air Force so that air power could be shifted around the battlefield as required.

Concepts of how to employ air power had improved before the invasion of France, but training had not. In Britain, there had been little opportunity to conduct large-scale regimental and division exercises with air support. Moreover, the U.S. air forces had had no time to train close-ground-support missions because they were busy clearing the European skies of German planes. By the time the air commanders informed General Bradley they were ready to conduct joint training with ground forces, it was too late because the assault divisions had already moved to the assembly areas for the invasion.

The poor state of air-ground coordination became apparent as soon as operations began in Normandy. For example, good G-3 air operations officers, the staff officers responsible for coordinating air support for ground operations, proved hard to come by. By the end of the first 2 weeks of the invasion, General Collins of the VII Corps and the other three U.S. corps commanders had all replaced their air operations officers.

In Normandy, the Ninth Air Force made improvements that enhanced close support. Very-high-frequency (VHF) radios were mounted in tanks so that the aircraft could communicate directly with units on the ground. But this provided no easy solution to existent problems. The VHF radios were not built to take the punishment of ground warfare with its dust, shock, and vibration, as well as a shortage of spare parts, that took a heavy toll on the fragile radio sets. To get the sets working for Operation Cobra, repair teams had to salvage parts from crashed planes, friendly and enemy. In addition to improving communications, the air forces modified planes to carry 2,000-pound bombs and rockets, beefing up the punch the aircraft could provide in support of the ground troops.

Modifications to equipment alone, however, were not enough to ensure that air and ground forces worked together smoothly. In July the Ninth Air Force reorganized ground-support personnel into parties staffed by experienced pilots to coordinate air attacks in the proximity of ground troops. Pilots were far from excited about the prospect of ground-support combat, but the innovation provided a tremendous boost in expertise for planning and coordinating air-ground operations.

Protecting the Force

The combat preparations based on planes, artillery, and tanks were only part of the combat power supporting U.S. infantryman at the front. It is a fact that most of a modern army's manpower is dedicated to protecting and sustaining the minority of the force that actually engages in combat. In World War II the United States had 3 million men in Europe of which only about 750,000 were combat infantryman. Because the number of these soldiers was proportionately so low, the loss of front-line soldiers represented the most significant drain on fighting power. All of the U.S. Army's VII

Corps infantry division commanders knew that measures to protect their soldiers were essential, and they knew they would need every experienced, veteran infantryman they could get for the breakthrough attack.

On the Normandy battlefield protecting soldiers was no small challenge. Even when not in battle, a soldier's daily life was cluttered with threats that included mines, booby traps, snipers, artillery, and aircraft. The Americans, however, possessed an impressive array of resources to protect the troops from these hazards of the battlefield.

Mines were perhaps the most common danger to the average soldier. To meet this threat, the U.S. Army included engineer units specifically trained and equipped to deal with the danger. In the days before Operation Cobra, combat engineers made an extra effort to clear mines from the projected routes for the spearhead attacks.[41] The engineers used the SCR-625 mine detector. Unfortunately, the SCR-625 had limitations that made mine clearing a difficult and dangerous occupation: it could not detect the smaller deadly antipersonnel mines because they contained little metal, nor could it find the tripwires used to detonate booby traps. In addition, during combat, where the Germans used minefields to channel enemy forces and make them lucrative targets for artillery attacks, clearing mines was even more difficult. In fact, most engineer casualties occurred in attempting to clear mines under German artillery fire. In short, the combat engineers could not always be relied upon to clear all dangers from the battlefield.

Avoiding mines relied more often on soldier savvy than technology. Troops had to invent their own methods. (One U.S. unit allegedly drove cows ahead of it to detect mines and booby traps.) Less innovative soldiers simply learned to move with care through the hedgerows and be wary of uncleared buildings, roads, and paths.

Snipers were another constant problem. The many trees and the thick undergrowth offered enemy marksman natural hiding places, and the Germans took full advantage of the opportunity. All soldiers detest snipers, and the Americans were no different. Despite the rules of war, soldiers often killed snipers who attempted to surrender, and even high-level officers shared a hatred for sniper tactics. As General Bradley's aide Major Hansen recorded:

> Talk of sniping and Bradley says he will not take action against anyone that decides to treat the snipers a little more roughly than they are being treated at present. Snipers cannot sit around and shoot and then be captured when you close in on him. That's not the way to play the game.[42]

The real key to dealing with snipers was security. "You must clean them out as you go," one commander warned, with every advance "followed by a sniper clean up."[43] Some units used antiaircraft guns to spray an area and make sure it was clear before units moved in to set up. Once an area was secure, units had to maintain vigorous patrolling to prevent enemy snipers from infiltrating their positions.

Another threat soldiers faced was unexpected harassing artillery fire by the Germans. Counterbattery fire (knocking out the German guns) was a mission for the U.S. field artillery, which found the enemy guns by using reports from ground and air observers and corps target acquisition detachments. Visual observation, photographic analysis, sound recorders, and analyzing shell craters all provided clues to finding the enemy batteries and directing attacks against them.[44]

Overall counterbattery operations were extremely successful. The German artillery was so fearful that they displaced their guns at the slightest indication of American fire. As one German commander complained: "In contrast with [our] experience in the First World War the [German] artillery had become more sensitive to enemy fire. A few shells into the firing position and its vicinity were sufficient to cause the young battery commander to order a change of position."[45] Even when the U.S. artillery did not destroy the guns, the mere threat of counterfire reduced the enemy's effectiveness.

Counterfire operations were largely successful, but they were mostly reactive. In other words, the enemy artillery first had to shoot to be detected, which meant that at least some rounds would land on U.S. lines. Protecting men against these fires involved the very basic soldier skill of digging in. During slow combat periods the basic bunker could become quite sophisticated; one battalion commander described his typical command post as 7 feet square and 5 feet deep, covered with logs and dirt. As an added comfort, on one side he had installed a shelf that could be used as a workbench and a bed.[46]

In the front lines fortifications were far more basic—a hole in the ground, the foxhole. Men used an entrenching tool, a small folding shovel, for this job. Digging a good foxhole was part of the art of war.

Enemy aircraft offered another threat to the ground forces. Before the invasion General Eisenhower had made a concerted effort to reassure soldiers that they would be protected from air attack. "If you see fighter aircraft over you," he often said, "they will be ours."[47] The general's prediction was not far off. The Allied air campaign took a heavy toll on the German Luftwaffe before the first GI stepped on Normandy's shore. One German prisoner commented that "for eleven days I saw seven Luftwaffe and seven thousand Thunderbolts."[48] By D-Day the Luftwaffe had been essentially destroyed, and the Allies enjoyed almost total control of the air over Normandy.

Allied air superiority, however, did not make U.S. soldiers immune from air attack, and in fact German fighter activity rose considerably during July.[49] One division reported air attacks on 16 different days. Avoiding Allied fighters and antiaircraft artillery, the German planes attacked in small groups at dusk, deploying flares to spot targets and then dropping bombs and antipersonnel mines or spraying American positions with machine gun fire.

U.S. fighter aircraft and antiaircraft artillery were the two principal means of protecting ground troops from air attack. The fighters were by far the most effective tool: in July they downed 75 percent of the enemy planes destroyed in Normandy. It was not unusual for soldiers to catch a glimpse of aerial combat overhead. In these aerial encounters the Americans usually won.

The remaining 25 percent of enemy aircraft losses came from antiaircraft artillery. At higher altitudes guns fired exploding rounds that created belts of flak, and at lower altitudes automatic weapons put out a blanket of bullets. At even lower levels, units used organic weapons like .50-caliber machine guns to provide local coverage. The density of antiaircraft fire was truly daunting. Some areas, for example, were covered by as many as forty-eight 90mm guns. When these systems were combined with Allied fighters and early-warning radar linked by wire and radio they represented an intimidating shield from enemy planes. Any German aircraft spotted in the Normandy skies drew a quick and savage response. One commander remembered that "there were sounds of airplanes, then suddenly streams of tracers, then the falling airplane on fire, the exploding crash and that was all. The whole thing was over in a matter of seconds."[50]

Although the air defense was awesome, sometimes it proved a danger to its own side: during the summer battles antiaircraft artillery units shot at fifteen friendly aircraft, twelve of which they brought down. Even when antiaircraft artillery was not a threat to friendly aircraft, it often proved a hazard to soldiers on the ground. When the dark erupted with fire, the least soldiers could expect was to lose a night's rest, but at worst troops were in danger from falling ordnance. As one commander concluded, "We find more men hit by our own flak than by enemy bombing."[51]

One potential danger turned out to be more imaginary than real—poison gas. Americans in World War II never had to face chemical warfare, but they had landed in Normandy prepared to protect themselves from gas attacks.[52] U.S. intelligence knew that Germany had the ability to conduct gas warfare, and as early as 1942 some predicted the Germans would employ chemicals against amphibious operations.[53]

The Allies took the threat seriously enough to order their own gas bombs readied for retaliatory strikes during the Normandy invasion. In addition, the U.S. First Army had planned for chemical mortar battalions and chemical service companies, as well as laboratories and decontamination units to support the lead elements of the Normandy invasion forces. In the assault phase, all troops wore specially treated uniforms and carried gas masks, eye shields, protective ointment, covers, a can of shoe impregnation material, and gas detector patches. After they had landed the Americans remained cautious: it was mid-July before they converted a 1,020-bed gas treatment unit into a regular hospital.

Even though the Germans never employed chemical weapons, there were some false alarms. In the days before Operation Cobra gas attack alerts reached epic proportions. Even General Bradley's U.S. First Army Headquarters was not spared. At 1:00 A.M. on 21 July the alarm sounded. General Bradley poked his head out of his sleeping trailer to see men donning gas masks and others, who could not find their masks, covering their heads with blankets. The general shook his head and went back to sleep.[54]

The panic and fear generated by the prospect of gas attacks threatened discipline and combat efficiency. General Hobbs, the 30th Infantry Division commander, dispatched sound trucks to assure the troops that they were not under chemical attack, but these announcements were sometimes misinterpreted as warnings of impending gas attacks, further exacerbating anxiety behind the lines. It got so bad that General Collins of the VII Corps issued an operations memorandum stating that "false alarms and the passing on of rumors is a sign of a lack of discipline and training in a unit and one of the earmarks of the amateur."[55]

In addition to alarms over nonexistent gas attacks, there were other such alarms that had no identifiable cause. They broke out, apparently spontaneously, all along the front on 21 and 23 July. The outbursts both reflected and contributed to the mounting stress of endless days of hedgerow fighting, and in fact medical statistics for the end of July show a significant increase in the cases of combat exhaustion.[56]

In war the environment, as well as the enemy, took its toll on the fighting force, and protecting soldiers from environmental threats was an important part of conserving combat power. In July, for example, the 30th Infantry Division lost well over 1,000 men, more than 15 percent of its casualties, to illness and noncombat injuries. These losses did not include the numbers who suffered from a weakened mental or physical condition and who had to remain in the front lines.

Bad weather also played a large part in weakening those who had prolonged duty at the front. The drenching Normandy rain, followed by blistering summer heat, made life miserable. As one soldier wrote:

> If I don't get a chance to bathe and change clothes pretty soon I'm going to have to burn the ones I'm wearing. I don't think the stink will ever come out of them. All I've had is a wash out of my helmet—what we call a whore's bath.[57]

The sharp end of battle was a collage of dirty, exhausted, foul-smelling men.

The living conditions in the hedgerows exacerbated the problem of hygiene. The battlefield was littered with the wreckage of war. Livestock was Normandy's principal livelihood, and in the summer of 1944 it was not unusual to see fields of dead men mixed with dead cows. The wastage of battle proved a boom to the insect population. Mosquito stories quickly became legion in the U.S. First Army.

> "Almighty God," I said politely to a nearby MP, "are they shooting these things at us, or are they self-propelled?"
> The MP said, "One touched down on the fighter strip near here today and they put 120 gallons of gas into him by mistake before he took off."[58]

Humor aside, the mosquitoes only added more misery to the appalling conditions of life in the hedgerows.

Poor hygiene invariably contributed to disease and illness, but despite the insect explosion U.S. troops in Normandy escaped southern Europe's scourge of war, malaria. Cases reported appeared mostly in the 1st and 9th Infantry Divisions, among men who had picked up the illness fighting in North Africa or Sicily. More common was dysentery, the soldier's universal disease. The soldiers in Normandy were fortunate in that they were in the combat theater that had lowest rate of this problem. Athlete's foot was more prevalent, and, while not life threatening, the itching and bleeding made life miserable and took men out of the line. Infantry commanders could not afford this, so the medics would paint the troops' feet purple with antifungal medicine and send them back to duty.

Problems of disease were not overwhelming, but they were persistent and detracted from combat readiness. So, as the summer passed, the U.S. First Army increased the laundry, repair, and bath units in the theater: it allocated to the VII Corps four laundry companies and a bath section. The 857th Quartermaster Company, for example, erected twenty-four hot showers that ran 15 hours a day. Combat engineers also set up shower points to supplement the quartermaster facilities.[59]

By July of 1944 soldiers could get not only a hot shower but a change of clothes. Quartermaster units issued new uniforms, an unimaginable luxury and a lift in morale for front-line soldiers. In addition, troops could get toilet articles and sundries through a sales store in Isigny and two mobile sales units. In forward areas, quartermaster units distributed free ration accessory convenience kits that contained basic items such as soap and shaving cream.[60]

Adequate, nutritious food proved equally important for protecting health. Although the GI's complaints about army chow were renowned, these were probably the best fed soldiers in the world. In combat soldiers received one of two standard battle rations, C rations or K rations. The C ration consisted of canned meals; K rations came in three small waxed-paper cartons. The rations provided about 3,400 calories a day, enough to sustain a man in combat, but only if he ate the whole ration. Rations were fairly tasteless unless heated, and at the front men had neither the time or energy to warm them up. "In practice," an officer wrote, "the soldier ate the part least offensive to his taste and discarded the rest."[61] Poor eating habits, combined with inadequate sleep and the stress of combat, resulted in a loss of appetite, and as a result, some troops suffered from malnutrition, primarily vitamin deficiency. Still, starvation, a common soldier's lot in previous centuries, was virtually unknown among the Americans in Normandy.

The adequacy of combat field rations, however, did little to sustain morale after weeks of bitter hedgerow fighting. Luckily, the pause before Operation Cobra offered an opportunity to get hot food to the front. The U.S. First Army set up field bakeries to provide fresh bread, and by the beginning of July, combat units could also get A or B rations, which contained fresh food that could be prepared in mobile field kitchens.

Hot food, in combination with sleep, the combat soldier's deepest craving, provided the most immediate relief from the debilitating effects of life at the front. The strain of fighting, combined with the disruptive sleep patterns of continuous combat duty, left men chronically fatigued. Units rotating out of the front line often spent their first days sleeping. These respites kept soldiers from total collapse from physical exhaustion after weeks of hedgerow warfare.

For the long term, to sustain the fighting strength of their soldiers commanders had to be concerned about the troops' morale as well as their physical well-being. In the rear areas, soldiers had access to a variety of diversion. For example, Special Services provided books, writing paper, and athletic equipment—in the rest area it was not unusual to find units playing a game of baseball or relaxing as if the war were a thousand miles away. At the 77th Evacuation Hospital, troops could catch movies like *Andy Hardy's Blonde Trouble*. Soldiers in the 30th Infantry Division's rear area listened to BBC radio broadcasts over Special Services loudspeakers; both the *Stars and Stripes* newspaper and *Yank* magazine were distributed free—and by 21 June troops could read the *Stars and Stripes* newspaper on the day of publication. There was even live entertainment. The first USO (United Services Organization) show arrived little more than a month after the first troops had landed at Omaha Beach.[62]

One area of entertainment that the army did not provide was sex. Soldiers had to make their own arrangements. As one commander wrote:

> If the soldier is in a headquarters unit, or a service support unit, stationed in a town for a relatively long period, he is in a position to satisfy his needs either with the native talent or imported WACs [Women's Army Corps]. But the poor soldier in a tactical unit is limited to contact with professional talent. No wonder he tends to grow embittered with his lot.[63]

Although the soldiers at the front would incessantly gripe about their misery, sex was not really a major concern in battle. Paul Fussell, in a study of World War II culture, concluded that men at the front were "too scared, busy, hungry, tired, and demoralized to think about sex at all. Indeed, the front was the one wartime place that was sexless."[64]

The greatest builder of a front-line soldier's spirit was not entertainment, sexual or otherwise, but mail call. After getting its first mail on 17 June, the 30th Infantry Division, for example, reported regularly receiving a steady flow of letters from home. True, the news did not always raise spirits. "Every day or so," a platoon leader wrote, "a soldier comes in and tries to find out how he can stop his allotment to his wife or get a divorce. So many of the wives are doing their husbands wrong."[65] On balance, however, most found mail a welcome relief from life on the front.

Spiritual care was also an important part of maintaining morale. Each infantry division was authorized fifteen chaplains (on average, two-thirds were Protestant and one-third Catholic; Jewish chaplains comprised less than 3 percent of the chaplain corps). Chaplains performed a range of pastoral services, ministering to the wounded and conducting services. The chaplain's jeep or the tailgate of a truck and a blanket would become an altar. Helmets, ammunition cases, and lockers served for pews. In addition to religious services, as many as 25 percent of the soldiers received personal counseling. Chaplains also wrote letters to relatives, fiancées, and friends and helped with inquiries through the Red Cross.[66]

An indicator of the collective success of all the U.S. Army's protective measures was the low desertion rate. Historically deserters had accounted for most noncombat losses, but in Normandy this was not a problem. The U.S. First Army had established a straggler line manned by the military police. The line picked up legitimate "stragglers," soldiers separated from their unit through no fault of their own, as well as men who had deliberately left the front without authorization. During Cobra the military police apprehended only forty-three stragglers.[67]

Another critical factor for maintaining the character of a division was the medical support system, which was essential for conserving combat power. The key to winning the next battle was to care for the sick and wounded, so that they could fight again. In contrast to previous centuries, in modern war wounded soldiers were less likely to be automatically considered a loss to the unit—commanders expected that wounded veterans would return and fight another day.

The linchpin of the U.S. military medical system was the medical battalion.[68] The battalion provided detachments to each regiment. The detachments, in turn, provided enlisted "medics" to the forward units. The life of the medic was difficult and dangerous. In the 2 weeks before Cobra the 9th Infantry Division, for example, had 21 medical personnel killed, 159 wounded, and 21 captured. Some units suspected that German infantrymen intentionally shot medics. An investigation concluded that the enemy did not have a deliberate policy of shooting medical personnel, but they did learn from German prisoners that it was almost impossible to pick out the medics' red cross armbands through the thick hedgerow underbrush. This started the tradition of painting an extra cross prominently on the helmet. Still, casualties remained high. In the European theater, in 6 months a typical division suffered 100 percent casualties in company medics.

Despite losses, medics continued to operate well forward. The reason they stayed up front was simple: seven of every ten wounds that had to be treated by medics resulted from combat—and most of these wounds were not fatal or debilitating if treated on the spot. Combat aid consisted of stopping the bleeding, treating for shock and pain, and evacuating the wounded.

The first step, controlling bleeding, was the most important and the easiest. Typical injuries were punctures, easy to plug, or amputations or cuts caused by hot, high-velocity shells or fragments that seared wounds shut. The most common wounds, over 50 percent came from shell fire (being shot accounted for barely 20 percent) usually in the arm or leg. The procedure for stopping bleeding was simple: applying a pressure bandage. The primary tool was the compress bandage that each soldier carried as part of his basic kit, but medics also improvised a good deal. For instance, medics would throw away their gas masks and use the containers to carry extra bandages, or a piece of raincoat would be used to cover a sucking chest wound to prevent respiration from drawing dirt into the wound.

After the medics treated the injured they had to deal with the next challenge, evacuating the casualties. Army doctrine called for companies to take the wounded to the battalion aid station. In battle there was no shortage of volunteers for litter duty. Litter parties, however, required four to six men to evacuate a wounded soldier. A company's combat power could quickly be whittled to nothing after evacuating its own wounded. Units ignored official doctrine, and instead the divisional medical battalion collecting company sent litter platoons forward to battalion aid stations, where the platoons were dispatched to collect the injured. Even this system had its drawbacks. Physical and mental exhaustion quickly drained the ranks of litter bearers. In heavy combat, corps and the First Army medical battalion collecting companies supplemented those from the divisions. During Operation Cobra the VII Corps attached fifteen ambulances to each division clearing company. Most units also retrained the division band as litter bearers and attached them to the medical battalion.[69]

The litter bearers carried the casualties to the battalion aid station where the battalion surgeon attended the wounded. The chaplain was usually also posted at the aid station, to provide spiritual support, although more often he could be found assisting the doctor and the medics. In the flurry of action that occurred at the aid station during battle, the lightly injured soldiers were quickly patched up and returned to duty. The seriously wounded were stabilized and evacuated to the rear.

The next stop for a wounded soldier was the regimental casualty collection point where the injured passed out of division control and were evacuated to an army field or evacuation hospital. For General Bradley's breakthrough attack, medical personnel anticipated at least 600 casualties per infantry division each day. To handle that rate of casualties the VII Corps was to have five hospitals supporting the offensive.

During periods of heavy combat the hospitals were a mass of ceaseless activity. Although the hospital staffs were far from the front and relatively safe from harm, they were not exempt from exhausting work and overwhelming responsibility. Personnel worked in two 12-hour shifts. The evacuation hospital maintained four operating tables for major surgery, two for fractures, and three for minor surgery. During a battle the tables would be in use 18 to 24 hours a day.[70]

Caring for battle casualties was only part of the medical support system. There were also illnesses and nonbattle injuries that required special care. Psychiatric casualties, self-inflicted wounds, and venereal diseases were treated separately. The army, for example, anticipated that there would be some psychiatric casualties, though the preparations made for these were perfunctory. The divisions did not have psychiatrists assigned to the divisional medical battalions; instead, the army directed divisions to appoint psychiatric officers, who were given a month-long course on medical psychiatry. Some of the divisions also arranged for briefings for the officers on "battle fatigue." Overall the training was minimal and unsatisfactory.[71]

Even though training was limited, units in Normandy developed fairly effective procedures for stress casualties. Most cases were relatively mild and could be treated at the battalion level. To deal with exhaustion, typically the battalion surgeon would hold the man at the aid station for 24 hours, often under sedation. Sleep, hot food, a change of clothing, and informal group therapy usually proved sufficient to return a soldier to a state where he could function in combat. Battalion surgeons evacuated only the most severely disturbed cases.

The percentage of psychiatric casualties increased substantially during July. There were 9,101 cases, more than four times the number reported in June. At the height of the campaign psychiatric casualties accounted for over 14 percent of admissions. A study concluded that the dramatic increase resulted from the combination of the difficult hedgerow fighting conditions and the prolonged exposure to constant combat. To address the large number of cases the First Army established two combat exhaustion centers, each with 250 beds. The centers had to be expanded, one to 750, the other to 1,000 beds.[72]

Commanders were sympathetic to the inevitable casualties caused by battlefield stress, but they were equally concerned with uncovering potential shirkers. General Patton allegedly once told his men, "We don't want yellow cowards in this Army. They should be killed off like rats. If not, they will go home after this war and breed more cowards." U.S. First Army commanders were less colorful, but equally obsessed with ensuring that every soldier pulled his weight. For example, General Bradley called for the inspector general to interview all officer casualties and ensure that fit leaders were immediately returned to combat duty. Bradley and other commanders understood there was a fine line between shirkers and soldiers suffering from mild combat exhaustion, and they invested considerable effort in trying to distinguish between the two.

Self-inflicted wounds were even more of a problem. At the 4th Convalescent Hospital there were 300 investigations of potential cases of self-inflicted wounds. Only fifteen were confirmed; this may have been due to the difficulty in documenting exactly how the wounds were incurred. In contrast to the official numbers, the VII Corps surgeon reported that preceding the breakout "self-inflicted wounds also were encountered in appreciable numbers for the first time."[73] Still, even allowing for a large margin of error, the number was an insignificant percentage of unit combat power.

Taken in total, the medical machine behind the U.S. Army in Normandy was impressive. Before the breakthrough attack, First Army medical units treated 95,639 patients, the equivalent of almost six infantry divisions. Of these, 22,639 (almost 24 percent) were returned to duty. This figure did not include the personnel treated for minor injuries at the front who might have become incapacitated if they had not received prompt medical attention. The army medical system provided a remarkable combat multiplier, the ability to put a wounded veteran soldier back into the line in fairly short order and in reasonable health.

When the army's medical capabilities were combined with the Americans' other abilities to protect the force the result was a truly daunting capability. In previous centuries far more soldiers had deserted or died of injury, sickness, malnutrition, exposure, and wounds than had fallen in battle. By contrast, in World War II that ratio was reversed: battle losses exceeded nonbattle deaths by three to one. In fact, General Bradley's army was so successful in limiting nonbattle losses, that a higher percentage of soldiers were lost to nonbattle deaths in the United States than in Normandy.

All together, it is difficult to overestimate the importance of the U.S. Army's ability to protect itself. After 7 exhausting weeks of combat every measure of safety, health, and comfort helped prepare Bradley's men for one more crack at the German hedgerow defenses.

Sustaining the Force

The last component of U.S. combat power for the next offensive was sustaining the force. As with the Americans' other material advantages, there was an overwhelming superiority in logistical support.[74] The greatest concern was getting all the supplies at the right time to the right place. To keep the lifeblood of war flowing, the Americans divided logistical demands into standardized classes of supply; the two most critical classes, the ones that decided the pace of battle, were class V (ammunition) and class III (fuel). In the case of class V the U.S. Army's only real concern was mortar and artillery ammunition because the Western Allies had seriously misjudged one critical logistical requirement for the opening phase of the campaign. Planners had assumed that fuel would be the initial priority as forces raced inland, but the slow-moving armies had burned only a fraction of the stockpiled fuel. On the other hand, hedgerow fighting consumed immense quantities of ammunition. For example, on 6 June the U.S. First Army fired 1,747 105mm howitzer rounds. On 12 June it fired more than ten times that, and firing increased exponentially as the Allies inched forward.[75] Ammunition expenditure rates had to be strictly controlled, which made nobody happy. Commanders complained incessantly, and General Bradley took to calling the problem his "disagreeable subject."[76] The chronic shortage of artillery ammunition persisted throughout the Normandy campaign.

On the other hand, despite the abundance of class III (fuel) during the opening weeks of the campaign, the U.S. Army also had problems in this area. At the start of the Normandy invasion the army had issued fuel based on written requisitions, but this method proved chaotic and unworkable. With experience, logisticians found the system more responsive if they anticipated requirements, allocated fuel based on commanders' priorities, and then pushed it to the units accordingly.

To deliver the fuel, support units carried it forward in trucks and dispensed it either in 55-gallon fuel drums or 5-gallon cans. The bulky drums were never popular. The 5-gallon can, usually called a "jerry can" (because the design was allegedly based on the German fuel can), was the preferred tool for transporting and issuing fuel. Support units simply exchanged empty cans for full ones. The cans proved so popular that there were 35 million in the theater by the end of the war. For the breakthrough all vehicles, except the tanks and tank destroyers, were fitted with carrying racks and filled cans before the attack. In the Normandy battles fuel never limited the progress of the campaign.

Issuing fuel and ammunition were not the only logistical requirements. The entire logistics base would have to expand to support the attacking troops—and the juggernaut of support men and materiel could not move on a moment's notice. To keep pace with the offensive, quartermaster depots awash with almost every class of supply needed to move about once every 4 days. The depots planned to use leapfrog tactics to maintain a continuity of support. Part of a depot would move up and establish a new base, while the rest remained in the original location and continued to issue supplies until the forward element was set.[77]

Men and supplies also had to be trucked from assembly areas to the front before the attack. This was another significant challenge. Although the U.S. Army had experimented with motorized divisions that were fully mobile, it had abandoned the initiative long before the Normandy campaign. And so the infantry divisions could not move themselves. Instead, 2 truck companies each split into 3 teams of 32 trucks were required to transport a division. Each team could move a battalion, with each truck carrying 25 to 30 soldiers. Keeping the divisions resupplied once the attack advanced required even more trucks. Supplying an armored division, for example, required an 84-truck column, with 12 trucks just for fuel.[78]

Trucking men and supplies was only one part of the logistical task. Supplies had to be ordered and organized so that they could be shipped to the front, and trucks had to be maintained so that they could keep the supplies moving. The combat divisions had only minimal organic assets to perform all these tasks: infantry divisions had a light maintenance company and a quartermaster company; the more vehicle-heavy armored divisions were authorized a supply battalion and a maintenance battalion. The organic units were enough to meet the divisions' immediate needs, but heavy support had to come from echelons above corps logistical units. These units issued all classes of supplies and performed a range of services from shoe repair to washing laundry.

The greatest challenge to pushing supplies and services around the battlefield was not the availability of support but traffic. All movement back and forth created a nightmare of congestion on the narrow Normandy roads. One observer described traffic as "hazardous and difficult to control. Vehicles could often be found speeding and cutting in and out of slow-moving columns."[79] Rotten weather, civilian traffic, and frequent road accidents exacerbated the problem.

For the big attack the VII Corps administrative order provided a volume of details on the restrictions, routes, and control points for moving through the corps area during the advance. The divisions had to strip out all nonessential equipment and reduce the length of their truck columns. The order also designated main supply routes, delineating which roads would be used for pushing supplies forward and which for evacuating prisoners, casualties, and damaged equipment.

The only problem with this deluge of directives was that someone had to enforce all the rules, and the mission of traffic cop fell to the military police. Each division had one military police platoon, and these men were constantly busy. One soldier in the 4th Infantry Division remembered that the MPs were always on the road enforcing two standing orders, "Keep the Frenchmen off and the trucks on."[80] Unfortunately, there were very few MPs with a lot of responsibility. (General Eddy, the 9th Infantry Division commander, tried to deal with the situation by keeping his military police platoon at 200 percent strength to handle all the required traffic control tasks.) Beyond the division rear, at field army level, military police units controlled military traffic. Even with a small army directing traffic, commanders had to anticipate that the narrow Normandy roads would be awash with friendly forces during the big attack. It would require all the skill commanders could muster to keep the U.S. advance from choking on its own mass of men and machines.

The Normandy traffic jams, while a challenge, were also the most visible symbol of U.S. might. The endless lines of trucks represented the unprecedented logistical, medical, and combat support backing up the U.S. infantryman. Without question, the First Army had more support than any other force on the Western Front, and, in fact, historian John Ellis credits the U.S. material advantages with the American victory.[81] General Bradley's battle to break through the Normandy defenses, however, does not support Ellis's thesis. While logistical support was a prerequisite for keeping the Americans in the fight, it could not carry the U.S. forces through the Normandy campaign. Grinding attrition warfare against the German defenses had effectively negated the American advantage. What was still needed to change the course of the campaign was for Bradley to figure out how to get his wealth of resources into play and turn a war of attrition into an unfair fight.

Bradley's Promise

Despite shortfalls in training, organization, equipment, and manning, it is clear that the U.S. units still held an overwhelming material advantage. So why could they not get past the hedgerows? In truth, the U.S. First Army simply lacked the room it needed to employ all its advantages to best effect. If it could have maneuvered more freely, in response enemy forces would have had to move out of their well-prepared defensive positions, exposing themselves to U.S. artillery, armor, and airplanes while stretching their own logistics to the breaking point. An operational maneuver would have also ended the debilitating small-unit battles in the hedgerows that were exacerbated by U.S. infantry squads' shortfalls in weapons and tactics. In turn, this would have led to fewer U.S. casualties and allowed the Americans to continue to build up the experience, training, and cohesion of combat units at the front. What the Americans needed, more than anything else, was the space to maneuver.

When the U.S. forces landed on D-Day they lacked the "operational flexibility" necessary to gain the ground they needed so desperately. Although there were veterans of North Africa and Sicily in the ranks of these forces, they were a fraction of the leaders and soldiers on the battlefield. In addition, their combat experience was from very different battlefields. It was going to take time to prepare leaders for the unique demands of the war in the hedgerows. It was also going to take time to gain a positional advantage and build up a preponderance of materiel and combat support to bring full combat power to bear.

It is clear that the U.S. Army was not prepared for hedgerow fighting, considering the state of training, the personnel replacement system in place, the level of experience among leaders, the limitations of fire-and-movement tactics, and the inadequacy of infantry weapons, but General Bradley's army adjusted to the requirements of Normandy fighting reasonably well. Commanders benefited from the army's tremendous capability to sustain and protect its forces. In addition, the 2 months of hard fighting had provided stiff lessons for the U.S. Army, which gave it the opportunity to correct its deficiencies and learn how to balance the strengths and weaknesses of its combat capabilities. By the end of July, measure for measure, the Americans had more than enough combat power to win the battle of the hedgerows.

More important, the U.S. forces had achieved what Bradley needed most, a degree of "operational flexibility," a balance in skill and power that gave them the measure of advantage they needed for an operational breakthrough. This flexibility derived from the confidence that leaders had gained in the dependability of their logistical and medical support and the ability of field-grade leaders to effectively command and control maneuver forces, overcome the shortfalls of the front-line infantry units, and effectively employ combat support (particularly close air and artillery support). Flexibility was the mental edge gained from knowing what the force could do, under the right conditions, to change the course of a campaign. The proof of the Americans' operational flexibility is well demonstrated in examining the planning and execution of General Bradley's big attack.

By the end of July Bradley had the place, the opportunity, and the forces to test the U.S. Army's new-found power. How he chose to do that is the subject of the next chapter.

Notes

1. Meindl, "II Parachute Corps," p. 43.
2. First U.S. Army (FUSA), Report of Operations, p. 117. For an overview of recent scholarship on the debate, see Colin Baxter, "Did Nazis Fight Better than Democrats? Historical Writing on Combat Performance of the Allied in Normandy," *Parameters* 25 (Autumn 1995): 113–118. A significant controversy surrounding the performance of U.S. soldiers in battle centers on the work of the combat historian S. L. A. Marshall and his influential book *Men Against Fire*. Critics were particularly concerned about Marshall's claim that only 25 percent of a unit's soldiers employed their weapons during a fight. See Roger J. Spiller, "SLA Marshall and the Ratio of Fire," *RUSI Journal* 133 (Winter 1988): 63–71; Fredric Smoler, "The Secret of the Soldiers Who Didn't Shoot," *American Heritage* 40 (March 1989): 37–45. For a defense of Marshall's work, see F. D. G. Williams, *SLAM: The Influence of S. L. A. Marshall on the United States Army;* John Douglas Marshall, *Reconciliation Road:*

A Family Odyssey of War and Honor. Despite the controversy over ammunition expenditure, many other of S. L. A. Marshall's conclusions, including his observations on the importance of cohesion and information distribution, remain unchallenged. Other criticisms of the performance of U.S. forces have been even more pointed. See Martin Van Crevald, *Fighting Power: German and U.S. Army Performance, 1939–45.* In *Brute Force: Allied Strategy and Tactics in the Second World War,* John Ellis argues in what he calls a "radical reappraisal" of World War II that the Allies won because of their material superiority. Recent, more balanced and systematic assessments of the performance of U.S. forces include Michael D. Doubler's *Closing with the Enemy* and Keith E. Bonn's *When the Odds Were Even: The Vosges Mountain Campaign, October 1944–January 1945.* Both undercut much of Van Crevald's and Ellis's analyses.

3. Recent studies on the combat performance of U.S. combat troops include Lee Kennett, *G.I.: The American Soldier in World War II;* Gerald F. Linderman, *The World Within War: America's Combat Experience in World War II;* Reid Mitchell, "The GI in Europe and the American Military Tradition," in *Time to Kill: The Soldier's Experience of War in the West, 1939–1945,* pp. 304–318; Stephen E. Ambrose, *Citizen Soldiers: The U.S. Army from the Normandy Beaches to the Bulge to the Surrender of Germany;* John C. McManus, *The Deadly Brotherhood: The American Combat Soldier in World War II.*

4. Unless otherwise cited, information on German forces organization and equipment is taken from the U.S. War Department, *Handbook on German Military Forces* and *German Order of Battle;* Max Simon, "Evaluation of Combat Infantry Experience," MS C-055. See also the English translation of the German manual on the infantry squad in combat in Matthew Gajkowski, *German Squad Infantry Tactics in World War II.* Information on U.S. forces and equipment was drawn from U.S. Forces, European Theater, *Report of the General Board: Organization, Equipment and Tactical Employment of the Infantry Division,* CARL. For a cogent and detailed comparison of the German and U.S. infantry regiment, see Joseph Balkoski, *Beyond the Beachhead: The 29th Infantry Division in Normandy,* pp. 94–116.

5. Activities of General Eddy, July 21, 1944, USAIM; Lida Mayo, *The Ordnance Department on Beachhead and Battlefield,* pp. 31,149–150, 155–156.

6. Letter from Major General Gillem to commanding general, AGF, September 4, 1943, CARL. See also U.S. Forces, European Theater, *Report of the General Board: Study of Organization, Equipment and Tactical Employment of Tank Destroyer Units, Study No. 60,* CARL. For an overview on tank destroyer employment in World War II, see Christopher R. Gabel, "Seek, Strike, Destroy: U.S. Army Tank Destroyer Doctrine in World War II," *Leavenworth Papers No. 12.* For case studies on infantry antitank fighting, see Allyn R. Vannoy and Jay Karamales, *Against the Panzers: United States Infantry versus German Tanks, 1944–1945.*

7. The addition of the U.S. regimental cannon company was a post–World War I innovation. The companies were supposed to provide the regimental commander immediately responsive fire support. In practice most units attached the guns to the nearest artillery battalion.

8. John S. Brown, "Winning Teams: Mobilization-Related Correlatives of Success in American World War II Infantry Divisions," thesis, U.S. Army Command and General Staff College, 1985, p. 31. See also Theodore A. Wilson, "Who Fought and Why? The Assignment of American Soldiers to Combat," in *Time to Kill: The Soldier's Experience of War in the West, 1939–1945,* pp. 284–303.

9. Charles E. Kilpatrick, "Lesley J. McNair Training Philosophy for a New Army," *Army Historian* (Winter 1990): 11–15.

10. Robert R. Palmer, Bell I. Wiley, and William R. Keast, *The Procurement and Training of Ground Combat Troops,* p. 444; see also pp. 443–444, 448–450.

11. R. L. Brownlee and William J. Mullen III, *Changing an Army: An Oral History of General William E. Depuy, USA Retired,* p. 8. See Brown, "Winning Team," pp. 13–18.

12. "Gen. McNair Talks," *Army and Navy Journal,* 11 October 1941, p. 144.

13. Morton J. Stussman, *60th Follow Thru,* p. 19.

14. John Colby, *War from the Ground Up: The 90th Division in WW II,* p. 4.

15. Christopher Gabel, *U.S. Army GHQ Maneuvers of 1941,* p. 187.

16. "Gen McNair Talks," pp. 143–144.

17. Ibid.

18. There was a very bitter controversy over the treatment of National Guard officers. This issue has received little attention in the World War II historiography. See, for example, Jim Dan Hill, *The Minute Man in Peace and War: A History of the National Guard,* pp. 423–443; Henry D. Russell, *The Purge of the 30th Division;* Bruce Jacobs, "Tensions Between the Army National Guard and the Regular Army," *Military Review* LXXII (October 1993): 11–16; Robert Bruce Sligh, *The National Guard and the National Defense: The Mobilization of the Guard in World War II.*

19. Gabel, *U.S. Army GHQ Maneuvers of 1941,* pp. 115–117.

20. Brownlee and Mullen, *Changing an Army,* p. 13. Ironically, England does have some countryside that resembles the Normandy hedgerow terrain that would have been ideal for training the U.S. forces.

21. *899th Tank Destroyer Battalion History,* pp. 32–36.

22. General George Patton, for one, was a very vocal critic of U.S. small-unit tactics. The problem, he argued, was that only part of the unit fired at a time. At the decisive moment of battle, two-thirds of the force were not firing their weapons— they were maneuvering or in reserve. Instead, General Patton advocated "marching fire." The unit should advance with the mass of men firing a round every two or three paces as they advanced. Unfortunately, Patton's idea was equally inappropriate for the hedgerow terrain. There was no room to maneuver a mass of men, and if there were, it would only have made the men better targets. See Paul F. Gorman, *The Secret of Future Victories,* pp. II-69 to II-70. Another technique suggested was "soft-spot" or infiltration tactics such as those used in World War I. See *Infantry in Battle,* pp. 307–323. This technique involved infiltrating a small force through a narrow gap or weak spot in the enemy line. The tactic might have been effective in the hedgerows, but required tremendously well-trained and disciplined forces and precise coordination to be employed effectively. Typically, this level of expertise exceeded most front-line U.S. infantry units.

23. Brownlee, *Changing an Army,* p. 8.

24. Donald J. Willis, *The Incredible Years,* p. 24.

25. U.S. Forces, European Theater, *Report of the General Board: Organization, Equipment and Tactical Employment of the Infantry Division,* p. 15, CARL.

26. For a cogent summary of U.S. tactical innovation in Normandy see Doubler, *Closing with the Enemy,* pp. 34–68, and *Busting the Bocage: American Combined Arms Operations in France, 6 June–31 July 1944;* Peter R. Mansoor, "Building Blocks of Victory: American Infantry Divisions in the War Against Germany and Italy," Ph.D. diss. (Ohio State University, 1995), pp. 273–325.

27. Meindl, "II Parachute Corps," p. 43.

28. The U.S. Army was so impressed with the attack that it issued a special how-to-fight history. See *St-Lo.* For details on planning, preparations, and mistakes made during the battle, see Frank T. Mildren, "The Attack of Hill 192 by the 1st

Battalion, 38th Infantry: Personal Experiences of a Battalion Commander," CARL; D. C. Little, "Artillery in Support of the Capture of Hill 192," *Military Review* XXVII (March 1948): 31–37.

29. Frank G. Ratliff, "The Field Artillery Battalion Fire Direction Center: Its Past, Present and Future," *The Field Artillery Journal* (May–June 1950): 116–119. For the most definitive account of the development of the fire direction center, see L. Martin Kaplan, "Harnessing Indirect Fire, 1905–1941."

30. For an overview of the employment of the field artillery groups and brigades in World War II, see U.S. Forces, European Theater, *Report of the General Board: Study of the Field Artillery Group, Study No. 51*, pp. 2, 8–10, 17, and *Report of the General Board: Study of the Organization and Equipment of Field Artillery Units, Study No. 89*, pp. 24–25, CARL.

31. Boyd Dastrup, *King of Battle*, p. 210.

32. The discussion on the development of U.S. armored forces is based on Kenneth Steadman, "The Evolution of the Tank in the U.S. Army, 1919–1940," *Combat Studies Institute Report No. 1*, pp. 11–12, 17; and Jonathan M. House, "Toward Combined Arms Warfare: A Survey of 20th Century Tactics, Doctrine and Organization," *Research Survey No. 2*, pp. 108–110. For a cogent summary on European developments, see Williamson Murray, "Armored Warfare: The British, French, and German Experiences," in *Military Innovation in the Interwar Years*, pp. 6–49. See also Belton Y. Cooper, *Death Traps: The Survival of American Armored Division in World War II*.

33. Steve E. Dietrich, "In-Theater Armored Force Modernization," *Military Review* 73 (October 1993): 36–37.

34. Dastrup, *King of Battle*, p. 205.

35. FM 71-5, pp. 32–33; see also pp. 44–45.

36. *Spearhead in the West, 1941–1945, the Third Armored Division*, p. 4.

37. *Activities of General Eddy*, 21 July 1944, USAIM.

38. For a summary of the problems in tank-infantry coordination, see H. L. Hillyard, "Employment of Tanks by the Infantry Division," *Military Review* XXVII (June 1947): 50–60; G-3 Section, Supreme Headquarters Allied Expeditionary Forces, "Employment of Tanks and Infantry in Normandy," *Military Review* XXIV (December 1944): 13–17.

39. Information on air-ground operations and the capabilities of U.S. aircraft is taken from Tactics and Techniques Developed by the United States Tactical Air Commands in the European Theater of Operations, 1 March 1945, Elwood R. Quesada Papers, Box 1, DDE; Robert H. George, Ninth Air Force, April to November 1944, microfilm K1005, AFHRA; U.S. Forces, European Theater, *Report of the General Board: The Tactical Air Force in the European Theater of Operations, Study No. 54*, pp. 5–15, CARL; Richard H. Kohn and Joseph P. Harahan, eds., *Condensed Analysis of the Ninth Air Force in the European Theater of Operations*, p. 13, 22; *Report of the General Board: The Control of Tactical Aircraft in the European Theater of Operations, Study No. 55*, CARL; Kenneth A. Steadman, "A Comparative Look at Air-Ground Support Doctrine and Practice in World War II," *Combat Studies Institute Report No. 2*, pp. 8–10; Daniel R. Mortensen, *A Pattern for Joint Operations: World War II Close Air Support, North Africa*; AGF Observers Immediate Report No. 40, pp. 1–2, CARL; *Report of the General Board: Organization and Equipment of Air-Ground Liaison in All Echelons from Division Upward, Study No. 21*, CARL; John J. Sullivan, *Overlord's Eagles: Operations of the United States Army Air Forces in the Invasion of Normandy in World War II*; Richard Hallion, *The U.S. Army Air Forces in World War II: D-Day 1944, Air Power over the Normandy Beaches and Beyond*; W. A. Jacobs, "The

Battle for France, 1944," *Case Studies in the Development of Close Air Support,* pp. 247–266, 272; Richard P. Hallion, *Strike from the Sky: The History of Battlefield Air Attack 1911–1945,* pp. 201–203; Jerry Scutts, *Republic P-47 Thunderbolt: The Operational Record.* For a summary of air support party operations, see Headquarters, IX TAC Air Command, 3 August 1944, Memorandum 20-2 Standard Operating Procedures for Air Support Parties, microfilm, Roll C5127, AFHSO.

41. The Americans also employed two other fighter aircraft in Normandy. The first, the P-38 Lightning, was the least capable of all the U.S. fighters, suffering from mechanical problems and lacking firepower. The P-38, however, did have advantages. A unique two-engine and twin-tail design made it highly survivable: the aircraft could lose an engine to ground fire and still make its way back to the airfield. The twin-tail silhouette also gave the aircraft a distinctive shape that was more likely to be noticed by nervous U.S. antiaircraft gunners, making it less probable that the planes would be shot down by mistake. The second U.S. fighter seen on the Normandy front was the P-51 Mustang. Designed for bomber escort, it carried a lot of fuel and could fly a long way. The plane's ability to loiter over the battlefield offered a real advantage in close air support. The P-51's disadvantage was a water-cooled engine with an exposed radiator underneath the airplane. One bullet from ground fire in the cooling system would incapacitate the plane in minutes.

41. Headquarters, 30th Infantry Division, U.S. Army, After Action Report, pp. 193–194. Information on the SCR-625 is taken from Blanche D. Coll, Jean E. Keith, and Herbert H. Rosenthal, *The Corps of Engineers: Troops and Equipment,* pp. 54–55, 477.

42. Hansen, War Diary, 8 June 1944, MHI.

43. Coates, "Notes on Interviews," p. 3, CARL. See also Willis, *The Incredible Years,* p. 21.

44. *Report of the General Board: Study of Field Artillery Gunnery, Study No. 64,* pp. 5, 7, 10–17, CARL.

45. Gerhard Treipel, "91st Airborne Division Artillery," p. 4, MS B 469.

46. Glover S. Johns Jr., *The Clay Pigeons of St. Lo,* p. 45.

47. Ellis, *Brute Force: Allied Strategy and Tactics in the Second World War,* p. 361.

48. Hansen, War Diary, 25 June 1944, MHI.

49. Statistics are from Headquarters, VII Corps, U.S. Army, The History of VII Corps, U.S. Army, Covering Operations in Normandy, France, from 1–31 July 1944, 6 August 1944, p. 21; FUSA, Report of Operations, Annexes 3–11, pp. 266, 274; Headquarters, Ninth Air Force, Air Force Logistical Data, 1946.

50. Carl I. Hutton, *An Armored Artillery Commander in the European Theater,* p. 90, USAFAS.

51. Coates, "Notes on Interviews," p. 4, CARL. For an overview of ground-air defense operations, see *Report of the General Board: Antiaircraft Artillery Techniques, Study No. 40,* CARL.

52. Information on chemical warfare operations are from Brooks E. Kleber and Dale Birdsell, *The Chemical Warfare Service,* pp. 70, 156, 167; and FUSA, Report of Operations, p. 95.

53. Alden H. Waitt, "Gas on a Hostile Shore," *The Infantry Journal Reader,* pp. 622–629.

54. Sylvan, War Diary, 21 July 1995, MHI.

55. VII Corps Operations Memo No. 46, 23 July 1944.

56. All information and statistical data on personnel are taken from *Report of the General Board: G-1 Reports and Reporting Procedures in European Theater of Operations, Study No. 8,* CARL; FUSA, Report of Operations, Annexes 3–11.

Medical statistics are extracted from John Lada and Frank A. Reister, eds., *Medical Statistics in World War II.*

57. Giles, *G.I. Journal,* p. 50.

58. A. J. Liebling, "St. Lo and Mortain," in *Danger Forward: The Story of the First Division in World War II,* p. 244.

59. FUSA, Report of Operations, p. 94; Headquarters, VII Corps, U.S. Army, Administrative Order, 8 July 1944.

60. FUSA, Report of Operations, p. 22; and *Report of the General Board: Organization, Operation and Supply of the Army Exchange, Service, Study No. 57,* CARL.

61. Charles R. Cawthon, *Other Clay: A Remembrance of the World War II Infantry,* pp. 69–70.

62. FUSA, Report of Operations, Annexes 3–11, pp. 71–72.

63. Hutton, *An Armored Artillery Commander,* pp. 19–20, USAFAS.

64. Paul Fussell, *Wartime: Understanding and Behavior in the Second World War,* p. 108. Homosexuality also does not appear to have been a significant issue in combat. For a brief discussion see Allan Bérubé, *Coming Out Under Fire: History of Gay Men and Women in World War II,* pp. 176–178. The army's only concerns about sex were in discouraging rape and limiting the spread of venereal disease, which was a particular problem. During World War II more soldiers contracted it than any other infectious illness. Commanders fought the problem with a "stick and carrot" approach, threatening soldiers with judicial action but at the same time issuing free prophylactics. The measures must have had some impact: the venereal disease rate was half that of World War I.

65. Charles E. Taylor, *Miss You: The World War II Letters of Barbara Wooddall Taylor and Charles E. Taylor,* p. 209.

66. *Report of the General Board: Chaplains,* pp. 9, 37, 42, 43, 56. For an overview on Catholic chaplains in World War II, see Donald F. Crosby, *Battlefield Chaplains.*

67. *Report of the General Board: Stragglers and Absentees without Leave, Study No. 105,* p. 4, CARL. FUSA, Report on Operations, Annexes 3–11, pp. 81, 96. These low statistics may be partially misleading, since most divisions recovered AWOL and straggler personnel within the division area.

68. Unless otherwise noted, the information on medical operations in the European Theater of Operations is taken from *Report of the General Board: Evacuation of Human Casualties in the European Theater of Operations, Study No. 92,* CARL; Graham A. Cosmas and Albert E. Cowdry, *Medical Service in the European Theater of Operations,* pp. 224, 226, 280, 229; AGF Observer Immediate Report No. 23, p. 1.

69. Headquarters, VII Corps, U.S. Army, Administrative Order No. 17, 12 July 1944.

70. Max S. Allen, ed., *Medicine under Canvas,* p. 111.

71. William S. Mullins, ed., *Neuropsychiatry in World War II,* vol.II, pp. 278–279; *Report of the General Board: Combat Fatigue, Study No. 91,* CARL; Paul Wanke, "American Military Psychiatry and Its Role among Ground Forces in World War II," *Journal of Military History* 63 (January 1999): 127–146.

72. Mullins, *Neuropsychiatry,* pp. 284–286. See, for example, the increases in the 4th Infantry Division in Private S. Hechter's Notebook, Statistical Summary of the 4th Medical Battalion, entries for 23–26 July, MHI.

73. FUSA, Observation Report No. 91, p. 3.

74. For a cogent overview of recent scholarship on U.S. Army logistics in World War II, see Charles R. Shrader, "World War II Logistics," *Parameters* 25

(Spring 1995): 133–137. Steve R. Waddell, *United States Army Logistics: The Normandy Campaign, 1944,* provides a scholarly and thorough overview.

75. U.S. Forces, European Theater, Study No. 61, p. 13.

76. Hansen, War Dairy, July 23, 1944, MHI.

77. Meredith L. Butterton, *Metric 16,* p. 121.

78. Charles F. Howard, AGF Observer Report, 27 July 1944, pp. 11, 12, CARL; Donald E. Houston, *Hell on Wheels: The 2d Armored Division,* p. 204.

79. Howard, AGF Observer Report, pp. 7–8, CARL.

80. Charles L. Dorst, *My Times and Service in the Military,* p. 61, MHI. For an overview of military police activities in the theater, see *Report of the General Board: Military Police Activities, Study No. 103,* CARL.

81. John Ellis, *Brute Force: Allied Strategy and Tactics in the Second World War.*

4

The Essence of Decisions

W hen it became clear that the Allies would not be breaking out of the Normandy lodgement area anytime soon, General Omar Bradley ordered a mess tent erected next to his headquarters with a nice dry plank floor so that he could spread out his maps and study them in quiet, Spartan comfort. Still, he was far from at peace. Modern combat, General Bradley believed, must be a fast war of movement, fought with swift, decisive campaigns that minimized friendly casualties and the expenditure of combat power. But that was not what was happening. The British Second Army had tried to push back the German defenses several times, but with very discouraging results. General Bradley's U.S. First Army had also given it a shot. In early July the Americans launched an all-out attack to broaden the lodgement area with a series of frontal assaults. Bradley threw twelve divisions into the fight. By the time the offensive finished it had cost 40,000 casualties, more men than the strength of two fully manned infantry divisions, but the attack had fallen far short of its objective.[1]

Even though the Americans had a decisive advantage in combat power, General Bradley believed that the army could not simply rely on a war of attrition to fight its way out of Normandy. After the Allies broke through the hedgerows there would be a lot of fighting to be done before they could ultimately defeat Germany. U.S. forces could not afford to waste their advantage in men and materiel on the coast of France. Bradley repeatedly told his aide, Major Chester Hansen, and the rest of the First Army staff that he did not want to stand and "slug it out" with the Germans.[2] The July offensive showed his inclination to be correct, frontal assaults offering no simple solution to the difficulties of the campaign. Now, in his solitary map room, Bradley searched for another means to break the German ring, change the course of the campaign, and allow the Allied armies to execute the bold operational maneuvers they had hoped to conduct across France and on to the German homeland.

The Planner

Before every battle there are commanders who stand at the nexus of the strategic, operational, and tactical levels of war. It is their task to harmonize the demands made by each level and make the fundamental decisions of when, where, and how the next battle is to be fought with the combat power at hand. For this operation the responsibility fell to Omar Bradley.

In his memoirs he glibly outlined what his forces needed to do. "First, we must pick a soft point in the enemy's line: next, concentrate our forces against it. Then after smashing through with a blow that would crush his front-line defenses, we would spill our mechanized columns through that gap before the enemy could recover his senses."[3]

In fact, the operation Omar Bradley described was one of the most complex and difficult missions that an army could hope to conduct. It would be hard to overestimate the depth of knowledge and skill required to effectively plan such an operation or the importance of Bradley's decisions to the next step in the campaign. Understanding the scope of the challenge that Bradley faced and the magnitude of his achievement in crafting a plan to break through the German defenses requires systematically walking through the process of how he decided what to do next.

The planning that went into making the decision to fight, particularly for Bradley, was fundamental to the U.S. Army's operational approach to war. The Americans were methodical planners. One contemporary U.S. Army text concluded that it was

> axiomatic that in war there will always be a plan. . . . In every operation there must run from the highest to the lowest unit the sturdy life-line of a guiding idea; from this will be spun the intricate web that binds an army into an invincible unit embodying a single thought and a single goal.[4]

In the U.S. Army planning was the essence of a decision. It was a lesson the Americans had learned well in World War I and then drummed into their officers during the interwar years and the early campaigns in North Africa and Sicily.[5] Every action, every innovation and modification that followed traced its origin to the plan that prepared the army for battle.

In preparation for the Normandy campaign Bradley had had 29 years of military experience in learning how to make plans. A 1915 West Point graduate, he had missed overseas service in World War I and learned his trade in the peacetime army. When war came again he got an early opportunity to take a division, and from 1942 to 1943 he successfully commanded two in rapid succession. His performance was rated as first class and General George Marshall sent him to North Africa, where he served as a deputy corps commander under George Patton. For the invasion of Sicily Bradley commanded his own corps. The campaign provided valuable experience: by the advent of D-Day General Bradley had had more time in combat than any other corps commander in the army.

General Bradley's star was rising. Dwight Eisenhower had great trust and confidence in his old friend and West Point classmate. After the Sicilian campaign Eisenhower wrote to Marshall:

> He [Bradley] is in my opinion the best rounded combat leader I have yet met in our service. While he possibly lacks some of the extraordinary and ruthless driving power that Patton can exert at critical moments, he still has such force and determination that even in this characteristic he is among our best.[6]

So, General Bradley was the right man for the job. Or was he? In Normandy, for the first time, Bradley was truly on his own. As the senior U.S. ground commander, there was no one to second-guess his decisions. He was facing exactly the kind of "critical moment" that Eisenhower had described in his letter, a moment requiring extraordinary, ruthless driving power—a moment of decision.

General Bradley was indeed facing some very difficult choices, and George Patton, for one, did not think that Bradley was up to the task (he called his old friend "Brad" mediocre and timid).[7] Bradley's plan for the big attack would prove a worthy test for the skill and determination of the U.S. First Army commander.

The Mission

In making the crucial choice of how to get beyond the Normandy beachhead, Bradley followed the army's official decisionmaking process, first preparing an estimate of the situation and then picking a course of action.[8] The first step in the estimate was to analyze the mission in order to determine the purpose of the operation and the critical tasks that had to be accomplished. The strategic, operational, and tactical situations (outlined in Chapter 2) all dictated to General Bradley that for the First Army to get the campaign back on course a breakthrough was essential.

A key objective of the Normandy campaign was to push out from the coast and into Brittany, securing a base of operations for the drive into Germany. General Bradley had to clear enough ground to launch the drive toward the Brittany ports with follow-on forces from the U.S. Third Army.[9] This meant getting out of the swamps and rough hedgerow terrain along the coast and on to higher, drier ground farther south. Therefore, Bradley concluded that the next attack had to push back the German defenses as far south as Coutances. Only a drive to Coutances, he told Major Hansen and other key First Army staffers, would allow "room for maneuver and greater

build up which will eventually permit the breakthrough," setting the conditions for the advance into Brittany.[10]

The Adversary

After determining the mission, the next step was to figure out how to best
accomplish the task. Commanders started by analyzing the capabilities of
enemy forces, battlefield conditions (terrain, time, and weather), and the
state of friendly troops. This evaluation was a prerequisite for determining
the best course of action. The estimate identified the strengths and weaknesses of friendly and enemy forces, so that commanders could select a
plan that best avoided the enemy's strengths and exploited his weaknesses
and, at the same time, took maximum advantage of the friendly forces'
strengths and limited their vulnerabilities. Finding the optimal balance of
strengths and weaknesses was the key to developing a winning plan, one
that would allow commanders to focus the fullest combat power at the critical point.

The most difficult part of conducting the estimate was gaining an
appreciation of the enemy. In Normandy, blocking the U.S. advance from
Caumont all the way to the coast, was the German Seventh Army. When the
Americans had landed on D-Day this army was commanded by Colonel
General Friedrich Dollmann. In 1940 General Dollmann had led the
Seventh Army to a brilliant victory against the French. But, 4 years and a
month of Normandy fighting later, things were very different. The German
Seventh Army had failed to stop the U.S. Army landings in Normandy, and
Hitler had determined that General Dollmann was no longer up to the chal-
lenges of war. Even those close to the general admitted that he looked
"tired and worn down."[11] On 29 June Hitler decided to relieve him, and he
would have had General Dollmann not dropped dead from a heart attack.[12]

For General Dollmann's replacement, Hitler selected a veteran armor
commander, Waffen SS Colonel General Paul Hausser.[13] General Hausser
was 64 years old, 13 years older than Omar Bradley. Hausser was a professional career soldier, a graduate of Berlin-Lichterfelde, imperial Germany's
West Point. After winning the Iron Cross in World War I, he had remained
in the army and then retired as a major general. He returned to service in
the Waffen SS and fought in the Polish and French campaigns. From 1943
to 1944, as a corps commander, he bounced from Russia to Italy to France,
back to Russia, then to Poland, and finally back to France. General Hausser
reported to his new headquarters at Le Mans on 28 June 1944, just in time
to witness the U.S. First Army's failed offensive in early July. Contemporary pictures show a distinguished-looking officer with wire-rim glasses, a
spotless uniform with SS insignia, and an Iron Cross around his neck. Were

it not for the Iron Cross and the insignia, the man in the pictures bore a passing resemblance to U.S. Vice President Harry Truman.

The new Seventh Army commander had a reputation as "an above-average divisional commander and a gifted and sometimes brilliant corps commander. . . . As a trainer, he had few equals anywhere."[14] General Hausser would need all these skills to succeed in Normandy. He received minimal guidance on how to defend his front. Even before his injuries, Marshal Erwin Rommel had not involved himself in the details of Seventh Army operations.[15] He visited General Hausser only once. Even Marshal Günther Kluge, the new Army Group B commander, despite his reputation as a meddler, gave little direction, so Hausser continued to follow the policies of his predecessor and hold fast. (The disposition of Allied and German forces is shown in Figure 4.1.)

The quality of Hausser's Seventh Army ranged from outstanding to inept. Some units were well trained, with veteran combat leaders; others were an odd assortment of old men, untrained youths, and inexperienced commanders. General Hausser rated only three of his nine divisions as good units.[16] One characteristic all the units shared, regardless of their fighting quality, was that they were woefully understrength after prolonged combat. The whole force totaled fewer than 35,000 men, equal to little more than two full-strength U.S. divisions and less than one-fifth of the force available to General Bradley. To make matters worse, replacements were few and far between. One regiment, for instance, was promised 1,000 replacements at the end of June: "170 men were lost while still on the march, from wounds, death, or in a few isolated cases, probably from desertion. The replacements were unarmed and their clothing and equipment were amazingly poor . . . their training and fighting spirit seemed inferior."[17]

The situation was discouraging. Want of combat support exacerbated the desperate conditions of the forward troops. In particular, lack of air support, General Hausser complained, "constituted a spiritual burden for the men."[18] Lack of artillery was also a serious problem. The 91st Division, for example, had lost so many guns that the artillery officers were sent off on reconnaissance duty because the division no longer needed an artillery staff.[19] Even the units that had artillery were not much better off because Allied air interdiction of supply lines had created chronic ammunition shortages.

The Germans' only advantage was their armored forces. But even here, the Allies, by design and by fortune, had early on limited the effective employment of the German tank divisions. In particular, Allied deception efforts played a key role in keeping the German armor out of the Americans' way.[20] The invasion deception plan, Fortitude North, had portrayed a fictional invasion army aimed at the Pas de Calais. A month after

Figure 4.1 Situation on the Normandy Front, July 1944: Order of Battle and Key Commanders for Operation Cobra

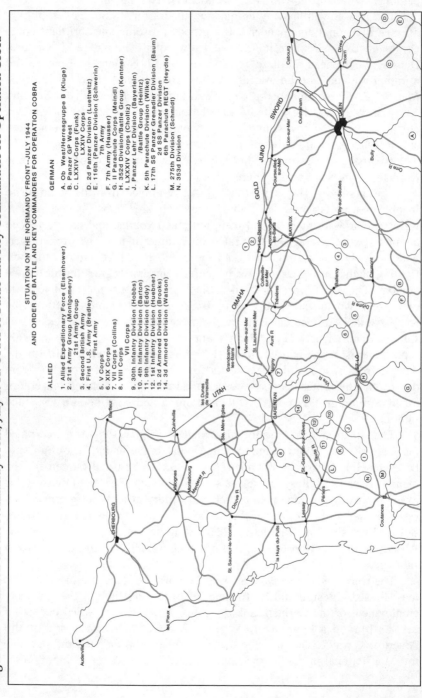

SITUATION ON THE NORMANDY FRONT—JULY 1944
AND ORDER OF BATTLE AND KEY COMMANDERS FOR OPERATION COBRA

ALLIED

1. Allied Expeditionary Force (Eisenhower)
2. 21st Army Group (Montgomery)
3. Second British Army
   21st Army Group
4. First U.S. Army (Bradley)
   First Army
5. V Corps
6. XIX Corps
7. VII Corps (Collins)
8. VIII Corps
9. 30th Infantry Division (Hobbs)
10. 4th Infantry Division (Barton)
11. 9th Infantry Division (Eddy)
12. 1st Infantry Division (Huebner)
13. 2d Armored Division (Brooks)
14. 3d Armored Division (Watson)

GERMAN

A. Ob West/Herresgruppe B (Kluge)
B. Panzer GP West
C. LXXIV Corps (Funk)
   LXXIV Corps
D. 2d Panzer Division (Luettwitz)
E. 116th Panzer Division (Schwerin)
   7th Army
F. 7th Army (Hausser)
G. II Parachute Corps (Meindl)
H. 353d Division/Battle Group (Kentner)
I. LXXXIV Corps (Cholitz)
J. Panzer Lehr Division (Bayerlein)
   Battle Group (Heintz)
K. 5th Parachute Division (Wilke)
L. 17th SS Panzer Grenadier Division (Baum)
   2d SS Panzer Division
   6th Parachute REGT (Heydte)
M. 275th Division (Schmidt)
N. 353d Division

D-Day Hitler, fearing a second landing, was still reluctant to shift the forces oriented on the Pas de Calais to Normandy. In fact, to help sustain the ruse at the same time that General Bradley planned to launch his big attack, the Allies' air forces conducted a diversionary bombing at the Pas de Calais.[21]

Meanwhile, the British Second Army's attacks around Caen succeeded in tying down most of the German Army Group B armor. Even after the British and Canadian forces had taken Caen, General Bradley anticipated that they would continue to hold the attention of the bulk of the German tanks. And General Montgomery had planned a major offensive south of Caen, called Operation Goodwood, timed to be launched in coordination with the U.S. First Army's big attack. Operation Goodwood would keep the Germans from shifting armor quickly against the Americans.[22]

In the German Seventh Army area, Hausser could not even concentrate the eighty or so armored vehicles in his command. Bradley's first offensive in early July, though unsuccessful, did have a significant impact on the German defenses, forcing Hausser to commit his only two armored divisions. Continuing pressure from the U.S. Army kept him from withdrawing his tanks and putting them in reserve.

In fact, the Seventh Army, LXXXIV Corps, and the forward divisions had only small reserves. Without a powerful counterattack force, General Hausser had little flexibility in how he could respond to the American's next initiative. Hausser believed that the U.S. forces were preparing for another offensive and that they would make their push west of St-Lô, right in his sector. To stop this attack Hausser put all his hopes on his main line of resistance, his front-line defenses. If these defenses were breached in depth, he would lose. His forces did not have the mobility or firepower to match that of the Americans. The Germans, for example, had horsedrawn artillery; the U.S. artillery was motorized. Likewise, U.S. forces relied mostly on speedy, flexible radio communications, but Hausser's troops used primarily wire lines. In virtually every respect, the Seventh Army could not match the Americans in a fast war of movement. General Hausser's goal was to make sure such a battle never occurred. Therefore, since Hausser did not have the combat punch to keep pace with the Americans, he had to rely on local counterattacks to maintain a cohesive area defense.

The Germans' ability to launch timely counterattacks with reserves depended on the command, control, and communications capabilities of their corps and division field headquarters. The headquarters and command posts had to be constantly apprised of the situation at the front so that they knew where the reserves were needed most. They also had to have the means to communicate with the reserves and to control the rear area so that counterattacks could be mounted quickly and launched at the front. Without firm command over the limited assets available, there was no way to ensure that reserves were thrown into battle at the right time and place.

How much General Bradley actually knew of the conditions in the German Seventh Army remains another of the controversies of the Normandy campaign. It was years after the war before the British and U.S. governments officially admitted their commanders had read many of the German high command (OKW) communications. At Bletchley Park, outside London, in the gracefully aging mansion that concealed the Government Code and Cipher School, U.S. and British cryptologists decoded thousands of the Germans' top secret radio messages. The Americans had long before broken the cipher of the Japanese Foreign Ministry. Because the Japanese ambassador to Berlin routinely provided Tokyo with comprehensive reports on military activities in Germany, he was the best spy the Allies had in occupied Europe. The Japanese decrypts, code-named Magic, along with Ultra, were disseminated only to high-level commanders and senior staff members. By restricting access to the information, the Allies hoped to prevent the enemy from discovering that the most secret German and Japanese codes had been broken. By D-Day senior Allied commanders routinely reviewed summaries of Magic/Ultra decrypts.[23]

While the story of this achievement is now in the public record, it remains unclear what the Allied commanders actually did with the intelligence. We know that General Bradley received Ultra intelligence reports. In the European theater of operations, Special Liaison Units (SLUs) were attached to all army group and army headquarters to distribute Ultra reports to the senior commanders and selected members of their staffs. SLU briefings usually took place once each morning. Lasting from 15 to 30 minutes, they covered salient intelligence received in the previous 24 hours.[24]

None of the senior commanders or staff officers who were still alive when the British finally declassified Ultra stated that the briefings played a critical role in tactical decisions. One problem was that the decoders at Bletchley Park were intentionally not told commanders' operational plans or priority intelligence requirements. Keeping the analysts in the dark kept them from being tainted by the perceptions of the field. The policy also kept them from being responsive to the field commanders' immediate needs. Bletchley Park never knew if what they produced could help win or lose a battle.

The SLUs were also far from perfect. They did not actually work for the commanders they supported; their first responsibility was safeguarding Ultra reports. As a result, one report concluded that "relations between the detachments and the commands to which they were attached were not always satisfactory."[25] Only two of the officers serving in the SLU detachments were regular army officers. Most had been lawyers in civilian life, and others were teachers, reporters, engineers, and even corporate executives—smart men, but not veteran intelligence analysts.[26]

In the last few days of June and the first 3 weeks of July, Bletchley

Park did not provide the SLUs with much intelligence on the German operations in Normandy. Decodings did increase during the end of July, but by then General Bradley had already completed the plan for his next attack.[27] In addition, most of the intercepted German message traffic was routine administrative reports, which rarely discussed future operational plans. Still, they could be helpful in that they revealed the general disposition and condition of the German forces. Sometimes the information affected current operations and was put to immediate tactical use. Ultra, for example, gave 36 hours' notice before an armored division moved into the U.S. First Army zone.[28]

Ultra, rather than guiding the course of the campaign, was used mostly by staffs to confirm intelligence gathered by other means. One officer concluded:

> At an Army HQ we maintained, however, that during battle we had not done our day's work properly unless we had beaten the Ultra. . . . This did not mean that we were not glad of its [Ultra] arrival, for at best it showed that we were wrong, usually it enabled us to tidy up loose ends, and at worst we tumbled into bed with a smug confirmation.[29]

It is apparent that the intelligence advantage certainly helped senior tactical commanders—providing useful background material, identifying the name and general location of units, and giving the status of supplies and command relationships—but Ultra was not exploited to its full tactical advantage, and it did not win or lose battles in Normandy.

General Bradley's appreciation for the enemy's capabilities and limitations came not from Ultra, but from his intelligence staff led by Colonel Benjamin Abbott "Monk" Dickson, the chief intelligence officer. Colonel Dickson, a 1918 West Point graduate, enjoyed a reputation as an extremely brilliant and thorough staff officer. Dickson could speak German, one of his fellow staff officers recalled, and more important, "think German." Colonel Dickson was also a colorful character, "a racketeer of the first order" and a "ham actor." Bradley tolerated his raffish intelligence officer. He respected the colonel's intellect, but he always thought that Dickson was poorly organized and drank too much. But Bradley admitted Dickson was "an excellent G-2."[30]

Colonel Dickson's intelligence estimate for Cobra reflected the quality of his work: it was not perfect, but it was close. The U.S. First Army intelligence estimate correctly identified all the German Seventh Army's major units.[31] The Seventh Army consisted of two corps, General Eugen Meindl's II Parachute Corps and Lieutenant General Dietrich von Choltitz's LXXXIV Corps. General Meindl's corps had only one infantry and one parachute division, and bits and pieces of five other divisions. General Choltitz controlled two armored, one armored infantry, one parachute, and three infantry divisions, plus an assortment of battle groups and independent regiments from four other divisions. Colonel Dickson, aided by Ultra intelligence, knew a great deal about the conditions of these forces, including the desperate German shortages in personnel and equipment. He also knew that Army Group B could reinforce the Seventh Army with only a handful of divisions, and even this commitment would take a few days.

While Colonel Dickson got a lot right, there were several critical pieces of intelligence he lacked. Thanks to the tenacity and skill of the Germans' forward defenses, he did not know the precise location of the enemy's main line of resistance. He also did not know the location of the intercorps boundary that divided operational responsibilities between the Seventh Army's two major subordinate commands, LXXXIV Corps and II Parachute Corps. Dickson failed as well to correctly identify all the command relationships in LXXXIV Corps or the location and identity of the corps reserves. In addition, the staff estimate concluded the enemy had more armored infantry and armor in reserve than was actually the case. In fact, the II Parachute Corps had no reserve. The LXXXIV Corps reserve was an infantry division supported by only a battalion of armor. The Seventh Army had only a small reserve (part of an infantry division positioned behind LXXXIV Corps). During the upcoming breakthrough, the omissions in Dickson's intelligence picture would lead to some surprising results for General Bradley once the big attack got underway, creating opportunities the Americans had never expected.

The Battlefield

Despite Colonel Dickson's shortcomings in piecing together the dispositions of the Seventh Army, General Bradley still had a great deal of useful information about the location and condition of the German forces. Analyzing the enemy, however, was only part of thinking about preparing for the next battle. Terrain, time, and weather were also important considerations and had to be measured with a military man's eye. It was not necessarily important to know a mountain's height, or how fast a river flowed, or how long it would rain. What was important, however, was knowing how the terrain, time, and weather affected the way both sides could employ their combat power. Bradley understood the importance of this aspect of planning extremely well. His campaign in Sicily had provided a stiff lesson in what it was like to fight a determined enemy in difficult terrain, and gave him an appreciation for what his corps commanders would be up against as they fought to breach the German lines.

For the Normandy battles terrain, especially the road network, had a particularly decisive impact on what commanders could and could not hope to accomplish. Terrain, in fact, pretty much dictated how the Seventh Army would defend its front. There were four major north-south roads in the army's sector. Two led out of St-Lô: one ran east of the Vire River heading straight south toward the city of Vire; the second ran west of the Vire River running southwest toward Avranches. A third north-south route went through Périers, and the fourth was a few miles west of the town. All but the first route passed through Coutances. They all headed to Bréhal and on to Avranches, where the roads turned toward the Brittany ports. To maintain a viable main line of resistance, General Hausser needed to keep the Americans off these routes and out of Avranches.

To guard the routes south Hausser considered the key terrain to be the ridges around St-Lô and along the Vire River. The ridge lines covered the eastern and center portions of the Seventh Army's front dominating the two most important roads near the city of Vire. Meindl's II Parachute Corps held the ridge lines. General Hausser was not concerned about this area. Even though the corps had only two divisions, comprising the least mobile elements of the Seventh Army, the corps's task was aided by the ridge's being the most defensible terrain in the whole sector.

General Hausser was also not worried about his extreme western flank, where swamps gave way to rolling hills leading to the sea. The ground was so bad that the Germans called it *wasserstellung* (water position). Traveling cross-country was difficult, with only one major road that could support a push south. This part of the front was the least critical terrain, and General Hausser covered the ground with the weakest elements of LXXXIV Corps.

The ground between the Vire River and the coastal plain held the Seventh Army commander's attention. The front in this area rested on marshy lowlands, crisscrossed by numerous streams, but farther south the ground gradually rose to hedgerow-covered hills and valleys rising toward good open ground that supported cross-country movement and allowed access to most of the major road networks. Hausser covered this area with the bulk of his combat power.

The roads not only defined how the Germans would defend, but where the U.S. First Army could best attack. General Bradley knew that only the terrain immediately west of St-Lô clearly offered the opportunity to mass his forces and push rapidly south. In this respect, time would also be a critical factor for the Americans. Bradley assumed that Army Group B would send in reinforcements to block the U.S. advance. Allied intelligence concluded that, at best, the U.S. Army had only a few days to cross this ground and secure the key roads before the enemy launched a major counterattack.

As for the weather, the most important factor was what affected visibility for air forces. If pilots could not see they could not fly, and if they could not fly, the Allies would lose their greatest advantage—air supremacy. The long summer days offered maximum flying hours, but the Channel coast weather often proved capricious. Sudden weather fronts could move in, blanketing the coastal terrain with thick fog or sudden downpours. In addition, in July 1944 low-pressure centers continually swept out of the Bay of

Biscay, bringing low cloud cover and light rains that frequently caused poor flying conditions.[32] As long as the weather held, Bradley could plan on owning the skies. But he also knew that a sudden spurt of bad weather would quickly even the odds of battle.

The Force

Taken in total, General Bradley had a fairly accurate knowledge of all the factors (enemy, terrain, weather, and time) that could thwart a drive to the south. The remaining step in the commander's estimate was weighing these factors against what his own combat power might accomplish. Here Bradley had an advantage. If he knew one thing, General Bradley believed he understood (as described in Chapter 3) what the U.S. soldier could achieve in battle. Bradley had been a direct participant in the hectic preparations to ready the first divisions for overseas duties, and he had observed and led the Americans in their first campaigns in North Africa and Sicily. This experience, combined with 2 months of Normandy fighting, left him confident of his appreciation of U.S. Army commanders and their soldiers. He believed that the army's strengths—the maturing of tactical commanders, the U.S. advantage in sustaining forces, and preponderance of combat support and air power—outweighed the limitations. General Bradley felt that if he set the conditions of battle right, his commanders and their soldiers could succeed.

To fight through the hedgerows, General Bradley had four corps totaling ten infantry and three armored divisions. U.S. V Corps held the east flank, stretching from the British Second–First U.S. Army boundary to the ridge line east of St-Lô. XIX Corps covered the ground from V Corps to the Vire River. VII Corps held a narrow front that ran from the west bank of the Vire River to a point about halfway between St-Lô and Périers. VIII Corps's zone stretched the rest of the way from the VII Corps to the coast. Four corps gave General Bradley a tremendous amount of combat power. It was thought that a three-to-one (friendly-to-enemy) force ratio was the minimum recommended for offensive operations. Although the U.S. forces were fewer than the Germans thought (General Hausser overestimated the Americans' combat power by two to three divisions), Bradley still had more than a three-to-one advantage in men and tanks plus overwhelming supply, air power, and artillery.

The Options

After completing the estimate of friendly and enemy forces, a commander turns his attention to the next step, picking a course of action. General

Bradley had three options for his big attack. The first and simplest option was the frontal assault. Army doctrine discouraged frontal attacks, concluding that "no decisive results can be expected from this plan of attack. The enemy's full strength is encountered simultaneously."[33] Frontal attacks against prepared defenses were particularly a bad idea because they pitted strength against strength, usually ensuring high attrition and little prospect for success.

The second alternative was the penetration attack. This attack was similar to a frontal assault, except that the commander massed the preponderance of his force on a small front, creating an enemy weak spot by breaching the enemy's defenses in depth through the overwhelming application of force on a narrow axis of attack. Even though the penetration seemed like a simple variation on the frontal assault, it was a significantly more complicated maneuver. Successful penetrations required concentrating combat power for the attack. Commanders also had to have a large dose of firepower to crack open the enemy defenses. Finally, the attacker needed sufficient mobility to exploit the breach before the enemy could seal the gap with counterattacks.

The third attack option was envelopment. In this maneuver the commander attempted to place his strength against the enemy's weakness by attacking a flank (normally the least heavily defended and therefore the most vulnerable area). By encircling the enemy, an attacker could disrupt supply lines and block reinforcements. The biggest problem with employing an envelopment in Normandy was that the Germans had no exposed flanks. Another difficulty was that an enveloping force had to have superior maneuverability: the attacker needed to be behind the defender before the enemy could react and reposition forces to defend or withdraw. Even though the Americans possessed powerful mechanized forces, the tough hedgerow country and stubborn German defenses denied them the opportunity to maneuver large armored units swiftly.[34]

The Decision

Each course of action had its advantages and disadvantages. Each option had to be weighed against the strengths and weaknesses of the friendly and enemy forces as well as the limitations of terrain, time, and weather laid out in the commander's estimate. Then came the hard part, making a decision.

General Bradley quickly discarded the frontal attack option. The Allies had tried that tactic and the German defenses proved too resistant. General Bradley wanted an alternative to the head-to-head struggles of brute force and attrition warfare. He required the force of a penetration attack to crack the enemy defenses, but the general also needed the decisiveness of an envelopment to give him enough ground to conduct his fast war of movement. Bradley decided that the U.S. First Army would conduct an attack with a combination of penetration and envelopment. The Americans would first penetrate the German defenses on a narrow front west of the Vire River, reach the good ground, and then envelop the enemy in front of Coutances.

The origins of General Bradley's decision generated another of the controversies of the Normandy campaign—who conceived the idea? In postwar interviews and memoirs, Bradley claimed that he had developed the plan himself while sequestered in his map room at First Army headquarters. Bradley always said that he was his own G-3 (operations) officer. "I make the decisions, draw-up the general plan," he asserted and then "turn it over to the G-3 to issue orders and go into the details."[35]

There are arguments contradicting Bradley's claim. One explanation suggests that British General Bernard Montgomery helped inspire and shape Cobra at a meeting on 10 July.[36] The evidence for this is, frankly, not conclusive. It is not clear exactly when the planning for Cobra began or how far the concept evolved before 10 July, but there is little to suggest that Bradley needed Montgomery's advice at the conference. In addition, General Patton, whose U.S. Third Army troops were to follow up the attack, did not significantly influence Cobra planning. In truth, opinions, suggestions, and ideas of how to best concentrate U.S. forces for the breakthrough proliferated around headquarters in the weeks before Operation Cobra.[37]

The penetration and envelopment maneuver General Bradley had decided on was not unprecedented. The Germans, British, and Russians had already conducted successful offensive campaigns using a combination of penetration and envelopment. In May 1940 the Germans defeated the French by penetrating the defenses in the Ardennes and enveloping the Anglo-French forces. In 1942 the British penetrated German defenses at El Alamein, although they moved too slowly to envelop the withdrawing German units. On the Eastern Front, the Red Army had developed penetration and envelopment to a fine art. One Soviet general boasted that "penetrating a defense zone to a depth of 10 or 15 kilometers on the first day of an offensive has become the customary rate of advance of our gallant troops."[38] General Bradley surely had plenty of military examples for inspiration, and there are no facts to convincingly suggest that the plan was anything other than his own.[39]

While the evidence supports General Bradley's probably conceiving the basic plan, he also makes clear in his memoirs that his subordinates played a significant role in shaping Cobra's final form. In addition to his "workmanlike" deputy commander, Lieutenant General Courtney H. Hodges, Bradley relied heavily on others, including the First Army chief of staff, Brigadier General William Benjamin Kean. The 47-year-old Kean, a 1919 graduate of West Point, had been Bradley's chief of staff since the fighting in North Africa and Sicily, and the army commander had high praise for him. General Kean was a fine organizer, with an infinite capacity for detail and hard work, though his demanding style made him very unpopular: he was ruthless with the staff, and they were afraid of him.[40]

The operations officer, Colonel Truman "Tubby" C. Thorson, was also considered an important part of Bradley's planning team. The tall, lanky Thorson had also served with Bradley during the Africa and Sicily campaigns, but he had known Bradley since they had worked together at Fort Benning's Infantry School before the war. A fellow staff officer described Thorson as a controversial figure on the First Army staff, an excitable character, "a bull in the china shop type" with no sense of humor, who could often be found in "open warfare" with the army's gregarious intelligence officer Colonel Dickson.[41]

Some officers claimed that the real strength of the G-3 section was Colonel Thorson's deputy, Colonel Robert A. Hewitt. A West Point graduate of the class of 1932, Bob Hewitt was also an old Bradley hand from North Africa and Sicily. Baldheaded since his cadet days, Hewitt had a reputation as a "thinking man's" officer. He was "the one in the G-3 section who always knew what was going on and never got rattled," a fellow officer remembered. Hewitt was the "brains and the backbone."[42]

By the recollection of most insiders, General Bradley's staff was a composite of unique characters who did not always get along, but shared a reputation as a bright, energetic, and loyal team that had served the general ably through a series of difficult campaigns. The fact that this eclectic group functioned so well together was a credit to General Bradley's ability to set a clear purpose and direction for the staff and then value their contributions. General Bradley rarely did anything without considering the advice and counsel of these trusted aides, and as he developed the plan for Cobra he called them in to critique his concept. In fact, Colonel Thorson proposed the name for the plan—Operation Cobra.[43]

While Bradley relied on his old hands, the man who most influenced the planning of Cobra was someone whom the General had worked with only a relatively short time, Major General Joseph Lawton "Lightning Joe" Collins, the VII Corps commander. The youthful, babyfaced General Collins was a 1917 graduate of West Point, only 2 years the junior of Eisenhower and Bradley. Commissioned in the infantry, he had missed combat in World War I, but had already seen more than his share of fighting in World War II. In the Pacific he commanded a division at Guadalcannal and New Georgia and led a corps in the Aleutian Islands campaign. General Collins took command of the VII Corps in March 1944 and quickly lived up to his reputation as a fighting general. In Normandy, he gave the U.S. Army its first notable victory, when the VII Corps seized the port of Cherbourg.

Bradley believed Collins to be his best combat commander. At times, perhaps a bit "cocky and sure of himself," the VII Corps commander was nonetheless a sound tactical leader, full of drive and energy.[44] And, in turn, Collins had enormous respect for the U.S. First Army commander. After the war he said that "fifty years from now people will think Georgie Patton won the war. He was a wonderful soldier but with all due respect to Georgie, he couldn't hold a candle to Bradley."[45]

Their mutual respect, trust, and confidence made the two generals an effective team. "The two men worked easily together," as Russell Weigley noted, "Bradley shaping the total design, but quick to accept Collins's proposal for modification."[46]

General Collins got his first look at the completed plan on 12 July, when he and the other corps commanders were briefed by the First Army staff. Cobra had three basic components: the pressure force, a penetration force, and an exploitation force. For the most part Collins liked what he saw, and the First Army published an outline of the plan on 13 July.[47] After studying Cobra with his staff and commanders, Collins wanted to review the plan further with the First Army commander. The operation must ensure, the VII Corps commander believed, that the right forces were at the right place at the critical points of battle. In subsequent meetings Collins reviewed each component of the plan with Bradley.

The pressure force's job was to hold the German defenses in place and prevent them from retreating until the envelopment was complete. The First Army planned for the other three corps to act as the pressure force, conducting frontal assaults to fix the enemy while the VII Corps completed the penetration and envelopment. General Collins had no suggestions for this aspect of the plan.

Collins's main issues were over the makeup of the penetration force, whose success was a prerequisite for the whole assault. After opening a gap, the penetration force was to hold open the shoulders (flanks) of the breakthrough and clear a route for the exploitation force. The penetration would be made by attacking on a narrow front of a little over 5 miles (the total Allied front at the time was about 100 miles) west of the Vire River. The VII Corps's 9th and 30th Infantry Divisions were assigned this task, while the 83d Infantry Division from the VIII Corps was to be attached to secure the breakthrough's west flank. As the plan for Cobra was being drafted, both the 9th and the 30th Infantry Divisions had been fighting steadily for weeks. On 19 July, when General Bradley discussed the plan again with General Collins and the division commanders, General Eddy, the never taciturn 9th Infantry Division commander, complained that the front for the penetration was too big for two beat up infantry divisions to handle.[48] (Figure 4.2 shows the final form of Operation Cobra.)

Both Collins and Bradley acknowledged that Eddy was probably right. The VII Corps needed another infantry division to ensure that the breakthrough was accomplished as quickly as possible. There was only one

Figure 4.2   Final Plan for Operation Cobra

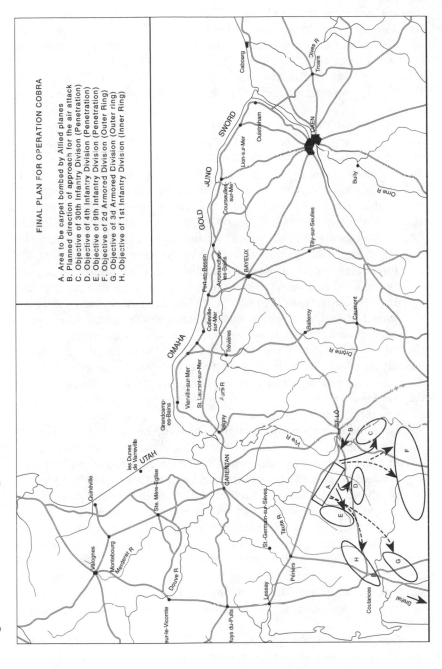

FINAL PLAN FOR OPERATION COBRA

A. Area to be carpet bombed by Allied planes
B. Planned direction of approach for the air attack
C. Objective of 30th Infantry Division (Penetration)
D. Objective of 4th Infantry Division (Penetration)
E. Objective of 9th Infantry Division (Penetration)
F. Objective of 2d Armored Division (Outer Ring)
G. Objective of 3d Armored Division (Outer ring)
H. Objective of 1st Infantry Division (Inner Ring)

division not committed to Operation Cobra, Barton's 4th Infantry Division (the First Army reserve). Without hesitation Bradley agreed to assign the division to the VII Corps. Then he asked Collins if there was anything else he wanted and joked, "Here [how] about my pistol."[49] Later reflecting on the incident, General Bradley remarked to Colonel Thorson, "Gosh, I never thought I'd ever be in the position where I could give away a division so easily."[50]

With the addition of another division, after an aerial bombardment and artillery barrage kicked off the attack (see Chapter 5), Collins planned to use Hobbs's hard-fighting 30th Division to secure the high ground along the Vire River and hold the east shoulder of the breakthrough (see Chapter 6).[51] Meanwhile, the recently assigned 4th Infantry Division under the dependable General Barton would attack in the center of the penetration and clear the enemy from the gap (Chapter 7). Collins's "old reliable," Eddy's 9th Infantry Division, would secure the west shoulder of the breakthrough and open the main route for the enveloping force (Chapter 8). The 83d Infantry Division was dropped from the plan: adding the 83d would have given Collins seven divisions, more than twice the number normally assigned to a corps. He did not want to be saddled with so many forces that they would exceed his ability to control them. Bradley and Collins agreed on a compromise. Rather than assuming command of the whole division, the VII Corps would only take temporary control of one regiment to secure the 9th Division's flank. With these final changes, the generals believed they had allocated sufficient combat power to open a decisive gap in the German lines.

The role of the exploitation force, the VII Corps commander believed, was also critical: a successful exploitation would put a hole in the German lines that could not be sealed. For Operation Cobra this force would consist of two parts, the inner and outer rings of the envelopment. First, one force would move through the penetration and form the inner ring, trapping the enemy. The second force would follow and establish the outer ring. Its mission was to protect the inner ring from enemy counterattacks attempting to relieve the encircled force. In Bradley's plan the VII Corps would turn west and encircle the enemy in front of the VIII Corps by forming the inner and outer rings with three divisions. One armored division would follow a route through Carantilly and then swing west, establishing blocking positions south of Coutances and forming the inner ring. A second armored division would be the outer ring, while the infantry division supported the armored forces.

General Collins redistributed the tasks for the envelopment. Wanting more infantry than armor for the inner ring, he assigned the task to Huebner's 1st Infantry Division, the heroes of the assault on bloody Omaha Beach, with Combat Command B, 3d Armored Division attached (see Chapter 9). He also mapped out a shallower and faster envelopment, a shorter route across the west side of the breakthrough, driving south only as far as Marigny and then west to the high ground north of Coutances. The change in the plan ensured plenty of infantry for close-in hedgerow fighting, while the shorter course would speed the tempo of the attack. Collins planned to protect the 1st Infantry Division's sweep with the two armored divisions in the outer ring. The remainder of Watson's 3d Armored Division (minus Combat Command B attached to the 1st Infantry Division), a largely untested unit, would move through the center of the breakthrough and follow a more southwestern route covering the 1st Infantry Division's flank (Chapter 10). Finally, Brooks's 2d Armored Division (see Chapter 11) would move on the routes in the eastern half of the breakthrough and drive south deep into enemy territory. It would complete the outer ring by establishing a string of blocking positions across the corps front from east to west, from the VII-XIX Corps boundary near Tessy-sur-Vire to Cérences (several miles short of the coast).

During the consolidation phase, after the encirclement of the enemy was complete, the pressure force would attack and destroy the enemy trapped by the inner ring. In this phase the V and XIX Corps would continue their attacks to the east of the VII Corps to hold the Germans' attention (the XIX Corps would be prepared to extend its boundary west of the Vire River and assume responsibility for guarding the east flank of the breakthrough). Meanwhile, on the west flank the VIII Corps would attack and finish off the Germans encircled by the VII Corps. By the time the operation was over the Americans would own Coutances and the U.S. Third Army would be on its way to Avranches and into Brittany.

The final change to the plan concerned General Bradley's concept for the consolidation. In Bradley's plan the VII Corps's outer ring was to attack all the way to Bréhal on the coast. This maneuver would completely block the withdrawal of the Germans in front of the VIII Corps, and would have the VII Corps monopolizing all the major routes heading south to Avranches. General Collins wanted to hold the VII Corps's attack at Cérences, farther east. This would leave one route to Avranches open for the VIII Corps to advance without having to pass through the VII Corps's units. General Collins admitted that this arrangement might let some Germans escape, but it would also simplify the operation by not risking the two corps' bogging down in a massive traffic jam on the coastal roads. General Bradley accepted the suggestion, and with that decision the planning for Cobra was complete.

Bradley's Choice

In analyzing Operation Cobra, General Bradley and subsequent historians credit General Collins's changes with significantly improving the plan.

Martin Blumenson gives Collins strong praise for his initiatives.[52] Another respected historian, Russell Weigley, wrote that Collins's proposals emphasized "further exploitation beyond the immediate operation, into an accelerating and expanding breakout. . . . Collins still more than Bradley was emphasizing breakout beyond breakthrough."[53] These approbations are overgenerous. The chapters that follow reveal that General Collins's suggestions actually contributed little to Cobra's dramatic success. His proposals were not bold measures of operational maneuver for precipitating a breakout, but conservative improvements designed primarily to ensure a safe and secure envelopment to complete the breakthrough that would open the roads to Brittany. In fact, given the extreme weakness of German LXXXIV Corps's west wing and the unlikelihood that it could generate much of a counteroffensive, Collins's preoccupation with successfully completing the envelopment was overcautious and unnecessary. In the end, completing the envelopment offered little of real worth in ensuring the breakthrough to Brittany. As the battle unfolded, the Americans would discover that it was the speed and depth of the penetration, rather than the success of the VII Corps's envelopment, that would determine whether the German defenses would be unhinged by the attack.

Indeed, historians have made far too much of the fact that Collins modified Bradley's plan: subordinate commanders were expected to refine the plans developed by higher headquarters. Commanders normally planned "two levels down." In other words, an army commander would consider how divisions would be employed when he drafted his plan. This was done to ensure that the tasks assigned and forces provided the subordinate corps commanders were suitable for the operation. Corps commanders then had the flexibility to use their own initiative and knowledge of the local situation to shape the final plan for employing their divisions as they thought best. There was nothing remarkable in a corps commander's modifying the general concept laid out by his superior. In fact, it would have been considered a mark of incompetence if General Collins had not sought to influence the detailed planning for the employment of the divisions under his command.

Even though Collins's efforts in planning Operation Cobra may have been both overemphasized and overrated, Bradley's contribution to bringing operational maneuver back to the Normandy battlefield has been thoroughly underappreciated. George Patton thought very little of Bradley's scheme for the breakthrough. "Cobra," Patton wrote, "is really a very timid operation." He added grudgingly, "At least it is the best operation which has been planned so far."[54] Historians have never seriously questioned Patton's opinion, and in fact, Bradley is given virtually no credit with having any significant operational skill. For example, Stephen Ambrose argues that Bradley always went for "the safer alternative, the small solution."[55]

Operation Cobra, however, demonstrated that Bradley could be a versatile operational planner. His concept for Cobra was startlingly different from the straight-ahead assault that the First Army had tried only a few weeks before. Presenting a totally different plan, a kind the U.S. Army had never attempted in battle, demonstrated Bradley's flexibility.

Bradley also proved that he could be a risk taker. An attack that combined penetration and maneuver was among the most complex maneuvers a commander could hope to execute. This was an operation on a scale far greater than the Americans had ever orchestrated in the past. In addition, it was not completely without danger. Once the offensive got under way, Bradley would have no reserve with which to influence the battle. At one time or another, he would have to put a third of the First Army's combat power at some risk to counter- or flanking attacks. In fact, the D-Day landings, where all the army had to do was get divisions ashore a few at a time, were from an operational perspective far simpler and safer than Operation Cobra. In Cobra, General Bradley proved that he could compose an operation that was well planned and not overly incremental.

Finally, and most important, Bradley showed he knew what had to be done to change the Normandy campaign from a battle of attrition into a war of movement. He had correctly identified the ground that offered the best opportunity to push south. His plan focused on exploiting the enemy's greatest weakness—their dependence on reinforcing the front at exactly the right time with the right force. His plan also capitalized on the U.S. Army's greatest strength—the ability to strike with massive firepower and exploit the strike with maneuver sustained by armor, air power, and superior logistics. Indeed, Bradley intended to do exactly what the Germans feared most—what commanders call the "most dangerous course of action"—to break through their lines at the place that could unhinge the entire German Seventh Army's front.

Without question, the success of Bradley's planning rested on the vast amount of combat information he had at his disposal and his firm grasp of the concept of the operation from the strategic to the tactical level. In addition, the First Army commander had a fair measure of the combat power available to both sides. He reasonably evaluated the options available against what the Normandy terrain would bear, and he made a sound decision.

After the last planning meeting with his corps commanders on 16 July, Bradley told them that he was more than ready to get going. This attack, he declared, was going to be "just the breakthrough we need."[56] With the plan now in place the battles of Operation Cobra were ready to begin.

There was only one "wild card" in General Bradley's plan, and that was the decision to conduct the carpet bombing before the big attack. Employing over 3,000 planes to lay down blankets of bombs less than a mile in front of U.S. troops was something no commander had ever attempted before. The consequence of his decision to employ firepower on such an unprecedented scale is the subject of the next chapter.

Notes

1. For an overview on British and Canadian operations around Caen, see John A. English, *The Canadian Army and the Normandy Campaign: A Study in Failure;* Henry Maule, *Caen: The Brutal Battle and Breakout from Normandy;* Alexander McKee, *Caen: Anvil of Victory.* A summary of the U.S. Army early July offensive can be found in Martin Blumenson, *Breakout and Pursuit,* pp. 52–102.

2. Hansen, War Diary, July 13, 1944, and July 16, 1944, MHI.

3. Bradley, *A Soldier's Story,* p. 318.

4. *Infantry in Battle,* pp. 138–139. This text was written at the direction of the then Colonel George C. Marshall when he served as commandant of the Infantry School at Fort Benning, Georgia. Bradley served under Marshall at the school. The book is an analysis of combat in World War I. The study contains twenty-seven short chapters, each highlighting a different aspect of warfare. It was widely circulated in the army before World War II. The book, in fact, is still in print today and used in the training of army officers.

5. Timothy K. Nenninger, *The Leavenworth Schools and the Old Army: Education, Professionalism, and the Officer Corps of the United States Army, 1881–1918,* pp. 134–144.

6. Hobbs, *Dear General,* pp. 123–124. General Marshall had thought highly of the First Army commander since Bradley had served under Marshall at Fort Benning. Marshall's efficiency report on Bradley for that period read, "General estimate: Quiet, unassuming, sound common sense. Absolutely dependable. Give him a job and forget it. Recommend command Regiment in peace, Division in war." Bradley remembered first coming to Marshall's attention after Marshall appointed him the head of the weapons section at the Infantry School and Bradley invented a method for laying machine guns. See Chester B. Hansen, Bradley's Commentary on World War II, efficiency report for 2 July 1929 to 24 June 1930, note 2-A, MHI.

7. Martin Blumenson, *The Patton Papers, 1940–45,* pp. 398–399, 588. See also Weigley, *Eisenhower's Lieutenants,* pp. 170–171.

8. The U.S. Army decisionmaking process was an integral part of the instruction at the army's Command and General Staff College at Fort Leavenworth, Kansas. See Philip Carlton Cockrell, "Brown Shoes and Mortar Boards: U.S. Army Professional Education at the Command and General Staff School Fort Leavenworth, Kansas, 1919–1940," Ph.D. diss. (University of South Carolina, 1987), pp. 181–203. Although in developing the plans for Operation Cobra General Bradley did not formally commit each step of the process to paper, study of the U.S. First Army records and recollections of the general and his staff suggest that Bradley followed the army's decisionmaking methodology.

9. For a recent assessment of the role of the Brittany ports in the campaign plan, see Ganz A. Harding, "Questionable Objective: The Brittany Ports, 1944," *Journal of Military History* 59 (1995): 77–95.

10. Hansen, War Diary, 16 July 1944, MHI.

11. Pemsel, "Comments," p. 1.

12. Bodo Zimmermann, OB WEST, Command Relationships (1943–1945), MS B-308, p. 116. There is some dispute over whether General Dollmann died on 28 or 29 June 1944. See also Samuel W. Mitcham Jr. and Gene Mueller, *Hitler's Commanders,* p. 131.

13. Paul Hausser, "Normandy Seventh Army," MS A-974; and Mitcham and Mueller, *Hitler's Commanders,* pp. 276–284.

14. Mitcham and Mueller, *Hitler's Commanders,* p. 285.

15. Rommel's instructions to the Seventh Army are summarized in *Armeeoberkommando 7, K.T.B. Entwurf und OB Chef-IA-Gespräche, 6 Juni–16 August 1944,* microfilm, T312, Roll 1568, NARA.

16. Unless otherwise noted the description of the German Seventh Army defenses is taken from *Armeeoberkommando 7, K.T.B. Entwurf und OB Chef-IA-Gespräche, 6 Juni–16 August 1944,* microfilm, T312, Roll 1568, NARA, pp. 176–189; Hausser, "Normandy Seventh Army," pp. 1–5, 15–16, 32–38; Supply Situation of Units Engaged on the Normandy Front, Army Group B, 1 July–31 July 1944, microfilm, T311, Roll 1, NARA. See also Eddy Florentin, *Stalingrad en Normandie: la destruction de la VIIe armée allemande dans la poche Argentan-Falaise, 31 juillet–22 août 1944.*

17. Friedrich-August Freiherr von der Heydte, "A German Parachute Regiment in Normandy Operations of the 6th Fallschirmjäger Regiment 6 June–15 August 1944," MS B-839, p. 26.

18. Hausser, "Normandy Seventh Army," p. 34.

19. Gehard Treipel, "91st Airborne Division Artillery," MS B-469, p. 7.

20. See William B. Breuer, *Hoodwinking Hitler: The Normandy Deception.* This recent work provides a useful introduction to the various deception efforts employed against the Germans.

21. At the same time as the Cobra bombings, a diversionary attack was staged with eighteen sorties and 60 tons of bombs near Marche and Grevelines with an objective of keeping German reserves in the Pas de Calais area. See Adjutant General's Office, World War II Operations, "Contribution of Airpower to the Defeat of Germany," 29 September 1945, Box 2240, RG 94, NARA.

22. For a summary of Operation Goodwood, see Carlo D'Este, *Decision in Normandy,* pp. 352–369.

23. For a cogent study of the use of Ultra, see Ralph Bennett, *Ultra in the West: The Normandy Campaign 1944–45.* For an overview on the use of Magic intelligence in the European Theater of Operations, see Bruce Lee, *Marching Orders: The Untold Story of WW II.* See also F. H. Hinsley et al., eds., *British Intelligence in the Second World War: Its Influence on Strategy and Operations,* vol. 3. pt. 2, *Summer 1944 to the End of the War with Germany,* pp. 210–235; A. S. Cochran Jr., "Magic, Ultra and the Second World War: Literature, Sources and Outlook," *The Journal of Military History* 46 (April 1982): 88–92; F. H. Hinsley and Alan Stripp, eds., *Codebreakers: The Inside Story of Bletchley Park.*

24. "Synthesis of Experiences in the Use of Ultra Intelligence by U.S. Army Field Commands in the European Theater of Operations," SRH-006, p. 17, CARL. See also Omar N. Bradley and Clay Blair, *A General's Life,* pp. 236–238; and Adolph G. Rossengarten Jr., "With Ultra from Omaha Beach to Weimar, Germany: A Personal View," *The Journal of Military History* 42 (October 1978): 127–132.

25. "Synthesis of Experiences in the Use of Ultra Intelligences," p. 7.

26. Colonel Adolph G. Rossengarten Jr. headed the U.S. First Army SLU section. For an introduction to relationships between the SLU and General Bradley's staff, see Thomas Parrish, *The American Codebreakers: The U.S. Role in Ultra,* pp. 207–217. For a list of reports received in theater, see G-2 Officer, Supreme Headquarters Allied Expeditionary Force, files, MHI.

27. Bennett, *Ultra,* pp. 10, 96, 98.

28. Ibid., p. 99. For an example of where Ultra was used to support tactical operations, see Bradley, *General's Life,* pp. 258–260.

29. "Reports Received by U.S. War Department on Use of the Ultra in the European Theater, World War II," SRH-037, p. 2, CARL.

30. Hansen, Bradley's Commentary on World War II, note S-22, MHI; Charles G. Patterson, Reflections on Courtney Hodges, pp. 102–103, 110, MHI.

31. Headquarters, First U.S. Army, Outline Operations Plan "Cobra," 13 July 1944. After the intelligence annex to the plan was completed, the 2d SS Panzer Division, which had started to arrive in theater in early July, moved into positions in front of the U.S. First Army's zone.

32. Historical Data, AAF Headquarters, Group Fighter, Fiftieth Fighter Group, 1 July to 1 August 1944, microfilm, Roll B0144, p. 2, AFHSO.

33. Cockrell, "Brown Shoes," pp. 216–217.

34. Envelopment from the air was also a possibility, or at least the Germans thought so. They did not know the status or location of the U.S. 82d and 101st Airborne Divisions (which had participated in the D-Day invasions). The Germans feared parachute drops behind their lines, and invested time and troops in defending potential landing sites. In reality airborne envelopment was not feasible. The U.S. airborne divisions were being reconstituted and were not then capable of conducting new operations. Any U.S. attack would have to be done on the ground.

35. Bradley, *A Soldier's Story,* p. 329; Hansen, Bradley's Commentary on World War II, note 22-B, S-14, MHI.

36. Blumenson, *Battle of the Generals,* p. 118. See also Richard Overy, *Why the Allies Won the War,* p. 171; Ulick Martin Hallinan, "From Operation COBRA to the Liberation of Paris: American Offensive Operations in Northern France, 25 July–25 August, 1944," Ph.D. diss. (Temple University, 1988), pp. 105–116. See also D'Este, *Decision in Normandy,* pp. 340, 347.

37. Bradley probably began detailed planning somewhere between 4–6 July. It does not appear that Bradley finalized his plan before 6 July, when he wrote to Eisenhower that he was "disappointed at the slow rate of progress . . . however, I feel that as soon as we can break this crust and get out of these bottle-necks our progress should be much more rapid." If Bradley had finalized his plan he would most likely have mentioned it in this letter. See Omar N. Bradley, Papers, Correspondence with Major Historical Figures, 1938–1960, MHI. Montgomery had written Eisenhower on 10 July stressing the need for hard and continuous attacks by the U.S. First and British Second Army. But it was Eisenhower who included in his response, "You might well have added 'We should like to kill them in big packets by breaking through his positions and cutting him off in sizeable elements.'" Eisenhower's letter left no indication that the U.S. First Army plan owed much to Montgomery other than the encouragement to push ahead in a major offensive. See Letter of Eisenhower to Montgomery, 21 July 1944, in Alfred D. Chandler Jr., ed., *The Papers of Dwight D. Eisenhower: The War Years,* vol. 3, p. 2018. In his memoirs Bradley claimed to have completed his basic plan by 10 July. See Bradley, *A Soldier's Story,* p. 330. See also D'Este, *Patton,* pp. 616–617, 620.

38. "Modern Warfare," *The Army and Navy Register,* 12 August 1944, p. 1.

39. In an oral history conducted after the war, General Bradley claimed that he did not draw on any historical examples to plan the operation. He recalled that the German invasion of France offered a fine example of a breakthrough operation, but that he had not studied it in any detail. Bradley also stated he had begun thinking about the concept for a breakout operation before the Normandy invasion and had begun detailed planning for the operation in early July. See Omar N. Bradley, Oral History Interview, Revised Transcript, tape 7, first reel, pp. 1, 2, 5–6, MHI; Hansen, Bradley's Commentary on World War II, note S-25, MHI.

40. Hansen, Bradley's Commentary on World War II, note S-20, S-22, A-22,

MHI. In contrast to General Kean, General Hodges was rarely closely involved with staff work; see Charles E. Hart, *Reflections on General Courtney Hodges,* pp. 13–14, MHI. General Collins, the VII Corps commander, recalled that Hodges played no significant role in planning or executing the breakout. See J. Lawton Collins, *Reflections on General Courtney Hodges,* p. 16, MHI. See also Courtney Hicks Hodges, Papers, DDE.

41. Charles G. Patterson, *Reflections on Courtney Hodges,* p. 102, MHI.

42. Ibid. For Hewitt's discussion of Cobra, see Robert A. Hewitt, *Interviews with Major General Robert A. Hewitt,* pp. 151–153, MHI.

43. Bradley, *A Soldier's Story,* p. 329.

44. Hansen, Bradley's Commentary on World War II, note 28-A, MHI.

45. J. Lawton Collins, Senior Officers' Oral History Program, p. 161, MHI.

46. Weigley, *Eisenhower's Lieutenants,* pp. 136–137.

47. In a postwar oral history General Collins stated that he assumed the idea for Cobra came from Bradley or Eisenhower, but claimed that Bradley had asked Collins to select the area for the breakthrough. Collins claims that in consultation with his corps artillery commander, Brigadier General Williston Palmer, and the corps G-3, Colonel Orlando Collette Troxel Jr., he had suggested that the attack take place north and west of St-Lô and suggested the jump-off point for the attack along the St-Lô-Périers road. Collins's claim contradicts Bradley's description of how the plan was developed. Collins's version is not substantiated by the recollections of Palmer or Troxel, nor does it square with the other evidence. In his oral history General Bradley says after he developed the plan he called in Colonel Thorson and then General Collins and General McNair (who happened to be visiting the command post). Bradley, however, gives no dates, nor did he state what comments or suggestions were made to the plan. Bradley did state, however, that he picked the road for the Cobra start line and that the plan was "well developed" before he showed it to Collins. General Collins's recollection is most likely in error, and he may have simply misspoken in the interview (in his autobiography he does not repeat the claim). See Collins, Senior Officers' Oral History Program, p. 192, MHI; J. Lawton Collins, *Lightning Joe;* Orlando Collette Troxel Jr., *The Papers of Colonel Orlando Collette Troxel, Jr.;* Williston Birkhimer Palmer, *Interview with Williston Birkhimer Palmer,* p. 63, MHI; Bradley, Oral History Interview, Revised Transcript, tape 7, first reel, pp. 4, 7, 117, MHI. See also John J. Walsh, Papers, letters July 1945, DDE.

48. Hansen, War Diary, July 19, 1944, MHI. Blumenson attributes the proposal to General Collins. See Blumenson, *Battle of the Generals,* p. 130; Blumenson, *Breakout and Pursuit,* p. 217.

49. Hansen, War Diary, July 19, 1944, MHI.

50. Ibid.

51. The VII Corps issued verbal orders for Cobra on 16 July. The plan was published on 19 July and revised on 20 July to include the 4th Infantry Division. All details on the VII Corps plan are taken from Headquarters, VII Corps, U.S. Army, Operation "Cobra," Field Order #6 (revised copy), 20 July 1944.

52. Blumenson, *Battle of the Generals,* p. 131; Blumenson, *Breakout and Pursuit,* pp. 218–219.

53. Weigley, *Eisenhower's Lieutenants,* p. 150.

54. Blumenson, *The Patton Papers,* p. 486.

55. Ambrose, *Citizen Soldiers,* pp. 89–90. See also Weigley, *Eisenhower's Lieutenants,* p. 177.

56. Hansen, War Diary, 16 July 1944, MHI.

PART 2

The Day of Infantry: 25 July 1944

5

The Firepower War

After 2 weeks of planning and coordination, General Omar Bradley was finally prepared to launch Operation Cobra. With the big attack about to start, it is not likely any of the senior commanders on the Normandy battlefield passed an unburdened night on 20 July, the eve of Cobra. General Bernard Montgomery, the Allies' 21st Army Group commander, had made a spectacular entrance into the U.S. First Army command post. This general enjoyed a reputation for dressing in his own eccentric style. "Striding in with his corduroy trousers," General Bradley's aide, Major Hansen, recalled, "his enormous loose fitting gabardine coat and his beret like a poorly tailored Bohemian painter."[1] Despite Monty's jovial appearance, the army group commander was not having a stellar day. Operation Goodwood, a major offensive by the British Second Army to push out from Caen, had began on 18 July but had not gone well.

Goodwood consisted of a heavy air (almost 2,000 planes) and artillery bombardment followed by a penetration along a narrow front. On the first day, the British Second Army lost 270 tanks and 1,500 men with almost no gains to show for the losses. The second day cost another 131 tanks and 1,100 casualties. On the third day, the sky ripped open with driving rains and the British and Canadian forces wallowed in a sea of Normandy mud. In total, the attack had gained only 32 square miles in exchange for the loss of 36 percent of the entire British armored force in Europe. Worst of all, the German lines remained unbroken.

When General Montgomery greeted his American comrades he had his best face on, but he could not have been pleased with Goodwood's disappointing and indecisive results. Still, Ultra confirmed that the attack had tied down a large contingent of German armor, and as far as General Montgomery was concerned that would have to be enough. It was out of his hands now, and as he told General Eisenhower, "It's up to Bradley to go ahead."[2]

Whether General Bradley's First Army would go ahead or not largely depended on the success of Operation Cobra's opening gambit. Montgomery's visit took place on the eve of the Cobra's first critical moment, the assault and opening of a gap in the German lines by the three lead infantry divisions. The planned carpet bombing was considered the single most crucial event of the attack, a blow that would cripple the enemy defenses, making them vulnerable to penetration by a ground assault. For Bradley this display of firepower would be the prelude to operational maneuver.

At U.S. First Army headquarters, as the Americans waited for the aerial bombardment that would lead off Cobra, there was little peace of mind during Montgomery's visit, and the distractions of protocol added to the day's tensions. Bradley had had a busy afternoon, not only with Montgomery, but also with a visit from Eisenhower and an award ceremony for Generals Leonard Gerow and Joseph Collins.

The greatest distraction of all, however, was not the VIPs, but the weather. Everyone was keeping an eye on the skies. Would the rains that drowned Goodwood in an ocean of mud continue on 21 July, the planned start date for Cobra? As evening approached the sky remained overcast— and the forecast for the next day was unpromising. At midnight General Bradley postponed the operation, to everyone's disappointment.

Across the hedgerows, the mood among the German high command was no better. The strain of command was not all that General Günther von Kluge, the Army Group B commander, had to worry about. On 20 July a cabal of German officers tried to assassinate Hitler. The next morning Hitler spoke on the radio, declaring that he was alive and well and that the bomb plot was the work of a "circle of small criminal elements which will be mercilessly exterminated." This declaration could have hardly proved comforting to General Kluge: on at least two occasions he had been contacted by the plotters.[3] Although not an active conspirator, the Army Group B commander feared that he might be a target for retribution.

How the assassination attempt affected Kluge's ability to command remains a subject of conjecture. In retrospect, however, as disturbing as the events of 20 July seemed, they paled by comparison with the tactical trials ahead for the German commander. Kluge was about to face something virtually unmatched in military history—firepower on an unprecedented scale, a blow that would not be equaled again until the Americans dropped the atomic bomb on Hiroshima.

Preparing for the Firepower War

Firepower, the massed fire to crack the heavily prepared defenses for a penetration attack, was a prerequisite for Cobra. In World War II the Americans had two means for massing fire, artillery and air power, and these were General Bradley's essential tools for a firepower war.

Of the two instruments for delivering a barrage of high explosives, U.S. artillery was given the supporting role. Normally for an offensive the U.S. Army allocated each corps its own slice of artillery, but Cobra was different.[4] Bradley stripped the corps of most of their supporting guns and allocated the lion's share of the First Army's artillery (twenty-three battalions) to the VII Corps (this was in addition to the twenty-two battalions already in the divisions). Support for the VII Corps's attack totaled over 550 artillery pieces, not counting additional fire from the other corps. In addition, Bradley assigned to the VII Corps six battalions of tank destroyers, not for antitank defense, but to further supplement artillery fire.

Brigadier General Williston Palmer, the VII Corps artillery commander, was responsible for organizing all supporting fire. General Palmer placed the light nondivision artillery and tank destroyer battalions under the control of the divisions. The light (105mm) artillery's short-range and smaller shells were best suited for attacking close-in targets.

In the close-in battle, the three infantry divisions leading the assault planned their own artillery fire, using both the First Army artillery battalions and the battalions from their own division artillery. Each lead division was to have an average of eleven artillery battalions in support; there was an artillery piece for every fourteen yards of front. In the attack's follow-on divisions, the 3d Armored Division artillery reinforced the preparatory fires of the 9th Infantry Division artillery, while the 2d Armored and 1st Infantry Divisions held back their guns to exploit the breakthrough.

General Palmer retained the medium and heavy battalions (134 tubes) constituting three field artillery groups. To control the groups the First Army assigned the 32d Field Artillery Brigade to support the VII Corps. Palmer planned to use the brigade to direct the three artillery groups, concentrating their guns on counterbattery fire (attacking enemy artillery) and counterflak fires (attacking enemy antiaircraft weapons), using the heavier guns' longer range and heftier firepower to attack the deeper targets behind the enemy lines.

To add more firepower for the penetration, the flank corps provided additional artillery support to the VII Corps. The VIII Corps planned fire in an area bounded in the west by a line from Périers to Lendelin and in the east along the VII-VIII Corps boundary. On the other flank, the XIX Corps scheduled fire in the eastern half of the VII Corps's zone to interdict any enemy reserves trying to move through Percy toward the penetration. The XIX Corps also planned artillery smoke on the high ground from La Calange to Le Mesnil-Herman to obscure the enemy's view of the main attack. Meanwhile, the XIX Corps's 35th Infantry Division artillery scheduled a 10-minute diversionary preparation to hold the attention of the enemy on the VII Corps's east flank.

The Americans planned to put a lot of fire across the hedgerows, having scheduled to shoot almost half of the artillery allocated in the first 40 minutes. The VII Corps alone (not counting the division fires) would shoot forty-one missions, more than 140,000 shells. The sophistication and complexity of the entire fire support plan was truly impressive, made possible only by the tremendous developments in the army fire direction center (FDC) and the army's flexible artillery organizations.

The mass of artillery, though impressive, was not enough to ensure Cobra's firepower punch for the simple reason that there was not enough ammunition. It would have required more than a million and a half rounds—equal to what was expended in the 10-day preparation for the Battle of the Somme during World War I—to saturate the breakthrough point. The difficulties in supplying ammunition and the high rate of consumption precluded the Americans from building up anywhere near that volume of ammunition. Even if U.S. forces had had the thousands of tons of ammunition they needed, it would have taken days for the artillery to fire it all. The preparatory artillery bombardment for Cobra would have to be delivered in a few hours to achieve the quick, powerful strike General Bradley desired, but it was physically impossible.

With the limitations in artillery, only air power offered the Allies the potential to achieve the sudden, mass disruption required for a penetration attack. A medium bomber, like the B-26 Mitchell or B-25 Marauder, could carry 4,000 pounds of bombs. The B-17 Flying Fortress, a heavy bomber, could carry a bomb load of 12,800 pounds, the equivalent of more than 100 howitzers firing at one time in a single planeload.[5]

There is no conclusive evidence to show how an air strike became part of Cobra. On 12 July, the day before the U.S. First Army published its plan, General Bradley declared, "I've been wanting to do this now since we landed. When we pull it [off], I want [it] to be the biggest thing in the world."[6] After the war he wrote that he had been thinking about saturation bombing since 1939. General Bradley also recalled that the results of air attacks supporting the VII Corps's assault on Cherbourg had furthered his interest in the idea. On 21 June he told his staff that he planned to use "air and masses of arty for [the] breakthrough when [the] time comes."[7] There was also a number of other precedents from past operations in both the Mediterranean and Europe that General Bradley might have drawn on for inspiration.

Carpet bombing (saturating a small area with an aerial bombardment) was not a new idea, but it was still controversial. Sorting out the mission priorities for the Allied bombing force was one of the most contentious issues of the war, complicated by the air forces' feudal command structures and the eccentric, often confrontational personalities of their commanders.

To resolve the conflicts in priorities between strategic bombing and the ground war, General Eisenhower appointed his deputy commander, Air Chief Marshal Sir Arthur W. Tedder, to arbitrate with the senior air commanders and inform them of Eisenhower's "wishes."[8] The problem with this notion was that Air Marshal Tedder had no formal authority, but, instead, had to cajole support from the air commands.

The tactical air forces were grouped under the Allied Expeditionary Air Forces headed by Air Chief Marshal Sir Trafford Leigh-Mallory. This air chief marshal relayed requests from the ground commander to the U.S. and British strategic air forces. Air Marshal Leigh-Mallory exacerbated the problems of air-ground coordination because he was the object of universal dislike. Bradley's aide, Major Hansen, described the air chief marshal as "the leanest of the top dogs, inclined to be curt."[9] Others simply found him insufferable. Even the British Air Ministry, which had insisted on his appointment, found Leigh-Mallory difficult to work with.

While not a popular leader, ground commanders who wanted bomber support had an advocate in the air chief marshal. Leigh-Mallory, who had started his career as a World War I foot soldier, was always sympathetic to the difficulties ground commanders faced in Normandy. He declared that "I have always taken the view that the Army should be given all the air support it desires. After all, it is a citizen army composed from the most part of men belonging to every walk of life to whom soldiering is neither natural nor easily learned."[10] As far as he was concerned, if commanders wanted heavy-bomber support, they should get it.

The problem was that neither of the senior bomber commanders agreed with him. "What I have been up against more or less since D-Day," Leigh-Mallory complained, "is the school of thought which takes the view that air support given to the Army should be the minimum rather than the maximum."[11] He heard this again and again from his counterparts in the strategic air forces, the Royal Air Force bomber commander, Air Chief Marshal Sir Arthur "Bomber" Harris, and U.S. Army Air Force Lieutenant General Carl A. "Tooey" Spaatz, commander of the U.S. Strategic Air Forces in Europe.

The debate over using bombers in Cobra was part of a larger controversy over employing air power, and this dispute had important implications for Operation Cobra. The most compelling argument against air support for ground forces was that it diverted the aircraft from their primary mission—the combined bomber offensive designed to destroy the German military, industrial, and economic systems, crippling Hitler's war machine and speeding Germany's capitulation. General Spaatz, in particular, complained about ground commanders

who visualize the best use of tremendous air potentialities is in plowing up several square miles of terrain in front of ground forces to obtain a few miles of advance. Our [ground] forces are far superior to the Germans opposing us, both in men and material. The only thing necessary to move forward is sufficient guts on the part of the ground commanders.[12]

General Spaatz did not want to waste his bombers on a handful of "half-baked German divisions."

In turn, General Bradley also had his differences with senior air commanders. For example, he loathed Major General Lewis Hyde Brereton, U.S. Ninth Air Force commander, whose planes provided tactical air support for the ground troops. Bradley considered the air commander an "air purist" and "a flop, not sincere or energetic, did not seem interested in the air-ground team." The two had rarely met before the invasion, and after the landings Bradley claimed his counterpart's vision of "fighting the war was a matter of finding a good place to live." Much to General Bradley's delight, General Brereton was ordered out of the command of the Ninth Air Force on 17 July, shortly before the scheduled kickoff for Cobra.

General Bradley also had unkind words for "Bomber" Harris. "Killer Harris," General Bradley quipped, "was called the greatest friend Russia ever had, destroyed the fabric of Europe's middle class." Bradley could not understand Harris's predilection for bombing cities when the air forces could be going after the real enemy, the German army.

To say the least, there was some friction among the senior ground and air commanders. Each from his own perspective was passionately dedicated to winning the war and had little patience for those they saw blocking his path.[13] It was not just strategy and personality, however, that argued against tactical carpet bombing: there was precious little practical experience and no doctrine on how to use bombers for supporting ground troops. The Allies had tried tactical bombings in the Mediterranean, but with poor results. The bombers' reputation as a tactical weapon did not improve in Normandy. General Montgomery had used bombers to support Operations Charnwood and Goodwood around the city of Caen, but both ground attacks failed to reach their objectives.[14]

To improve on past experiences, General Bradley's plan had to address the many difficulties in employing bombers in a tactical role. One of the greatest challenges was the craters caused by exploding bombs. Heavily cratered roads could stop friendly armor as effectively as any enemy obstacle (during Operation Charnwood, for example, craters slowed the advance considerably). To avoid this problem, Bradley proposed using only light 100-pound impact-detonation bombs. These would still produce craters, but smaller and shallower, easier to repair, and easier for the armored force to get around.

Another challenge was coordinating the time of air attacks. Unlike land battles, weather conditions rather than the ground tactical situation always determined when an air attack could start. Complicating the problem was the Allies having to deal with two weather systems, one in Britain at the airfields and the other in Normandy, which were often out of synch. The U.S. ground forces would have to wait for acceptable weather conditions that would support air operations in both places.

Bradley would have preferred an early morning jumpoff for Cobra, so that the attack could take maximum advantage of the long summer days. He

realized, however, that getting an effective bomber strike was the most crucial consideration. Bradley conceded that the air attack should be when it
was best for the bombers, and that the ground troops should make do with
whatever daylight was left after the aerial assault. Bradley deferred to
Leigh-Mallory in designating the best time for the attack based on the
weather situation.

In terms of the weather, cloud cover above the target area was particularly important. The lower the clouds, the lower the bombers would have to
fly to see the target—and at lower altitudes antiaircraft fire was a greater
threat. For a fleet of heavy bombers below 15,000 feet of altitude, heavy
flak was not only deadly, but it forced formations to disperse and thus
decrease bombing accuracy. Disrupted formations also raised confusion,
increasing the probability of accidental or inadvertent bomb releases.

Flying too high created other problems. Planes at higher altitudes were
safer, but had more difficulty in finding their targets—and target sighting
was especially critical in this case. Even small errors could mean big problems. Each flight followed a lead bombardier. When he released his bomb
load, the others followed. If he missed, everybody missed.

Even if the air forces attacked at the right time and place, there was
still no guarantee that they would hit the enemy. Accuracy was always
problematic. For medium bombers to have a 95 percent chance of hitting a
6,000-square-foot target, they had to drop 600 bombs (medium bombers
were considered more than twice as accurate as Cobra's main punch, the
heavy bombers).[15] On average, regardless of the type of bomb employed,
only 90 percent of the bombs fell within a thousand yards of the target. At
best, even if the lead bombardier attacked with perfect accuracy, the odds
were that at least 10 percent of the ordnance would fall over a thousand
yards away from the target. As for the bombs that hit the target, they might
land anywhere within that 1,000-yard radius—and this was the crucial limitation of aerial bombardment: the explosive effects of the bombs did not
extend much further than the bombs' craters. A direct hit would devastate a
target with explosive effect, shrapnel, and concussion from the detonation,
but all there was to show for a miss was a hole in the ground and a lot of
dirt in the air.

Accuracy was a double-edged problem: commanders had to worry
about protecting their own forces. A "no-bomb line" was used to mark the
forward line of friendly troops and thus protect them from aerial attacks
by their own planes. Ground commanders had limited flexibility in moving or marking the line, which had to be placed on terrain recognizable
from the air. In addition, to shift the line air units had to be alerted over the
air support radio net 1 hour prior to the effective time to ensure that the
order reached all the air units, and this alert only took care of the forward-
placed fighter-bombers. Medium and heavy bombers could not communicate with ground forces, and so messages had to be relayed to England and

then to the planes. These requirements dictated that no-bomb lines be coordinated well ahead of time and placed on the most prominent terrain available.

The ground commanders knew that marking the bombing limits was a problem. On 17 July General Eddy, the 9th Infantry Division commander, and his air support officer went to the VII Corps headquarters to give General Collins a "first hand appreciation" of the problem.[16] The two commanders had good reason to be concerned. The most common method for marking the no-bomb line was by firing colored-smoke artillery rounds. This technique had severe limitations, however. The 4th Infantry Division, for example, in a report dated more than 3 weeks before Cobra, observed that "smokes [sic] and dusts present on the field of battle may lead to confusion on the part of the pilot."[17] Smoke, the division concluded, should only be used if there was no other way for marking a target. The air forces people also knew that marking targets with smoke was a problem. Initially they did not want to use smoke to mark the northern boundary, but after conducting a reconnaissance they changed their mind and requested a series of smoke targets along the front at 1-mile intervals for 10 minutes, starting 5 minutes before the initial attack. Even with this measure, the air staffs remained deeply concerned about the danger of "short" bombings.[18]

In fact, there was no safe, effective means to mark the no-bomb line, though this was not news to anyone. The Infantry Board at Fort Benning, Georgia, had experimented with the problem only a year before. Marking positions with smoke, phosphorescent paint, mirrors, colored lights, flares, and even flags was tried, but no technique worked very well. The best that pilots could do was identify targets at 2,000 feet (13,000 feet lower than the planned attack altitude for the bombers in Cobra). In addition, only direct radio communication proved effective in coordinating air and ground operations.[19]

During combat, even radio did not completely solve the problem of air-ground coordination. In Normandy, where ground units had radio contact with tactical aircraft through their attached air support parties, short bombings or strafings were endemic. In the first week of the campaign there were nine official reports of accidental attacks. The actual number of incidents was probably much higher. Just about every combat soldier had a story to tell. As one veteran remembered: "I always knew our Air Force was pretty good, because twice we were strafed by our own planes. We tried to put identification panels out where our pilots could see them, but in the apple orchard country of Normandy that was kind of hard to do."[20] During the assault on Cherbourg (the attack General Bradley said had helped inspire the idea for the Cobra bombing), planes bombed one friendly position 2,000 yards behind the no-bomb line (almost twice the safety distance planned for Cobra) three times.

Communication was not a panacea, because pilots found it difficult to fix their exact positions even under ideal conditions. Fighter pilots went into battle with their maps strapped to their knee—reading coordinates, flying their aircraft, and watching out for enemy planes, antiaircraft fire, friendly troops, civilian noncombatants, and enemy targets all at the same time. Fighter pilots, when asked how they decided when they were behind the enemy lines, claimed:

> It was quite simple. All they [pilots] did was watch the roads and when they saw a Frenchman flogging a horse and drawing a cart down the road they knew they were over German held territory. On our side of the line, trucks and transportation lined the road, generally bumper to bumper.[21]

As imprecise and haphazard as the task of locating and identifying the enemy lines was for the fighters, the difficulty increased exponentially for medium and heavy bombers flying at much higher altitudes.

Despite such limitations, General Bradley relied on the no-bomb line as his primary tool for protecting the ground forces. The U.S. First Army's no-bomb line, marked A-B on the operations overlay, was easily identifiable because it ran parallel to the St-Lô–Périers road running straight east to west across the VII Corps's front. The line would be in effect from the designated start time for the attack plus 20 minutes (H+20). After H+20, as the troops advanced, the line would shift farther south to a line marked C-D and then continue to shift south as the attack progressed.

General Bradley wanted the bombers to attack parallel to the road and use the St Lô–Périers road to mark the boundary between friend and foe. In addition, by taking a parallel approach the bombers would not fly over the VII Corps's forces, thus reducing the chance that bombs released at the wrong point would land on friendly troops. To further identify the no-bomb line, U.S. units would mark their forward positions with florescent panels, while the artillery would fire red smoke along a 250-yard strip along the road. Drivers were also told to paint white stars on the top of their vehicles to help low-flying planes identify friendly units.

Fixing the distance between the forward line of troops and the no-bomb line was another important factor in safeguarding the soldiers. If the ground force withdrew too far to avoid the bombing, the enemy might recover from the effects of the attack before friendly troops could assault. For example, during Operation Charnwood the Allied forces had withdrawn 6,000 yards, and by the time the attackers got back to the front the German defenders had already recovered.

General Bradley compromised between distance and caution. He wanted troops to withdraw only 800 yards, 1 hour before the attack, whereas the air commanders wanted more than six times that distance, almost 3 miles. They then proposed 3,000 yards and finally compromised at 1,200 yards. For additional safety, only the smaller fighter-bombers would attack targets in the 250-yard strip directly adjacent to the road (making the bomber safety distance 1,500 yards).

Friendly troops were not the only concern on the battlefield. Just days before Cobra, General Bradley had briefed the press at the First Army press camp at Vouilly, and reporters had asked whether the civilians had been warned. In response General Bradley remembered: "I shook my head as if to escape the necessity of saying no. If we were to tip our hands to the French, we would also show it to the Germans. . . . The success of Cobra hung upon surprise; it was essential we have surprise even if it meant the slaughter of innocents as well."[22]

Employing firepower incurred a heavy moral responsibility. Although many civilians had evacuated the area, the target included a number of sizable villages. Those who remained may have lacked the resources to leave or feared the hardships of becoming refugees more than the dangers of remaining at the front. Not every villager could or would flee to safety and any attack behind the German lines had the potential to endanger the local populace. Allied bombs had already killed many civilians in the area including more than a dozen in a strike on Marigny in late June. As a result, when the Americans executed Operation Cobra noncombatant casualties were likely. Bradley's decision to bomb them without warning adhered to the laws of war. It is unacceptable to intentionally target civilians, but casualties may be incurred in pursuit of legitimate military objectives (in fact, civilians who willingly remained in a combat zone were considered adequately warned). The laws of war also recognized the necessity of secrecy and the inherent right of commanders to weigh the safety of their troops against the danger of revealing their intentions for an operation. Commanders could take prudent precautions, even if it meant noncombatants were put at risk. This did not mean that civilian lives and property were forfeited. Commanders had a responsibility to take all practical measures to safeguard the innocents. But, in this case, General Bradley felt security concerns precluded any warnings to civilians.[23]

With the safety measures determined to General Bradley's satisfaction, the final air plan for Cobra took shape. It was divided into five phases employing a mix of fighter-bombers and medium and heavy bombers from the U.S. Eighth and Ninth Air Forces. From H-80 to H-60 seven groups (350 fighter-bombers) would attack the part of the target area labeled strip A and several strong points north of the St-Lô–Périers road. From H-60 to H hour, 1,800 heavy bombers were to bomb the southern portion of the target area, farther away from the friendly troops. From H hour to H+20 seven groups of planes, 350 fighter-bombers, would again attack strip A. Eleven groups of medium bombers (396 planes) would then bomb the southern half of the target again from H+30 to H+75. After H+6 hours, the mediums would rearm and refuel for additional bombing as needed.

All together, General Bradley thought this plan provided an adequate balance between the need for firepower and the safety of his troops. On 19 July General Bradley and Major General Elwood R. "Pete" Quesada, commander of the IX Tactical Air Command, boarded a small two-engine plane and flew to Marshal Leigh-Mallory's headquarters in a ramshackle old mansion at Stanmore, outside London, to review the plan with the air commanders and staff. In addition to Leigh-Mallory, Air Chief Marshal Tedder, General Spaatz, and General Brereton, a host of high-ranking air staff officers and commanders joined in the meeting that started at about 3:30 P.M. Even though both Bradley and Leigh-Mallory left before the meeting ended, General Bradley left feeling upbeat, believing that potential problems had been addressed, including the two most contentious issues, the distance the troops would withdraw from the no-bomb line and the direction of flight for the attacking planes. Bradley's aide, Major Hansen, recorded that the "conf[erence] went well, came out by five [P.M.] with Brad speaking amiably, laughing."[24] Spaatz even ordered up a C-47 for Bradley's return flight to Normandy, insisting that it was not proper for the First Army commander to be running around in a tiny two-motor plane. As Bradley returned to his headquarters in style, he assumed everything was set for the big attack.

The Bombing

Finally on 24 July, despite continued poor weather, Marshal Leigh-Mallory and General Bradley gave the go-ahead to Cobra, gambling that the weather would clear up over the target area before the planes arrived.[25] By midmorning the weather had gotten worse, and before noon Leigh-Mallory and Bradley thought it best to recall the planes. Not all the aircraft received the message, and some of the uninformed pilots completed their bombing runs with disastrous results. One pilot bombed a U.S. Army ammunition dump, another an Allied airfield, and other planes dropped their payloads north of the road on the 30th Infantry Division (see Chapter 1).[26]

Later that afternoon, Marshal Leigh-Mallory met with General Bradley at the U.S. First Army field headquarters. General Bradley was furious. It was not just that the attack was postponed, and it was not just that bombs had fallen on U.S. soldiers. It was because General Bradley claimed that he had learned for the first time that the heavy bombers had flown perpendicularly to the target area, right over U.S. troops. This was not what he had agreed to. The air chief marshal claimed that he did not know about the change in plans. His directive for the bombing, in fact, had not even designated the direction of attack.[27] He thought that it had all been agreed to at the Stanmore meeting on 19 July.

Apparently, without clearly relaying their final decision to General Bradley, the air commanders decided that the bombers needed to approach perpendicularly to the target, rather than fly a course parallel to the U.S. positions. The perpendicular course, they concluded, would minimize the time aircraft would be over enemy lines and exposed to antiaircraft fire. More important, the target box was narrower on the parallel axis, and so on a parallel approach fewer planes could fit over the target area. It was simple geometry. It would take much longer to complete the bombing on a parallel course. A parallel bombing run would be more like a shifting steady rain (requiring several hours to complete, more than triple the time Bradley had allocated), rather than the single powerful strike General Bradley needed. To maximize shock effect and deliver the most bombs in the shortest time, the bombers needed to attack perpendicularly to the target. In addition, a perpendicular course would be safer for the aircraft because they would spend less time over the target exposed to antiaircraft fire.

The reason the air commanders had not pressed their case on General Bradley more clearly at the conference at Stanmore on 19 July, or in the days following the meeting, is far from apparent—and remains one of the unresolved controversies of the campaign. There is evidence to suggest that some senior air staff officers had raised the issue at the Stanmore meeting. Notes made by air force people after the conference even stated that they thought General Bradley had understood the risks of short bombings and that he said he was "prepared to accept such casualties no matter which way the planes approached." On the other hand, officers recalled that at the same meeting Leigh-Mallory had quickly rejected the proposal of bombing on a parallel course. In short, while it is clear that the air commanders decided to conduct the perpendicular bombing at the Stanmore meeting, General Bradley and Air Chief Marshal Leigh-Mallory were probably not present when the final decision was made.

Confusion persists. Leigh-Mallory's deputy, U.S. Army Air Corps Major General Hoyt Vandenberg, claims in his diary to have contacted the air chief marshal after the meeting to confirm that General Bradley would accept a perpendicular bombing. After the aborted attack on 24 July, a team of air staff officers again met with General Bradley to impress on him the imperative of a perpendicular bombing, but there appears to be no record of senior air commanders ever taking up the issue personally with the First Army commander. In fact, there appear to be no joint army-air force records of the precise coordination agreed to during the period of 19–24 July. Either someone lied or, if both sides are to be believed, each left the 19 July meeting believing exactly the opposite thing. Indeed, misperception on both parts may be the answer. The bulk of the evidence suggests that the confluence of mismatched personalities, the convoluted relationship between air and ground commanders, and the lack of a sound doctrine created a situation in which, at the end of the day, commanders simply failed to understand what the others were doing.[28]

Now that the damage was already done, Bradley and Leigh-Mallory had to decide what to do next. They had simple alternatives. They could repeat the perpendicular bombing run, bomb on a parallel course that would not give Bradley the quick, powerful strike he wanted to lead off the attack, or call off the aerial bombardment. These contained a difficult choice. General Bradley had already seen the tremendous disruption that could be caused by a short bombing. If he had any hopes that the other safety measures he had put in place would be sufficient, he now had incontrovertible evidence that they were inadequate. If the planes attacked the same way again, Americans would most likely die from American bombs.

General Bradley had to make a decision. The long-range forecast indicated that weather conditions were probably going to diminish. The day of 25 July might be the last clear one for a week. Reluctantly he gave the go-ahead. After all, Cobra without the carpet bombing would be just another bloody frontal assault into the hedgerows. They would try it all again the next day.

The Bombers Again!

Bradley's aide, Major Hansen, was not among the troops at the front on 25 July when a smaller contingent from the First Army staff returned to the house outside Pont Hébert to watch the bombing. Hansen was back in England running errands for General Bradley. The skies over London were gray and overcast. He wondered if the planes would be able to fly and if the skies over Normandy were clear.

Not far away, Captain Stewart Reid and his ten-man B-24 Liberator crew from the 493d Bomber Group had similar thoughts. After the disastrous day on 24 July they were preparing for another run at the target in Normandy. They had been thoroughly briefed on their mission and knew that their bombs would be falling within sight of the U.S. infantry. They hoped that this time when they got over the target area that they would find open skies—and no German antiaircraft fire.

By dawn the spotter planes over Normandy were already reporting rapidly clearing weather. At 7:59 A.M. the front-line infantry divisions were flashed the code "Charlie is confirmed." Once again Cobra was on and the troops were told to get ready for the big attack. Among the anxious soldiers waiting for the attack, Lieutenant George Tuttle had returned to his post as liaison officer to the 119th Infantry Regiment. He and thousands of other Americans waited for the bombing to start again.

In Normandy, at 9:36 A.M. the first fighter-bombers banked for their run at the 250-yard strip south of the St-Lô–Périers road. Behind them came the heavy and medium bombers. Throughout the battlefield men could see and feel the effects: observer described the sound of approaching bombs as "clacking like dry peas shaken in a wooden basket."[29] Two miles away from the road the concussion from the explosions felt like "gale-force winds."[30] General Bradley, who was observing the bombing with General Collins in the VII Corps command post, could watch each successive wave of bombers whip a pair of lace curtains through an open window.[31] A reporter 5 miles away wrote that the force of the explosions "kept my shirt sleeves fluttering."[32] One officer remembered he could see the bombing from 10 miles away.[33] The display of firepower was nothing short of breathtaking.

Meanwhile, Captain Reid's B-24 headed for the target area. His squadron was not in the first wave, and when it reached the target area the battlefield was already totally obscured by smoke, fire, explosions, the flash of artillery, and billowing dust. The preplanned bombing altitude had been set between 15,000 and 16,000 feet, but cloud cover forced the bombers to drop down to 12,000 feet. Bombing data had to hurriedly be recomputed and sites readjusted. On cue, Reid's Liberator dropped its 2-ton bomb load according to plan and wheeled away from the target area.

The Germans did little to interfere with the air attacks. Before the battle had started, they were already critically short of antiaircraft ammunition and had fired off a good deal of their precious supply the previous day during the aborted bombing run. U.S. artillery had also taken a serious toll on German antiaircraft guns, having fired sixty-nine counterflak missions before the canceled attack on 24 July. After the weather had cleared later that same day, air photographs showed "excellent effects" from the artillery fire. The artillery repeated the counterflak firing on 25 July, but the German units that were not hit the day before had moved and the first aircraft encountered some flak. Aerial observers now called in artillery fire on the new antiaircraft positions and flak against the subsequent waves subsided. One German division, for example, opened fire as soon as they spotted U.S. planes, but half their antiaircraft guns were immediately knocked out by U.S. artillery, and the commanding officer ordered the rest to cease fire immediately. Overall, antiaircraft fire had a minimal affect on the attack: Five bombers were lost and fifty-nine damaged.[34]

As Captain Reid banked away from the target area below, bombardier Charles W. McArthur could see behind the plane waves of bombs heading toward the hedgerows below. He recalled that "it was a sight one does not forget."[35] The 1,495 B-17s and B-24s dropped more than 3,370 tons of bombs;[36] 380 medium bombers and 550 fighters also joined in the attack. The total tonnage of bombs approached 4,700, the equivalent of a good-sized, modern tactical nuclear weapon. The only problem with this overwhelming display of firepower was that not all the bombs landed on the enemy. In the front lines each of the assault infantry divisions had its share of disaster.

The 9th Infantry Division's Disaster

In the 9th Infantry Division, on the VII Corps's west flank, division commander General Eddy had had the word passed the night before the bombing that every man should be in a foxhole or shelter until H-Hour. Despite this precaution the division's 47th Infantry Regiment still took heavy casualties, its most forward-positioned unit, the 3d Battalion, getting hit the hardest. Bombs struck the battalion command post and wounded the entire command group, except for the commander and his executive officer. The battalion had thirty men killed or wounded in a few minutes' time.[37]

Support units also felt the effects of the bombing. B Company, 899th Tank Destroyer Battalion reported bombs landing only three fields away. The 196th Field Artillery Battalion reported bombs all over its area, one explosion being within 100 yards of its command post.[38] The 9th Infantry Division artillery lost all its wire communications and could only talk with its battalions by radio, but most of the artillery units reported only light casualties and they could still fire—except for the 957th Field Artillery Battalion.[39]

The men of the 957th may have had the most luckless day of any unit in the VII Corps. They called it "black Tuesday at Purple Heart Corner." The morning had started out with German shelling killing one soldier and wounding two; a short while later, the men watched the fighter-bombers make their attack. One plane had a bomb hung up on its rack, and, just as the plane cleared their area, the gunners saw the dangling bomb break loose, landing less than 100 yards to their rear. It was a close call, but that was just the start. When the planes arrived over the 957th Field Artillery Battalion, gunners "swarmed out of their dugouts and foxholes" to view the attack. One plane's bombs hit the battalion command post, killing thirteen and wounding twenty-two, including the commander and operations officer. Men set up smoke pots to mark their position and ward off the planes. The smoke mixed with black clouds from burning wreckage around the headquarters, covering the area in a dense, greasy, acrid fog.

Despite confusion and disaster the war went on: the division artillery called for fire missions. Even though the battalion's FDC was completely destroyed, the uninjured frantically tore through the wreckage searching for the artillery plans. They found them, and a half an hour later the guns were firing. It was the first thing that had gone right all day for the ill-fated battalion. All in all, it was a harrowing start for the 9th Infantry Division's attack, the division's total casualties already being ten dead and eighty wounded.

The 4th Infantry Division Under Fire

Disaster also visited the center of the U.S. lines at the 4th Infantry Division. The day before, General Barton, the division commander, had lost only one man to short bombings, a liaison officer at the 120th Regimental command post in the 30th Division area. On 25 July Barton was not as fortunate. Bombs landed on the 8th Infantry Regiment, hitting the 1st Battalion and causing serious casualties.

Other units were luckier. The 3d Battalion was late moving up to its position. Bombs crushed the spot where the battalion was supposed to be when the planes attacked. The 70th Tank Battalion was also lucky: bombs landed all around it but missed most of the battalion, and only one tank in A Company took a direct hit. Even with their good fortune, many of the tankers were shaken by the attack, including Captain Robert Crisson, the battalion executive officer: "A bomb exploded 30 feet from me. I was flat in a ditch beside the road. I can remember looking up after the explosion and seeing dirt and rocks raining down all around me. When I got up, I was half out of my senses." Captain Crisson jumped up and rushed to extinguish a fire before the flames attracted more bombers. "That's the way it affects you," he recalled, "You're not rational. Many of the men were out of their heads the same way I was. . . . We found them just wandering around and unable to understand clearly when you spoke to them."[40] For all the confusion, the division was fortunate to have only twenty-two men wounded.

Calamity in the 30th Infantry Division

General Hobbs's 30th Infantry Division on the VII Corps's eastern flank took the worst of the short bombings. Hobbs was already deeply upset about the short bombings on 24 July; both his lead regiments had taken losses in the attack. During the night, he ensured that the troops had been pulled back the planned 1,200 yards, over half a mile. It did not help. Casualties from short bombings on 25 July proved to be a lot worse. The 119th Regimental combat post near Le Mesnil-Durand was hit, causing forty casualties, and twelve vehicles carrying gas and ammunition exploded. To add to their misery, units took German artillery fire shortly after the bombing had started. Nearby, a light tank from the 743d Tank Battalion's Company D was set ablaze.[41]

Lieutenant Tuttle, the 120th Infantry Regiment's liaison officer to the 119th's command post, found himself being bombed for the second time in two days. He counted three bombing runs on his position, one from heavy bombers and two from fighter-bombers. Seven vehicles were burning in the immediate vicinity and men were hit. "Some men, who received direct hits," he recalled, "were blown to bits and no evidence of their existence remained."[42] The 119th Infantry Regiment suffered a total of 133 casualties from the short bombing.

Not far away, at the 120th Regiment command post, soldiers waited anxiously. After taking casualties on 24 July, they had become very cautious. The command post was dug in on the reverse slope of a hill, which proved to be a good idea because bombs landed twice nearby. Luckily no one was hurt.

Not all the soldiers of the 120th Regiment were so fortunate. Captain Ernest Bell, the operations officer for the regiment's 2d Battalion, was standing next to his command post when a bomb struck, killing him instantly. At the same time German artillery hit the position; several trucks loaded with gasoline ignited in a spectacular blaze. Troops were confused and disoriented. As one officer vividly remembered:

> One man was trying to dig a hole in the side of a hedgerow. His squad leader told me he was badly shaken up, wanted to know if he should be sent back. I went up to the man, and tried to talk to him. His face was as yellow as the dead ones that lay near him, and his eyes seemed to be on fire. He tried to answer my questions, but his vocal cords were uncontrollable and he couldn't utter a sound. He went on digging.[43]

Another officer from the regiment recalled that "my men stumbled ahead— as if walking in their sleep. . . . Their hands and feet lacked coordination. They had the look of punch drunk fighters—and that's just what they were at that time."[44] Others reported that "some men simply dropped everything—rifles personal gear—and ran blindly."[45] Soldiers tried to signal the aircraft with yellow flares, smoke grenades, and signal panels, while officers scrambled to assess the damage.

The concentration of forces for the attack was so great that it was hard to find an empty field on the U.S. side. Any bombs that fell landed on or near a friendly unit, hitting the support battalions as well as the attacking regiments. Bombs were reported within a thousand yards of the 18th Field Artillery Battalion and two batteries of the 230th Field Artillery Battalion. The 92d Chemical Mortar Battalion was hit particularly hard. Friendly planes struck four times, leaving five dead and twenty-three wounded. A Company lost nine of its twelve mortars; B company lost half its ammunition and four mortars. The battalion suffered so many casualties that it was knocked completely out of action.[46] On 25 July the 30th Infantry Division's total losses from the air attack were 61 killed, 374 wounded, and 60 missing—a battalion's worth of men lost before the battle had even started! The total losses in the VII Corps were approximately 108 dead and 472 injured.[47]

The most famous casualty of the day occurred not far from the small house where Bradley's aide, Major Hansen, had been watching the bombing the previous day. Every history of the battle mentions the death of General Lesley J. McNair, though none provide the full details of his death. It all began about 11:30 A.M. when two officers from General McNair's staff rushed up to the observation post and reported to the deputy First

Army commander, General Hodges. Their first words were, "We're a bit worried about General McNair."[48]

Only weeks before Cobra the press had reported that General McNair, the Army Ground Forces (AGF) commander, had been reassigned to an important, but unannounced, post. The blue-eyed field artillery officer, who had graduated near the top of his 1904 West Point class, was well known throughout the army. As the AGF commander, General McNair had supervised the organization and training of forces before they were deployed overseas. It was not widely known, but General McNair's new secret assignment was to replace General Patton as the commander of a fictitious army in the deception plan, Fortitude North.

This new command would give General McNair his second opportunity to see for himself the performance of the troops he had trained for battle. In 1943 he had visited the front in North Africa, only to be wounded by German artillery. He hoped for better luck this time. He was present for the short bombings on 24 July and decided to return to the front the next day, when he watched the attack from the 2d Battalion, 120th Infantry Regiment command post. The general was in a foxhole only 30 yards from the command center when the bombs hit. His aide rushed to the spot, but there was nothing there, only a crater. A rescue detail dug up the area but could find no trace of the general.

It was 12:25 P.M. before the last wave of aircraft had passed over and General Hodges thought it was safe enough to begin searching for General McNair. He did not get far. His command car was stopped after less than a mile by mortar fire and the chatter of German machine guns. General Hodges's aide cautioned they did not need two dead generals in one day. So, reluctantly, Hodges decided to delay his search until U.S. troops had secured the area. He waited at the 30th Infantry Division command post, while officers were dispatched to check the clearing stations and hospitals.

Later that day General Hodges went back to the front, parking not far from the devastated 92d Chemical Mortar Battalion, and a short distance from where Lieutenant Tuttle had experienced his two near misses at the 120th Infantry Regiment headquarters. General Hodges met Colonel Tory Roberts, the 2d Armored Division artillery commander, who asked whether Hodges was "looking for, or had heard of, the body of the Ground Forces General." The colonel then led Hodges to McNair's body. The force of the explosion had thrown McNair over 60 feet from the slit trench he had occupied during the bombing. His remains were completely unrecognizable, except for his shoulder patch and stars.

Upon his return from London Major Hansen had planned to meet General McNair at the airfield, only to find out that the general had been killed not too far from the spot Hansen had been the previous day. Hansen entered the following in his diary: "Everyone upset about the thing. Strict secrecy on the X [McNair's] death. No one knows and the funeral arrangements are secret. No talk. No comment. . . . I learned inadvertently. His aides feel badly and walk around somewhat lost with themselves."[49] General McNair was buried quietly in a temporary cemetery at La Cambe.[50]

McNair's death and the other casualties were not the divisions' only problem. Despite the fact that less than 3 percent of the bombs dropped had hit U.S. lines, the attacks created a near crisis in the VII Corps. In addition to the outrage and frustration at the tragic killing and wounding of soldiers, the disaster threatened the whole offensive. The first effect was the obvious physical damage and the disruption of attack plans. Just as serious was the psychological injury: "friendly fire" undercut unit morale, creating a heightened sense of fear and hopelessness in soldiers and a mistrust and apprehension about again employing friendly fire support systems. In some cases such results had been severe. The 30th Infantry Division, for example, reported an additional 164 cases of combat exhaustion. The short bombings were indeed a disastrous start for the beginning of the breakthrough.[51]

The Burden of a Firepower War

Half a century later, the debate over the Cobra bombing disaster has lost none of its vitality. Today, typing on a keyboard far from and long after the terror of the hedgerows, it is simple to point out the shortcomings of the bombing plan. On that July day it all seemed very different. An officer at the front concluded: "I believe every man in the company will agree that if we have such an attack again they would want the bombing just where it was, right to our lines. We would rather take the ones that fall on us to get the effect on the Germans in front of us."[52] The issue, however, was not whether the bombing should have been conducted but whether the commanders had done everything possible to mitigate the risks.

General Eisenhower, for one, was concerned about the implications of assigning blame for the disaster. He wrote to General Marshal that "complete investigations are underway. . . . In the meantime I am anxious that treatment in the newspapers, if the matter becomes one of public discussion, be moderate and sensible so that we do not get a ground versus air war started that is completely senseless and harmful."[53] At the time no one was anxious to fix responsibility on any senior leader. In fact, Lieutenant Colonel Alvin B. Welch from the U.S. First Army's inspector general's office conducted an official investigation of the incident, finding "no delinquencies on the part of the ground units." His report specifically did not address at all the activities and decisions by senior air and ground commanders.[54]

Official reports offered no criticisms of senior commanders. Martin Blumenson has also absolved the First Army commander of any responsibility for the short bombings. More recent studies, including those by John Sullivan and Richard G. Davis, are more critical of both Bradley and Leigh-Mallory, stressing their lack of experience in planning air-ground operations and inadequate coordination with the air commanders.[55] These historians, however, do not go far enough. A thorough review of the evidence suggests not only that General Bradley must bear major responsibility for the disaster, but that his failure was more than simply inexperience or an inadvertent lack of proper oversight.

Why did things go so terribly wrong? The issue has too frequently focused on the simple issue of parallel versus perpendicular attack. General Hobbs, the 30th Infantry Division commander, has blamed the route taken by the heavy bombers. He claims that "bombers that flew parallel to our front lines dropped their bombs on the target. Many of the bombers who flew across our line dropped their bombs short and it was these that caused our casualties."[56] But the general's assessment and that of the historians who generally followed his reasoning are incorrect.

A parallel attack was no "magic bullet" for solving the challenge of bombing in close proximity to ground troops. In fact, with the battlefield totally obscured by smoke, dust, and fire there was no guarantee that a parallel approach would have been any more successful in preventing short bombings. In addition, even on a parallel course there was a risk of the bombers' hitting U.S. troops. If the bombers had overshot or undershot the target area, bombs might have landed on U.S. forces holding positions to either the northeast or northwest of the target area. In addition, planes on a parallel course might have drifted north of the no-bomb line, passing over American troops. All the previous Allied experience in air-ground coordination suggested that a parallel approach was not a sufficient precaution to preclude a serious threat from short bombings.

Although the seeds of disaster were sown by the lack of clear understanding between the ground and air commanders over the direction of the aerial attack, there is more to the story. Some of the most tragic short bombings were made by the supposedly more accurate fighter-bombers, and some of these planes had flown parallel, not perpendicularly, to the target and at an altitude of only 2,000 feet.

In fact, neither the parallel bombing nor any of the other precautions General Bradley ordered had proved sufficient. The smoke markings actually worsened the situation. When the corps artillery fired red-smoke shells to mark the no-bomb line, the smoke clouds drifted north, obscuring the line. After the first bombs hit their targets, dust from the explosions mixed with the smoke, further exacerbating the problem. The panel markers placed in front of the friendly positions and white stars painted on the vehicles were equally useless. In fact, all the marking and coordination techniques employed by the Americans were inadequate, even for marking targets for the fighter-bombers. This was not a new discovery: these techniques had consistently failed to prove themselves earlier in the campaign.

Another problem during Cobra was that commanders had not ensured that the ground troops were adequately prepared. Even though troops were supposed to withdraw 1,200 yards from the no-bomb line, some units were still positioned as close as 800 yards or less. Others had pulled back shortly before the air strike, but were not told to dig in. The 2d Battalion, 120th Infantry Regiment, for example, which was hit hard on 24 July, was deployed in battle formation preparing to attack, not dug in and protected. Lieutenant Chester H. Jordan in the 3rd Battalion, 47th Infantry Regiment, recalled that "I reasoned the Germans would be in no shape to throw anything at us so why dig a hole." When the attack started, his platoon "cheered the bombers on like kids at a football game," until the first short bombs began to land.[57] The failure to take protective cover was an invitation to disaster.

Neither the First Army nor the VII Corps had ordered additional precautions on 25 July or warned units that heavy bombers were flying a route perpendicular to the U.S. lines and that there was an increased likelihood of short bombings. In fact, the VII Corps issued a message on 25 July at 1:55 A.M. reassuring commanders that there would be no bombings north of the road. Some units, however, on their own initiative had ordered troops to dig in. Foxholes did protect soldiers from bomb fragments, but even then no one could be completely safe. As the death of General McNair illustrated, entrenchments were not sufficient protection from direct hits.

General Bradley had appreciated the necessity of closely integrating aerial bombardment with the other elements of the plan, but on this occasion he failed. All the U.S. military experience with employing close air support in World War II up to this point had indicated that known safety measures would be inadequate. Nevertheless, official inquiries into the bombing absolved senior air and ground commanders of any culpability. The reports catalogued twelve separate incidents (not including short bombing and strafings by the fighter-bombers), determining that the causes of the short bombings were human error or confusion and disorientation of pilots and bombardiers.[58]

The preconditions for the bombing disaster were the cumulative result of three critical failures: inadequate coordination with supporting air forces, inability to mark the forward positions of ground forces, and the lack of warning to and protection of the troops. But what the reports fail to fully emphasize is that none of these failings were beyond General Bradley's control. In particular, he had made the most important and tragic decisions about the bombing: how far the troops would withdraw from the no-bomb line and what precautions had to be taken. Considering the Allies' history of problems in short bombings and strafings, particularly in Normandy, Bradley's failure not to pay more attention to the issue and work harder with the air commanders until the issue was fully resolved was inexcusable. The overall fire support plan was his initiative and it was seriously flawed.

In his memoirs, Bradley goes to great lengths to absolve himself. For instance, in the text his stated preference for having the bombers fly a *parallel course* is italicized, suggesting that if the air commanders had just followed his wishes there would have been no casualties. Bradley also included curious statements in his account of the pre-Cobra planning, such as a remark that General Eddy, the cautious 9th Infantry Division commander, had "balked initially at this order to withdraw. After having fought hard for that mile he disliked giving it up with the prospect of having to fight once more to regain it. But I was unwilling to chance a bombing any closer to our lines."[59]

The account of this conversation fails to note that the actual safety distance General Bradley had decided on was 1,200 yards (1,500 for the heavy bombers), a distance well short of a mile. Bradley also does not reveal that he himself had initially argued for only an 800-yard separation. In addition, he does not point out that if the U.S. troops had withdrawn the 3,000 yards suggested by the air commanders, there would have been minimal front-line casualties from the short bombings. Finally, Bradley's description of Eddy's concerns hardly squares with Eddy's complaints on 17 July about the danger of short bombings.[60] Nor does Bradley mention that Brigadier General F. H. Smith, the director of operations for the Allied Expeditionary Air Force, at the 19 July meeting at Stanmore, had briefed Bradley that there might be "gross bombing errors causing troop casualties."[61] In short, General Bradley's own accounts of the Cobra bombing did much to obfuscate his personal responsibility. The evidence suggests that he knew the front-line troops would take casualties. He was willing to take that risk. He was not, however, prepared to acknowledge this truth publicly—and his explanations are a disingenuous moment in what is regarded as an otherwise honorable and distinguished career.

Why General Bradley made such poor choices about this particular aspect of the campaign cannot be confidently ascertained from the available evidence. However, it is clear that whether due to a serious tactical misjudgment, intentionally assuming the terrible risk of killing and maiming his own troops, or unrealistic wishful thinking on his part, Bradley failed to adequately address the issue of protection for his ground forces.[62]

In the end, there was no question that 25 July had started as another terrible day. Commanders were left wondering after everything that had gone wrong—could the infantry still break through? That could only be answered by the skill and determination of the regiment and battalion commanders who were about to launch their men into battle.

Notes

1. Hansen, War Dairy, July 20, 1944, MHI.

2. Eisenhower, *Eisenhower at War*, p. 369. For a treatment of Operation Goodwood, see John J. T. Sweet, *Mounting the Threat*.

3. Blumentritt, "Three Marshals," pp. 92–94. For one account of General Kluge's reaction to the plot, see Speidel, *We Defended Normandy*, p. 130–132.

4. Unless noted otherwise, the information on the fire support and air support plans for Operation Cobra was extracted from U.S. Forces, European Theater, *Report on Study of Field Artillery Operations, Study No. 61*, pp. 15–22, CARL; Headquarters, VII Corps, U.S. Army, Operations Memo 45, 22 July 1944, "Field Artillery, Anti Aircraft and Tank Destroyer," Annex No. 3, and "Air Support Plan," Annex No. 4, Field Order #6. See also Robert H. George, "Normandy," in *The Army Air Forces in World War II*, vol. 3, *Europe: Argument to V-E Day January 1944 to May 1945*, pp. 185–227; Robert W. Ackerman, The Employment of Strategic Bombers in the Tactical Role, 1941–1945, microfilm K1010, 1953, AFHRA; Headquarters, Allied Expeditionary Force, Subject: Operation "Cobra," 20th July 1944, microfilm, Roll A5129, AFHSO; Headquarters, IX TAC Operations Order for Operation Cobra, 19 July 1944, microfilm, Roll B5731, AFHSO.

5. Ian Gooderson, "Heavy and Medium Bombers: How Successful Were They in Tactical Close Air Support During World War II?" *The Journal of Strategic Studies* 15 (September 1992): 369. The figures cited here were optimal loads. Actual combat loads varied and could be considerably less. The air forces had to balance fuel and bomb load requirements for each individual mission.

6. Hansen, War Diary, 12 July 1944. John Sullivan suggests that Professor Solly Zuckerman, an RAF scientific advisor, played a significant role in planning the air strike. See John J. Sullivan, *Overlord's Eagles: Operations of the United States Army Air Forces in the Invasion of Normandy in World War II*, pp. 137–138; and Solly Zuckerman, *From Apes to Warlords: The Autobiography of Solly Zuckerman*, pp. 278–280, 284–285. The evidence for this is not convincing. Neither the recollections of the First Army staff nor Bradley and Zuckerman's memoirs support this conclusion. It appears that Zuckerman's only significant role was in the contentious debate over the minimum safe distance that troops should withdraw from the no-bomb line.

7. Hansen, War Diary, 21 June 1944. See also Bradley, *Soldier's Story*, pp. 309, 338–339.

8. W. A. Jacobs, "The Battle for France, 1944," in *Case Studies in the Development of Close Air Support*, p. 240. See also Eisenhower, *Eisenhower at War*, pp. 152–153. For a concise overview of the complicated command and control relationships between the ground and strategic air forces, see Richard G. Davis, *Carl A. Spaatz and the Air War in Europe*, pp. 354–363. For the organization of theater air support, see *Report of the General Board: Air Power in the European Theater, Study No. 56*, CARL. See also Frederick Lewis Anderson, Papers, HHI.

9. Hansen, War Diary, 19 July 1944, MHI. On the eve of Cobra, Eisenhower himself offered a lukewarm endorsement of Leigh-Mallory, writing,

I entertained some doubts as to the qualifications of Air Chief Leigh-Mallory for the post. . . . In justice to him I want to tell you now that I've liked the way he has operated and cooperated. While, possibly, his experience in support technique may be somewhat limited this is rapidly being eliminated and is, moreover, more than balanced by his fighting heart and desire to pull his weight in the team.

See the letter from Eisenhower to Charles Frederick Algernon Pearl, 22 July 1944, in Alfred D. Chandler Jr., *Papers of Dwight David Eisenhower,* p. 2025.

10. Davis, *Carl A. Spaatz,* p. 268.

11. Ibid.

12. Ibid., pp. 267–268.

13. The quotes in this paragraph are taken from Hansen, Bradley's Commentary on World War II, notes 30-A, 30-B, S-22. See also Davis, *Carl A. Spaatz,* pp. 466–467; Thomas Alexander Hughes, *Overlord: General Pete Quesada and the Triumph of Tactical Airpower in World War II,* pp. 120–121; Sullivan, *Overlord's Eagles,* p. 136.

14. Operation Charnwood was the British and Canadian attack toward Caen from 7–9 July, spearheaded by 460 British bombers hitting an area 4,500 by 1,500 yards. In the 2-day attack that followed, the assaulting forces reached the Orne River, but failed to take all of Caen. More than 2,000 planes preceded the Operation Goodwood assaults.

15. Gooderson, "Heavy and Medium Bombers," p. 372.

16. *Activities of General Eddy,* 17 July 1944.

17. Headquarters, 4th Infantry Division, U.S. Army, Letter to G-3 Air, VII Corps, "Air in Support of Infantry," 1 July 1944.

18. The Battle for Normandy, File 8-3.1 AF, p. 170, CMH.

19. Office of the Infantry Board, Report, "Artillery-Infantry Test," p. 27, USAFAS.

20. Dorst, *My Times,* p. 56, MHI. There were probably many more unreported attacks by friendly aircraft. The Military History Institute at Carlisle Barracks, Pennsylvania, for a number of years has been collecting surveys of World War II veterans. In a random search of forty surveys, I found that thirty-five of the respondents claimed to have been attacked by friendly aircraft. See *World War II Survey,* MHI.

21. Charles F. Howard, AGF Observer Report, 27 July 1944, pp. 6–7, CARL.

22. Bradley, *Soldier's Story,* pp. 157–158. Colonel Dickson remembered the briefing in his memoirs. He recalled that Bradley was "calling his shots" with the press like a pool player. See Benjamin A. Dickson, "Algiers to the Elbe," Dickson Papers, p. 139, MHI. In another encounter with the press, General Patton's staff inadvertently leaked news of the big attack before General Bradley had authorized discussion with the press. See Blumenson, *The Patton Papers,* pp. 482–484.

23. There is very little scholarship to evaluate the implications of Bradley's decision. Françoise Dutour, *The Liberation of Calvados 6th June 1944–31st December 1944,* provides a summary of archival records on civilian casualties, but no specific figures for Operation Cobra.

24. Hansen, War Diary, July 19, 1944, MHI. See also Bradley, Oral History Interview, Revised Transcript, Tape 7, pp. 10–11, MHI. Davis, *Carl A. Spaatz,* p. 720, n. 70, questions whether General Spaatz was in attendance. General Bradley's recollection claims he was (see Bradley, *Soldier's Story,* p. 340), as does General Quesada (see Elwood R. Quesada, Interviews of Lt. Gen. Elwood R. Quesada, USAF Oral History Interview, 12–13 May 1975, AFHRA). Spaatz also visited

Bradley's headquarters on 20 July 1944; see Sylvan, War Diary, 20 July 1944, MHI. There is no record that Spaatz discussed bombing tactics for Cobra.

25. For General Spaatz's criticism of the decision, see Carl A. Spaatz, *The Papers of Carl A. Spaatz*, Memorandum for General Spaatz's Diary, Subject: Operation "Cobra," 24 July 1944, Box 168, LC.

26. It was a B-24 Liberator that bombed a Ninth Air Force airfield at Chippelle when the bombardier accidentally hit the release toggle switch. The bombs destroyed two P-47 Thunderbolts parked on the ground, killing four and wounding fourteen men.

27. Headquarters, Allied Expeditionary Force, Subject: Operation "Cobra," 20th July 1944, microfilm, Roll A5129, AFHSO.

28. The account of General Bradley's coordination with the air staff was reconstructed from Bradley, Oral History Interview, Revised Transcript, Tape 7, pp. 10–11; Quesada, USAF Oral History Interview, AFHRA; Hoyt S. Vandenberg, *The Papers of Hoyt S. Vandenberg*, Diary, Box 1, entries 19–24 July 1944; memo for General Spaatz's Diary, Subject: Operation "Cobra," July 24, 1944, Carl Spaatz Papers, LC; Blumenson, *Breakout and Pursuit*, pp. 220–221, 231–233; Davis, *Carl A. Spaatz*, pp. 465–471; Hughes, *Overlord*, pp. 199–201. In addition, Hansen, War Diary, contains a memo, Subject: "Combined Air and Ground Operations west of St. Lô on Tuesday 25 July 1944." The memo lays out General Bradley's interpretation of the coordination. Davis, *Carl A. Spaatz*, p. 720, n.60, suggests that the memo was composed sometime after the event (though the memo is dated 25 July 1944). Davis has no evidence to support this assertion; in fact, it would seem to be exactly the kind of document that Bradley would have wanted to put together in light of the investigation that was sure to follow. Official Eighth U.S. Air Force memos on the coordination also appear to have been written after the event. See also Blumenson, *Battle of the Generals*, pp. 136–137.

29. John D. Hess, *Move Out, Verify: The Combat Story of the 743rd Tank Battalion*, pp. 63–64.

30. Barry W. Fowle and Floyd D. Wright, *The 51st Again! An Engineer Combat Battalion in World War II*, p. 55.

31. Robert A. Hewitt, *Interviews*, p. 195, MHI.

32. A. J. Liebling, "St. Lo and Mortain," in *Danger Forward: The Story of the First Division in World War II*, p. 247.

33. Carl I. Hutton, *An Armored Artillery Commander in the European Theater*, p. 105, USAFAS.

34. First United States Army, Report of Operations, 20 October 1943 to 1 August 1944, Annex 3, p. 182; Carl A. Spaatz, *The Papers of Carl A. Spaatz*, Headquarters, Air P/W Interrogation Detachment, Subject: Enemy Intelligence Summaries, 29 May 1945, Box 134, p. 7, LC.

35. This quote and the account of Captain's Reid's mission are taken from Charles W. McArthur, *Operations Analysis in the U.S. Army Eighth Air Force in World War II*, pp. 192–193. For more on the warnings to the air crews that they would be bombing in proximity to ground troops and the difficulty pilots experienced in identifying targets, see the numerous excerpts from postoperation reports in Carl A. Spaatz, *The Papers of Carl A. Spaatz*, Headquarters Eighth Air Force, Special Report of Operations 24 and 25 July, 1944, 11/9/44, Bombing Errors Committed on Normandy Battlefront, 25 July 1944, Box 168, pp. 1–15, LC. See also Report of the Tactical Bombing 25 July 1944, Box 84, Carl Spaatz Papers, LC; John J. Sullivan, "The Botched Air Support for Operation Cobra," *Parameters* XVIII (March 1988): n. 24.

36. The bomber force attacked in 3 divisions in this order: 2d Bomber

Division (45 tactical units), 3d Bomber Division (36 tactical units), 1st Bomber Division (43 tactical units). Each unit contained 12 to 14 planes. Under each division 3 to 4 units were organized into a wing. There were 3 wings in each wave, and each division consisted of 4 waves. Bombers attacked with 2 minutes between waves. There were 1,586 bombers in the force, though only 1,485 dropped bombs. The 2d Division dropped from 10:00 to 10:17 A.M. at 11,300 to 13,000 feet. Twelve B-24s dropped 2,800 yards short when a bomb sight failed and the lead bomber released visually. Eleven B-24s bombed 3,000 yards short when the lead bomber's bomb sight failed and they dropped on the first group's mark. The 2d Division dropped at 13,000 to 12,000 feet between 10:19 and 10:36 A.M. Fourteen B-24s dropped short when the lead pilot ordered bombs released by mistake after he saw the bombs from another wing release and thought it was the lead bomber from his wing. The 1st Division bombed at 13,000 feet between 10:40 and 10:55 A.M. Five units did not attack because they could not see the target through the smoke and clouds. Approximately one-half of the division's bombs fell south of the southernmost edge of the bomb box (on the German lines). See Adjutant General's Office, World War II Operations, Operation Cobra, Air Support, Box 24245, RG 94, NARA.

37. David Gillespie, ed., *The 47th Infantry Regiment;* Joseph B. Mittelman, *Eight Stars to Victory: A History of the Veteran Ninth U.S. Infantry Division,* pp. 199–200.

38. *899th Tank Destroyer Battalion History,* p. 37, MHI.

39. The events at the 957th Field Artillery Battalion on 25 July 1944 are taken from Headquarters, 9th Infantry Division Artillery, U.S. Army, Combat Log, entry for 25 July 1944; D. G. Dively, *End of Mission: 957th Field Artillery Battalion,* pp. 40–41.

40. Headquarters, 8th Infantry Regiment, U.S. Army, S-3 Journal, 25 July 1944; Headquarters, 4th Infantry Division, U.S. Army, After Action Report, entry titled "Interview with Lt Joseph L. Gude and Lt William Woodruff, ETO, C Co, 8th Infantry on 14 Aug 1944"; and Chester B. Hall, *History of the 70th Tank Battalion.*

41. Robert L. Hewitt, *Workhorse of the Western Front: The Story of the 30th Infantry Division,* pp. 36–37; *Combat History of the 119th Infantry Regiment,* p. 22.

42. *History of the 120th Infantry Regiment,* pp. 34–35.

43. Ibid.

44. Ibid.

45. Hess, *Move Out,* p. 64.

46. Brooks E. Kleber and Dale Birdsell, *The Chemical Warfare Service,* p. 468; Elmer Hale, *History of the 18th Field Artillery Battalion, World War II,* p. 6; Headquarters, 30th Infantry Division Artillery, U.S. Army, *History of the Thirtieth Division Artillery,* p. 24.

47. Casualty figures for the attack vary. The figures given here are from the official Inspector General office investigation. See Headquarters, First U.S. Army, Air Support Report, Investigation of Bombing of Ground Troops by Friendly Planes on 24 and 25 July 1944, 16 August 1944, Adjutant General Section, General Correspondence 1940–47, Box 119, RG 338, p. 1, NARA.

48. The events surrounding the death of General McNair are taken from Sylvan, War Diary, 25 July 1944, MHI.

49. Hansen, War Diary, 25 July 1944, MHI.

50. Bradley wrote to Eisenhower with the details of the funeral. It took place at 8:30 P.M. on the evening of 26 July in a small cemetery just west of the town. In addition to Bradley, Generals Hodges, Patton, Royce, Kean, and Quesada, and McNair's aides attended the funeral. Colonel McNamara, a quartermaster officer,

made all the arrangements. Bradley's letter included photos of the funeral that he thought Eisenhower might want to pass on to Mrs. McNair. See the letter dated 28 July 1944, Bradley Papers, Correspondence with Major Historical Figures, MHI. See also Blumenson, *The Patton Papers,* p. 489. After the bombing McNair's death was kept a secret. When a newspaper reporter asked General William Harrison in the 30th Infantry Division about the rumors of a death of a general in the vicinity, Harrison replied, "I'm the only general around here and I ain't dead yet." See William K. Harrison, Oral History, p. 327, MHI. Although General McNair's death was not announced immediately, it did not remain a secret long. In a few days, his death from the accidental bombing was announced in the press and appeared in U.S. papers on 28 July. On 29 July a public ceremony was held at the AGF headquarters. The troops assembled on the parade field in the shadow of the general's old house. Brigadier General James Christiansen, the AGF chief of staff, gave the eulogy. The colors were dipped slowly to the strains of the Field Artillery anthem "The Caissons Go Rolling Along." See "The Late GEN McNair Honored," *Army and Navy Journal,* 5 August 1944, p. 1488. After the war, McNair's body was moved to the U.S. military cemetery established above the cliffs on Omaha Beach.

51. For a useful introduction to the problems of fratricide on the modern battlefield, see Charles R. Shrader, "Friendly Fire: The Inevitable Price," *Parameters* XXII (Autumn 1992): 29–44.

52. Headquarters, 4th Infantry Division, U.S. Army, Actions Against Enemy/After Action Reports, 10 August 1994, Combat Journal, "Interview with Lt Gude."

53. Chandler, *Papers of Dwight David Eisenhower,* p. 2032.

54. Headquarters, First U.S. Army, Air Support Report, Investigation of Bombing of Ground Troops by Friendly Planes on 24 and 25 July 1944, 16 August 1944, Adjutant General Section, General Correspondence 1940–47, Box 119, RG 338, NARA.

55. The official U.S. First Army after action air support report called the Cobra carpet bombing "a complete success" and did not even mention the short bombings. See Headquarters, First U.S. Army, Air Support Report, 6 August 1944, Section V. Operation Cobra, microfilm, Roll C5127. Marshal Leigh-Mallory also rated the mission a success, arguing that it proved the value of strategic bomber support for ground operations. See *The Papers of Carl A. Spaatz,* Despatch by Air Chief Marshal Sir Trafford Leigh-Mallory, Box 104, pp. 57–58, LC. A report by commanding general of the Army Air Forces did not mention the short bombing in its narrative of Cobra; see *Second Report of the Commanding General of the Army Air Forces to the Secretary of War,* pp. 11, 14. For a photographic analysis of the bombing coverage and the pattern of the short bombings, see U.S. Strategic Bombing Survey, Europe War, G-2 Target File, 2478, Box 140, RG 243, NARA. Experiences late in the war demonstrated that strategic bombing could support tactical operations without fratricide. The 8th U.S. Air Force eventually developed an extensive air-ground marker and communications system that was used to support Operation Queen in November 1944. See *Report of the General Board: Air Power in the European Theater of Operations, Study No. 56,* p. 17, CARL; Gooderson, "Heavy and Medium Bombers," pp. 390–391. Blumenson absolves General Bradley of responsibility for the short bombings: his assessment can be found in *Battle of the Generals,* p. 131. For another assessment of the responsibility for the failure to adequately coordinate air support for operation Cobra, see Sullivan, "The Botched Air Support for Operation Cobra," pp. 97–110. See also Davis, *Carl A. Spaatz,* pp. 463–479.

56. AGF Immediate Report No. 16, CARL.

57. Chester H. Jordan, *Bull Sessions World War II Company K, 47th Infantry Regiment, 9th Infantry Division from Normandy to Remagen,* p. 42. Instructions given to soldiers across the front were not uniform. Some were told to dig in and did so. See, for example, Robert C. Baldridge, *Victory Road,* p. 110.

58. See *The Papers of Carl A. Spaatz,* Harold W. Ohlke, Report of Investigation of Bombing, 24–25 July, Box 168, LC; Headquarters, Eighth Air Force, Special Report of Operations 24 and 25 July 1944, 11/9/44, Box 168, p. 7, LC. In fact, poststrike air force analysis rated the overall bombing as technically accurate with less bombing errors than anticipated. In total forty-two planes (thirty-five bombers) dropped bombs on friendly positions. See Eighth Air Force, History of Operations Analysis Section, October 1942–June 1945, AFHRA. See also Walter E. Todd, Report of Investigation of Bombing July 24–25, Box 71, RG 243, NARA.

59. Bradley, *Soldier's Story,* p. 341. The italicized passage on parallel bombing is on p. 330.

60. Activities of General Eddy, 17 July 1944.

61. Headquarters, Eighth Air Force, Special Report of Operations 24 and 25 July 1944, 11/9/44, Box 168, *The Papers of Carl A. Spaatz,* p. 1, LC.

62. There is one other potential source of evidence that may provide insight on the controversy. John L. Walsh, General Collins's aide-de-camp, wrote his wife shortly before and after the bombing. The letters have not been released to the public, but they may offer further insight into General Collins's knowledge concerning Bradley's actions. See John L. Walsh, letters for 24, 26, and 27 July 1944, DDE.

6

Taking the High Ground

While the U.S. Army corps on his flanks attacked on 25 July to capture German attention and prevent any shift to counter the U.S. penetration of German positions, the soldiers of General Collins's three lead infantry divisions stood poised along the fringe of the Allied carpet bombing that was preparing the breakthrough assault. Leading the attack, the troops of the U.S. 30th Infantry Division massed on the eastern edge of the penetration, readying for the first battle of the day of the infantry.

At the 30th Infantry Division's command post Major General Leland Stanford Hobbs, the division commander, gathered reports on the unfolding events. He had a well-earned reputation for operating on a short fuse. His histrionics had earned him the nickname of "Hollywood Hobbs." But when the results of the carpet bombing reached the command post, the edge in his voice was not theatrical. "There's absolutely no excuse," he fumed, "no excuse at all. I wish I could show some of those boys [in the Army Air Force] . . . our casualty clearing stations."[1] After all his division had been through, General Hobbs thought his men deserved better.

General Hobbs, a 1915 West Point graduate and career infantry officer, had missed the fighting in World War I. In 1942 he took command of the 30th Infantry Division and prepared to lead troops into battle for the first time. Two years later, on June 15, the division debuted in its first campaign of the war. The baptism proved to be a bitter summer of close combat over some of the toughest Normandy ground, a crisscross of waterways and hedgerows west of St-Lô. In the worst fighting, from 13 to 17 July, the division lost 3,200 in dead, wounded, and missing. Now the first moments of Cobra, despite the tremendous planning and preparations that took place in the weeks before the operation, seemed to promise only more casualties.

A Plan to Take the High Ground

On 15 July the U.S. First Army assigned the 30th Infantry Division to support the VII Corps during Operation Cobra. General Collins, the VII Corps commander, gave the division a tough, threefold mission. The first, and most important, task was to establish the left flank of the corps's attack on the high ground near Hebecrevon. The second part of the mission required clearing part of the gap for the breakthrough by seizing an objective south of St-Gilles to open routes for the U.S. 2d Armored Division. The third task was to secure the bridge on the Vire River to block potential counterattacks from the east.

None of the objectives would be easy to reach. Including the hundreds of yards the division would have to pull back from the no-bomb line, its initial objectives were more than 2 miles away, a far distance in hedgerow warfare. If the plan went according to schedule, by the end of the attack the division would advance 12 miles, an unprecedented gain for an offensive in the Normandy terrain.

General Hobbs's mission was one of the most critical of the campaign. The bombing would briefly paralyze communications and the movement of German reserves within the target area, but if the 30th Division could not penetrate the defenses and open up an avenue for the penetration attack before the enemy recovered, the effects of the bombing would be wasted. In addition to cracking open the German defenses, the division would have to seal the flank of the penetration to prevent enemy units outside the bombing box from counterattacking. If the division failed, the likelihood of General Bradley's plan succeeding was greatly diminished.

On 21 July unit commanders reported to the 30th Infantry Division command post to be briefed on their part in Operation Cobra. Even as the officers huddled to hear about the plan from General Hobbs for the first time, the Germans knew that something was up. From 18–20 July German intelligence had intercepted radio traffic indicating that an important briefing was scheduled for 21 July.[2] All the signs indicated that the Americans were preparing another offensive. A 21 July entry in the Seventh Army war diary concluded that "the enemy will launch another large-scale attack west of the Vire [River]."[3] While they suspected what was coming, the Germans did not have much combat power to stop it. The 30th Infantry Division was about to attack one of the most vulnerable parts of the Seventh Army's line, the boundary between its two constituent corps.[4]

In the II Parachute Corps area, the 352d Division covered the eastern half of the intercorps boundary. Like many of the divisions guarding the coast, the 352d Division was a makeshift division. It had been created from the remnants of the 268th and 321st Infantry Divisions after those units had been decimated on the Eastern Front. The 352d Division had limited artillery and virtually no transport, armor, or reconnaissance. As for the troops, as one officer wrote, the divisions guarding the Normandy coast frequently did not get the best.

> Most of the soldiers belonged to older age classes and were not physically fit. On three separate occasions the units and staffs in the West had been "combed out" for the sake of the Eastern Front. In return the West received . . . soldiers with second and third degree frostbite, and in some cases even men suffering from malaria and stomach ailments. . . . Soldiers with heart trouble or other physical defects, and even officers with artificial limbs were not infrequent.[5]

The 352d Division's readiness was typical: it had only 6,000 men, only a few officers had combat experience, and 30 percent of the noncommissioned officer positions were unfilled. Troops lacked physical conditioning and training averaged barely 3 hours a day. When the battles had started things only got worse; the division lost a sixth of its men the first day. By July, even after being supplemented with the remnants of five other units, the division had only 1,900 men and forty artillery pieces, covering a division-sized front (6 miles wide).

Despite their impoverished organization and initial losses, the unit fought well. General Eugen Meindl, the II Parachute Corps commander, who had little respect for the U.S. infantry, recalled that the soldiers of the 352d Division were "quite useful."[6] The division had distinguished itself in tough fighting with the Americans on Omaha Beach and in the hills around St-Lô. Nevertheless, after weeks of constant fighting, General Meindl believed the division was so weak that if the Americans opened a gap in their lines, it could not be closed.

On the west bank of the Vire River, facing the 30th Infantry Division, the 352d Division positioned one of the units attached to the division—a battle group (*kampfgruppe*). In 1943 the Germans had decided that the *bodenständige* (static) defense divisions along the Normandy coast were not sufficiently mobile to hold the Atlantic Wall. OB West ordered units in Brittany to form battle groups that could be rapidly deployed to supplement the *bodenständige* defenses. One of the battle groups, composed of elements of the 266th Division, was called Kampfgruppe Kentner after the 56-year-old Colonel Kentner, commander of the division's 987th Regiment. The son of a pastor, Colonel Kentner had a reputation for being "not much of a soldier." Previously, he had served on the Eastern Front as a bridging officer.[7]

Arriving on the Normandy front shortly after D-Day, Battle Group Kentner's ranks were thinned in unrelenting hedgerow fighting. The unit even lost men from the German artillery, because there were no more trained observers to accurately call in fire. On 14 July the regiment's strength was listed as 316 men, less than the strength of one U.S. infantry battalion. On 25 July two decimated companies (about 30 men each) of the battle group were dug in forward of Hebecrevon, right in the path of the 30th Infantry Division.

On the west side of the intercorps boundary another *kampfgruppe* stood in the way of the Americans, Battle Group Heintz attached to the Panzer Lehr Division of LXXXIV Corps. The *kampfgruppe* commanded by Colonel Gebhardt Heintz had also been deployed to Normandy on D-Day. It was composed of the 984th Grenadier Regiment with two infantry battalions, the 275th Fusilier Battalion and the 3rd Battalion of the 275th Artillery Regiment, the 275th Pioneer Battalion, and an antiaircraft battery from the 275th Infantry Division. The Angers Battalion, a unit made up from the Seventh Army's engineer school, was later added to the command.

Although Colonel Heintz had started the battles of Normandy with a fair amount of combat power, by late July his command was down to 600 men. The division commander reckoned that the battle group was little more than "a lot of other scraps thrown together."[8] What was left occupied five strongpoints near Hebecrevon. Each position was no bigger than a reinforced platoon, backed up by a few tanks, tank destroyers, or antitank guns.

While the battle groups' poverty suggested that Allied victory was assured, something kept it all from being that simple—terrain. The 30th Infantry Division's front rested only a few hundred meters from the St-Lô–Periers road that was comprised of tough hedgerow-covered ground. Starting in the west, the division's boundary was confined by a ridge along the near bank of the Terrette River. From the river, the front followed a line from Haut-Denier to the northeast past La Houcharderie, where the division's eastern boundary was abruptly blocked by the Vire River. The high ground near Hebecrevon dominated the zone. The only way to get to the town was across a small creek near La Nouillerie and up the steep bank of a draw. The area was not only difficult to traverse, it was extremely narrow: the 30th Infantry Division's front line covered only about a mile.

General Collins had assigned the 30th Infantry Division this narrow zone for a very specific reason: it would allow General Hobbs to mass combat power for the breakthrough. All the division's supporting artillery (108 pieces), for example, could range targets anywhere on the division's front. The only problem with the small front assigned to the division was that there was not much room for maneuver.

The task of deciding how to cover this tough ground fell to General Hobbs's division staff, a veteran team that had been together for over a year. The team included the widely respected assistant division commander, Brigadier General William Kelly Harrison Jr., whose father had attended the U.S. Naval Academy and won the Medal of Honor. Harrison, himself a 1917 West Point graduate, had served in backwater posts from the Philippines to Fort Riley, Kansas. Starting in 1939, he spent 3 years on the Army General Staff, for which his performance earned him recognition and the present assignment with the 30th Infantry Division. In combat, General Harrison had a reputation as a first-rate professional; he was a "soldier's soldier," one veteran remembered, always on the front lines with the troops, showing confidence and leadership.

The plan that the staff had developed for Cobra called for two regiments attacking abreast.[9] The 119th Infantry Regiment would attack southeast past La Nouillerie toward Hebecrevon to secure the flank of the VII Corps's penetration. To help it take and hold the high ground, the 199th received B Company, 105th Engineer Combat Battalion, plus C Company and a platoon of D Company from the 743d Tank Battalion (the rest of the battalion's tanks would be with the 120th Infantry Regiment). The 120th Infantry Regiment (with the 3d Battalion, 117th Infantry Regiment and C Company, 105th Engineer Combat Battalion attached) would attack in the western part of the zone through Haut-Denier in the direction of St-Gilles. Meanwhile, the 120th had the mission of clearing the way for the advance of the 2d Armored Division. It was a critical task and General Harrison would personally accompany the attacking troops.

To help get the attack of the 119th and 120th Infantry Regiments started, the division's plan called for plenty of firepower. In addition to the carpet bombing and artillery fire from Brigadier General James Malcolm Lewis's 30th Infantry Division artillery, the corps assigned the 188th Field Artillery Group to provide reinforcing fire. During the battle, the division would also receive support from the 823d Tank Destroyer Battalion, the 92d Chemical Mortar Battalion (less C Company), the 18th and 203d Field Artillery Battalions, and supporting fires from the 35th and 4th Infantry Division artillery. All in all, the division would have three times the artillery normally assigned to a division. (The 30th Division's attack is shown in Figure 6.1.)

Before the attack, the artillery fired missions to harass the enemy defenses. During the bombing, the guns would fire concentrations on suspected German antiaircraft positions and mark targets for air attack. After the bombing, the artillery fire would shift to suspected enemy positions and counterattack routes. Meanwhile, the 230th Field Artillery Battalion would provide a rolling barrage in front of the 120th Infantry Regiment. Perhaps the most important part of the fire support plan was a smoke screen across the high ground near Hebecrevon to block enemy observation of the division's attack. This important task was assigned to the 92d Chemical Mortar Battalion, commanded by Lieutenant Colonel Ronald LeVerne Martin.

While the main attack was underway, the 117th Infantry Regiment (minus the battalion with the 120th Infantry Regiment), commanded by Colonel Henry E. Kelly, would be in reserve. Supported only by A Company, 105th Combat Engineer Battalion, the regiment would, on order, clear out the area in the loop of ground formed by the Vire River just west of St-Lô. Meanwhile, the last element of the division's combat power, the

Figure 6.1 Attack of the 30th Infantry Division

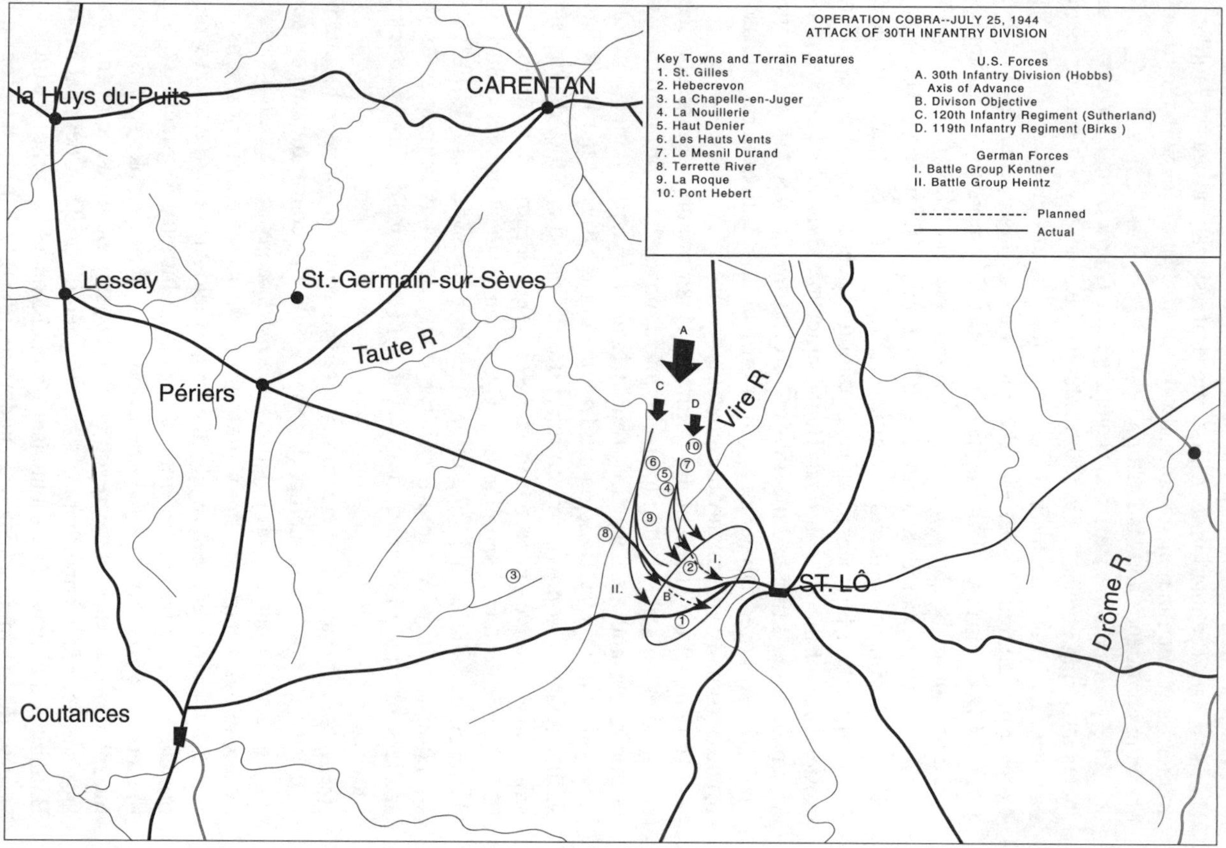
OPERATION COBRA--JULY 25, 1944
ATTACK OF 30TH INFANTRY DIVISION
Key Towns and Terrain Features
1. St. Gilles
2. Hebecrevon
3. La Chapelle-en-Juger
4. La Nouillerie
5. Haut Denier
6. Les Hauts Vents
7. Le Mesnil Durand
8. Terrette River
9. La Roque
10. Pont Hebert
U.S. Forces
A. 30th Infantry Division (Hobbs) Axis of Advance
B. Divison Objective
C. 120th Infantry Regiment (Sutherland)
D. 119th Infantry Regiment (Birks)
German Forces
I. Battle Group Kentner
II. Battle Group Heintz
Planned
Actual
la Huys du-Puits
CARENTAN
Lessay
St.-Germain-sur-Sèves
Taute R
Périers
Vire R
Coutances
ST. LÔ
Drôme R

30th Reconnaissance Troop, would remain in the assembly area (reconnaissance troops were designed to do mounted patrolling and security, not fight in heavy combat). Each of the troop's teams had only two quarter-ton trucks and an armored car; after the attack began, the troop would be brought up to clean out any enemy forces bypassed by the assault units.

The 119th Infantry Regiment Leads the Assault

With the division plan set, Colonel Edwin Malcolm Sutherland and his 119th Infantry Regiment prepared to lead the Cobra attack. Colonel Sutherland, West Point class of 1919, had taken over the regiment only 10 days before the battle, but he was no stranger to combat. He had already seen more of the war than most, serving in China and the Aleutians. Normandy was his third campaign.

Colonel Sutherland planned to attack with his battalions in column through Le Mesnil-Durand, across the creek near La Nouillerie and up the draw toward Hebecrevon. His troops had already secured a bridge across the creek, and engineers had cleared mines from the road so that the regiment could attack unimpeded by obstacles. Colonel Sutherland intended to lead with the 3d Battalion followed by the 2d and 1st Battalions. As the attack progressed, he expected to swing the 1st Battalion east toward Hebecrevon, while the rest of the regiment pushed south. By attacking with two battalions abreast, the regiment would be able to assault the key high ground from two directions at once, taking the town and securing the flank of the VII Corps's penetration.

Despite the promise of the carpet bombing on the enemy lines, Colonel Sutherland knew there were at least three factors that might disrupt his plan. First, the terrain was not ideal for swift movement. The battalions would have to attack down into the draw and then up the other side, fighting through hedgerows all the way. Since there were not many roads, maneuvering the tanks would be particularly tough.

The second problem was that the 119th Regiment's whole attack would be under the eyes of enemy observers on the high ground near Hebecrevon. If the German artillery and mortars were not destroyed in the bombing, his troops would be easy targets and they would have to run a gauntlet of fire all the way to the objective. To address this serious threat, Colonel Sutherland planned to use a smokescreen delivered by the 92d Chemical Mortar Battalion to cover the advance.

The third problem was his biggest concern: Colonel Sutherland did not know where the enemy was. The regiment had counted on intelligence from field reconnaissance before the attack, but the ground patrols had encountered determined resistance in the Germans' security zone and had failed to discover the location of the enemy's main defensive positions.

Without knowing the enemy's exact locations, Colonel Sutherland could not know where to focus his combat power until the battle had been joined, and that might give the Germans an early advantage.

Each problem threatened the one thing that the regiment could least afford—slowing the advance, thus giving the enemy time to recover from the bombing and mount a counterattack before the U.S. infantry reached the high ground. With his plan in place, however, there was little more Sutherland could do than wait for the operation to begin. Once the battle was on he would see how best to keep up the tempo of the attack.

Concerns and unknowns aside, on 25 July, as U.S. planes pounded the target area, Colonel Sutherland ordered the 119th Infantry Regiment to move out. But almost immediately the first pieces of his plan began to fall apart as U.S. bombs hit the regiment's positions and command post. The friendly bombers also knocked out Lieutenant Colonel Martin's 92d Chemical Battalion before the mortars could fire the smokescreen to cover the advance. Nevertheless, without covering smoke and despite the short bombings, the 119th Regiment kicked off its attack at 11:14 A.M., only 14 minutes behind schedule. Tanks and infantry rumbled past the steeple of the church at Le Mesnil-Durand, heading south.

The regiment's 3d Battalion, led by Lieutenant Colonel Courtney P. Brown, spearheaded the attack with K Company and tanks from the 743d Tank Battalion. Lieutenant Colonel Brown had a choice of the only two roads leading to the creek, one paved, the other no more than a dirt path. He elected to move on the paved road so that his troops and tanks could swiftly follow up the effects of the bombing.

Before the battalion cleared Le Mesnil-Durand U.S. fighter-bombers attacked the column. Quickly recovering from the accidental air assault, Lieutenant Colonel Brown's advance resumed, though it stopped again only 200 yards past the village where patches of teller (tank) mines blocked the road. At the same time, German fire began to fall on the column, directed from the unobscured heights near Hebecrevon.

To make matters worse, the enemy had not left the road to the creek undefended. When the Americans had pulled back from the area before the bombing, the Germans had returned and laid more mines. Now queued up behind these obstacles, the Americans made a perfect target. The tanks idled and the infantry huddled under any available cover while German fire harassed the U.S. combat engineers attempting to clear the road ahead. Finally the 30th Infantry Division artillery, joined by the VII and XIX Corps artillery, fired on the enemy guns, reducing the enemy shelling enough to allow the mines to be cleared and the attack to advance.

By noon Lieutenant Colonel Brown's 3d Battalion reached the creek at la Nouillerie with I and K Companies abreast and L Company trailing. At the creek they found more mines strewn over the crossing site covered by artillery fire. Not wanting to waste time fighting through another obstacle,

Brown shifted his attack to the west, farther upstream, but there the troops found even more mines and behind them a strongpoint covered by dug-in troops from Battle Group Kentner. Again, Brown tried to outmaneuver the enemy, ordering L Company around the strongpoint. The Germans, however, had planned artillery fire to cover their flank, and L Company took heavy casualties, gaining little ground. Lieutenant Colonel Brown ordered the troops to pull back and call in an artillery strike, but as the soldiers withdrew more men fell from German artillery and mortar fire.

It was one of the most terrible moments imaginable. Before the battle commanders had prayed that, for once, charging the hedgerows would not be another bloody, frustrating day. In less than 1 hour Lieutenant Colonel Brown saw everything come apart, with soldiers falling back, wounded piling up, and all covered in shattering sound, white-hot metal fragments, acrid smoke, and blinding dust. The initiative was lost, and every decision seemed likely to bring only more casualties. Unbelievably, despite tons of U.S. bombs, the Germans positions were holding strong. The advance of the 3d Battalion and the rest of the 119th Regiment had gone nowhere.

The 120th Infantry Regiment Attacks

While the attack by Colonel Sutherland's 119th Infantry Regiment sputtered in front of apparently well-prepared defenses, the 120th Infantry Regiment on his flank was having a little better luck. General Hobbs's plan had called for Colonel Hammond D. Birks's 120th Infantry Regiment to move to the west of the 119th Regiment, along the top of the ridge and down the main road toward St-Gilles. Colonel Birks's intent was to commit each battalion in turn, leapfrog fashion, until they reached the objective at the intersection of the St-Lô–Périers road and the Les Hauts-Vents–St-Gilles road. The regiment's 2d Battalion was to lead the attack followed by the 1st and 3d Battalions with the attached 3d Battalion, 117th Regiment, trailing. The two units leading the attack, the 1st and 2d Battalions, had relatively new commanders, but both men were veterans of the campaign and Birks believed they would acquit themselves well.

Although Colonel Birks had had hopes for a swift advance, a crisis right at the start threatened his whole plan: before the first soldier was able to attack, short bombings devastated the 2d Battalion and the attached 3d Battalion of the 117th Regiment. In the opening moments of the battle Colonel Birks had to make a critical choice. For the second time in 2 days his plans had been upset by the ill luck of being struck by U.S. bombs. Both he and the regiment were in a difficult situation: when the 46-year-old University of Chicago graduate had arrived at the division in 1942, he had received mixed reviews from his men, with some questioning his ability to command in combat. This day would be a critical test of his leadership.

With his lead element crippled, he now had to make a critical combat decision. Should he wait for the battalion to reorganize or replace it with one of his follow-on units? Waiting would slow the attack, but any changes might cause even more confusion and delay.

The initial reports looked bad. In fact, Colonel Birks did not have to go very far to see the devastation. The destroyed 2d Battalion command post was very close by. He could see himself the chaos caused by the bombing. The area was littered with screaming casualties, fires roaring out of control from burning ammunition vehicles, and dazed, hollow-eyed soldiers stumbling around the area. Birks feared that the battalion had suffered too hard a blow to carry out the attack. General Harrison, the assistant division commander, who had sat through the bombing at the regimental command post disagreed. "Colonel, if you've got three men you jump off. I'll get a reserve unit to help you if you need it."[10] Colonel Birks clearly had his marching orders. The attack had to press ahead.

Colonel Birks left Lieutenant Colonel Eads Hardaway's 2d Battalion in the lead, but he replaced the 3d Battalion, 117th Regiment (last in the march order), with the 1st Battalion, 117th Regiment, from the division reserve. Despite the disruption, the 120th Regiment reported starting moving at 11:30 A.M., only 30 minutes late. F Company, 2d Battalion, accompanied by Lieutenant Donald H. Ticknor's platoon of light tanks from D Company, 743d Tank Battalion, were the first to get organized and get going—the rest gradually followed.

That the regiment's attack started at all was a major achievement, and part of its success can be credited to the determination of General Harrison. During the aerial attack one bomb knocked the general off his feet, while another had destroyed a halftrack loaded with ammunition parked right behind him. At one point he thought he had been hit by shrapnel, only to discover that he had been smacked by wad of bone, flesh, and blood from another man.

General Harrison was unfazed by the danger; he moved about organizing and motivating the men—just getting them going. Sergeant Floyd Montgomery had just finished digging out from the debris of the short bombing, when he looked up to see the general standing over him.

"Sergeant, where are your men?" Harrison asked.

"Sir, I've only got five left, counting me."

"Well, we've got five hedgerows to take . . . I'll go with you."[11]
It was typical Harrison—restoring order and confidence among the dazed and bewildered troops. When more fighter-bombers appeared and strafed the attacking U.S. troops, he stormed back to the regimental command post to radio the air forces and tell them that they could go home now. The division could win the war without them.[12]

The 120th Regiment's attack was under way, but even with General

Harrison's presence problems continued. The Germans had sowed the fields surrounding the roads with antipersonnel mines. One officer recalled that "a man a few yards in front of me stepped on one, and his entire lower legs were blown off. As I passed by him, he asked me for help. A medic was summoned and everyone kept moving."[13] While the troops continued to dodge mines, the unit was hit again by U.S. bombers. The explosions set fire to a light tank from D Company, 743d Tank Battalion. The crew quickly returned the tank to action, but the frustration of being hit by more friendly fire was a further blow to the troops' confidence.

After a few hundred yards, F Company, 2d Battalion, found something even worse—three German tanks blocking the road flanked by infantry and machine guns from Battle Group Heintz. The planned rolling barrage by the 230th Field Artillery Battalion was a wasted effort. Blocked by the German strongpoint, the U.S. infantry could not follow the advancing artillery strikes without the risk of being cut down by enemy fire. As soon as the U.S. rounds passed the German position, the enemy gunners would be back at their posts and ready for the Americans. Outgunned, F Company pulled back and reported the disheartening news to the 2d Battalion commander, Lieutenant Colonel Hardaway.

Following the demoralizing short bombing, Lieutenant Colonel Hardaway had been relieved to be able to get the battalion going. The last thing he wanted to hear was that the troops now faced stiff resistance at the front. After finding that F Company's way was blocked, Hardaway decided to attempt to outflank the enemy. While F Company held its position, Companies E and G with the light tanks from D Company, 743d tank Battalion, swung east of the roadblock. Unfortunately, the companies could not get around the machine gun, mortar, and artillery fire that had held up F Company.

Lieutenant Ticknor, whose light tanks had been accompanying the infantry, decided to attack the enemy position on his own. He planned to advance without the support of Lieutenant Colonel Hardaway's men and run the flank of the German strongpoint. Ticknor was taking an incredible, almost suicidal risk, especially since the guns of his light tanks had little chance of penetrating the armor of a German tank. Nevertheless, his force maneuvered to a spot where they had a clear shot at the Germans. After one U.S. tank opened fire a voice screamed over the radio net, "Good God, I fired three rounds and they all bounced off."[14] The enemy returned fire, hitting two tanks and killing Lieutenant Ticknor. The other U.S. tanks immediately withdrew. The young lieutenant's brave but futile gesture had failed to displace the enemy.

Now, without any tank support, infantrymen, led by a bazooka team, crawled forward and took a crack at the German roadblock. They too failed. Lieutenant Colonel Hardaway then tried a full-scale assault with F, G, and E Companies attacking in unison, but the Germans still held fast. At this point Hardaway had just about run out of options. It was his first big battle as battalion commander, and, so far, he little to show for his efforts. The German roadblock had thoroughly frustrated the 2d Battalion's advance.

The 2d Battalion's situation prompted Colonel Birks to discard the remainder of his plan. He was not going to be able to leapfrog his units to victory over disorganized enemy defenses, but was going to have to fight through the enemy strongpoints or find a way around them. To keep the attack going, Birks ordered the 1st Battalion under Lieutenant Colonel James W. Cantey and another platoon of D Company tanks to slide east of the 2d Battalion and push on.

Lieutenant Colonel Cantey's battalion also found rough going, but not from the enemy. As the 1st Battalion, 120th Regiment, slipped to the east to move around the roadblock on the Les Hauts-Vents–St-Gilles road, the 2d Battalion, 119th Infantry Regiment, was moving west along a small stream around the enemy. The U.S. units collided and created a tactical logjam. The best Lieutenant Colonel Cantey (also commanding in his first major engagement) could manage was to push B and C Companies of the 1st Battalion into a space only sufficient for a platoon, through the maze of friendly and enemy fire.

At the same time, Colonel Birks ordered his 3d Battalion, led by his most experienced commander, Lieutenant Colonel Paul W. McCollum, to move west of Lieutenant Colonel Hardaway's 2d Battalion. When McCollum's battalion entered the line, moving in a column of companies, it also drew the attention of enemy armor. The enemy tanks, however, where in the open. The battalion called for artillery fire, destroying one German tank in its path and forcing the remaining enemy to withdraw. McCollum's battalion then continued to advance behind the screen of friendly artillery fire. Thanks to the timely artillery support, the 3d Battalion achieved the 120th Regiment's first modest gains in enemy territory.

Anxious Moments at Higher Headquarters

When General Hobbs, the 30th Division's commander, received reports on the situation of Lieutenant McCollum's 3d Battalion and the other units at the front, he was not encouraged. The slight progress by the two attacking regiments seemed feeble in comparison to the massive bombing that had preceded the assault. At 3:30 P.M. General Hobbs, with his famous temper clearly evident, called the VII Corps commander, General Collins. As far as Hobbs was concerned the bombing had failed: "There is no indication of bombing," he complained, "in where we have gone so far."[15] Both Collins and Bradley were clearly disturbed by this. The terrible casualties from the short bombings, combined with the disappointing reports of the infantry advance, left them both wondering whether the success of the whole mission was in doubt. Without control of the left flank of the axis of advance, there was little likelihood that they could risk pushing their armor forward to attempt a breakthrough.

Although it was not apparent to General Hobbs and other senior commanders at the time, the reason the bombings had had no effect was simple. The German positions encountered were well forward of the no-bomb line. The effects of the bombing on the enemy units were not too different from those on the Americans. Unless a bomb landed directly on a German position, there was going to be no effect from the hit.

What the Americans did not know was that farther back in the bombing box chaos reigned among the German forces. Medical Sergeant Walter Klein in Battle Group Heintz was at his company command post near St-Gilles when Allied air dropped a "rain of bombs." He had spent the morning shuttling wounded to the dressing station:

> When a wave of planes had passed, one could hear the crying of the wounded and shouting for help of medical personnel. . . . On that day my company lost 1 officer, 34 noncommissioned officers and enlisted men. Many of my young comrades lost their heads. . . . Worse than the loss of weapons was the effect that the attack had made on our morale.[16]

Casualties were not the only problem. Vehicles were destroyed, command posts hit, and wire communications were disrupted. All this incredible destruction, however, was out of the Americans' sight. At the front the German positions held fast, successfully holding off the attacks by the 30th Infantry Division.

The 120th Infantry Regiment—Attack Before Dark!

In the fading light of a late Normandy afternoon, attacking with three battalions abreast, Colonel Birk's 120th Regiment doggedly continued to pressure German defenses. The 1st Battalion under Lieutenant Colonel Cantey crawled forward in the eastern part of the zone, fighting for space the whole way with elements from the 119th Regiment. Lieutenant Colonel Hardaway's 2d Battalion remained blocked by Battle Group Heintz's roadblock in the center. Lieutenant Colonel McCollum's 3d Battalion advanced slowly in the west. Meanwhile, the division's reconnaissance troop moved up and extended the regiment's flank from the 3d Battalion down to the Terrette River. At the same time, the attached 1st Battalion, 117th Regiment, commanded by Lieutenant Colonel Robert Frankland, followed as the reserve. Even though Colonel Birks had a whole battalion of infantry left to throw into the fight, and the attack was making little progress, he held back his reserve. He had a good reason. With three battalions fighting in the space where one battalion might normally be employed, there was no room for more forces on the front.

Colonel Birks also had had trouble finding a place to employ the armor from Lieutenant Colonel William D. Duncan's 743d Tank Battalion. Throughout the day of 25 July the medium tanks of A Company, commanded by Lieutenant Ernest Aas, dodged mines, "friendly" bombers, and German artillery fire, but had not yet engaged the enemy. Finally, reaching the roadblock that had held up the advance by Hardaway's 2d Battalion since the start of the attack, the tanks got a chance to join in the offensive.

The rush to battle proved futile. Lieutenant Aas lost one tank in a direct assault on the enemy strongpoint and quickly withdrew the rest of his vehicles. The frontal armor of the German tanks had again proved superior to the guns of the U.S. Sherman tanks. Lieutenant Aas was not ready to give up, but he needed an angle of attack that would give his men a shot at the weaker side or rear armor of the German tanks. He decided to conduct a reconnaissance on foot before taking on the enemy strongpoint a second time. He found a concealed route to bring his tanks up on the east side of the road, where they took out one German tank with a flank shot. Surprised by the maneuver, the remaining two enemy tanks withdrew.

When the German armor abandoned the strongpoint the way seemed clear. After consulting with Lieutenant Colonel Duncan and Colonel Birks, Lieutenant Aas continued his advance, outflanking the strongpoint by sending his tanks one at a time across the open country east of the road. As the U.S. armor dashed across the open field, they found the German tanks straddling the Les Hauts-Vents–St-Gilles road. Aas's armor destroyed another enemy tank, and the remaining German tank retreated.

Lieutenant Aas could be well satisfied with the results of the engagement and the performance of his men. They had outmaneuvered and outfought three superior German tanks. With the roadblock uncovered by the advance of U.S. armor, Hardaway's 2d Battalion resumed its advance. Meanwhile, Lieutenant Aas swung his armor farther east to support Lieutenant Colonel Cantey's 1st Battalion. Colonel Birks reported that the 120th Regiment was finally on the move.

The 119th Infantry Regiment Prevails

While the 120th Infantry Regiment with the aid of Lieutenant Aas's tanks pushed along the ridge road toward St-Gilles, the 119th Infantry Regiment was still stuck at the bottom of a draw, held up by roadblocks and the enemy's indirect fire. Half the day was gone, and the regiment was nowhere close to Hebecrevon, one of the most important objectives in the kickoff of Cobra. Colonel Sutherland was attempting everything he could think of to move his attack forward. At 1:00 P.M. he launched a platoon of light tanks from D Company and a platoon of medium tanks from C Company against the roadblock. He also sent Lieutenant Colonel Edwin E. Wallis's 2d Battalion to the west of Lieutenant Colonel Brown's 3d Battalion, bypassing the enemy. Under the cover of tank fire, the 2d Battalion worked its way up the draw, but got caught with 120th Infantry Regiment soldiers in the mob competing for maneuver space on the ridge.

Frustrated by the traffic jam with the 120th Regiment, Sutherland decided to try another alternative. He launched the 1st Battalion, commanded by Major Robert H. Herlong, east into the difficult terrain at the base of the draw. Starting at 1:13 P.M. Herlong's battalion advanced with C, B, and A Companies, attacking in column, supported by a rolling barrage from the 197th Field Artillery Battalion. After crossing the stream, the 119th's 1st Battalion bypassed the strongpoint holding up Lieutenant Colonel Brown's 3rd Battalion and moved up the draw.

At the lip of the draw, Major Herlong's men of the 1st Battalion found German positions clustered around a small group of buildings. As the U.S. infantry approached, mortar fire began to fall on the advancing column. Rather than take the Germans on directly under a withering rain of mortar rounds, Herlong elected to outflank the position: B Company swung to the east, while C Company found a steep gully and advanced one man at time to the west of the buildings. The companies surrounded the enemy and captured fifty prisoners.

After securing the buildings, Herlong's men continued to advance to the top of the hill where they dug in to face south and southwest. Colonel Sutherland's decision to attempt an advance through the draw with the 1st Battalion had proved a sound decision. This was the first U.S. unit to reach the high ground on the shoulder of the Cobra breakthrough.

The 120th Infantry Regiment Digs In

As dark approached, the 30th Division was finally making progress, though neither the 119th nor the 120th Regiment had secured its objective. The 120th had given up any hope of reaching its goal, St-Gilles, and only two of its battalions were on high ground. The regiment's 1st Battalion, commanded by Lieutenant Colonel Cantey, was at the crossroads of the St-Lô–Périers road and the Les Hauts-Vents–St-Gilles road, while Lieutenant Colonel McCollum's 3d Battalion had only reached La Roque—more than a mile and a half from St-Gilles.

The 120th Regiment's objective was too far away to reach by dark, but at least the men were on a good, defensible piece of high ground. The Germans most likely still had enough force in the zone to mount a counterattack, so Colonel Birks ordered his men to consolidate positions and take up a defensive posture. It proved a sound precaution. After dark Battle

Group Heintz counterattacked with tanks and infantry, but the assault came too late. The 120th Infantry Regiment was prepared and held its ground. Some may have questioned Colonel Birks's leadership many months before, when he had first joined the regiment, but in this battle he had proven that he and his battalion commanders could carry an attack through difficult terrain and against a determined enemy.

The 119th Infantry Regiment Attacks into the Night

Meanwhile, despite the success of Major Herlong's battalion in reaching the high ground on the flank of the Cobra breakthrough, the 119th Infantry Regiment was not even close to Hebecrevon—and not taking Hebecrevon was a problem. This was the key to holding the east flank of the penetration. "The important thing," General Hobbs had reminded Colonel Sutherland, "was to gain control of the crossroads in the town [Hebecrevon]."[17] At 3:50 P.M. General Hobbs was on the phone to General Collins telling him that the success of the mission was in doubt. Collins wanted to call in an air strike to clear the way for the advance, but Hobbs, fearful of more short bombings, disagreed. "If we should have more of the same," he cautioned, "then our troops are finished."[18] Hobbs believed that generals could not fight the battle from their headquarters and that only the commanders at the front had sufficient appreciation of the situation to decide what to do and the immediate resources to accomplish the task. Instead, Hobbs gave Colonel Sutherland the last of the division reserves, 2d Battalion, 117th Regiment, commanded by Lieutenant Colonel Ben Ammons, and told the colonel to press on to Hebecrevon.

At the 352d Division command post, the Germans also viewed the situation with grave concern, knowing that a successful attack would leave a gap in the intercorps boundary. Even worse, they had no contact with the units to their west and no reports of any counterattacks against the U.S. penetration. The division ordered Colonel Kentner, backed by supporting fire from the 135th Artillery Regiment, to counterattack to Hebecrevon. Division did not think the gap could be closed, but it hoped to block what was wrongly feared to be an attempt to encircle the II Parachute Corps.[19]

While the Germans were finally organizing a counterattack, the U.S. 119th's Colonel Sutherland was considering his own situation. His men had already fought hard and long, but they had to push on. In the western part of the regiment's zone, Lieutenant Colonel Wallis's 2d Battalion continued to make slow progress. In the center, Lieutenant Colonel Brown's 3d Battalion was still at the start line, held up by the enemy strongpoint by the small stream. Brown's men had been fighting and dying in place all day. Meanwhile the reserve battalion assigned by the division was still far from the front. The best progress had been in the east with Major Herlong's 1st

Battalion. Sutherland decided to push the 1st Battalion all the way to Hebecrevon, but to do that he needed to get his armor back into the fight.

Earlier in the day the tanks of C Company, Lieutenant Colonel Duncan's 743d Tank Battalion, had tried to follow the 1st Battalion through the draw, though it was some of the worst terrain on the regiment's whole front. The tanks had found a sunken overgrown dirt path, but then got stuck on a sharp curve and had to withdraw. The regimental tank liaison officer was dispatched to find another path where the armor could ford the creek and link up with the 119th's 1st Battalion. When he guided the armor forward the first tank turned the wrong way. Another slid off the road north of the stream and got stuck in a ditch. A third was hit by enemy fire. Despite all the setbacks, the armor was ordered to continue the advance, and, finally, by dusk, the tanks managed to scale the draw's slopes and set up in an orchard behind the 1st Battalion.

When the tanks finally linked up with Major Herlong's 1st Battalion, their crews found an exhausted and depleted outfit of slumping, gaunt men, who were filthy, unshaven, sweat stained, and sore of foot. With little daylight and a worn-out battalion, Major Herlong had to decide how best to continue the attack. Only his A Company, commanded by Captain Ross Simmons, had not been chewed up in the day's fighting. Herlong faced tough calls. He had to consider how much combat power he could reasonably muster to push forward, and he had to reckon with the possibility of a German counterattack.

Because of the lack of counterattacks so far, he hoped that if he moved right away, he could still steal a march on the Germans and seize Hebecrevon before the enemy could secure it in strength. Herlong created "Task Force A" with Captain Simmons's company and the newly arrived tanks, and assigned them the task of taking the town.

Task Force A launched its attack at 8:00 P.M. on 25 July. In the twilight the infantry fanned out to the front and flanks, while the tanks followed at 20-yard intervals down the main road toward Hebecrevon. Craters from the U.S. air strikes and German mines had turned the road into one long obstacle course. A mile from Hebecrevon Captain Simmons's infantrymen found something to add to their woes, a roadblock of wire and mines backed up by a German 88mm antiaircraft gun and machine guns. The "88", as always, was a formidable foe: it could stop a tank or shred a human body beyond recognition.

As the Americans grimly prepared to attack the position, a German flare inadvertently silhouetted the antiaircraft gun and the U.S. tankers quickly took aim and destroyed it. Captain Simmons and a small party of men rushed forward, drove off the German infantry, and cleared the wire and mines. After that taking the town proved to be the easiest part of the battle.

By 1:00 A.M. on 26 July Task Force A had cleared Hebecrevon, and the

1st Battalion had dug in east of the town. Lieutenant Colonel Wallis's 2d Battalion took up a position to the south. Finally, Lieutenant Colonel Brown's luckless 3rd Battalion crossed the stream and by dawn reached a position north of the town, completing the regiment's advance. The 25th had cost the 119th Regiment 40 dead, 220 wounded, and 10 missing, but Colonel Sutherland was able to report that they had the town. His new command had done well.

Late that night news of the U.S. advance reached the 352d Division command post. Colonel Kentner had been barely able to generate any counterattack at all, and it had failed to hold Hebecrevon. His battle group reported that U.S. forces had occupied the town and their tanks were advancing on the road from Pont-Hébert to St-Gilles.[20] The Americans had penetrated the main of line resistance and held off the Germans' attempts to push them back.

What It Takes to Take the High Ground

Although General Hobbs's division had failed to reach all its assigned objectives, its accomplishments were noteworthy. In what turned out to be a typical day of hedgerow fighting, the troops fought past well-organized and determined defenses made up of mines, machine guns, tanks, mortars, and artillery. Most significant, though, the 30th Infantry Division had achieved a critical objective for the offensive, securing the high ground at Hebecrevon on the east flank of the breakthrough. It was a significant achievement for a battle-weary division.

As for the carpet bombing, though it had not cleared a path for the ground attack, it did do something equally crucial. The air attack had thoroughly disrupted command and control in the Germans' rear area and severed contact between the command posts and the front. German counterattacks were significantly delayed and reduced in force. No battle group mustered any kind of reinforcements or counterattack until well after dark—and by then it was too late. The Americans were already on the high ground in strength.

In reaching Hebecrevon, the 30th Infantry Division demonstrated that Cobra was a great plan and that General Bradley had chosen well. The operation had struck the enemy where it could least afford it, demolishing effective coordination between forward troops, headquarters, and counterattacking forces. The chaos created by the bombing had significantly impaired the Germans' ability to launch timely, powerful counterattacks, thus creating a "window of advantage" for the U.S. infantry. The 30th Division used this advantage to good effect.

Although the division's attacks were successful, they were not without fault. Commanders had not expected that the Germans would again place mines and obstacles in the way before the attack. U.S. commanders had no contingency plan for the mortar battalion's failure to screen the high ground near Hebecrevon with smoke, and had not anticipated the minimal affect of the bombing on the German main line of resistance. In addition, with little knowledge of the location and strength of the enemy positions in their path, the regiments' maneuvers encountered the enemy on the worst possible terms, when the lead troops were greeted by overwhelming German artillery, tank, and machine gun fire. U.S. commanders' failure to foresee all the dangers that lay ahead and to plan for likely contingencies demonstrated that their tactical judgement was still far from perfect.

On the other hand, despite these setbacks, U.S. commanders did demonstrate critical combat leadership skills. The 30th Infantry Division's regiment and battalion commanders exploited the advantage of the bombing by concentrating on maintaining a high tempo for their attacks and breaching the enemy defenses before the Germans could reorganize and counterattack. Maintaining the tempo of the attack was the key to winning the day—and effectively orchestrating combat power on a crowded, confusing battlefield was the key to maintaining tempo. U.S. commanders stayed focused on what was important and applied the mass of their combat power accordingly, showing perseverance, flexibility, discipline, and initiative. When they discovered that the main line of German resistance had not been disrupted, rather than continuing to push strength against strength and dissipate their combat power by forcing enemy positions head on, the commanders used their infantry to search out gaps in the German defenses. In addition, when the infantry could not get through, the commanders managed to get their armor and artillery to the critical points on the battlefield, reducing or bypassing the German positions and opening the way for the advance of the ground troops.

For his part, the 30th Infantry Division's General Hobbs supported his commanders well by not trying to fight the battle from his headquarters. Even though the initial reports from the front were discouraging, Hobbs had the patience and confidence to give his assistant division commander and the regiment and battalion commanders the opportunity to use their leadership and skill to decide what to do next. General Hobbs knew that even if he wanted to, he could not direct tactical operations effectively from his headquarters or greatly influence the course of a day's fighting. This was aptly demonstrated in his commitment of the division reserve. By the time a battalion from the 117th Infantry Regiment had reached the front, it was too late in the day to influence the action. Hobbs's decision would bolster the 119th Regiment for the next day's attack, but would not win the first day's battle. From their position closer to the front, where they had access to the most current combat information and control of the reserves and supporting arms that could be thrown into the fight quickly enough to affect the outcome of an engagement, the regiment and battalion commanders were the only ones who could fight and win the battles of the hedgerows.

Although they had not anticipated well, the U.S. commanders had reacted with confidence and skill. On this day the 30th Infantry Division's regiment and battalion commanders demonstrated how combat leadership enabled an operational vision. Their attack toward the high ground made the first critical step in turning the promise of Cobra into a reality.

Notes

1. Sylvan, War Diary, 25 July 1944, MHI. See also Leland Stanford Hobbs, Papers, DDE.

2. Fritz Ziegelmann, "The Battle for St. Lo," MS B-464, p. 2.

3. *St-Lo,* p. 128. See also Ziegelmann, "The Battle for St. Lo," p. 4.

4. Meindl, "II Parachute Corps," p. 40.

5. Hans Speidel, "OB West: A Study in Command," MS B-308, pp. 29–30. Information on the status of the 352d Division is from Fritz Ziegelmann, "History of the 352d Infantry Division," MS B-432, p. 4; and Ernst Blauensteiner, "Commitment of the II Parachute Corps in Northern France," MS B-346, p. 1. No operational records are extant for this unit.

6. Meindl, "II Parachute Corps," p. 15.

7. The information on Colonel Kentner and his kampfgruppe was compiled from *Armeeoberkommando 7, K.T.B. Entwurf und OB Chef-IA-Gespräche, 6 Juni–16 August 1944,* microfilm, T312, Roll 1568, p. 122, NARA; First U.S. Army and VII Corps periodic and intelligence reports; and prisoner of war interviews and Ziegelmann, "The Battle for St. Lo," pp. 1–2. There are no operational records of this German unit extant for this period.

8. The information on Battle Group Heintz was compiled from several postwar interviews with Fritz Bayerlein; 30th Infantry Division order of battle notes and the First U.S. Army and VII Corps periodic and intelligence reports; and prisoner of war interviews. There are no operational records of this German unit extant for this period.

9. Unless otherwise cited, the description of the division's plan and the conduct of the attack are taken from the 30th Infantry Division and 30th Infantry Division Artillery after action reports; William K. Harrison, Oral History, pp. 325–328, MHI; Robert L. Hewitt, *Workhorse of the Western Front,* pp. 37–41; *History of the Thirtieth Division Artillery,* pp. 23–25; *History of the 120th Infantry Regiment,* pp. 33–37; Hess, *Move Out,* p. 65; and *Combat History of the 119th Infantry Regiment,* pp. 22–23.

10. Harrison, Oral History, p. 327, MHI.

11. Alwyn Featherston, *Saving the Breakout: The 30th Division's Heroic Stand at Mortain,* p. 36.

12. Harrison, Oral History, p. 326, MHI. See also testimony of Brigadier General W. K. Harrison, Exhibit A, Headquarters, First U.S. Army, Investigation of Bombing of Ground Troops by Friendly Planes on 24 and 25 July 1944, 16 August 1944, Adjutant General Section, General Correspondence 1940–47, Box 119, RG 338, p. 28, NARA. In his testimony General Harrison also noted that "neither Col.

Birks or the Battalion Commander Lt. Col. Hardaway showed anything other than complete self-possession and a willingness to go ahead in spite of the obvious damage done by such reprehensible bombing."

13. *History of the 120th Infantry Regiment,* p. 36.

14. Hewitt, *Workhorse of the Western Front,* p. 37.

15. Blumenson, *Breakout and Pursuit,* p. 245.

16. Walter Klein, "Bombing and Operation Cobra," MS A-910, pp. 2–3.

17. Blumenson, *Breakout and Pursuit,* p. 244.

18. Hewitt, *Workhorse of the Western Front,* p. 40.

19. Fritz Ziegelmann, "Operations from 25 July until 30 July," MS B-489, p. 1.

20. Ibid.

7

Beyond the Field of White Crosses

The 30th Infantry Division's progress had been important, but not enough by itself to ensure the success of the operation. The U.S. Army units needed to secure both the flanks of the penetration and open up sufficient room to pass through the exploitation force—and all this had to be done before the Germans could react. All three of the VII Corps's infantry divisions had to succeed in order to give General Bradley's plan a chance to achieve its ambitious objectives. West of the 30th Division, the 4th Infantry Division was trying deliver its share of the mission by widening the split in the German Seventh Army's lines.

Like all the divisions in Normandy the 4th Infantry Division carried its own legacy into the battle, the legacy of what it took to get the U.S. Army to the eve of Operation Cobra—the sacrifice of soldiers. Perhaps the most profound moment of the division's legacy had taken place on 14 July, 2 weeks before Cobra. On that day, General Raymond Oscar Barton, the 4th Infantry Division commander, had stood outside the village of St-Mère-Eglise with the boys of his division. General Barton's men had missed the opening rounds of the war in North Africa and Sicily, but then they were making up for it. They had been the first wave ashore on Utah Beach, and weeks of continuous combat were to follow. The division's losses for the first 2 months of the Normandy fighting were to total 8,754, 60 percent of the division's effective strength, more than those of any other division in the VII Corps. Many of the fallen were here in a temporary cemetery at St-Mère-Eglise.

On 14 July General Barton buried another loss, assistant division commander Brigadier General Theodore Roosevelt Jr., eldest son of the late President Theodore Roosevelt. Soldiers had loved and admired Roosevelt even though his 56 years and handlebar mustache had made him look like anything but a battlefield commander.[1] The grueling demands of hedgerow warfare proved too much, and he had died in his sleep from heart failure. General Barton, along with Captain Quentin Roosevelt, Brigadier General

Roosevelt's son, and a group of other generals attended the funeral. Afterward, the generals surveyed the rows of shallow graves, silent statements about the cost of war and a terrible reminder of the price of learning how to fight in the Normandy hedgerows.[2]

As the ceremony ended, General Barton could at least take some consolation in his division's finally getting a well-deserved rest. By 18 July the last of the 4th Division had pulled out of the line and headed to St-Jean-de-Daye to form the U.S. First Army reserve. General Barton planned to rehabilitate his exhausted command and train over 6,000 new replacements. But the promise of a respite was short-lived: at the last minute, the generals had decided that they needed more infantry to secure the breakthrough in Normandy. Effective 7:30 P.M. on 19 July the 4th Infantry Division was reattached to the VII Corps to be the spearhead of the breakthrough for Operation Cobra.

General Collins was glad to have General Barton back under his command. When Barton was a cadet at West Point, the future 4th Infantry Division commander had won a letter in football and been captain of the wrestling team. Sports showed that he was a good-natured man, but a tough and determined fighter. As a friend remembered, "How can a man with such a veritably sweet disposition be so devastating?" Barton carried his no-nonsense style throughout his career, and in taking over the 4th Infantry Division in 1942 he had earned good marks as a commander. In the Normandy battles, despite heavy casualties, his command had also earned a reputation as a first-class fighting outfit.

Preparing to Take the Center

General Collins had selected a challenging task for the proven fighters of the 4th Infantry "Ivy" Division. They would assault in the center of the corps's zone between the 30th and 9th Infantry Divisions. The 4th Division's objective was to take the high ground south of the Marigny–St-Gilles road and hold off any German counterattacks. At the same time, the 4th Division was to maintain contact with the 30th Infantry Division and clear routes for the attack of the 3d Armored Division.

Although the assault by this division was the least critical of those by the three lead infantry divisions, its mission was still crucial for the success of the operation. By attacking in the center, the 4th Division would allow the 30th and 9th to concentrate on the decisive tasks of taking and holding the shoulders of the breakthrough. In addition, the 4th Infantry Division's attack would cover the back of the other two divisions. Without a strong advance by Barton's men, the Germans still trapped in the breakthrough area might counterattack the flanks of the penetration or withdraw and set up new defensive positions, thus impeding the advance of the U.S. follow-on forces. Even minor counterattacks from inside the breakthrough could be more than a nuisance; they might slow the tempo of the attack and prove the death of Cobra.

For the initial phase of the operation, the 4th Infantry Division would assault with only two regiments (the 22d Infantry Regiment was attached to the 2d Armored Division). The lack of a third regiment was not considered a problem. The zone for the assault was less than 2,000 yards wide. Barton's forces also were not facing much of an enemy. Waiting on the other side of the hedgerows were the last of the 13th and 14th Regiments of the German 5th Parachute Division. On paper the regiments, part of the Luftwaffe ground forces, were even more formidable than a regular German infantry regiment. They had three battalions (regular German army regiments had only two battalions), each with three rifle companies and a weapons company with heavy machine guns and mortars. Parachute units also had two machine guns and three submachine guns per squad. In addition, the regiment had its own organic antiaircraft guns, antitank weapons, engineers, and reconnaissance, for a total strength to 4,500 men. In reality, the units, commanded by Lieutenant General Gustav Wilke, were under-equipped and undermanned, and still being organized when the Allies landed in Normandy. According to one German commander, the 13th and 14th Regiments' officers were "extremely poor. They consisted for the most part of officers from the Air Force who had no infantry experience."[3] When the invasion started the regiments were not even rated ready for combat.

General Wilke's division was thrown into battle piecemeal. The 13th and 14th Regiments reached the front on 12 July and were assigned to the LXXXIV Corps reserve. The following day, the 13th Regiment was sent to hold down the Panzer Lehr Division's western flank. The 14th Regiment went into battle on 15 July, taking up a position between the 13th Regiment and the 17th SS Panzergrenadier Division. Once in battle the regiments' limitations quickly became apparent: the Seventh Army's chief of staff rated them complete failures, complaining that they lacked *fallschir-mjägergeist* (paratrooper spirit).

General Wilke's division headquarters did not even reach the front until 19 July. On the evening of 21 July General Choltitz, the LXXXIV Corps commander, directed Wilke to retake command of his regiments and establish a sector between the Panzer Lehr Division and the 17th SS Panzergrenadier Division. Unfortunately for Wilke, there was not much division left to command. The 13th Regiment had suffered so many losses that it could no longer be considered a regiment. What was left was consolidated with the 14th Regiment. Meanwhile, the division's third regiment was tied down supporting the II Parachute Corps, and there was no plan to return it to General Wilke's command. To make matters worse, Operation Cobra started while the 5th Parachute Division was shifting west and turning over its front to the 901st Panzergrenadier Regiment, Panzer Lehr

Division. The bombing disrupted the withdrawal. Only the 1st Company, 901st Panzergrenadier Regiment, actually moved into position. The rest of the front was held by two companies of the decimated 14th Regiment.

To add to General Wilke's woes, he had to hold some of the least defensible ground on this front. The terrain was a flat blanket of hedgerow fields and orchards, crisscrossed by secondary roads and small streams and rising steadily toward high ground farther south. There were few obstacles in the U.S. 4th Division's path, mostly small clusters of farm buildings like those at La Courdes-Landes a short distance from the St-Lô–Périers road. The 4th Division's eastern boundary with the 30th Infantry Division followed the bank of the Terrette River to the St-Lô–Coutances road, and from there headed southeast to the rail line south of Canisy. The western boundary with the 9th Infantry Division followed a line that ran southwest and started at the St-Lô–Périers road going east of La Chapelle-en-Juger toward Marigny.

To carry the assault against General Wilke's beleaguered paratrooper force, General Barton planned to have the 8th Infantry Regiment leading, while the 12th Infantry Regiment and the 4th Reconnaissance Troop followed as the division reserve. The 4th Division's attack would be augmented by the 801st Tank Destroyer Battalion (towed); Company C, 634th Tank Destroyer Battalion (self-propelled); Company B, 87th Chemical Mortar Battalion; the 377th Antiaircraft Artillery Automatic Weapons Battalion; and the 70th Tank Battalion.[4]

Most of the division's combat support was behind the 8th Infantry Regiment, which would be supported by A and C Companies (less one platoon) from the division's 4th Combat Engineer Battalion (twice the engineer support usually allotted). The extra engineers would help breach the hedgerow defenses and clear routes to speed the advance for the follow-on forces. In addition, the 8th Infantry Regiment had all of Lieutenant Colonel John C. Welborn's 70th Tank Battalion (less one platoon of Company D's light tanks). This was a lot of armor support; normally an attacking regiment received only a company of tanks. Also supporting the 8th Regiment was B Company, 87th Chemical Mortar Battalion, and C Company, 634th Tank Destroyer Battalion (self-propelled). All the extra combat support was designed to give the regiment's commander everything he would need to press the attack to the enemy.

The 8th Infantry Regiment had a reputation as an aggressive, hard-fighting unit, earned under an outstanding commander, Colonel James Alward Van Fleet. Colonel Van Fleet was an innovative tactician and a fanatical trainer, and even in a combat zone he insisted on rigorous training to keep up tactical proficiency and unit cohesion. On 2 July he had been promoted and transferred to a new assignment.

The 4th Division's chief of staff, Colonel James S. Rodwell, replaced Van Fleet. Operation Cobra would be Colonel Rodwell's first big battle with the regiment. When Rodwell issued his attack plan on 23 July, in addition to all the extra combat power, he had another significant advantage: he knew where the enemy was. The division had identified the two main enemy strongpoints in his zone. These positions were supported by a few dug-in self-propelled guns, Mark V tanks, and a little artillery. Division had missed only one thing, the repositioning of the 5th Parachute and Panzer Lehr Divisions and the fact that the German defenses were in a state of flux, even weaker than suspected.

Faced with a very narrow zone that was crowded with friendly units, Colonel Rodwell planned to advance against the enemy by battalions in column. The route he mapped out passed through a stand of woods and across the St-Lô–Périers road. His 8th Regiment would charge across the road, with Lieutenant Colonel Welborn's 70th Tank Battalion moving with the lead elements, and C Company, 634th Tank Destroyer Battalion, would follow, setting up successive defense positions in case of enemy counterattacks.

In his planning, Colonel Rodwell emphasized the importance of speed, taking maximum advantage of the bombing, moving fast and bypassing enemy elements. He expected the columns to advance without halting at a rate of 100 yards every 3 minutes so that they would be 500 yards from the St-Lô–Périers road by H-Hour+15. Once the columns had crossed the road they would continue south to their objective beyond the St-Gilles–Marigny road.

The plan also called for Brigadier General Harold W. Blakely's 4th Infantry Division artillery to provide support for the assault. Beginning at H-Hour, the support included a series of targets running south, starting at the line of departure. The volume of fire would not be great. The division artillery was left with only two 105mm and one 155mm battalions (one artillery battalion was detached to the 22d Infantry Regiment). Most of the targets would have to be engaged by only one firing battery. To help out, A Company, 801st Tank Destroyer Battalion, and the assault guns of the 70th Tank Battalion were also assigned targets. In addition, at the last minute, the division received additional fire support from an 8-inch artillery battalion and a 240mm gun battalion for H-15 minutes to H-Hour. After the preparation firing was complete, the 29th Field Artillery Battalion would support the attack of the 1st Battalion, and the 42d Field Artillery Battalion would support the 3d Battalion. Meanwhile, the 20th Field Artillery Battalion, the 155mm battalion, would provide general support. Despite the last-minute additions, on the whole the artillery support was not impressive for a major attack. With the promise of an immense aerial bombardment, however, the limited artillery support seemed adequate.

Colonel Rodwell had only one serious concern. The division's front was screened by elements of the 39th Infantry Regiment from General Eddy's 9th Infantry Division. Reaching the enemy would involve passing one friendly unit through another. This "passage of lines" in the presence of the enemy was a difficult and treacherous task. There was always the danger that the enemy might launch a counterstrike before friendly troops were organized and ready to go. An even more important consideration for this operation was that a passage of lines required additional time and could slow the tempo of a regiment's advance.

To get the attacking troops to the front quickly, Colonel Rodwell decided to conduct a forward passage of lines, with his attacking battalions moving through the units already in contact with the enemy. This was an aggressive move, and it demanded very close teamwork with the in-place unit to avoid congestion and preclude friendly units from firing on each other by mistake. Before the battle, the colonel and his staff shuttled back and forth to the 39th Regiment, coordinating the details, artillery fire, signals, and link-up points.

All the preparation for the passage of lines had been done through good staff work, but very quickly it all had to be changed. After the bombing on the morning of 24 July, General Barton ordered the 8th Infantry Regiment to retake the ground that had been given up for a safety zone. At 1:00 P.M. Lieutenant Colonel Yarborough's 2d Battalion, 8th Infantry Regiment, passed through the 39th Infantry Regiment and conducted a hasty attack all the way to the St-Lô–Périers road.

The 2d Battalion's unexpected advance gave Colonel Rodwell an opportunity to modify his plan: he now had room to push more firepower into the initial assault and even increase the tempo of the attack. Rather than attacking with battalions in column, he now elected to advance with battalions abreast (side by side). Lieutenant Colonel Meyer's 1st Battalion would attack in the west. Lieutenant Colonel Strickland's 3d Battalion would attack in the east. Armor from Lieutenant Colonel Welborn's 70th Tank Battalion would support both attacks. With his new scheme of maneuver, Rodwell would get twice as much force into the fight at the outset. The only problem was that there would now have to be two passages of lines, with part of the attack passing through the 2d Battalion, 8th Infantry Regiment, and part through the 39th Infantry Regiment, 9th Infantry Division.

The short bombing on 24 July also forced Colonel Rodwell to adopt a more cautious plan for the passage of lines. Units were ordered to pull farther back before the bombing on 25 July. The 2d Battalion withdrew several hundred yards and established the division's new front along a stream parallel to the St-Lô–Périers road. At 9:30 A.M. on 25 July the 2d Battalion would withdraw again and become the regimental reserve, while Lieutenant Colonel Strickland's 3d Battalion attacked. Meanwhile, the 39th Infantry Regiment would also withdraw and make room for Lieutenant Colonel Meyer's 1st Battalion to attack. (See Figure 7.1 for a map of the 4th Infantry Division's attack.)

Figure 7.1 Attack of the 4th Infantry Division

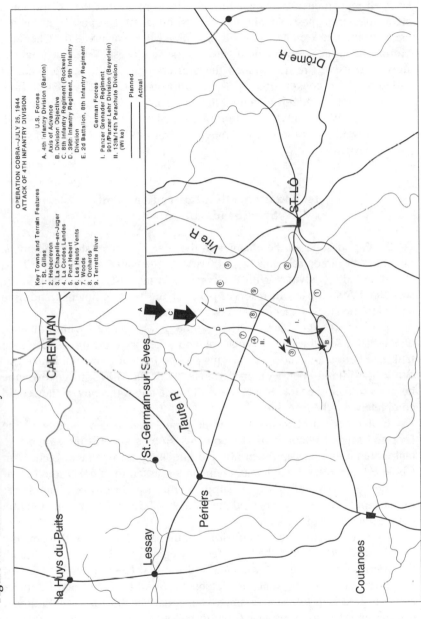

OPERATION COBRA—JULY 25, 1944
ATTACK OF 4TH INFANTRY DIVISION

Key Towns and Terrain Features
1. St. Gilles
2. Hebecrevon
3. La Chapelle-en-Juger
4. La Cordes Landes
5. Pont Hebert
6. Les Hauts Vents
7. Woods
8. Orchards
9. Terrette River

U.S. Forces
A. 4th Infantry Division (Barton)
B. Division Objective
C. 8th Infantry Regiment (Rockwell)
D. 39th Infantry Regiment, 9th Infantry Division
E. 2d Battalion, 8th Infantry Regiment

German Forces
I. Panzer Grenader Regiment 901/Panzer Lehr Division (Bayerlein)
II. 13th/14th Parachute Division (Wilke)

Planned
Actual

To compensate for the extra ground that had to be covered, Colonel Rodwell repositioned the attacking units forward so that they could jump off as quickly as possible. He also moved his command post right behind the 2d Battalion. Colonel Rodwell positioned B Company, 87th Chemical Mortar Battalion, a few hundred yards to the southwest to provide immediately responsive fire. He wanted the mortars close by to act as what he called his "hip-pocket artillery."[5] In addition, C Company, 634th Tank Destroyer Battalion, moved behind the 2d Battalion prepared to set up anti-tank defenses. Meanwhile, Lieutenant Colonel Welborn's 70th Tank Battalion waited for the word to move up from its assembly area near La Capalainerie.

1st Battalion, 8th Infantry Regiment, Spearheads the Attack

On 25 July, despite all the changes in the plan and more short bombings, the attack began on schedule at 11:00 A.M. Lieutenant Colonel Meyer's 1st Battalion led the advance with B Company in the east, C Company in the west, and A Company in reserve. Each of the lead companies had nine tanks attached (seven medium and two light tanks).

Even though the attack started on time, it was plagued with problems. One infantry squad waved down a tank and asked the crew for a shovel; the tank had buried a member of the squad when it burst through a hedgerow. While the infantrymen worked furiously with the shovel to uncover the helpless soldier, the tank then had to pull a tree out of the way so they could completely dig the man out.

In another act of misfortune, three planeloads of U.S. bombs hit the first and second platoons of B Company. Bombs also hit the supporting tank column, holding up the armor and knocking out one tank. Lieutenant Clyde Eddinger, the B Company commander, asked for a delay to reorganize the company and his tank support, but 1st Battalion commander Lieutenant Colonel Meyer denied the request. The attack had to get moving to take advantage of the bombing.

Despite the chaos and confusion, Lieutenant Eddinger's B Company spearheaded the attack of the 8th Infantry Regiment. He moved out with all the troops he could muster, two squads of the first platoon and a section of machine guns from the weapons platoon followed by Lieutenant Eddinger and the three men from the company headquarters. All together, Eddinger had an embarrassingly meager force to follow the massive bombardments by airplanes and artillery.

This kind of war, Lieutenant Eddinger had learned in his brief career, was what real combat was like. The neat doctrinal manuals that envisioned the well-coordinated advance of three elements backed by supporting fires were useless on an actual battlefield. Battles were not fought by units, but by remnants of units, a hodgepodge of replacements following a few battle-weary veterans. Every advance was a pick-up game, carried forward on the shoulders of a few experienced and aggressive men prepared to meet the test of battle. Fortunately, Lieutenant Eddinger's tiny force found that it would not face the test right away. It encountered no enemy artillery or ground troops and crossed the stream and the woods to its front without opposition.

Meanwhile, at 11:13 A.M., C Company of Lieutenant Colonel Meyer's 1st Battalion also reported that its attack was underway, although it too had had a tumultuous beginning. Company commander Lieutenant Joseph L. Gude had stepped on a nail and had to be evacuated. Lieutenant William Woodruff, the executive officer, took over. For the first 500 yards Woodruff's company had no contact with the enemy; his left platoon crossed the stream and passed through the woods ahead without any resistance. The right platoon received rifle and machine gun fire as it entered the woods, but the enemy seemed disorganized and quickly withdrew.

At 12:10 P.M. the 1st Battalion's artillery liaison officer reported that Lieutenant Colonel Meyer's lead elements were moving without opposition and nearing the St-Lô–Périers road. By 12:30 P.M. Meyer reported that troops were 300 yards north of La Courdes-Landes. Behind the battalion engineer teams from A Company, 4th Combat Engineer Battalion, cleared the battlefield debris left by both the Germans and the bombing. The engineers cleared mines and filled craters, and that day they would build 4 miles of road to provide enough room for the follow-on troops.[6]

3d Battalion, 8th Infantry Regiment, Joins the Attack

While the 1st Battalion continued to advance, Lieutenant Colonel Erasmus H. Strickland's 3d Battalion moved with equal swiftness in the east. The battalion reported that the companies were moving so fast that the wire lines could not keep up with the company command posts. Colonel Rodwell was pleased. He alerted the 2d Battalion to be ready to follow on 30 minutes notice. C Battery, 634th Tank Destroyer Battalion, moved a platoon forward behind each of the attacking battalions to guard against unexpected counterattacks. Everything was going well for Rodwell's big attack until the first 8th Infantry Regiment soldiers found the enemy's main defenses.

1st Battalion, 8th Infantry Regiment, Finds the Front

A patrol from C Company of Lieutenant Colonel Meyer's 1st Battalion pushed out all the way to the St-Lô–Périers road, where they found a German squad on guard. After a short fight the squad surrendered, except for one man hiding behind a vehicle. He killed a patrol squad leader, and was killed in turn by the Americans.

After the brief but tragic engagement on the road Lieutenant Woodruff's C Company continued to advance, but when it reached a small bridge on the St-Lô–Périers road it took fire from isolated German positions to its rear.

At higher headquarters the idea of moving quickly and bypassing resistance had seemed a simple and effective way to maintain momentum. In actual practice, advancing units found that bypassing the enemy was difficult and dangerous. C Company was well out in front of the regiment, and thus had passed German positions in the woods behind. The Germans had unimpeded fields of fire onto the exposed flanks of the company. Lieutenant Woodruff's could not advance without coming under fire from several directions at once. He was facing the most terrible situation imaginable, and for the moment he had no options for carrying out the attack or protecting his men.

While C Company appeared to be all but surrounded, Lieutenant Eddinger and a handful of men from B Company found themselves virtually cut off in the woods north of the St-Lô–Périers road. The Germans in front of them appeared well entrenched and showed no signs of retreating. Rather than pressing the enemy, Eddinger stopped at the edge of the woods to wait for the rest of his men. A short while later he was joined by his executive officer and seventeen men, but there was no sign of the rest of the company or the supporting tanks. Remembering the emphasis his commanders had placed on keeping up the momentum of the assault, Lieutenant Eddinger decided to continue the attack even though he had less than half of the 130 men assigned to his command.

The company began a tough, confusing battle in the woods. During the fight the Americans trapped a squad of Germans in the corner of a hedgerow. The Germans indicated that they wanted to give up, but when one of the U.S. squad leaders moved forward to accept the surrender he was shot—and a second squad leader was wounded by a grenade. This was a difficult situation. "We could not see just what part of the enemy position this fire was coming from," Lieutenant Eddinger recalled, "and we couldn't risk anyone else, so we shot down the Germans who wanted to surrender." It was another of those brutal moments of hedgerow combat that would be hard to forget. But, for the time being, like the men of C Company who had lost a good sergeant in a similar incident just down the road, the troops put the incident behind them and moved on.

3d Battalion, 8th Infantry Regiment, and Death in the Orchard

The 1st Battalion's C and B Companies under Lieutenant Colonel Meyer were not the only units having problems. At 12:35 P.M. Lieutenant Colonel

Strickland's 3d Battalion reported receiving machine gun and artillery fire. Then they found German defenders dug in an orchard 300 yards north of the St-Lô–Périers road. The Germans had selected their position well, and attempts to outflank it failed. To make matters worse, the 3d Battalion's supporting tank platoons had lost contact during the advance and were nowhere to be found. Without tank support a direct assault offered little hope of success.

At the regimental command post, Colonel Rodwell was faced with the critical decision all commanders must make at some point in battle. Should he commit the reserves? Both his battalions had stalled, and a third of his combat power was waiting and ready to go. Passing a new unit through one already in battle could prove difficult and time consuming. On the other hand, every passing moment that the attack failed to progress diminished the advantage provided by the carpet bombing. Hoping to speed up the tempo of his attack, Colonel Rodwell decided to have the 2d Battalion move up, pass through Lieutenant Colonel Strickland's 3d Battalion, and then assault the German position in the orchard. Before the 2d Battalion could move out, however, reports began to filter back to the command post that the assault battalions were on the move. Rodwell immediately decided to hold back the reserve. He had confidence in his leaders. His commanders had already demonstrated they could handle a complicated passage of lines, numerous changes in the plan, and the surprise of the short bombings with discipline and confidence. If his battalion commanders said they could do the job, he would have faith in them.

Lieutenant Colonel Strickland was renewed in his optimism because he had gotten his armor back under his control. After losing sight of the supporting tanks for 2 hours, the 3d Battalion had finally reestablished contact and coordinated an assault on the German strongpoint blocking the advance in the orchard by the St-Lô–Périers road. With the aid of armor the 3d Battalion attack quickly regained momentum: by 2:25 P.M. Strickland reported advancing with I Company in the lead. The attack continued for another 700 yards before K Company on the battalion's flank encountered another German strongpoint supported by two dug-in tanks and infantry along a sunken road.

Before K Company was ready to tackle the strongpoint, coordination with the supporting armor from Lieutenant Colonel Welborn's 70th Tank Battalion failed again. The tanks could not keep up with the infantry's pace of advance across cratered roads and hedgerow terrain. Strickland, anxious not to lose the attack's momentum, decided this time not to wait for armor, and he also rejected the regiment's offer to send up tank destroyers. The German tanks were too well dug in, meaning that the tank destroyers would have to move within point-blank range to get a shot across the sunken road—and they wouldn't stand a chance. On the other hand, the 3d Battalion's infantry had demonstrated tenacity and skill in advancing against the small, isolated German positions that they had encountered so far. Strickland decided to send in the infantry, though in pitting men against tanks he knew he was running the risk of heavy casualties. Still, he felt that he had little choice if the regiment was to keep up the tempo of the attack.

The assaulting companies tried to outflank the positions on either side with bazooka teams. Considering the many complaints that soldiers in Normandy had about the effectiveness of the bazooka (which had to be fired from almost point blank range to penetrate the armor of a German tank), this was a desperate maneuver. The infantry, however, managed to get close enough to destroy two of the enemy tanks. But, despite having lost their armored support, the Germans refused to withdraw and the Americans had to wait for their own tanks to come up again before the strongpoint could be reduced.

German resistance at the sunken road proved to be the last major obstacle in the 3d Battalion's path. To not slow the attack, any remaining small, unsupported German positions were ignored. A task force consisting of a platoon of infantry, two tank destroyers, and two or three tanks was left behind to mop up the bypassed German defenses. The job took the rest of the day, but the tiny force captured twenty-nine Germans without losing a man.

1st Battalion, 8th Infantry Regiment, Pushes Through

Lieutenant Colonel Meyer's 1st Battalion, led by B and C Companies and the intrepid Lieutenants Eddinger and Woodruff, also continued to advance. The battalion eventually reached La Courdes-Landes, where it encountered another German strongpoint. Meyer called for artillery support, and behind the fire support C Company prepared to assault the strongpoint's buildings. There was still plenty of daylight, and Lieutenant Colonel Meyer had standing orders to keep up the pace of the attack, exploit the bombing, and push to the regiment's objective before the Germans could counterattack. Here again, the shortage of radios that could communicate between tanks and infantry proved to be a serious shortcoming. The assaulting infantry could not talk directly to the armor, and did not know whether support was around the bend or miles away. All that the infantry knew for sure was that, tanks or no tanks, the battalion had to move forward.

Fortunately, only moments before this assault was to begin the battalion's supporting tanks roared down the road. Since the enemy positions lacked armor or antitank support, the U.S. tanks were able to pull right up to the buildings and fire into them at point-blank range. With the aid of the armor, by 1:30 P.M. Lieutenant Woodruff's C Company had cleared the buildings and captured fifteen prisoners. Unluckily for Woodruff, the bulldozer tank was damaged in C Company's attack on La Courdes-Landes, and without the 'dozer blade to break through the hedgerows, the tankers were reluctant to continue the advance into the fields beyond and withdrew to get the bulldozer tank repaired.

For the second time in Woodruff's first day of command, C Company was on its own without armored support. It moved south another 700 yards and encountered a German tank emplaced in a sunken road. Without supporting armor, and remembering that his orders were to keep up the tempo of the attack, Woodruff had little choice but to go it alone and try to take out the German position with the means at hand—one bazooka team.

Attacking tanks with bazookas was a traumatic experience. Unless the bazooka's rocket hit a German tank in a weak spot (side or rear), the odds were that the tank would suffer little or no damage. In addition, the back blast from a firing bazooka produced a cloud of smoke and debris that was not hard to spot, quickly drawing the attention of the enemy tank or any accompanying German infantry. Despite the tremendous risks and long odds, a bazooka team did work its way around the enemy tank, hit a track, and disabled the vehicle. The German crew immediately surrendered.

While C Company pushed past the defeated enemy tank, Lieutenant Eddinger's B Company was still held up back at the woodline by enemy fire. Finally, about 2:30 P.M. the tank platoon supporting the company caught up and advanced along a road through the woods, then skirted east past B Company to outflank the Germans. The U.S. 'dozer tank took the lead, punching holes through the hedgerows. Two tanks followed, fanning out to cover the 'dozer as it advanced. Eddinger's infantry closed after the tanks, reducing the German position and capturing twelve prisoners.

After B Company had pushed past the woods enemy resistance diminished. At about 4:30 P.M. B Company, accompanied by the tanks, closed the gap with Lieutenant Woodruff's C Company along the St-Lô–Périers road and continued the advance south. The tanks, however, could not find a suitable place to cross the stream by the road, so again the infantrymen advanced alone. Amazingly, they saw no sign of the enemy, though Lieutenant Eddinger's company had another near miss from bombs dropped by U.S. fighter-bombers. There were no casualties, and the assault continued.

It was almost 2 hours before the attack encountered the German defenders again. As B and C Companies advanced, the slope turned uphill toward a small group of farm buildings bordering an orchard. Enemy fire from the houses blocked further progress by both companies. It was another discouraging moment for the exhausted infantrymen. Once again they faced the prospect of a direct assault against a protected position.

In probing for weaknesses in the German position, fire was exchanged for about 20 minutes. Then the desultory firefight was drowned out by the sound of tanks. All eighteen tanks supporting the U.S. assault companies suddenly rumbled into view, and for the U.S. infantry the sight was awe inspiring. For the Germans the roar of tank engines, grinding of tracks, report of guns firing, and spectacle of smoke and explosions were overwhelming. The Germans immediately withdrew.

An Unexpected Turn for the 8th Infantry Regiment

By 6:00 P.M. the whole 8th Regiment had reached a line just southeast of La Chapelle-en-Juger. Although they were only halfway to their objective on the Marigny–St-Gilles road, the attack was going well. Then, unexpectedly, Colonel Rodwell received a change in orders. General Collins ordered the 4th Infantry Division to move east of the division boundary into the 9th Infantry Division's zone and take La Chapelle-en-Juger, a key corps objective. It had to be secured to clear the way for the armor breakthrough, and by the end of the first day's attack it was apparent that General Eddy's 9th Infantry Division would not be able to reach the town. Since Colonel Rodwell's command was the closest unit, General Collins shifted the mission to the 4th Infantry Division.

From the division's command post General Barton could see that the new assignment would not be an easy task. Intelligence reports had indicated that the Germans were defending La Chapelle-en-Juger in strength. In addition, aerial reconnaissance had confirmed that there definitely were German tanks in the town. A plan was quickly thrown together, with an air strike to open the attack followed by an assault by the 1st Battalion of Colonel Rodwell's 8th Infantry Regiment. Colonel Rodwell also ordered the 2d Battalion to follow the 1st Battalion, and the 3d Battalion to shift its attack toward the town as well. The units swiftly issued new orders. By 7:30 P.M. the bomb run was complete and Lieutenant Colonel Meyer's 1st Battalion reported that the strike had been on target.

Then the word came down—Halt. At the 30th Division command post General Barton had monitored the attack. He was a hard-driving leader and he had confidence in his field commanders, but he did not like to continue operations late in the day. He strongly believed that "attacking troops should halt at least an hour before dark on favorable ground in order to permit reorganization and establishment of security and anti-counterattack measures before dark."[7] The lead battalions had been attacking for 12 hours without pause, and now night was falling.

In theory, a bold and aggressive commander would want to keep the initiative and carry the offensive into the dark. In reality that was more often impractical. Carrying a nighttime battle into an urban environment is particularly ill-advised: narrow streets and stone buildings offer a lot of cover for a defending enemy and obstacles to the attacker, as well as restricting the opportunity to employ tanks and artillery. There were few actions more difficult than coordinating an advance through a town—

particularly at night. In addition, after a day of continuous hedgerow fighting, Barton's troops were exhausted, hungry, dehydrated, and mentally drained.

General Barton knew that there were limits to both human endurance and a commander's initiative. The 8th Regiment's assault had outpaced the progress of the units on the division's flanks. Rodwell's 8th Regiment had established a salient sticking out in the dark—a prime target for counterattacks. Since it was apparent that the regiment had already gotten through the enemy's main line of resistance, continuing the offensive seemed an inordinate risk. It was not worth jeopardizing the vital high ground that had been gained for an uncertain, bitter firefight in the streets of La Chapelle-en-Juger in the dark.

Although General Barton also had a regiment in reserve, it would do him little good at this point. Although the Germans often used their reserves at night, these reserves were employed in counterattacks that usually followed well-established routes, linking up with their own stationary units already at the front. In the 4th Infantry Division's case, General Barton would have had to marry up two regiments moving forward, in the dark and on the fly. This, too, seemed inordinately risky.

The 4th Division ordered its units to consolidate their gains. Between 10:00 and 11:00 P.M. the troops occupied positions and prepared defenses, with the 1st and 3d Battalions dug in on the high ground just north of La Chapelle-en-Juger. As night fell on the battlefield, General Barton could look back with some satisfaction. Colonel Rodwell had done well in his first attack, and his troops had broken through to close on the high ground to the south, opening the center of the gap for the Cobra penetration.

Leaving the White Crosses Behind

Several factors contributed to the success of the 8th Infantry Regiment's attack. Much like the defenses in the 30th Infantry Division's zone, the enemy north of the St-Lô–Périers road had not been greatly disrupted by the aerial attacks.[8] However, the Cobra bombing campaign once again proved its value by disrupting the commitment of German reserves and any hope of organizing an effective counterattack to the U.S. 4th Division's assault. In addition, the interrupted reorganization of the parachute and Panzer Lehr units at the front left the German defenses facing the 4th Infantry Division uncoordinated, with no artillery support or reserves. As a result of this disorganization and the bombing, the only opposition offered by the Germans was by a handful of small, isolated strongpoints.

On the other hand, the U.S. 4th Infantry Division did not have an easy task. There were, for example, at least four significant failures in infantry-armor cooperation, illustrating again the difficulty of coordinating attacks in the hedgerows even against weak opposition. The lack of radios to effect close coordination between armor and infantry exacerbated the problem. This was another reminder of how poorly the U.S. Army had prepared to conduct integrated infantry-armor operations. Small-unit infantry commanders were often left helpless behind a hedgerow unaware of whether armored support was on the way or nowhere to be found.

The fact that a regiment had managed to complete a complicated passage of lines and initiate an attack despite the breakdowns in infantry-armor cooperation and the short bombing was an affirmation of the infantry's determination and the confidence commanders had in their own judgement of what their soldiers could accomplish. Even though confusion, adversity, and breakdowns in coordination with supporting arms complicated the commanders' task, the commanders kept control of the situation and the attacks continued.

The obstacles faced by the 8th Infantry Regiment also highlighted another important contribution to the conduct of the day's fighting, the efforts of small U.S. units and their leaders. Without question, winning a battle required the orchestrated combat power controlled by regiment and battalion commanders. As the day's attack demonstrated, it took the application of supporting arms and the direction by field commanders to string small victories among the hedgerows into a sustained advance.

On the other hand, as the 8th Regiment's assault also showed, small units on their own could make the difference in individual engagements. Even when stripped of the robust combat support that usually accompanied an offensive, seasoned small U.S. Army units could fight with aggressiveness and initiative. When they faced the Germans on even terms, force against force, without the aid of artillery, tanks, or counterattacks, the U.S. infantry, veterans of 2 months of hard campaigning, proved more than the equal of their adversaries.

In particular, the performance of the 8th Regiment's 1st Battalion B and C Companies was noteworthy. Both units were woefully understrength when they attacked, and both had been disrupted by the short bombing. C Company had lost its commander. Finally, both companies had found themselves frequently isolated and without armor or artillery support. In spite of these obstacles, both units continued to advance, retaining their discipline and cohesion. They demonstrated courage and skill, even successfully taking on enemy tanks and fortified positions even though they carried only small arms and the unpopular bazookas. Even though the particularly chaotic state of the German forward defenses in this sector allowed the U.S. infantry companies to make far more progress than could normally be expected on the hedgerow battlefields, small-unit leaders must be credited with having the drive to take advantage of the situation. In short, both these units demonstrated that they could advance and maneuver when given the chance to fight on even terms.

Such small-unit battles also showed how poorly the U.S. Army had prepared its infantry for the Normandy campaign. How the U.S. units fought that day in Normandy did not resemble in the slightest the ballet-like tactics of fire and movement the units had been taught before the campaign. The Americans advanced not because of the soundness of their tactics or the quality of their individual weapons, but because of the courage and individual skills of soldiers and leaders—and because the enemy's overwhelming advantage in small-unit combat (the well-prepared German machine gun positions in the hedgerows that could not be flanked) had been taken away by the collapse of the German's main defensive perimeter.

In addition, in that day's fighting, the U.S. infantry also showed that it could attack and win hedgerow country battles without the later sophisticated, rehearsed, and orchestrated hedgerow-busting techniques developed by U.S. forces during the campaign. This suggests, once again, that although U.S. Army tactical innovations were praiseworthy, they were not a prerequisite for the Normandy breakout. Small, unsupported, and unrehearsed, but aggressive groups of U.S. soldiers could, given the right tactical conditions, win a battle among the hedgerows. Without the threat of serious counterattacks, the Americans moved swiftly and fearlessly, bypassing the enemy where they could and risking exposed flanks, keeping the tempo of the attack as rapid as possible. Such initiative and persistence alone could not win the war or even ensure operational success, but when they were brought into battle at the right time and place they could achieve spectacular results.

The maturing of the American infantry was also a reflection of the great material strengths that the Americans brought to the battlefield. Despite heavy casualties throughout the Normandy campaign, the Americans had used their advantages in combat power to sustain and protect ground troops, as well as hone their hedgerow fighting skills. Small unit combat in the 4th Infantry Division suggests that, for at least some units, this effort bore fruit. The ranks of the squads, platoons and companies were sprinkled with enough veterans of the campaign to provide the core leadership to rally and focus the efforts of the infantry.

The field of white crosses showed the bitter cost of learning the lessons of war, but despite heavy casualties and a flood of replacements the 4th Infantry Division demonstrated that it could field small units that would fight and function like veteran combat outfits. This was a reaffirmation of General Bradley's confidence in the operational capabilities of U.S. forces and it brought the U.S. First Army one step closer to breaking through to victory in Normandy.

Notes

1. Francis L. Ware, Family Doctor to 2nd Battalion 12th Infantry Regiment, 4th Infantry Division, p. 18, MHI.

2. Descriptions of General Roosevelt's funeral are found in Sylvan, War Diary, 14 July 1944, MHI; Hansen, War Diary, 14 July 1944, MHI; "Theodore Roosevelt, 56, Dies on Normandy Battlefield," *New York Times,* 14 July 1944; Blumenson, *The Patton Papers,* pp. 480–481. The cemetery at St-Mère-Eglise was a melancholy place. One soldier recalled that "at the time it was an open cemetery and was a terrible sight. There were many open graves and I actually saw a POW who was working there, throw an arm or a leg into a grave where he thought the poor soul needed it. The stench was terrible." See Dorst, *My Times and Service in the Military,* p. 53, MHI.

3. Heydte, "A German Parachute Regiment in Normandy," pp. 33–34. The information on operations of the 5th Parachute Division are drawn from *Armeeoberkommando 7, K.T.B. Entwurf und OB Chef-IA-Gespräche, 6 Juni–16 August 1944,* microfilm, T312, Roll 1568, pp. 172, 180, NARA; Pemsel, "Comments on the Study," pp. 4–7; Gustav Wilke, "5th Parachute Division (6 June–24 July 1944)," MS B-820, pp. 6–8; Hausser, "Normandy Seventh Army"; Headquarters, 4th Infantry Division, U.S. Army, Actions Against Enemy/After Action Report, 10 August 1944, order of battle notes and interrogation of prisoner of war reports. There are no operational unit records extant for this period.

4. The plan and operations of the 4th Infantry Division described are from Headquarters, 8th Infantry Regiment, U.S. Army Field Orders No. 22 and 23, July 1944; Headquarters, 8th Infantry Regiment, U.S. Army, S-3 Journal, 25 July 1944; Headquarters, 4th Infantry Division, U.S. Army, Actions Against Enemy/After Action Report, 10 July 1944, entries titled "Interview with Lt Joseph Gude," "Interview with Lt Clyde Eddinger," and "Interview with Lt Bauer, Lt Brody, Lt Kleekamp"; Chester B. Hall, *History of the 70th Tank Battalion,* p. 75.

5. AGF Observer Immediate Report No. 1, p. 3, CARL. For an overview of chemical mortar employment, see *Report of the General Board: Chemical Mortar Battalions, Study No. 70,* CARL.

6. Photo analysis of the road showed that the aerial bombing cut the road in at least twenty places. See U.S. Strategic Bombing Survey, Europe War, G-2 Target File, 2478, Box 140, RG 243, NARA.

7. AGF Observer Immediate Report No. 1, p. 1, CARL.

8. On the other hand, the bombs that landed forward of the no-bomb line and made a direct hit on a German front-line position were devastating. One eyewitness observed a U.S. bomb hit a German observation strongpoint and saw four German soldiers buried alive. See M. C. Adair, Combat Diary, 2d Battalion, 8th Infantry Regiment, 4th Infantry Division, 25 July 1944, MHI.

8

One Tired Division

T he attacks of all three of the VII Corps's front-line infantry divisions had to succeed to complete the penetration of the Germans' main line of resistance, but the U.S. 9th Infantry Division's assault in particular was essential. To create the opportunity for maneuver on an operational scale, the U.S. forces had to cut the German Seventh Army into two unsupported parts—but General Collins, the VII Corps commander, believed that could not be done unless the 9th Infantry Division reached its assigned objectives. It was a lot of responsibility for one tired division.

Unlike the 30th and the 4th Infantry Divisions, when the 9th first arrived in Normandy it was already a veteran outfit. The generals always expected big things from the division. When the first elements of the 9th Division landed on Utah Beach, General Collins immediately assigned them the mission of cleaning out the last of the enemy beach defenses. The 9th Infantry Division commander, Major General Manton Eddy, protested. He had only a third of his division ashore; he needed time to organize for the attack. General Collins gently grabbed his arm laughing, "Why Manton you don't need a division . . . you can do it with a regiment."[1] General Eddy relented and ordered the attack. But this would not be the last time that General Collins would demand that the 9th Division do more with less—nor would it be the last time General Eddy complained about the burden.

General Eddy was different from most of his contemporaries. When the Allies invaded Normandy, he was 56 years old, a little old for a division commander, 4 years older than his corps commander General Collins, a year older than U.S. First Army commander General Bradley. Age was not the only thing that distinguished Eddy from his contemporaries. He had graduated from the Shattuck Military School, not West Point. He also had more combat experience than most, having commanded a machine gun battalion during World War I.

In 1942 General George Marshall had personally selected Eddy to command the 9th Infantry Division, one of the first units headed overseas for North Africa, where General Bradley first met Eddy. Bradley's first impression was not entirely favorable. He thought that General Eddy "was a good leader and a well-schooled tactician but, as it developed, inclined to be cautious."[2] The division's poor performance in its first battles did nothing to raise Eddy's stock. In North Africa, however, General Eddy was under General George Patton, not Bradley. Patton believed that "a man should not be damned for an initial failure with a new division. Had I done this with Eddy of the 9th Division in Africa, the army would have lost a potential corps commander."[3] Eddy was given the chance to prove himself, and by the end of the campaign even Bradley had to admit that despite his cautious nature Eddy was probably the best all-around division commander in the theater. While General Eddy and his command earned a reputation as a dependable and capable outfit, he himself never lost his reputation for caution. After the war, Bradley wrote that "Manton liked to count his steps carefully before he took them."[4]

In large measure General Eddy's caution came from experience. He knew the cost of mistakes in battle—casualties. In Normandy the 9th Infantry was a veteran division, but it was not a division full of veterans. Casualties changed its makeup every day, and the division lost 2,359 men before the end of the first month of battle. Replacements came in large numbers as the wounded left: counting the 10 days before Operation Cobra alone, the division received over 2,000 replacements, the equivalent of changing out an infantry regiment.

General Eddy knew that the loss of every experienced soldier was a problem. It was for that reason that Eddy and the other infantry commanders were constantly concerned about measures to protect and sustain the welfare of their men. They needed the veterans. To win in the hedgerows, General Eddy believed that "the individual soldier or small groups of soldiers play a dominant part. Success comes to the offensive force which employs the maximum initiative by individuals and small groups."[5] This kind of performance required well-led, experienced soldiers. The problem with Operation Cobra was that Eddy was not sure he had enough of them for the difficult task General Collins had assigned his division—securing the west flank of the breakthrough.

The Plan to Take Marigny

General Collins established a number of ambitious and critical objectives for the 9th Infantry Division. It had to seize the high ground beyond Marigny along the Tribehou–Marigny road. Holding the high ground would give the VII Corps free use of the road and secure the west flank of the breakthrough. The division was also tasked with taking the vital terrain along Marigny's southern ridge. This was critical to opening the way for the envelopment. Because the dominating ground south of the town commanded key routes heading south and west, it was one of the most important and decisive objectives of the first phase of the attack.

Once the penetration was secure, the 9th Division had to clear routes for the 1st Infantry Division's attack and maintain contact with the encirclement force as it advanced. Considering all the tasks assigned, General Collins was asking a lot from one division. Marigny was the southernmost objective in the breakthrough, more than 2 1/2 miles of tough *bocage* countryside away, and the division could expect that Marigny would be heavily defended.

Blocking General Eddy's route to Marigny was an assortment of German forces ranging from inept to formidable. On the west side of the Tribehou–Marigny road, General Wilke, the 5th Parachute Division commander, was attempting to organize his shattered forces. His troops had to hold two key chokepoints, a roadblock and a strongpoint covering the road to Marigny. Behind the 5th Parachute Division, General Choltitz, the LXXXIV Corps commander, positioned the last of his reserve, the 353d Division. The reserve, held in an assembly area south of Périers, had five woefully understrength combat battalions. To the east of the 5th Parachute Division, on the vital high ground near Marigny, stood the U.S. 9th Division's toughest opposition, the Panzer Lehr Division.[6] The panzers covered a critical 2-mile front along the St-Lô–Périers road.

The Panzer Lehr Division was commanded by Lieutenant General Fritz Bayerlein, who had impeccable credentials for a panzer commander: he had been Rommel's chief of staff during the North Africa campaign. After the withdrawal from North Africa, the short, stocky, energetic Bayerlein was given his own command, one of the choicest in the German army. The Panzer Lehr Division was organized in January 1944, with the 901st and 902d Panzergrenadier Regiments, the 130th Panzer Regiment, and artillery, reconnaissance, antiaircraft artillery, and antitank battalions. General Bayerlein boasted that the division "was the best equipped panzer division that Germany ever had."

The strength of General Bayerlein's division was in its Mark IV and Mark V tanks. The *Panzerkampfwagen* (Pzkw) IV, usually called by the Americans the "Mark IV," was armed with a 75mm gun. Even though it had been in service since the beginning of the war, the tank had undergone a series of upgrades, making it a dependable armored system. Even more formidable was the Pzkw V, the "Mark V." Fielded in 1943, the Mark V was capable of speeds of up to 30 miles an hour and packed a 75mm high-velocity gun. The tank's mechanical reliability could not match that of the American Sherman tank, but once it got to the battlefield it outclassed its American counterpart in almost every way. What made the German tank so superior was its virtually invulnerable sloping frontal armor.[7]

Before the invasion, General Bayerlein's division had been part of the OKW reserve stationed at Le Mans, but on D-Day it was ordered to the front. After fighting the British for 4 weeks, the division was shifted to the U.S. Army zone. Two more weeks of constant battle left the Panzer Lehr Division in poor shape. Authorized over 15,000 men, the division had fewer than 2,200 and forty-five combat vehicles remaining. The only reinforcements received were the remnants of other commands. Logistical problems were as perplexing as the shortage of men and guns. "I had to haul my fuel from a point east of Paris," General Bayerlein complained, "and my ammunition from south of the Loire." He was running out of force to fight with and supplies to keep them going.

General Bayerlein had another significant problem to overcome. The *bocage* was terrible terrain for his tanks. Their wide tracks and long gun barrels made it difficult to negotiate the narrow, sunken Normandy roads. In addition, the constricted fields of observation created by the hedgerows limited the panzers' ability to exploit their superior gun range. As Bayerlein complained, "We simply used them [tanks] more as armored antitank guns or armored machine guns." Because of the limitations of terrain and U.S. air power, "there was no possibility of moving on the battlefield." Rather than performing sweeping armored counterattacks the tanks "had to stand and fight." The armored infantry vehicles, the *schützenpanzerwagen* (halftracks), were of even more limited use than the tanks. The halftracks were open at the top and vulnerable to enemy artillery fire, and in battle they had to be left behind.

Although his armored units were not designed to fight in static defenses, General Bayerlein shrugged with a "What else can you do?" To compensate for the lack of opportunity to maneuver, he layered his defenses in depth. North of the St-Lô–Périers road Bayerlein left a line of infantry outposts; his main defenses remained south of the road, organized around the tanks. The armor was dug in and camouflaged. "Each tank was surrounded by a group of armored infantry. The defense was built up around the tank like a *perlenschnur* [string of pearls]." Behind the strongpoints, Bayerlein positioned supporting mortars, and farther back his regimental reserves and artillery.

On the vital high ground between Marigny and St-Gilles, General Bayerlein established three roadblocks and three strongpoints, the roadblocks covering the high-speed approaches into his sector. Two covered the road to St-Gilles. The third was near La Chapelle-en-Juger. To back up these positions, the regiments had small company-sized reserves (sufficient to conduct local counterattacks). General Bayerlein knew that his forward defenses had to hold because there was very little left to their rear. General Hausser, the Seventh Army commander, positioned part of the army reserve, the 275th Division, behind the Panzer Lehr Division. The 275th consisted of only three battalions—not much of a force at all.[8]

General Bayerlein expected the Americans to make another push in his sector. To closely coordinate his division's defenses on 24 July, he moved to his advanced command post in the tower of a Norman castle at Le Mesnil-Amey. Unfortunately, as soon as he moved in U.S. artillery and air attacks disrupted communications. After the bombing, General Bayerlein inspected the damage, and he did not like what he saw. He found "nothing left" at the 902d Panzergrenadier Regiment headquarters at Bernardier, north of St-Gilles. From there General Bayerlein walked down to the Battle Group Heintz positions near Hebecrevon and found out that they had also been "wiped out" by the bombing. In total, he estimated a loss of 350 casualties and ten vehicles. His forward defenses were still intact, but they were an empty shell. Behind them, where the main force of the bombs had landed, was nothing but air and chaos.

General Bayerlein had another problem as well. After the Germans had responded to the U.S. air and artillery fire on 24 July with their own artillery and antiaircraft fire, they found their ammunition stocks critically low. Unintentionally, the aborted U.S. attack had further crippled the division by depleting the Germans' meager ammunition supplies.

General Bayerlein expected the Americans to follow up the bombing on 25 July. He called General Choltitz, the LXXXIV Corps commander, to brief him on the situation and request reinforcements. Choltitz replied that "he had nothing and could send nothing."[9] General Bayerlein would have to make do.

While Choltitz closely monitored developments in the Panzer Lehr Division sector, he viewed the situation with concern but not alarm. The 50-year-old veteran of World War I was relatively new to his job, having assumed his command on 18 June. He was the third commander the corps had seen since the invasion on 6 June. General Choltitz was one of the few commanders left on the front who was unconvinced that the Allies would launch their main effort in his sector. Still, the activity on 24 July disturbed him, and he dutifully reported the results of the Allied bombing and artillery fire to General Hausser, the Seventh Army commander.[10]

When Hausser briefed General Kluge, the OB West commander, he relayed Choltitz's assessment. Kluge asked Hausser whether he expected heavy fighting ahead. Hausser's reply was noncommittal: "We've got to expect something."[11] The OB West commander was perplexed: "We have got to expect a heavy offensive somewhere." Still, if General Kluge was greatly worried, his actions did not show it. The next day he planned to inspect the positions of Panzergruppe West, and he would be several miles away from the front when Cobra kicked off.

Faced with the threat of renewed attacks on 25 July, General Bayerlein of the Panzer Lehr Division reorganized his defenses. In the Battle Group Heintz sector he decided to keep the main line of resistance forward of Hebecrevon. This was essential, for if he lost this ground, he would lose the capability to tie his defense into the flank of II Parachute Corps. He could not risk the enemy's breaking through on the flank and getting behind him. In the rest of the division sector, he left only outposts forward of the St-Lô–Périers road and pulled back to his main line of defense closer to Marigny.

Bayerlein also ordered his tanks back south of the road and coordinated with the 5th Parachute Division so that it would pull back its main line of resistance to coincide with the Panzer Lehr Division. With these adjustments, Bayerlein thought he had achieved as cohesive a defense as possible with the forces at hand. He did not know that there were six U.S. divisions aimed at his front and that the bombing on 24 July was only a mistaken prelude. Bayerlein's modifications in fact pulled more troops into the center of the target area for U.S. planes and artillery.

If General Bayerlein still had any advantage, it was that the ground he defended was some of the most difficult and important terrain in the LXXXIV Corps sector. Across the hedgerows, the U.S. 9th Infantry Division's front rested a few hundred meters north of the St-Lô–Périers road near the village of Le Mesnil-Eury. In the west the Lozon River marked the division's boundary with the U.S. VIII Corps's 83d Infantry Division. In the east the boundary with the 4th Infantry Division followed a line running north to south past La Chapelle-en-Juger to Marigny, leaving both these key towns in the 9th Infantry Division's zone.

There were three terrain features in the division's area that were critical to Cobra's success. The first was the major road running down the center of the division's zone north to south from Tribehou to Marigny. This road would be needed for the U.S. armored forces to exploit the breakthrough. The second dominant feature was the spur that ran parallel along the ridge east of the Tribehou–Marigny road. The 9th Division would have to control this high ground to be able to use the road. The third piece of terrain was the most important, a high ridge running from east to west just beyond Marigny. Controlling this high ground was a prerequisite to any further attacks to the east, south, or west. To the east the ridge led to the banks of the Vire, where the river could be easily crossed. To the west the ridge dominated the road toward the town of Coutances. There were also several secondary roads leading south. Any way U.S. VII Corps wanted to go, Marigny was the way out of the *bocage* or a decisive roadblock for holding it in.

To help reach Marigny, despite General Eddy's concerns over the difficulty of the mission, General Collins provided the 9th Infantry Division with only a modicum of additional combat power. Eddy's forces received the 376th Antiaircraft Artillery Automatic Weapons Battalion; the 746th Tank Battalion commanded by Lieutenant Colonel G. Hupfer; Lieutenant Colonel Herbert J. McChrystal's 899th Tank Destroyer Battalion; A Battery, 129th Antiaircraft Artillery Battalion (Gun); C and D Companies,

87th Chemical Mortar Battalion; and the 196th and 690th Field Artillery Battalions.

The 9th Division's plan for accomplishing a tough mission with limited combat power was sketched in a brief order of only three pages and a paper overlay.[12] Even putting together this brief plan took a monumental effort. One of General Eddy's biggest problems was that he was a victim of his own success. His most successful staff officers had been siphoned off for other assignments. Colonel George Bittman Barth, the division chief of staff, had been pulled out early in the campaign to take a regiment in the 90th Infantry Division. He was replaced by Colonel Noah Brinson. Brigadier General Donald A. Stroh, the assistant division commander, had been tabbed to take over the 8th Infantry Division. He was replaced by Brigadier General James E. Warton. All the changes in the division's senior leadership only increased the already heavy burden on the junior staff officers.

The heaviest burden fell on the G-2 and G-3 sections, small staff groups led by lieutenant colonels. General Eddy's staff sections were typical of those found in the U.S. divisions. Lieutenant Colonel Robert W. Robb headed the G-2 section; his job was to determine the enemy's dispositions, capabilities, and intentions. Knowing the enemy was challenging and often frustrating work for the G-2. The staff complained that "even with the use of all possible sources of information it is difficult to get much. Front line units have little time to gather G-2 information. . . . The division reconnaissance troop is seldom under direct G-2 control."[13]

The G-2 staff members tried to supplement intelligence with whatever was available. For example, they made extensive use of aerial photography to identify positions behind the lines. From French civilians, they also learned that the road from Tribehou to Marigny was heavily mined and that the enemy had a strongpoint at La Chapelle-en-Juger.[14] Intelligence collecting seemed chaotic. G-2 personnel scribbled the incoming reports on message forms and spent their time piecing the often contradictory pieces of information together. The process was like assembling a giant, living jigsaw puzzle where the pieces constantly shifted and changed shape.

The focus of the G-2 effort was to build the order-of-battle book (OB). The OB contained everything known about the enemy—organization, tactics, strength, dispositions, even the history of units and commanders—as much detail as possible. And even though the 9th Infantry Division staff members did not know it, they usually started off each battle with a fairly good list of the enemy units in the area, thanks in part to the Ultra decrypts. This intelligence came to them through the OB published by army headquarters, which the division supplemented with whatever information it could gather about the enemy in its sector.

The division rarely found enough time to publish a detailed intelligence plan. Usually G-2 would take the OB and supplement it with any recent information. For Cobra, G-2 published a periodic report covering each 24-hour period. Despite the difficulties in collecting and sorting information, in this battle the division's reports proved accurate. The periodic report of 20 July identified forty-three enemy locations, picking out all the major forces facing the 9th Infantry Division.

The division G-2 staff was also quite successful at uncovering the enemy's intentions. On 17 July the section identified the commitment of elements of the 5th Parchute Division; G-2 correctly guessed that the paratroopers had been committed to relieve Panzer Lehr units on the front. Lieutenant Colonel Robb concluded that this reorganization demonstrated the enemy's intention of not giving up ground easily and trying to build up armored reserves.

There was only one major piece of the puzzle that 9th Division G-2 failed to uncover: the 5th Parachute Division was getting its own sector west of the Panzer Lehr Division. Since G-2 had not located many of the division parachute units listed in the OB, it assumed that the whole division had not been committed yet. In fact, these units were not in the line because they no longer existed—everything the 5th Parachute Division had left was already at the front.

The 5th Parachute Division's shift to the west, though not complete, was important. The reorganization meant that the 9th Infantry Division would primarily face Panzer Lehr units. When the Americans attacked they would find Marigny covered by a string of strongpoints manned by veteran, battle-tested infantry and Panzer Lehr armor.

After the G-2 section had laid out its take on the enemy dispositions, it fell to the G-3 staff under Lieutenant Colonel Frederick C. Feil to determine the best course of action. After the commander approved the course of action, Feil's staff would prepare a written order, brief the subordinate commanders, and then monitor the order's execution. Operations planning was a lot of work for a very small staff: the task of planning dragged on 24 hours a day, week after week, and Feil had only two majors and one captain to assist him in running the division's daily operations. Normally the two majors split the "crucial daily hours," under Feil's supervision, while the captain worked the "six quiet hours of the night."[15]

The division published its order for Cobra on 20 July. The plan called for the 47th Infantry Regiment to make the main attack in the eastern half of the 9th Division's zone and secure the first of the objectives, taking the high ground near Marigny and clearing the routes for the attack by the 1st Infantry Division. After the 47th Infantry Regiment had seized its objective and reached a point 1,000 yards south of the St-Lô–Périers road, it would pass through the division's 9th Reconnaissance Troop. From that point the troop would lead the attack, passing back word of the enemy locations and racing toward the second, and southernmost, objective, a blocking position on the west flank of the Cobra breakthrough. (The planned attack by the 9th Infantry Division is shown in Figure 8.1.)

Figure 8.1   Attack of the 9th Infantry Division

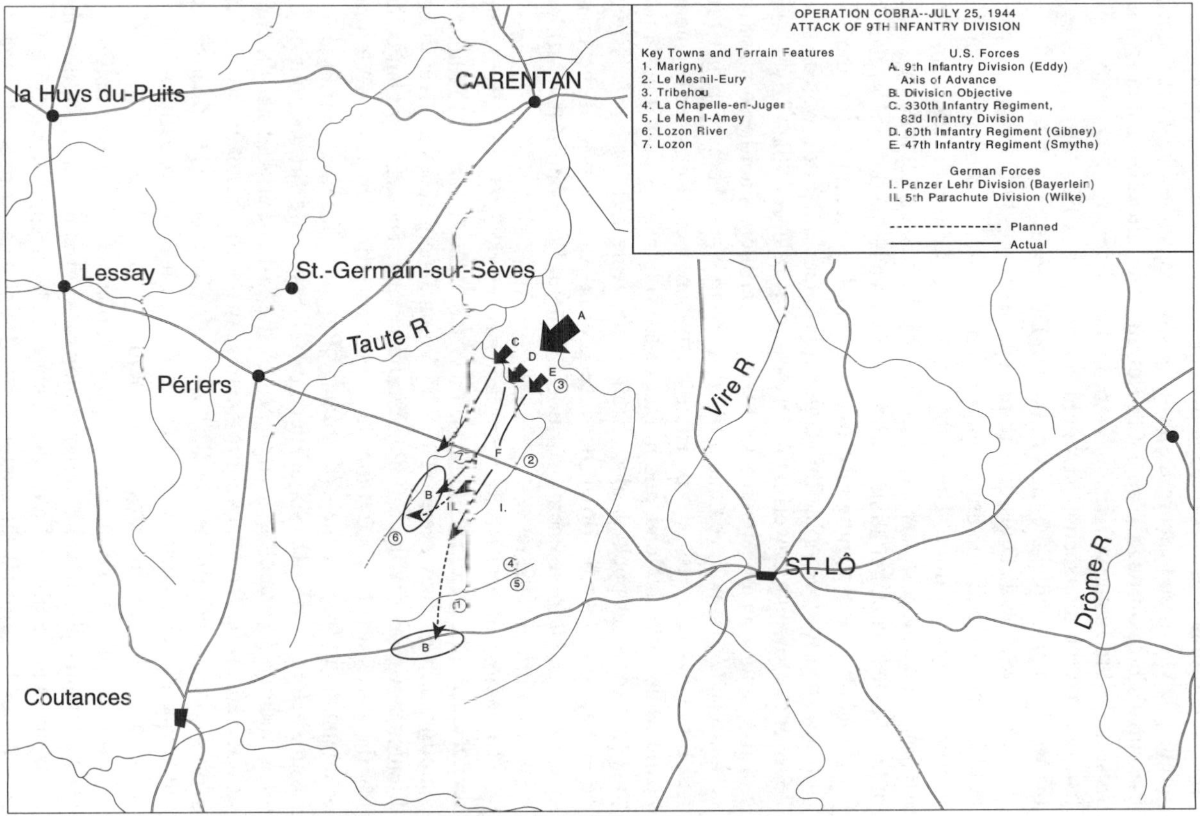

OPERATION COBRA--JULY 25, 1944
ATTACK OF 9TH INFANTRY DIVISION

Key Towns and Terrain Features
1. Marigny
2. Le Mesnil-Eury
3. Tribehou
4. La Chapelle-en-Juger
5. Le Mesnil-Amey
6. Lozon River
7. Lozon

U.S. Forces
A. 9th Infantry Division (Eddy)
    Axis of Advance
B. Division Objective
C. 330th Infantry Regiment,
    83d Infantry Division
D. 60th Infantry Regiment (Gibney)
E. 47th Infantry Regiment (Smythe)

German Forces
I. Panzer Lehr Division (Bayerlein)
II. 5th Parachute Division (Wilke)

------- Planned
————— Actual

Meanwhile, the division's 60th Infantry Regiment would attack in the west in coordination with the 330th Regiment from the VIII Corps's 83d Infantry Division and secure the last division objective, the west flank of the corps's breakthrough. The 330th Regiment would seize the crossroads west of the 9th Infantry Division on the St-Lô–Périers road. Once the 330th had secured the intersection, it would set up a blocking position facing to the west and protecting the flank of the 9th Division.

Initially, the 9th Division's third regiment, the 39th Infantry, would hold its position until the 8th Infantry Regiment, 4th Infantry Division, had passed through its lines. The 39th would then follow the 47th Infantry Regiment and mop up any bypassed enemy. The 39th Regiment was also ordered to leave one battalion in an assembly area as the division's reserve.

In addition to assigning maneuver tasks and allocating forces, the division also had to develop a fire support plan. General Eddy was a strong believer in providing powerful artillery support for every attack. Ever since North Africa, he had been impressed with the artillery's ability to mass fire on a target, and he believed that artillery support would be particularly critical for this attack. Also, the division knew there were a number of enemy positions north of the road, and in fact on 20 July had requested air bombings to "clean out pockets of resistance that were left."[16] The missions, however, could not be flown because ground haze obscured the front. Concerned about these enemy positions, General Eddy hoped that artillery could substitute for the task.

Brigadier General Reese Maughan Howell, West Point 1915, commanded the 9th Division artillery. Much of the credit for developing the fire support plan went, however, to Howell's young, energetic executive officer, Lieutenant Colonel William Childs Westmoreland. The artillery plan called for the corps artillery's 240mm howitzer battalions to fire on German strongpoints in front of the 47th Infantry Regiment from H − 60 to H − 5. From H-Hour to H + 18, six artillery battalions would fire in front of the 47th Infantry Regiment as it advanced to the St-Lô–Périers road. In addition to supporting the attacking regiments, two artillery battalions were to provide preparatory fire for the 330th Infantry Regiment. The final part of the preparation included 10 minutes of fire on a 300-yard strip along the same road before the infantry charged across.

The 9th Infantry Division's fire support plan was the most ambitious of all the infantry divisions'. It suffered, however, from the same shortcoming as all the other artillery plans: the gunners did not know the precise location or condition of all the enemy units. There was no guarantee that the rounds would land on German positions or that the enemy would not be protected from the fire by field fortifications. Artillery rounds had to hit within 50 yards of an unprotected target to be effective. Precision fire could normally be obtained only by visual corrections from artillery observers, but all the 9th Division preparatory fire for Cobra would be unobserved. It remained to be seen how much the bombardment would help break down the German defenses. Only when the infantry had reached the enemy would it be known if the division's comprehensive fire plan had done any good.

Uncertain Start for the 47th Infantry Regiment

With the plan issued all that remained was to wait for the bombers. Everything seemed to be ready, but on 25 July the short bombings played havoc with the division's assault. Colonel George Winfered Smythe's 47th Infantry Regiment took the worst of this friendly fire. Colonel Smythe, West Point 1924, had commanded the 47th Infantry Regiment since North Africa.

After the aborted bombing on 24 July Colonel Smythe had launched his 2d Infantry Battalion, commanded by Lieutenant Colonel Woodrow W. Bailey, with A Company, 1st Battalion attached, to retake the ground given up before the bombing as a safety zone. The attack had met stiff resistance and heavy enemy artillery fire, and Colonel Smythe expected another tough fight on 25 July. To start the offensive, he elected to lead with a fresh unit, Lieutenant Colonel Donald C. Clayman's 3d Battalion. To help the battalion advance, regimental support included A Company, 746th Tank Battalion; C Company, 899th Tank Destroyer Battalion; B Company, 15th Combat Engineer Battalion; B Company, 9th Medical Battalion; and C Company, 87th Chemical Mortar Battalion. In addition, the 34th Field Artillery Battalion commanded by Lieutenant Colonel Alvar B. Sundin would be in direct support. When not firing for the division, the 196th Field Artillery Battalion would also provide reinforcing fire. Colonel Smythe hoped that these forces, in combination with the carpet bombing, would be enough to ease the advance of Lieutenant Colonel Clayman's 3d Battalion.

Colonel Smythe's confidence was shaken after the short bombings on 25 July. Clayman's 3d Battalion suffered terrible casualties. To make matters worse, every moment the 3d Battalion delayed its advance meant more time for the enemy to recover. Smythe had to make a quick decision. Would it be faster to reorganize the 3d Battalion and continue the advance or try to pass another unit through the disorganized battalion to lead the attack? Smythe made his choice immediately after receiving the first bombing reports. He expected stiff opposition on the enemy's main line of resistance, and it was unlikely that a battalion shattered by the friendly bombing would be able to fight its way through. He ordered the 1st Battalion, commanded by Lieutenant Colonel Wendel T. Chaffin, to pass through the 3d

Battalion and attack. In addition, after conferring with General Eddy, Colonel Smythe received the 1st Battalion, 39th Infantry Regiment, from the division reserve to replace Clayman's devastated 3d Battalion.

Meanwhile, at the 3d Battalion command post a stunned Lieutenant Colonel Clayman was wondering what to do next. The entire command section, except for himself and his executive officer, were wounded. At that moment, General Eddy appeared accompanied by two armed guards, carrying word that Clayman's battalion was to re-form and follow the attack. After surveying conditions in the battalion, Eddy shuttled back and forth between the 60th Infantry Regiment's command post and Smythe's headquarters assessing the damage and improvising changes.

General Eddy's actions on 25 July were one example of how division commanders, if they chose, could effectively influence a day's fighting, particularly at the outset of an operation. The division commander had to go to the critical point of the battle where he could observe the operation from the same perspective as the regiment and battalion commanders. Good commanders, like General Eddy, would work with commanders, not getting in the way and undercutting their leadership, but facilitating operations, speeding resources and reinforcements where they were needed most, and, most important, giving a more detached perspective to the pressure cooker of immediate combat decisionmaking. Eddy's favorite saying was, "Things are never half as good or half as bad as they look at first."[17] This battle seemed to fit that assessment. Despite the disasters and the difficult task ahead, he hoped that firm leadership and a steady hand from the regiment commanders would be able to get the plan back on track.

Although Colonel Smythe had made a timely decision, the confusion caused by the short bombing and the time required to move up the 1st Battalion postponed the attack until 12:30 P.M., a delay of an hour and a half. Even after the assault got under way bad news continued to come into Colonel Smythe's command post. At 1:00 P.M. the 1st Battalion reached the road north of Calentinerie, but met tough resistance from the enemy blocking the Tribehou–Marigny road.

Although the German forward positions had been marked for destruction by the 9th Infantry Division's artillery, they were still in place. This was surprising in light of the extensive artillery fire planned for the area, and in fact the artillery preparation, except for that of the luckless 957th Field Artillery hit by U.S. bombs, had been on schedule. Lacking precise target locations, however, the unobserved fire had failed to destroy or suppress the key front-line German defensive positions blocking the regiment's advance.

Colonel Smythe gave up any idea of executing the division's original plan of passing the 9th Reconnaissance Troop ahead to race south. The enemy had not been disrupted by the air and artillery attack. Smythe's 47th

Regiment was less than an hour into the offensive, and it was already clear that Cobra was not going to be a race to Marigny, but a typical day of fierce hedgerow fighting.

The 60th Infantry Regiment on the Move

Fortunately for the 9th Division, to the west of the 47th Regiment, the 60th Infantry Regiment's attack set off on schedule. Colonel Jesse Lewis Gibney, West Point 1918, had his 60th Regiment assault with two battalions abreast, the 2d Battalion in the east and the 3d Battalion in the west, supported by B Company, 746th Tank Battalion; B Company, 899th Tank Destroyer Battalion; C Company from Lieutenant Colonel John G. Schermerhorn's 15th Combat Engineer Battalion; C Company from Lieutenant Colonel Abraham S. Kaufman's 9th Medical Battalion; and D Company, 87th Chemical Mortar Battalion. The 60th Field Artillery Battalion was in direct support, with reinforcing fire from the 690th Field Artillery Battalion.

The obligatory barrage of German artillery and mortar fire greeted the assault. The fire, however, was far less than the division had seen during the aborted attack on 24 July, reflecting the severe shortages of the German artillery. The 60th Regiment's advance continued, but then slowed considerably when it encountered the first German positions. The regiment's 3d Battalion was stopped by machine gun fire and lost a tank to artillery fire at the crossroads southeast of Le Mesnil-Eury.

While enemy fire stopped the 3d battalion, the 60th Infantry Regiment's 2d Battalion commanded by Major Max Wolf continued to push forward despite enemy resistance. Major Wolf's battalion had been spared the worst of the short bombings, but the confusion and the Germans made difficult the start to the offensive. Moments after beginning the attack, Major Wolf realized his men would be facing another day of harrowing, and mortal, combat. As the first companies of the 2d Battalion moved to the attack, however, Major Wolf got some unexpected assistance. Captain Matt Urban, commander of the battalion's F Company (and still limping from a wound he had received earlier in the campaign), had hitched a ride from the hospital at Utah Beach in time to rejoin the unit and help lead the assault. Captain Urban had a reputation as a fearless and irrepressible leader; when he heard that a big attack was about to commence Urban commandeered a jeep and driver and headed for the front. The young captain's face was the first positive sign of hope Major Wolf had seen all day, and Urban's abrupt appearance reassured and heartened the men. More important, an extra leader proved to be an immeasurable help in organizing the advance.

An Unexpected Opportunity

On the west flank of the 60th Infantry Regiment, the 330th Infantry Regiment, 83d Infantry Division (temporarily attached to the 9th Infantry Division), also made some progress. In the first 40 minutes it had advanced 800 yards. After this initial success, however, the attack was held up by elements of the German 5th Parachute Division. The Germans stopped the 330th several hundred yards short of its objective at the crossroads along the St-Lô–Périers road.

The 330th Infantry Regiment's stalled advance left an unexpected gap between it and the 60th Regiment. At the same time, the 60th Regiment's progress left the 47th Infantry Regiment behind. The 60th Regiment's exposed flanks offered a chance for a German counterattack, but it also presented an opportunity for maneuver. Colonel Gibney, the 60th Infantry Regiment commander, now faced a serious situation. Should he reorient his attack to tie in more closely with the units on his flank and preclude any openings for a German counterstrike or should he push ahead? Remembering the importance of the division's objective for the success of the overall operation, he decided to push forward as quickly and aggressively as possible. Gibney sent Major Wolf's 2d Battalion around the regiment's open west flank to continue the drive south.

Wolf launched his command into unknown territory. Anything resembling the original plan was long gone. The maneuvers now were all ad hoc, and the situation his troops faced was totally unpredictable. They could be heading right into the teeth of a German counterattack, run straight into a prepared defense line untouched by the bombing, or maybe effortlessly skirt German defenses. Whatever they did, they would most likely be on their own, ahead of the regiment and with no friendly forces on either flank.

Major Wolf had to make some quick decisions. The faster the battalion moved, the better, but he knew he still had to keep control of the companies and maintain discipline. He was facing an unknown situation and he needed to be flexible. There would be little time to react, and the battalion would need all its forces ready to go in the direction it was needed. He ordered the battalion to slip the advance to the west and keep going.

The 2d Battalion skimmed the edge of the area blanketed by the carpet bombing, but ran into a German strongpoint, which one company managed to outflank. The rest of battalion followed quickly behind and continued the push forward. At 3:00 P.M. Wolf's battalion reached its objective near the town of Montreuil, where it held to wait for flank units to catch up. By the end of the day, Colonel Gibney's regiment had pushed back the remnants of the 5th Parachute Division and secured the west flank of the breakthrough.

The 60th Infantry Regiment's advance, spearheaded by Major Wolf's 2d Battalion, had also opened up an avenue for the 47th Infantry Regiment.

Colonel Smythe shifted his 1st and 3d Battalions to the west into the 60th Infantry Regiment's zone. By 3:00 P.M. the 1st Battalion reached a point southeast of Le Mesnil-Eury. At 4:00 P.M. the 1st Battalion's first elements finally crossed the St-Lô–Périers road. As the attack picked up momentum, Colonel Smythe committed the attached 1st Battalion, 39th Infantry Regiment, on his eastern flank. This battalion pushed south to the outskirts of La Chapelle-en-Juger, where it made contact with the 8th Infantry Regiment, 4th Infantry Division.

Finally, as night settled on the battlefield, the last battalion reached the front. Lieutenant Colonel Clayman's 3d Battalion, 47th Infantry Regiment, which had taken the worst of the short bombings, had made a hard night's march to catch up with the rest of the force. After recovering from the aerial bombardment the battalion had been on the move for 16 straight hours. It was now 4 A.M. Lieutenant Chester H. Jordan remembered that every time his platoon in K Company stopped he would fall asleep. Reaching the final position for the day, he passed the order from Lieutenant Colonel Clayman for the troops to dig in and had his men prepare positions outside a small church surrounded by recently dug German graves. The lieutenant also put half the men on guard, wanting 50 percent of the men on the alert. He recalled, however, "I am sure it was 0% in just a few minutes."[18] The lieutenant found a spot next to his men and joined in the sleep of the dead. The young lieutenant and the rest of the 47th Infantry Regiment had reached the high ground 1,000 yards south of the St-Lô–Périers road, but they were still over 2 miles short of the vital objective at Marigny.

Measuring What Can Be Done by One Tired Division

During the afternoon of 25 July General Eddy made his final rounds of the regimental command posts. At 5:45 P.M. he returned to division headquarters, where General Collins, VII Corps commander, joined him. Over dinner the two leaders reviewed the progress of the day's attack and, deciding the division could not carry through the attack to Marigny, discussed the plan for passing the 1st Infantry Division forward through Eddy's men of the 9th Division to complete the assault.

That evening General Eddy ordered the division's advance to halt. He did not want the lead units maneuvering at night with exposed flanks. On the move they lacked the power, and he did not have the reserves to fight off any unexpected counterattacks; this was one time that he would fail to come through for General Collins. The combination of German defenses and difficult terrain made it too tough to finish the job.

Still, a modicum of success was better than a bushel of disaster. Without question the 9th Division had dented the Panzer Lehr and 5th Parachute Divisions' defenses, and that the U.S. infantry had made any

progress at all after the casualties caused by the short bombings was a significant accomplishment. In particular, the 60th Infantry Regiment's
advance spearheaded by Major Wolf's 2d Battalion had demonstrated that
the division was still an aggressive, dependable fighting outfit.

Why did the 9th Infantry Division fail to reach its objective? Certainly
there were flaws in the division's plans. In particular, the artillery preparation that began the attack was inadequate: the unobserved artillery fire did
not, as the division had hoped, unhinge the Germans' forward defenses.

Commanders knew well that unobserved fire could often prove ineffective, because artillery had to hit within 50 yards to affect a target. The
artillery needed either a precise location or an observer who could adjust
fire onto targets to ensure that enemy positions were suppressed or
destroyed. Knowing the limitations of supporting fire, it is worth considering why the division bothered with preparatory artillery fire at all. Part of
the answer was in the psychological. The immense power of an artillery
barrage created the impression that guns were delivering a devastating
blow. The boom of firing howitzers and the crunch of exploding rounds
reassured the attacking troops. Part of the answer may also have been
moral. Why risk the life of a soldier when ordnance could do the job? After
all, commanders knew the general location of the enemy, and the possibility of an artillery round making a lucky hit seemed worth the chance when
the alternative was finding enemy positions only after German machine
guns cut down U.S. soldiers leading the attack. Together, moral and psychological factors seemed to suggest that a plan using unobserved fire was
better than no preparatory fire at all.

On the other hand, unobserved fire wasted the army's limited stocks of
ammunition and offered little opportunity to dislodge the enemy. Barrages
could unsettle and demoralize inexperienced soldiers, but experienced
fighters, such as the troops facing the 9th Infantry Division, would react
quite differently to artillery fire. They could tell, for example, by the dura-
tion and movement of the exploding rounds whether they were being
harassed by unobserved fire or whether they were facing observed fire and
an impending ground assault. Unobserved fire that did not directly affect
their location did little more than alert the Germans to an impending
ground operation. In contrast, accurate, observed fires coordinated directly
with a ground attack represented a serious threat to a defensive position.

Considering all the advantages and disadvantages of unobserved
preparatory fires, the 9th Division's fire plan was probably a wasted effort.
Commanders would have been better off massing their fire on precisely
located enemy positions, then husbanding their artillery and integrating
support more closely with the assaulting infantry.

Still, even accounting for missteps like the poorly designed artillery
preparatory fire, the failure of the 9th Infantry Division to seize its objectives is not apparent from judging the division's performance. When the

battle did not unfold as expected, regiment and battalion commanders modified their plans, exploiting the situation and opportunities at hand. In the same manner as leaders in the 30th and 4th Infantry Divisions, regiment and battalion commanders handled their units with discipline and confidence. Close to the front, armed with timely, relevant combat information, they made decisive, prudent decisions—changing the order of attack, shifting the route of advance, and adjusting plans as the situation required. Where they could, the unit commanders did everything possible to keep up the tempo of the attack and press the German defenses.

It was not that the division had done anything terribly wrong. But, then neither had Panzer Lehr's forward defenses. Not all battles end in clear-cut victories or defeats. Decisive victory requires applying overwhelming combat power at the decisive point, and in this case General Eddy lacked an advantage to give him that kind of success. Cobra provided an edge by disrupting communications and holding off German reinforcements with the carpet bombing. The carpet bombing had given the Americans at least a full day's march to assault the German lines before the enemy could organize an effective counterattack. But if the U.S. forces were not strong enough to break through the enemy's forward defenses, this advantage was wasted.

When it came to piercing the enemy's main line of resistance, the divisions were pretty much on their own, and here General Eddy was at a disadvantage. It was not that his commanders were overly cautious or lacked skill and initiative; what they lacked was the time and resources to get the job done. In contrast to the other assaulting infantry divisions, the 9th had a much more difficult mission against much greater opposition over very difficult terrain, without commensurately greater forces for the mission. When the generals measured out the combat power for this battle, General Eddy simply did not get enough for the job he had been handed.

Having a preponderance of power in an operation was useless if this force was not applied at the right time and place. Although Martin Blumenson and others have failed to emphasize this point, General Collins's apportioning of missions for the first phase of the attack was a significant flaw in the Cobra plan. Expecting the 9th Infantry Division to take Marigny in a lightning advance was thoroughly unrealistic.

General Eddy had understood well the magnitude of the challenge he faced. He had appreciated, perhaps more than any other senior commander, that the carpet bombing would not take out German forward defenses and that the task for breaking through would fall to the infantry. It was for that reason that Eddy had insisted on adding a third infantry division to the breakthrough attack, narrowing the responsibility for his own division. In fact, it was only with Eddy's urging that Collins had requested the additional division for the attack. Even with the addition of the 4th Infantry Division, the 9th Division's task in Cobra was impossible. General Eddy was right: the enemy's main line of resistance was too strong and the objectives too deep inside German defenses for one tired division.

The End of the Day—The State of the Battle

While the results of the day's fighting appeared ambivalent for the 9th Infantry Division, to Panzer Lehr Division they were an unqualified disaster. General Bayerlein found that his outposts north of the road were not badly hit by the bombing, and they offered some resistance. Farther north from the St-Lô–Périers road, however, things were far worse. When Bayerlein inspected his positions he described them as *mondlandschaft* (the surface of the moon). "I don't believe hell could be as bad as what we experienced," he later recalled.[19] Luckily, the regimental reserves in the main defense line were still in good shape and were committed at once. They had done most of the day's fighting for the division and to their credit slowed the 9th Infantry Division's advance considerably.

Initially, General Choltitz, the LXXXIV Corps commander, remained entirely in the dark with regards to the fate of the Panzer Lehr Division. Communications had gone with the first Allied bombs. Choltitz then had sent a runner to Bayerlein's headquarters, but received no answer. General Choltitz was worried.[20] He then ordered part of his corps reserve, a reinforced regiment of the 353d Division to attack from an area south of Périers toward La Chapelle-en-Juger. General Choltitz was not aware that he had just assigned these troops an impossible task. To succeed, the regiment would have to attack across the front of at least three U.S. divisions and the width of the Allied bombing box, an incredible feat.

Meanwhile, General Hausser, the Seventh Army commander, was also surprised and concerned. He was most worried about the ground between La Chapelle-en-Juger and Hebecrevon. It was the linchpin holding the II Parachute and LXXXIV Corps together. Hausser could accept being pushed back, but his defenses could not survive a major breach. A break in the line would lead to a repeat of the horrors on the Eastern Front where German units were regularly encircled and annihilated by the Soviet hordes.

To shore up the front, Hausser released part of the 275th Division to LXXXIV Corps to counterattack toward La Chapelle-en-Juger. General Schmidt, the 275th Division commander, ordered his 985th Grenadier Regiment with an infantry battalion and artillery and antitank support to make the attack. But U.S. air power prevented them from moving an inch. Unable to advance, the 985th Grenadier Regiment dug in northwest of Marigny and tried to set up a new line of defense.[21]

General Hausser had no idea of the inadequacy of his response. Although he had anticipated that a major attack west of the Vire River would be the Americans' main effort, he did not know how much force was massed against him. The problem, in addition to the breakdown in communications caused by the bombing, was that his intelligence gave no hint of the strength of the attacking U.S. force. In fact, the Germans' U.S. forces order of battle for 24 July was just plain wrong, showing that the U.S. VII Corps had only four divisions, rather than the six it actually contained. Hausser did not know that there were three infantry divisions attacking his front, because the faulty order of battle showed only two. In addition, the order of battle indicated only two divisions in reserve, whereas there actually were three poised to conduct the Americans' follow-on attack.[22] In total, the U.S. corps had about a quarter more infantry, twice the tanks, and four times the artillery that General Hausser suspected. If he had known the true ratio of forces, he would have quickly recognized how feeble his reserves were to handle the U.S. offensive.

Despite the Americans' overwhelming advantages, on the other side of the front, at General Bradley's U.S. First Army headquarters, there was scant optimism after the day's fighting. The tragic short bombings and the death of General McNair seemed to drain everyone's spirit. Bradley's aide, Major Hansen, and others discussed the lessons of the day, agreeing that using heavy bombers for tactical air support was probably not workable. General Eisenhower, who had come to observe the first day of the operation, declared, "I don't believe they [bombers] can be used in support of ground troops. I gave them the green light on this show, but this is the last one."[23]

The tragedy of the bombing had been bad enough, but for all that sacrifice the first reports from the front-line infantry divisions were less than positive, showing heavy fighting and, in some places, scant progress. In particular, General Eddy's failure to make much of an advance toward Marigny was worrisome. Still, there was little General Bradley could do at this point to affect the outcome of the operation; he would have to wait for dawn and see whether General Collins's forces could continue to exploit the dent they had made in the German lines on 25 July. The following day would also put Bradley's faith in the VII Corps commander, his tactical commanders, and the American soldiers in Normandy to the test.

General Collins too faced a difficult situation on the evening of 25 July. The corps on his flank had attacked all day but showed no dramatic successes. However, the fact that the other corps were not advancing rapidly was not all bad news, because that meant that the German Seventh Army was holding its positions, and was still vulnerable to penetration and envelopment. The U.S. VII Corps's infantry divisions, however, had not opened the door for the armor. In particular, the essential route to Marigny had not been cleared.

General Collins had to decide whether to commit his follow-on forces and use them to complete the breakthrough or to wait for the situation to develop. If he waited, the attack might lose its momentum and become bogged down in fighting off German counterattacks. If he pushed his forces in too early, he might feed in his exploitation force piecemeal or choke his attack by trying to push too much force into too narrow a space.

Collins had a reputation as the right kind of commander to make this kind of decision. He had long ago developed the habit of visiting each of his divisions every day to get the feel of the battle, trying to get closer to the front where he could gain fresh, relevant combat information on the situation from the perspective of regiment and battalion commanders. He knew that if he wanted to discover whether a battle was going to be won or lost, the place to find that out best was from the field commanders at the key points of the operation.

At the same time, General Collins always maintained communications with his headquarters, where he left matters in the able hands of his corps artillery commander, General Williston B. Palmer. General Collins's aide habitually carried a field telephone and would tap a division's line back to the rear to receive a situation update and issue any required orders.[24] In short, Collins's command style was always a balancing act—get to the front and see the battle from that vantage point, but never losing his own perspective or neglecting his responsibilities as corps commander.

General Collins knew that simply planning a battle was not enough. Even in a methodically thought-out operation like Cobra, commanders' estimates could prove wrong. The 9th Infantry Division's overambitious mission to take Marigny offered a good example. Once the battle was underway commanders needed to reassess the situation, get closer to the regiment and battalion commanders who were going to win or loss the day's fight, measure the conduct of combat, and decide when more decisions had to be made.

On 25 July Collins weighed the requirement for another decision. At the end of the day, he saw no signs of the usual determined German counterattacks. General Collins's reading of the battlefield told him that his tired but determined divisions had made enough progress to hold the flanks. But he needed an open road to Marigny to complete the penetration of the German defenses, and the 9th Infantry Division was not up to the task.

The first day's fighting had showed that it would take a lot more combat power to reach the vital high ground to the south. Therefore, Collins decided to give the 1st Infantry Division the mission to complete the breakthrough to Marigny, and 26 July would reveal whether or not he made the right decision. He passed the order to General Clarence Huebner, the 1st Infantry Division commander. Years later Collins wrote, "I have always said that an order is but an aspiration, a hope that what has been directed will come true."[25] That July day would be the start of General Collins's aspiration—the clash of armor.

Notes

1. Hansen, War Diary, 9 June 1944, MHI. For another example of General Collins's relationship with General Eddy during the Normandy campaign, see J. Lawton Collins, "Answers to Generalship Study Questionnaire," A Study of Requirements of Senior Commanders for Command-Control Support, 16 November 1966, p. 22, CARL.
2. Bradley, *A General's Life*, p. 136.
3. Martin Blumenson, *The Patton Papers*, p. 479.
4. Bradley, *A Soldier's Story*, pp. 101.
5. AGF Observer Immediate Report No. 5, CARL.
6. Unless otherwise noted, information on the Panzer Lehr Division is taken from interviews with Fritz Bayerlein in "An Interview with GENLT Fritz Bayerlein: Panzer Lehr Division Jan–28 Jul 44," pp. 1–4, 12–13, 34, 38, 48, and "An Interview with GENLT Fritz Bayerlein: Panzer Lehr Division at the Start of Operation COBRA," pp. 1–2; Headquarters, Air P/W Interrogation Detachment, Subject: Enemy Intelligence Summaries, 29 May 1945, Box 134, *The Papers of Carl A. Spaatz*, pp. 7–9, LC; *Panzer Lehr Meldungen, Befehle, Anordungen and Fernschreiben*, microfilm, T315, Roll 2292, NARA; *Armeeoberkommando 7, K.T.B. Entwurf und OB Chef-IA-Gespräche, 6 Juni–16 August 1944*, microfilm, T312, Roll 1568, pp. 185–189, NARA; Frank Kurowski, *Die Panzer-Lehr Division bei grösse deutsche Panzer Division und ihre Ausgabe: die Invasion zerschlagen— die Ardennen schlacht entscheiden*, pp. 117–128; Helmut Ritgen, *Die Geschichte der Panzer-Lehr-Division im Western, 1944–1945;* Headquarters, 7th Armored Division, U.S. Army, Appendix A to 7 Armd Div, Intelligence Summary No. 40, "Translation of Enemy Document, Panzer Lehr Division, Report on Experiences"; Hausser, "Normandy Seventh Army," p. 38; War Journal of Headquarters Army Group B, 1–31 July 1944, entry 24 July and 25 July 1944, microfilm, T311 Roll 1, NARA.
7. U.S. War Department, *Handbook on German Military Forces*, pp. 386–389. See also reports on armor tactics in *Panzer Lehr Meldungen, Befehle, Anordungen and Fernschreiben*, microfilm, T315 Roll 2292, NARA.
8. Hausser, "Normandy Seventh Army," p. 38.
9. Blumenson, *Breakout and Pursuit*, p. 238, contradicts Bayerlein's stating that the Panzer Lehr Division requested and received 200 replacements from the 275th Division. I could not confirm this and found no record of reinforcements before 25 July. On 24 July the 275d Division was still the Seventh Army reserve. These reserves were committed on 25 July. See *K.T.B. Entwurf und OB Chef-IA-Gespräche, 6 June–16 August 1944,* microfilm, T312, Roll 1568, pp. 185–189, NARA.
10. Pemsel, "Comments on the Study," pp. 4–5. There are no LXXXIV Corps records extant for this period. For General Choltitz's recollection of events prior to the breakout, see Dietrich Choltitz, "LXXXIV Corps (18 Jun–15 Jul 1944)," MS B-418. See also Dietrich Choltitz, *Un Soldat Parmi des Soldats.*
11. The English translation of this discussion can be found in Blumenson, *Breakout and Pursuit*, p. 239. See also *K.T.B. Entwurf und OB Chef-IA-Gespräche, 6 Juni–16 August 1944,* microfilm, T312, Roll 1568, pp. 187–189, NARA; War Journal of Headquarters Army Group B, 1–31 July 1944, entry 24 July 1944, microfilm, T311, Roll 1, NARA.
12. Unless cited otherwise, the 9th Infantry Division operations are taken from Headquarters, VII Corps, U.S. Army, The History of VII Corps, U.S. Army, Covering Operations in Normandy, France, from 1–31 July 1944, pp. 28–29;

Mittelman, *Eight Stars to Victory,* pp. 200–201; Headquarters, 9th Infantry Division, U.S. Army, G-3 Journal, 25 July 1944; Matt Urban and Charles Conrad, *The Hero We Nearly Forgot: The Matt Urban Story,* pp. 311–334; Activities of General Eddy, 20 July to 25 July 1944, USAIM; Jordan, Bull Sessions, pp. 42–43, MHI.

13. AGF Observer Immediate Report No. 23, p. 2, CARL.

14. The division's intelligence picture is drawn from Headquarters, 9th Infantry Division, U.S. Army, G-2 Reports, 17–20 July 1944.

15. AGF Observer Immediate Report No. 23, p. 3, CARL.

16. Activities of General Eddy, 20 July 1944, USAIM.

17. Ib Melchior, *Case by Case*, p. 40.

18. Jordan, Bull Sessions, p. 43, MHI.

19. *Report of the General Board: Air Power in the European Theater of Operations, Study No. 56,* pp. 16–17, CARL; Bayerlein, "An Interview with GENLT Fritz Bayerlein: Panzer Lehr Division Jan–28 Jul 44," pp. 47.

20. An officer from General Kluge's staff did contact General Bayerlein and stated that General Kluge wanted the line from St-Lô to Périers held at all cost. General Bayerlein answered, "With what?" See Paul Carell, *Invasion—They're Coming! The German Account of the Allied Landings and the 80-days Battle for France*, pp. 234–235. See also *Kriegestagebuch des Oberkommandos der Wehrmacht. Band IV. 1. Januar 1944–22. Mai 1945,* p. 327.

21. Hans Schmidt, "Battles in Northern France," MS A-973, p. 1.

22. *Heeresgruppe B* OB Map for 24 July, Intelligence Reports and Estimates of the Situation on the Front of Army Group B 1 July–1 December 1944, microfilm, T311, Roll 1, NARA.

23. Hansen, War Diary, 25 July 1944, MHI.

24. Gary Wade, transcribed "Conversations with General J. Lawton Collins," *Combat Studies Institute Report No. 5,* p. 6. See also J. Lawton Collins, "Answers to Generalship Study Questionnaire," A Study of Requirements of Senior Commanders for Command-Control Support, 16 November 1966, CARL; Palmer, Interview, pp. 65–66, MHI.

25. Collins, *Lightning Joe,* p. 243.

PART 3

A Clash of Armor:
26 to 30 July 1944

9

A Scheme of Maneuver

On 25 July, while the lead divisions from General Collins's VII Corps had penetrated the German defenses, the other corps in the U.S. First Army conducted supporting frontal attacks, holding in place the rest of the German Seventh Army's forces and preventing them from reinforcing the target area. On 26 July the U.S. First Army's other corps would continue their attacks while General Patton's Third Army prepared for the push to Brittany. At the same time, the U.S. VII Corps would focus on the task of finishing the breakthrough. To complete the operation one critical task remained—the most important task of all—prying open the gap in the German lines. That task fell to the 1st Infantry Division, the "Big Red One."

No U.S. infantry division commanded more attention than the 1st Infantry Division. After a distinguished record in World War I, the division had remained on active service, and it was a prestigious command. When it was sent to North Africa, Major General Terry de la Mesa Allen wore the green patch with the red "1" in the center.[1] Although he led a great division, General Allen had a talent for infuriating his senior commanders. He drove George Patton to distraction in North Africa, and during operations in Sicily he proceeded to annoy Patton's replacement, Omar Bradley. Neither general cared for Allen's histrionics nor his reputation for slack discipline. Eventually, Bradley relieved Allen, deciding that the division could fight just as well without its troublesome commander. In July 1943 the 1st Infantry Division got its new leader, Major General Clarence Huebner. Unlike most general officers, Huebner had begun his military career as an enlisted soldier, and had been commissioned as a lieutenant in 1916. By the end of World War I he was a highly decorated lieutenant colonel. In the peacetime army Huebner had picked up a reputation as a "flinty disciplinarian." In short, he was no Terry Allen.

General Huebner found a less than warm welcome when he took over his veteran division. Its soldiers resented the change in command and resented even more being slated for the Normandy campaign. After Sicily, rumor had had it that the division had done its share of the fighting and would be rotated back to the States; but, instead, the Big Red One was sent to England to prepare for Normandy. The invasion plans fueled a popular complaint: "The Army consists of the 1st Division . . . and eight million fucking replacements." Only after reaching the beaches in Normandy did the general and his division become accustomed to one another and get on with the business of war. On 13 July, after weeks of continuous combat, the division was pulled out of the line, but only to be resupplied and to get ready to attack again as part of Operation Cobra.

Rethinking the Route to Marigny

Before the battle, General Collins assigned the 1st Infantry Division what he believed the most critical task of Operation Cobra. The Big Red One would drive through the gap created by the 9th Infantry Division, turn southwest, and establish blocking positions between Coutances and Fontenay, trapping the Germans in front of the U.S. VIII Corps. This was to be the "inner ring" of the envelopment. General Collins directed that the division be ready to move on 2 hours' notice. He could not predict exactly when the breakthrough would come, but he did not want to waste a minute. To speed the advance, Huebner's infantry would go forward by truck and then dismount for the exploitation.

Collins also augmented the division with more combat power than any other force in the attack. This included a field artillery group, a chemical mortar company, and tank, antitank, and antiaircraft battalions. Collins also gave the division two very special units—a cavalry squadron and an armored brigade. The cavalry squadron was a unique force. Unlike other units that would normally be attached to a division, the 4th Cavalry Reconnaissance Squadron, led by Lieutenant Colonel John F. Rhoades, constantly shifted around the battlefield to wherever its special talents as a long-range reconnaissance and security force were needed most. For Cobra, the squadron would provide the Big Red One with a significant capability to extend the range of operations.

Combat Command B (CCB), 3d Armored Division, was an even more unusual supplement to the division. Adding an armored column made General Huebner's command the largest division in the operation, with six times more tanks than the average infantry division. All together, for Cobra, the 1st Infantry Division would be one big, combat-capable force.

General Huebner's plan for exploiting all that combat power was based on the 9th Infantry Division's attack penetrating the Germans' defenses.[2] Huebner expected that the 1st Infantry Division's main enemies would be the press of time and unexpected counterattacks rather than well-prepared

German strongpoints. As a result, he planned on pushing the 4th Cavalry Squadron ahead to Marigny as an advance guard, and its mission would be to move fast, find clear routes for the armor, and provide security. One troop would move east of the Tribehou–Marigny road, and the rest of the squadron would deploy west of the road. After reaching Marigny, the squadron would screen the division's movement and maintain contact with the U.S. 3d Armored and 9th Infantry Divisions. If the Germans launched a counterattack, the 4th Cavalry Squadron would be there to detect the enemy advance.

Behind the cavalry, CCB, 3d Armored Division, would lead the attack out of Marigny toward the division objective, followed by the 18th, 16th, and 26th Infantry Regiments. General Huebner divided the division's ultimate objective into the three subordinate objectives. The first was at Camprond. The second and third were along the high ground farther west. CCB would advance on each objective in turn, securing them until relieved by the 18th Infantry Regiment, which would hold the objectives until relieved by the 16th Infantry Regiment. The 26th Infantry Regiment (except for the 2d Battalion attached to the 3d Armored Division) would follow, eventually taking up a position between the first and second objectives. After the objectives were secured, CCB would attack north along a line from Coutances to Périers to disrupt the rear of the enemy defenses.

Huebner's plan was striking in two respects. First, it was incredibly complicated. The plan called for a combination of no fewer than five passages of lines. Second, and very remarkable, was that it overwhelmingly emphasized security at the expense of speed. Rather than CCB racing behind the Germans to cut their lines of communications, the plan called for a cautious process of inching forward into the enemy's rear. No unit was to move until another came from behind to relieve it, and the division was never to offer an exposed flank. It would also take a year and a day to reach the final objective. General Huebner may have been a great disciplinarian and a determined combat leader, but he had come up with a complicated, timid, awful plan. Its only saving grace was that the division never got a chance to execute it.

On 25 July the men of the 1st Infantry Division waited all day for an order to move. It never came. But rumors flew fast, some claiming the German defenses had held, others reporting that the roads had been wiped out by the bombing. The only thing known for sure was that it was a real SNAFU ("Situation normal, all fucked up").[3] Finally, a few minutes after 8:00 P.M., General Collins ordered the 1st Infantry Division to pass through the 9th Infantry Division on 26 July and continue the attack. But, rather than exploiting a penetration, Collins ordered the Big Red One to become the point of the spear, complete the rupture in the enemy lines, and move on to capture Marigny.

Martin Blumenson portrays General Collins's decision to send in the

1st Infantry Division as a bold "gamble," committing part of his exploitation force before the situation was "ripe for an exploitation maneuver."[4] In truth, Collins had little option. It was clear that General Eddy's 9th Infantry Division would not be able to reach Marigny rapidly, so Collins had no other choice than to throw more forces in to complete the breakthrough. He undoubtedly made the right decision, but it was hardly a great risk or the mark of a truly aggressive commander. Rather, it reflected a reasonable attempt to overcome a serious mistake in not initially weighting Eddy's 9th Division with enough combat power to carry its attack all the way to the objectives at Marigny.

The only risk in Collins's decision, as Blumenson admits, was the possibility of congestion—too much force trying to squeeze into too narrow an attack zone. Ensuring that that did not happen would be the responsibility of the 1st Infantry Division's commander, Clarence Huebner. Huebner and his staff spent the night revamping their plan and studying intelligence reports. From the attacks by the 9th, 4th, and 30th Infantry Divisions, Huebner had a good idea of the enemy conditions along the front. Resistance was "moderate" with some artillery and heavy-weapons fire. Most important, tanks were not employed in organized counterattacks but in small uncoordinated groups. Some prisoners had even confessed that their line was only a thin shell and that there was nothing to keep the Americans from breaking through.

In fact, conditions behind the German lines were as desperate as the Americans suspected. If the 1st Division had been privy to Ultra reports, it would have known that LXXXIV Corps had reported very heavy casualties.[5] Still, even without that detailed knowledge there was sufficient evidence to indicate the turmoil in the German defenses. Air reconnaissance, for example, showed enemy troops behind the lines drifting south. The Germans could be broken, but a study of the map showed that it would not be an effortless task. Ahead of the division, on either side of the Tribehou–Marigny road, lay the same spider's web of hedgerow countryside and Panzer Lehr Division defenses that had frustrated Eddy's 9th Infantry Division. Intelligence also reported that Panzer Lehr antitank and artillery units were setting up around the road junctions in Marigny.[6]

The weather prediction offered no comfort: the forecast for the next few days was for generally overcast skies with low clouds and intermittent rain. The weather report suggested the division might lose one of its real advantages in the coming attack—dedicated tactical air support. Despite all the airplanes available ready to respond to calls from the Big Red One, it did not look as though the weather would allow much chance to employ them.

Breaking what remained of the German defenses would be a task for a combination of infantrymen and tankers, and General Huebner believed the situation called for a new plan. It would not do to lead with the 4th Cavalry

Reconnaissance Squadron. The division would have to fight its way through with CCB and the 18th Infantry Regiment attacking abreast, while the 4th Cavalry Squadron followed to screen the flanks and the 16th and 26th Infantry Regiments trailed as reserve. Huebner's new attack plan again emphasized caution and security. By pushing two regiments through a narrow zone Huebner minimized the risk of exposed flanks and got a lot of combat power into the fight early, but the plan also left limited room and opportunity to maneuver. (Figure 9.1 shows the plan of attack for the U.S. 1st Infantry Division.)

Ten minutes before midnight, the division issued the new scheme of maneuver. In the CCB headquarters, Colonel Truman E. Boudinot briefed his commanders with enthusiasm. "We're going to make a breakout of the dammed beachhead," he announced, "and it's got to be successful even if it means the annihilation of CCB."[7] A World War I veteran, Colonel Boudinot had a reputation for the characteristic flamboyance of armor leaders in the Pattonesque tradition. Just after Boudinot took over CCB, one officer remarked that the new commander made quite an impression. Colonel Boudinot "had a faculty for appearing dapper in whatever uniform he chose to wear. . . . He carried a stick (later replaced by a riding crop), which he used as a pointer on the maps."[8]

The CCB commander sketched out the task forces' routes and objectives. They were going past Montreuil down the Tribehou–Marigny road, through Marigny, and onto the high ground north of that town. CCB would then cut west through the 1st Division's objectives down the main road toward Coutances. The advance would have to cover more than 18 miles. Colonel Boudinot wanted to move fast. The armored infantry would stay mounted and only dismount if heavy opposition was met. Isolated enemy units would be bypassed.

Boudinot planned to lead his attack with the 33d Armored Regiment's reconnaissance company, under Lieutenant James Cleveland, reinforced by a platoon of medium tanks. Behind it followed Task Force Roysdon and Task Force Lovelady. Task Force Roysdon consisted of D Company, 33d Armored Regiment; D Company, 36th Armored Infantry Regiment; and headquarters, 2nd Battalion, 33d Armored Regiment. Task Force Lovelady contained E Company, 33d Armored Regiment; E Company, 36th Armored Infantry Regiment; and headquarters, 2d Battalion, 36th Armored Infantry Regiment. Each task force had a battery of Lieutenant Colonel George C. Garton's 391st Armored Artillery Battalion attached, as well as a company of self-propelled tank destroyers from the 703d Tank Destroyer Battalion, and a platoon from the 23d Armored Engineer Battalion. In addition to the ground power, if the weather cleared, the army air forces promised a constant stream of four P-47 Thunderbolts to cover the armored column's advance.

On the night of 25 July the 1st Infantry Division's 18th Infantry

Figure 9.1   Attack of the 1st Infantry Division

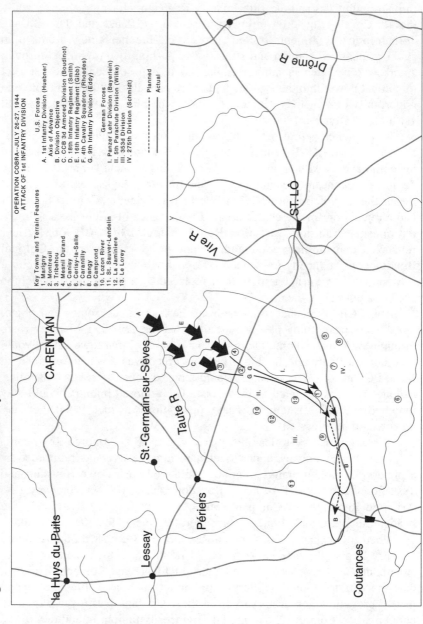

OPERATION COBRA—JULY 26-27, 1944
ATTACK OF 1st INFANTRY DIVISION

Key Towns and Terrain Features
1. Marigny
2. Montreuil
3. Tribehou
4. Mesnil Durand
5. Canisy
6. Cerisy-la-Salle
7. Carantilly
8. Dangy
9. Camprond
10. Lozon River
11. St. Sauveur-Lendelin
12. La Jaminiere
13. Le Lorey

U.S. Forces
A. 1st Infantry Division (Huebner)
   Axis of Advance
B. Division Objective
C. CCB 3d Armored Division (Boudinot)
D. 16th Infantry Regiment (Smith)
E. 18th Infantry Regiment (Gibb)
F. 26th Infantry Regiment (Seitz)
F. 4th Cavalry Squadron (Rhoades)
G. 9th Infantry Division (Eddy)

German Forces
I. Panzer Lehr Division (Bayerlein)
II. 5th Parachute Division (Wilke)
III. 353d Division
IV. 275th Division (Schmidt)

- - - - - Planned
———— Actual

Regiment, commanded by Colonel George Smith Jr. also prepared for the assault on the German lines. Smith's regiment would advance past Mesnil-Durand, east of the Tribehou–Marigny road, with the 1st, 2d, and 3d Battalions in column. The force would be supported by the 32d Field Artillery Battalion; Battery C, 103d Antiaircraft Artillery Automatic Weapons Battalion; Company B from Lieutenant Colonel William B. Gara's 1st Engineer Combat Battalion; B Company, 1st Medical Battalion; one platoon from D Company, 1st Medical Battalion; a detachment from the 1st Signal Company; B Company, 634th Tank Destroyer Battalion (self-propelled); B Company, 635th Tank Destroyer Battalion (towed); B Company from Lieutenant Colonel Wallace J. Nichols's 745th Tank Battalion; and the 1st Battalion, 33d Armored Regiment, 3d Armored Division.

Since the German defenses had not been penetrated in depth, the 18th Infantry Regiment's infantry would walk rather than be trucked into battle. To speed the attack, Colonel Smith directed that the troops move closer to the front, over half a mile farther south. To help speed the move, the VII Corps ordered the 9th Infantry Division to hold off evacuating wounded until the 18th Infantry Regiment had cleared the roads and was set in its new positions. While all this shifting was taking place, bombardment from the 9th Infantry Division artillery drew enemy return fire, peppering the road and holding up the 18th Infantry Regiment's move. By the time the firing was stopped and the troops got to their new positions, it was 1:00 A.M., more than 2 hours for the short walk to the front and a sleepless night for the infantry.

At 5:45 A.M. the VII Corps added another complication to preparations for the attack: if the weather cleared it would have another air strike on Marigny. The corps artillery planned to mark the no-bomb line with smoke at 2-minute intervals beginning 5 minutes before the attack. The air strike meant greater coordination, and the 1st Infantry Division had to make sure that everyone knew the no-bomb line's location and that the division artillery did not shoot any smoke rounds until it was time to mark the bomb run. The coordination had to be done quickly: the attack was to begin in just over an hour.

The 18th Infantry Regiment on the Road to Marigny

The next morning, on 26 July, at 7:00 A.M. the 18th Infantry Regiment and CCB attacked. At the 18th Regiment command post Colonel Smith was anxious to get the offensive moving. Colonel Boudinot, the CCB commander, planned to push south fast, and Colonel Smith did not want his walking infantry to fall too far behind CCB's rolling armor.

The first indications of the day left Colonel Smith hopeful that his men would be able to keep pace with the tankers. Less than a mile north of the St-Lô–Périers road, Smith's 18th Infantry Regiment reported making contact with the U.S. 8th Infantry Regiment, 9th Infantry Division, and passing quickly through its lines. At 7:15 A.M. the 18th Regiment's 1st Battalion reported first contact with the enemy, a force of about 150 German soldiers south of Mesnil-Durand. Smith ordered them bypassed and mopped up by the 3d Battalion.

The news coming into General Huebner's 1st Infantry Division command post was equally encouraging. Attacking units were hitting pockets of resistance rather than impervious belts of interlocking German positions. At 9:00 A.M. the U.S. 32d Field Artillery Battalion reported knocking out an enemy antitank gun, another isolated position. This mission was the first of only eight that the gunners would fire all day. The fact that the infantry was not requiring heavy fire support was another very good sign.

As in most battles, however, news was never uniformly good or bad. There was still no word on the progress of CCB or the bombing of Marigny. Colonel Smith feared his regiment was being left behind. Meanwhile, it took an hour and a half for the 18th Infantry Regiment's follow-on units to clean out the Germans bypassed at Mesnil-Durand and link up with the 1st Battalion. In addition, the regiment's advance still had not reached the St-Lô–Périers road. Despite the "rhino" metal hedgerow cutters fitted on the attached tanks from B Company, 745th Tank Battalion, the countryside was as difficult to navigate as ever—and to make matters worse the roads were cratered by bombs.

The 1st Infantry Division command post reported that "they are having a helluva time with the roads." One of the routes that the division had planned to use appeared to no longer exist. A combat engineer described the scene looking like "the craters of the moon . . . everything has been flattened. The road is chewed to pieces."[9]

Before the carpet bombing for Operation Cobra, General Bradley had requested that the air forces use light 100-pound bombs and Air Marshal Leigh-Mallory's directive had declared that "cratering is not acceptable." Despite these precautions both the fighters and the heavy aircraft planned for and used ordnance that ranged up to 500-pound bombs. The result was that the carpet bombing had demolished the route to Marigny. Aerial photographs showed that the road had been cut in at least twenty-five places by exploding bombs.[10]

Fixing roads quickly become a high priority. The division ordered all its engineer companies to the front to fill in the craters. Engineer Corps bulldozers cleared away the debris; dump trucks and bulldozers filled the holes with rubble; the dozers then compacted the fill and covered it with a layer of gravel or crushed rock. The task was not complicated, but it took time and effort, slowing the advance.

CCB's Dash to Nowhere

While the 18th Infantry Regiment stumbled over broken ground, Colonel Boudinot found that his CCB's breakout was not proceeding with the dash he had hoped for. In fact, the tankers' progress had been no quicker than the advance of the 18th Infantry Regiment. CCB's column was still north of Montreuil on the Tribehou–Marigny road, and slowed down by a fair amount of enemy fire from the flanks. Bomb craters impeded CCB's advance as well. The lead tank mounted with a 'dozer blade filled in the holes as the column advanced, but a half-hour after the attack started enemy artillery fire crippled the 'dozer tank, slowing the advance even more. Finally, at 10:35 A.M., CCB made contact with the 18th Infantry Regiment and the two units moved abreast toward Marigny. In the next few hours, their attacks made slow but steady progress.

The Enemy Reacts

While the 1st Infantry Division's attack struggled to pick up momentum, General Choltitz, the LXXXIV Corps commander, and General Hausser, the commander of the German Seventh Army, were trying to forestall any U.S. advance. General Choltitz had committed the last of his reserves, the remainder of the 353d Division, from south of Périers eastward toward Montreuil on 25 July. After moving 6 miles under the cover of early morning darkness, the force set up positions on the outskirts of the town and waited to spring on the Americans.

The 353d Division was going into battle with the odds against it. The division had been fighting on the Normandy front since 4 July. By 25 July the division was a tired outfit. The Seventh Army listed the division's strength as little more than five weak infantry battalions with only sixty men per company, less strength than half a U.S. infantry regiment. To make matters worse the division had just two weak artillery battalions for support.

Meanwhile, the only other force available to oppose the U.S. 1st Infantry Division was General Hans Schmidt's 275th Division, the Seventh Army reserve.[11] Having fought on the front since 11 July, the 275th Division was also understrength. In truth, from his command post at a farm southwest of Dangy, General Schmidt had very little to command. His force had been distributed piecemeal throughout the front. Battle Group Heintz was holding down the right wing of the Panzer Lehr Division. The 983d Regiment was near Canisy, and the 985th Regiment, except for one battalion, was southeast of Marigny. This battalion was southeast of St-Lô guarding the left flank of the 352d Division on the east bank of the Vire

River. The division artillery was under LXXXIV Corps's control, except for one battalion supporting the 5th Parachute Division.

General Hausser ordered General Schmidt to reinforce the front on the line from Hebecrevon to La Chapelle-en-Juger with the last of the 985th Regiment, but the regiment's movement was stopped cold by air attacks, and the Germans had to shift to a less ambitious effort—helping Panzer Lehr hold the high ground northwest of Marigny. The Seventh Army also ordered General Schmidt's 983d Regiment from positions near Canisy into the counterattack with the 353d Division. In addition, Hausser threw in the last of his reserves, a tank company and a company of infantry from the 2d SS Panzer Division. Even though the forces were modest, both Choltitz and Hausser believed that they would be enough to limit the U.S. forces' penetration. Both were still unaware of the size of the U.S. force pushing toward Marigny.

Unfortunately for the Germans, when dawn came on 26 July the promise of poor weather turned out to be wrong. Rather than overcast, dark skies, it was a clear day with only occasional intermittent showers. U.S. planes were out in full force: six groups of aircraft, each with 36 medium bombers, hit the northernmost part of the division zone near Marigny. P-47s supporting CCB attacked the enemy tanks south of Marigny that had been blocking the road into the town. These attacks quickly dispersed the Germans, leaving at least one tank smoking. This was only the beginning.

General Bayerlein, the Panzer Lehr Division commander, estimated losing 1,200 men from the constant fighter attacks in his rear area from Carantilly to Cerisy-la-Salle and along the Canisy–Dangy road. Throughout the morning air attacks rained havoc on German positions, and in fact, the U.S. 1st Infantry Division never felt the force of the 275th and 353d Division counterattacks because the German columns were crushed by U.S. air power. General Schmidt, the 275th Division commander, summed up the situation by saying, "All movements, even in the rear area were paralyzed."[12] His troops could not get through to counter the U.S. forces' penetration.

CCB Struggles Forward

While air attacks cleared the way to Marigny, when CCB's reconnaissance company, under the command of Lieutenant Cleveland, reached the town it found signs of organized defenses. Two German 75mm towed antitank guns blocked the main road near Montreuil, but the company skillfully outflanked the guns, destroying them and taking twelve prisoners. With the road open, CCB's main body was on the outskirts of Marigny by late afternoon, but there it found the way blocked by a handful of Mark IV tanks and self-propelled guns. Colonel Boudinot's advance had hit what was left of the moribund counterattack against the U.S. advance, two companies of the 2d SS Panzer Division and the 353d Division.

The CCB commander did not know that U.S. air attacks had spared him having to fight off a German armored counterattack. To Boudinot the scattered German positions his men encountered were just some more frustrating obstacles blocking his cavalry dash to Marigny. So CCB's air support parties called for additional air strikes. After U.S. fighters hit the enemy positions, the column tried to swing west of the roadblock, but German fire held it back despite the air support. Lieutenant Colonel Roysdon's task force was no closer than a mile west of the town. Not wanting to lose momentum, Boudinot ordered Task Force Lovelady, commanded by Lieutenant Colonel William B. Lovelady, to move up and reinforce Lieutenant Colonel Roysdon's tankers. But before the attack started Colonel Boudinot had second thoughts. With darkness approaching the armored columns would be vulnerable to German antitank weapons, and he did not want Germans sneaking up and ambushing his tanks. He ordered the command to hold up and continue the attack at first light.

Behind CCB, the 4th Cavalry Squadron (less troop C) received word that the attack had ground to a halt. The squadron set up a screen on the division boundary along the high ground west of the Marigny–Tribehou road. A Troop stopped near Les Hérouards. B Troop covered the road from Marigny toward Tribehou. The meager day's advance had come to an end.

The End of the Day

Even though CCB had stopped for the night, division told Colonel Smith, the 18th Infantry Regiment commander, that Boudinot's armor was still on the move. Coupled with a rumor that U.S. tanks had been spotted in Marigny as early as 2:05 P.M., Smith concluded that the town was secure and that his attack was again lagging. Despite approaching darkness, Smith decided to continue and swing east of the town to take the crucial high ground beyond. With his 1st Battalion still leading the advance, the 18th Regiment skirted between Marigny and the border with the 8th Infantry Regiment, 4th Infantry Division. At 7:00 P.M. the 1st Battalion reported receiving mortar and small-arms fire, but encountering no organized ground resistance. The infantry pressed on and at midnight sent back word it was at the objective above Marigny. The 8th Regiment also reported that the 3d Battalion was on the outskirts of the town. At last, by the end of the day on 26 July, the 1st Infantry Division had Marigny—or did it?

Reports of progress near Marigny encouraged Bradley and Collins. In fact, reports from across the U.S. First Army front on 26 July were uniformly good.[13] On the VII Corps's west flank the VIII Corps had been attacking with three infantry divisions abreast. The divisions had made modest progress, with forward units reaching the Lessay–Périers road, pressing elements of the 17th SS Panzergrenadier and 2d SS Panzer Divisions (with the 6th Parachute Regiment attached) and preventing them from threatening the U.S. VII Corps's flank. Instead, the enemy forces were withdrawing steadily south.

Meanwhile, General Eddy's 9th Infantry Division had established control over the shoulder of the VII Corps's breakthrough. Despite giving ground over to the 1st Infantry Division for the attack to Marigny, the 9th Division had finished the day more than 2 miles south of the St-Lô–Périers road. Working in tandem with Allied air power, the division had also helped blunt the German 353d Division's aborted counterattack. Perhaps the 9th Division's greatest accomplishment of the day, however, was that it had cleanly passed the 1st Infantry Division through its own lines and kept the routes open for the advance south.

At the same time, to the 1st Infantry Division's east, General Barton's 4th Infantry Division continued its attack where it had left off the day before, driving on to La Chapelle-en-Juger. By day's end, the 4th Infantry Division took the town, pushing 5 miles south of the St-Lô–Périers road. With the help of U.S. air strikes, 4th Division units were cleanly through the Germans' main line of resistance and chasing what was left of the Panzer Lehr artillery and the 985th Regiment, 275th Division, off the battlefield.

On the same day General Hobbs's 30th Infantry Division took an important prize. After a day of tough fighting division elements were 2 miles beyond their initial objective and across the Coutances–St-Lô road, splitting the LXXXIV–II Parachute Corps boundary. The last of Battle Group Heintz, by now only 200 men, withdrew in the face of the advance. Battle Group Kentner also fell back, and in the withdrawal Colonel Kentner was struck by small-arms fire, was captured, and died of wounds.

While the 30th Infantry Division held the door open, General Brooks's 2d Armored Division drove toward St-Gilles to begin the outer ring of the encirclement. By midafternoon, the division was in the town and heading south against light opposition. The 2d Armored Division was moving so fast that when the 897th Grenadier Regiment counterattacked from the east to shore up the II Parachute Corps's flank all the regiment found was a smattering of the Panzer Lehr Division's rear-echelon units near Canisy and charging columns of U.S. armor. During the night, the German regiment cautiously withdrew to Soignes, giving the Americans undisputed control of the German intercorps boundary.[14]

Of all the good news, the report that the 1st Infantry Division was in Marigny was considered the most important. The stories of tanks in Marigny had reached all the way to U.S. First Army headquarters. After his initial pessimism the day before, by the end of 26 July, General Bradley believed that a breakthrough had been made. In addition, intelligence reports indicated that the Germans were reacting to the penetration and committing the last of their reserves. This meant that the enemy defenses were being drawn even tighter. First Army G-2, Colonel Dickson, confided to Bradley's aide, Major Hansen, that "if we are able to make a break through we may be able to go on through for some considerable distance."[15] Even General Patton, making a brief visit to Bradley's headquarters, was apparently impressed by the First Army's achievement. Before the big attack Patton had privately concluded that Bradley's plan was "timid," but he now publicly mused that he needed to get his Third Army into the fight quickly, before the war was over. General Bradley was the most pleased of all; he considered Cobra well on its way to being an unqualified success.

U.S. forces in Marigny meant that the breakthrough was complete. Now the VII Corps commander was ready for his next big decision—completing the encirclement. He ordered General Watson's 3d Armored Division (less CCB) to roll on 27 July, charging through the gap between St-Gilles and Marigny to complete the envelopment's outer ring. General Collins redrew the boundary between the 9th and 1st Infantry Divisions to make room for the 3d Armored Division. He also ordered the 1st Infantry Division to continue its attack through the night. He was in a hurry to push past Marigny and close the door on the retreating Germans. The VII Corps was so confident of success that the 18th Field Artillery Group reinforcing the 1st Infantry Division artillery was swapped for one battalion, the 188th Field Artillery. The infantry would no longer need heavy artillery support because it was in a fast war of movement now.

Although General Collins believed he had chosen a prudent and low-risk course of action, there was a problem with his decision. The pivotal piece of information he had been waiting for, the news that Marigny had been taken, would turn out to be 100 percent wrong. The Germans still held Marigny. In sending in the remainder of the 3d Armored Division, Collins was crowding more forces into the gap, leaving less and less room for maneuver. At the same time, as the last of his armor moved into battle, Collins irrevocably committed himself to a course of action that continued the VII Corps's main effort toward the west to complete the envelopment according to the original plan for Cobra.

Preparing for Dawn

Anticipating success on 27 July, the 1st Infantry Division commander, Clarence Huebner, changed his plan again to speed up the division's attack even more. He issued new orders at midnight. Taking advantage of the ground opened up by moving the 9th and 1st Infantry Division boundary, CCB would turn immediately toward Camprond to encircle the enemy, while the 18th Infantry Regiment finished securing Marigny. After taking the town, the regiment would send a battalion to relieve the armor at Camprond, and CCB would finish the drive toward Coutances. Meanwhile, the 16th Infantry Regiment would swing east of the 18th Infantry Regiment around Marigny and shadow CCB's left rear all the way to Coutances, establishing blocking positions north of the town. At the same time, the 4th Cavalry Reconnaissance Squadron would continue to screen the division's west flank, while Colonel John F. R. Seitz's 26th Infantry Regiment would remain in reserve.

All these plans and decisions were based on the belief that the 1st Infantry Division had Colonel Boudinot's CCB and two of the battalions from Colonel Smith's 18th Infantry Regiment controlling Marigny. In fact, CCB's columns were still a mile and a half short of Marigny. The 3d Battalion, 18th Infantry Regiment, was also still well short of its objective. Meanwhile, the 1st Battalion, 18th Infantry Regiment, had discovered that it was on the wrong hill and not overlooking Marigny at all. To say that the information flow to higher headquarters had been less than perfect would be an understatement. The commanders had done a miserable job of tracking and managing the battle.

On 27 July, at 6:00 A.M., still unaware that it did not control Marigny, the 1st Division resumed the offensive. The first news received at the division command post did not indicate a good start. At 6:40 A.M. the 3d Battalion, 18th Infantry Regiment, reported that not only was it short of its objective in Marigny, but when it sent a company into the town the two lead platoons were cut off.

The 16th Infantry Regiment Tries to Join the Fight

At 7:00 A.M., on 27 July, the 16th Infantry Regiment reported problems as well. Even though it was finally committed to battle, there was no place for it to go. The front was swamped with men and vehicles, and at one point, the 16th Regiment's 1st Battalion had to halt its attack while a convoy of vehicles pushed through to carry critical supplies of gasoline and ammunition to CCB. After allowing the trucks to pass, the 16th Regiment not only had to compete for space with the rest of the 1st Infantry Division, but also had to make room for 3d Armored Division's CCA attack.

Lieutenant Colonel Frederick W. Gibb, the 16th Infantry Regiment commander, had a tough task ahead. In addition to his own battalions he had the 7th Field Artillery Battalion; B Battery, 103 Antiaircraft Artillery Automatic Weapons Battalion; A Company, 1st Medical Battalion; A Company, 1st Engineer Combat Battalion; a detachment for the 1st Signal Company; Reconnaissance and A Companies, 634th Tank Destroyer

Battalion (self-propelled); A Company, 635th Tank Destroyer Battalion (towed); and A and B Companies, 87th Chemical Mortar Battalions. Lieutenant Colonel Gibb had to figure out how to pack all these units on the few overcrowded roads leading south.

At 7:15 A.M. the first good news of the day came in, with the 16th Infantry Regiment reporting that somehow its battalions had found room to maneuver and that "they are now going in." Open trucks shuttled the regiment's soldiers to dismount points. Rain pelted the column as it threaded its way along the roads jammed with vehicles of all descriptions. The rain "felt as if someone were throwing a handful of rice in our face," one soldier complained.[16] It was a miserable day to go to war. The 16th Infantry Regiment dismounted among apple orchards and hedgerows, the men forming up and marching toward the front.

Trailing after the battle, the men were slowed more by minefields and a sea of mud than by the Germans. When, occasionally, small-arms fire halted the advance the companies would take up skirmish formation and drive off some small, isolated enemy force bypassed in the general breakthrough. Then the move continued, with pauses for brief showers of German artillery fire, the clash of tanks, or an accidental strafing by U.S. planes.

The 4th Cavalry Squadron on the Flank

While the 16th Infantry Regiment advanced the 4th Cavalry Squadron spread out on the west flank of the division. B Troop headed toward La Jaminière along the Lozon River. From there, the troop was to head southwest to secure an objective across the Marigny–St-Sauveur–Lendelin road and cover CCB's move toward Coutances. The troop found Germans holding the river crossing at La Jaminière. This resistance ended the Americans' forward progress. B Troop spent the rest of the day sparring with the Germans and looking for another crossing site, as well as sending out patrols to tie in with the 9th Infantry Division. At the same time A Troop, 4th Cavalry Squadron, headed northwest. En route they found about a hundred German defenders and tanks concentrating at Le Lorey, a mile and a half west of Marigny. The sight of organized German defenders repositioning themselves to the south should have been a sure sign that the Germans west of the breakthrough were beginning to react to the penetration and that the U.S. envelopment of the west wing of the German LXXXIV Corps was in doubt.

A Troop spent the rest of the day in bitter combat with the Germans, as well as skirmishing with enemy elements retreating in the face of the advance by CCB, 3d Armored Division. A troop received help from E

Troop's assault guns and Lieutenant Colonel George C. Garton's B Battery, 391st Artillery Battalion, positioned only a few hundred yards away. During the firefight, available artillery personnel went as infantry to aid A troop, while the remainder continued to fire the guns to knock out German tanks. The 1st platoon, A Troop, lost four vehicles, including two tanks. The 3d platoon lost every vehicle, except for four of its armored cars. To make the troop's task even more difficult, while it continued to fight the Germans, orders came from the 1st Division adding another mission—reconnoitering the secondary roads west from Marigny to CCB's objective north of Camprond. The division had changed the direction of CCB's attack again. The Big Red One was taking the war to the west.

The Road "Away" from Marigny—CCB Heads West

While the 4th Cavalry Squadron skirmished along the Lozon River, CCB resumed its attack on 27 July with Task Force Lovelady and Task Force Roysdon advancing abreast, led by the intrepid Lieutenant Cleveland's reconnaissance company reinforced with two squads of engineers. After contacting A Troop, 4th Cavalry Squadron, the force continued to head west on the road out of Marigny as the troop guarded its flank. While the cavalry squadron battled with the Germans on the division's flank, the weather cleared and CCB made good use of air cover to aid its advance. The planes bombed and strafed enemy positions, radioing the German ground locations to CCB. In turn, when the armor hit trouble spots it would call in an air strike and then continue to advance. After moving 4 miles in 4 hours (practically a road march in hedgerow country) CCB turned north near La Chapelle and headed across country straight for Camprond. There CCB found open ground for the first time in the operation.

Colonel Boudinot's CCB finally reached the Big Red One's first objective (Hill 177) at 3:40 P.M. Again there were problems. The bare gravel and clay on the hillside made it difficult for the infantry to dig in, and occasional German artillery fire did not make the job easier. In addition, supplies, particularly fuel and ammunition, were running short. The growing number of prisoners the column had picked up along the way was also becoming an unmanageable burden. There was little CCB could do on its own to solve these problems. Colonel Boudinot would have to wait for the resupply column to thread its way through enemy forces and friendly traffic to deliver fuel and ammunition and take back the enemy prisoners.

Late that night, a convoy of twenty-one trucks escorted by a company of medium tanks and squads of military police reached the objective. Getting the trucks to the front had proved to be a little microwar in itself, battling enemy troops to clear the way and squabbling with friendly units for room to maneuver, justifying American fears that the crushing traffic on the Normandy roads might slow the attack. Finally reaching CCB, the trucks delivered their supplies and the military police loaded the prisoners into the empty vehicles for the equally perilous return trip. The resupply solved the immediate supply crisis, but the troops at the objective still had orders to wait for relief from Colonel Smith's 18th Infantry Regiment before continuing the attack. It was a frustrating time: the longer they waited, the more time the Germans in front of the U.S. VIII Corps had to retreat through Coutances.

The 18th Infantry Regiment at Marigny

The reason that the 18th Infantry Regiment had not reached CCB was that it was still fighting its way through Marigny. Since midmorning on 27 July, two battalions from the regiment were in the town, but the Germans continued to hold the high ground south of the crossroads. The division artillery moved up and pounded the German positions, but despite the fire the Germans held fast. Traffic congestion around the major crossroads at Marigny also slowed the attack. It would take all day for Colonel Smith to get one battalion through town, move down the St-Lô–Coutances road, and cut north of Camprond. It was not until 11:00 P.M. that the first elements of the 18th Regiment reported linking up with CCB. By then it was too late for Colonel Boudinot to continue his attack. CCB would have to wait for dawn and then resume its frustrating drive west.

The 16th Infantry Regiment at Maringy

On 27 July Lieutenant Colonel Gibb's 16th Infantry Regiment was also crawling toward Marigny. By darkness the first soldiers had reached the town, where the regiment found Germans still holding the high ground covering the crossroads and blocking the regiment's move west to cover CCB. This obstacle put Lieutenant Colonel Gibbs even more desperately behind schedule. During the night, however, patrols from the regiment discovered a 300-yard gap northwest of the crossroads. The engineers used bulldozers to clear the trail and the regiment filed through, heading west on the road to Coutances right past the German defenders. By dawn of the next day, the regiment's 3d Battalion reached La Chapelle, covering CCB's flank and thickening the outer ring of the U.S. VII Corps's envelopment.

Elements of Huebner's 1st Infantry Division were finally through the German lines in depth, but it had taken longer than he had hoped. Even with the commitment of General Watson's 3d Armored Division that morning, the two commands had failed to close the envelopment on the west wing of the German lines.

What Went Wrong with the Scheme of Maneuver

The 1st Infantry Division had pushed past Marigny, breaking through the last of the organized German defenses, but it was still short of capturing all its assigned objectives. In addition, and most important, the enemy forces were already withdrawing, escaping the encirclement, and attempting to reestablish their defensive line. Considering the tremendous combat power at the Big Red One's disposal and the fragmented German defenses it faced, the division's success was clearly less complete than it could have been.

General Huebner's plan had been to get the bulk of his combat power through and beyond the enemy's main defenses and establish blocking positions before the Germans could react. To meet this goal, the scheme of maneuver needed to balance the necessities of assuming risk, maintaining tempo, ensuring adequate control, and providing security. Huebner's answer to this dilemma was to seal the penetration and envelopment with a continuous wall of armor and infantry, pushing all the division's combat power into a very small space at a very slow tempo. It was a poor scheme, and execution, particularly the capture of Marigny, was not well managed. The division's failure to take advantage of the lack of any effective German counterstrikes and push CCB's advance more aggressively was particularly disappointing.

In general, the U.S. forces' poor battlefield reporting and uncoordinated advances suggested that the units available exceeded the capabilities of the Big Red One's commander to command and control the entire force effectively. The Americans had learned a good deal about fighting in the hedgerows, but it was apparent that there were still lessons to be learned about managing large forces in combat. In this battle, the shortcoming in the U.S. attack was not that the commander lacked the combat power for the task, but that he failed to execute an appropriate scheme of maneuver.

In Normandy, the division and corps commanders' greatest influence on battles was to set the conditions before an engagement and assign the field commanders reasonable, appropriate tasks. In this respect both Generals Collins and Huebner failed. This failure was exacerbated by the mediocre performance and mistakes of subordinate commanders, particularly Colonel Boudinot, who proved unable to fulfill his promise of a CCB cavalry dash in the face of cratered roads, harassing enemy fire, and determined German roadblocks. If anything, the attack of the 1st Infantry Division demonstrated the synergy that was lost when the link between the general's decisions and the field-grade commander's execution broke down, and, most important, how quickly operational maneuver could falter under ineffective leadership and poor execution.

The Germans' Dilemma

While the Americans pondered how to follow up the results of the 1st Infantry Division's efforts on 26 and 27 July, on the German side, General Choltitz, the LXXXIV Corps commander, and his superior, General Hausser, the Seventh Army commander, conferred on how best to stop a breakthrough. The two leaders correctly concluded that the Americans were heading west to encircle the flank of LXXXIV Corps. The generals decided to reorient 17th SS Panzergrenadier and 2d SS Panzer Divisions to form a protective wall so that the remaining forces to the east could withdraw and establish a new defense line farther south. The only problem with their decision was that each time they selected a new line for the front, word came in of new U.S. advances that made the choice untenable. The generals finally settled on anchoring their new line on Coutances, running from there to Cambernon, Savigny, and Cerisy-la-Salle. With a new defense line in place the U.S. attack would only mean a defeat, not a disaster. The Seventh Army could conduct an organized, disciplined withdrawal, maintaining a cohesive defense and denying the U.S. forces an open flank or road to Brittany. All the German generals needed to make their plan work was for the Panzer Lehr Division to hold the line around Pont-Brocard.

Standing not far from Pont-Brocard, as far as the Panzer Lehr Division's General Bayerlein was concerned, the battle was already lost. He had set up a new command post in Dangy, several kilometers south of Marigny, and had vainly tried to reorganize his division. Most of what was left of the command, the 901st Panzergrenadier Regiment with 2,300 men assembled from the remnants of various commands, twelve tanks, and six self-propelled guns, had already fled farther south to Villedieu-les-Poeles. All that stayed behind with General Bayerlein was a small battle group with a few engineers and antiaircraft guns at Pont-Brocard. To make matters worse, communications were virtually nonexistent; motorcyclists carried messages back and forth, but harassment by U.S. fighters made their task virtually impossible. Even when riders got through the orders were usually too late, overcome by other disasters.

While Bayerlein conferred with his staff, elements of the U.S. 82d Reconnaissance Battalion leading CCB, 2d Armored Division, broke into Dangy. Tanks swept past the command post on either side. Bayerlein and his staff scrambled for cover while the 82nd Reconnaissance Battalion, unaware that it had just overrun the German division command group, rumbled south and drove off the last of the Panzer Lehr forces at Pont-Brocard. By the time General Bayerlein's superiors decided to hold at Pont-Brocard, the Americans had already liberated the town. Reaching Percy about midnight, Bayerlein finally found a radio and reported that his division had been all but annihilated. With Panzer Lehr virtually destroyed, a real crisis loomed for the Seventh Army. The only question that remained was how well the Americans could exploit the situation when they resumed their offensive on 28 July.

Notes

1. For a comparison of Allen's and Huebner's leadership styles, see Bryce F. Denno, "Allen and Huebner: Contrast in Command," *Army* 34 (June 1984): 62–70.

2. Unless otherwise cited, the plans and operations of the 1st Infantry Division are taken from Headquarters, 1st Infantry Division, U.S. Army, After Action Report, pp. 10–22; Headquarters, 1st Infantry Division Artillery, U.S. Army, Unit Report of Action 1 July to 31 July 1944, p. 2; Headquarters, 1st Infantry Division, U.S. Army, G-2 Journal, 26 July 1944; Headquarters, 26th Infantry Regiment, U.S. Army, Unit Journal, 26 and 27 July 1944; Headquarters, Combat Command B, 3d Armored Division, U.S. Army, Report of Action C. COMD. B 3RD ARMD. DIV. for Period 25 July to 31 July 1944; Thomas T. Crowley and Gerald C. Burch, *Eight Stars to Victory: Operations of the First Engineer Combat Battalion in World War II*, p. 67; Paul H. Bowdle and Edward R. Broadwell, *Combat History of the 391st Armored Artillery Battalion*, pp. 59, 60; Nelson W. Toby, *History, 7th Field Artillery, World War II*, p. 55; Headquarters, 4th Cavalry Group, U.S. Army, After Action Reports, entries 11–31 July; John F. Rhoades and Dale E. Strick, *The History of the Fourth Cavalry Reconnaissance Squadron, European Theater of Operations*, p. 6; Harold D. Howenstine and George E. Troll, *History of the 745 Tank Battalion, August 1942 to June 1945*, pp. 45–46.

3. Liebling, "St. Lo and Mortain," p. 248.

4. Blumenson, *Breakout and Pursuit*, p. 252.

5. Bennett, *Ultra in the West*, p. 102.

6. Headquarters, VII Corps, U.S. Army, G-2 Periodic Reports, 25 July.

7. A. Eaton Roberts, *Five Stars to Victory*, p. 20.

8. Ibid.

9. Giles, *The G.I. Journal of Sergeant Giles*, p. 65.

10. U.S. Strategic Bombing Survey, Europe War, G-2 Target File, 2478, Box 140, RG 243, NARA; Headquarters, Allied Expeditionary Force, Subject: Operation "Cobra," 20 July 1944, microfilm, Roll A5129, AFHSO; Headquarters, IX TAC Operations Order for Operation Cobra, 19 July 1944, microfilm, Roll B5731, AFHSO; Headquarters, 97th Combat Bomb Wing, 25 July 1944, Field Order No. 143-44, microfilm, Roll B5788, AFHSO.

11. Information on operations of the 275th Division and Panzer Lehr Division and German activities on 26 and 27 July are from *Kriegstagebuch des Oberkommandos der Wehrmacht. Band IV. 1. Januar 1944–22. Mai 1945*, p. 327; *Armeeoberkommando 7, K.T.B. Entwurf und OB Chef-IA-Gespräche, 6 Juni–16 August 1944*, microfilm, T312, Roll 1568, pp. 191–193, NARA; Schmidt, "Battles in Northern France," MS A-973, pp. 1–3; War Journal of Headquarters Army Group B, 1–31 July 1944, microfilm. T311, Roll 1, NARA.

12. Schmidt, "Battles in Northern France," p. 3.

13. For a summary of activities across the U.S. First Army front on 26 July, see Blumenson, *Breakout and Pursuit*, pp. 247–251, 252–255.

14. Zeigelman, "Operations from 25 July until 30 July," p. 2.

15. Hansen, War Diary, 26 July 1944, MHI. See also Blumenson, *The Patton Papers*, p. 489.

16. John Hurkala, *The Fighting First Division*, pp. 124–125.

10

A Tank Show, at Tank Speed

O n 27 July, as General Bayerlein's Panzer Lehr Division collapsed, General Bradley's U.S. First Army spread across the German lines like an expanding ink blot. In the far west the U.S. VIII Corps continued to act as the main "pressure force," attacking to hold the enemy in place so that the German defenders would be enveloped by the VII Corps. Assaulting straight ahead toward Coutances on a 15-mile front, the VII Corps was completing the third day of its offensive and finally making rapid progress.

On the far eastern side of the U.S. First Army zone, the U.S. V Corps completed a modest set of attacks along the front from the outskirts of Caumont to St-Lô, successfully holding the Germans' attention and preventing them from shifting to counter the VII Corps's penetration.

Meanwhile, immediately east of the VII Corps, XIX Corps was completing its domination of the high ground around St-Lô and heading west of the Vire River to take advantage of the ground uncovered by the VII Corps's attack. The progress of the flank corps pleased General Bradley and reinforced his conclusion that the German defenses were on the brink of a major setback.

While the flank corps renewed their attacks, the divisions of General Collins's VII Corps widened the gap in the center created by the collapse of Panzer Lehr.[1] In the east General Brooks's 2d Armored Division continued to advance rapidly. General Hobbs's 30th Infantry Division moved into the loop along the Vire River south of St-Lô, making contact with the XIX Corps and wiping out the last resistance on the breakthrough's eastern flank. Meanwhile, in the center of the VII Corps zone, General Barton's 4th Infantry Division pushed 7 miles south of the St-Lô–Périers road, clearing out all organized resistance in its path. At the same time, General Huebner's 1st Infantry Division and the 3d Armored Division under General Watson were still slowly pushing west, while General Eddy's 9th Infantry Division (sandwiched between the flank of the VIII Corps and the

1st Infantry Division) had just about run out of room to maneuver and enemy to fight.

Of all the results on 27 July, the most important development of the day for the culmination of Operation Cobra was east of the 9th Infantry Division on the VIII Corps front. While the VIII Corps continued to press the offensive, by the night of 27 July there did not seem to be much of an enemy to pressure. Resistance was characterized as "light." The whole corps had taken less than a hundred prisoners. The enemy forces were not waiting to be enveloped; they were pulling back, running away faster than the VIII Corps was advancing.

While the VIII Corps moved forward, Colonel Eugen Koenig, acting commander of the German 91st Division, the westernmost unit in the LXXXIV Corps, was leading the Germans' withdrawal south as rapidly as possible.[2] After weeks of fighting, his skeleton force included all that was left of LXXXIV Corps's west wing, the remnants of the 91st and 243d Divisions, a battle group from the 265th Division, and bits of several other units. His men had only held on so long because they defended some of the absolutely worst terrain in Normandy. Now, with the threat of Americans' moving on their flank (the advance of the VII Corps), it looked like even that advantage was lost. Colonel Koenig, fearing envelopment, ordered everyone to pull back. He only hoped that the shattered defenses to his east could slow down the Americans long enough to give his men time to retreat.

At U.S. First Army headquarters, radios picked up a German broadcast from Calais reporting that the Americans had made a "slight" penetration west of St-Lô and that efforts were being made to contain the attack. General Bradley's aide, Major Hansen, noted the report and added one word in his diary: "understatement."[3] Bradley concluded that Cobra was a success and that he had the breakthrough he needed. The lack of resistance in front of the VIII Corps was clear evidence that the Germans were moving their defenses south and that they were afraid of being enveloped by the First Army's sudden advance. General Bradley now turned his attention to determining how best to exploit the success of the operation.

In particular, the slow progress on the VII Corps's western flank caused General Bradley to reevaluate his plan. It appeared less and less likely that Watson's 3d Armored Division and Huebner's 1st Infantry Division were going to move fast enough to trap the enemy rapidly withdrawing from the VIII Corps's front. General Bradley now believed that the best opportunity for exploiting Cobra's success was to further widen and deepen the gap as quickly as possible, rather than worry about completing the envelopment. By widening the gap, General Bradley saw an opportunity not only to open the door into Brittany, but also to threaten the entire flank of the German Seventh Army.

Bradley ordered General Collins's VII Corps, along with the XIX

Corps, to turn its efforts south. He also directed the VIII Corps to put more pressure on the enemy and punch south down the coast to Granville. He told them to "push hard" and gave the VIII Corps more room to maneuver by assigning it the 1st Infantry Division's objectives near Monthuchon and Coutances.[4]

Despite General Bradley's orders and the VIII Corps's new orientation, the VII Corps's Collins did not change his plans for the 3d Armored Division's attack on 28 July. The division (minus CCB attached to the 1st Infantry Division) was to pursue its original course, moving to Montpinchon and then toward Coutances with a final objective of sealing the VII Corps's outer ring on a line from Hymouville to Montpinchon to Cerisy-la-Salle. General Collins hoped that an aggressive move by the division would loosen up the opposition facing the 1st Infantry Division and allow the Big Red One to complete the envelopment's inner ring. Collins believed that the 3d Armored Division's advance could still prove decisive, cutting off German forces in the west and quickly uncovering an open road to Brittany.

The 3d Armored Division's Plans—A Drive to Destiny

Before the battle, when Major General Watson, the 3d Armored Division commander, briefed General Hodges, the First Army deputy commander, on his division's part in Operation Cobra, Watson declared it was going to be a "tank show, conducted at tank speed." Not even the hedgerows would slow him down. Hedgerows, Watson told Hodges, were more of a "psychological hazard" than anything else.[5]

Two new innovations never used before in the Normandy fighting, "rhinos" and "armored column cover," bolstered General Watson's confidence. They were an important part of the division's plans and contributed to the high expectations for Cobra's success. The hedgerow-busting "rhinos" were scrap-metal prongs that had been fabricated in Normandy and welded to the front of the tanks. The prongs acted like a bulldozer, ripping a path through the dirt berms, bushes, and trees. General Bradley was amazed when he saw a demonstration of how they worked and ordered the invention held in reserve until the breakout. A third of the 3d Armored Division's tanks were outfitted with the new secret weapon before Operation Cobra.

Another cause for confidence was a new form of air support promised for the armored forces called "armored column cover." The ambitious air plan was in large part attributable to Major General Elwood R. "Pete" Quesada, the commander of IX Tactical Air Command (TAC), a subordinate headquarters of the Ninth Air Force. IX TAC provided air support for the U.S. First Army. As far as the army was concerned,

General Quesada was a Godsend. General Bradley's aide recorded that "Quesada and General [Bradley] agree perfectly on the use of air power. For essential missions at the front, for delaying employment of enemy reinforcements and destroying roads of supply and communications."[6] When it came to close air support the army and air commander saw "eye to eye."[7] Quesada even located his headquarters near the First Army command post so that he could coordinate ground and air operations as closely as possible.

General Quesada cut a singular figure around the army headquarters. Frequently not even wearing rank insignia, he liked to drive his own jeep or race about in a P-38 Lightning. He was a popular fixture at General Bradley's mess table, telling stories that showed a strong sense of humor. But it was airplanes, not Quesada's jokes, that made him Bradley's indispensable general. By the start of Cobra, there were eighteen fighter-bomber and reconnaissance groups, a radar control system, and fifteen airbases and additional temporary airfields in Normandy.[8] General Quesada could help bring a lot of firepower to the fight.

The challenge of providing air support for Operation Cobra was figuring out how to harness all that air power in support of fast-moving armored columns. During the campaign there had been only two kinds of requests that ground commanders could use to get air support, preplanned and immediate. Preplanned requests worked their way by radio, telephone, or teletype up through the division and corps G-3 air officers and the representatives of the tactical air command until they reached the First Army, where the IX TAC maintained a joint combined operations center. Requests reaching the center between 6:00 and 9:00 P.M. were reviewed jointly by the army and army air corps intelligence and operations officers. Approved requests were sent to the fighter-bomber groups. At the groups, army ground liaison officers briefed the pilots on the next day's targets.

Immediate requests were made by the air support parties via very high-frequency (VHF) radio directly to the joint combined operations center. Higher headquarters monitored the requests by listening in on the communications net. Approved requests were forwarded directly to the tactical control center, which alerted its forward command posts, which in turn contacted the fighters and directed the aircraft to their targets by radar.

Both the preplanned and immediate request processes had their advantages. The preplanned system allowed for the precise allocation of assets and detailed coordination; the immediate request, however, was much more responsive to rapidly changing situations where firepower needed to be shifted quickly around the war zone.

Both systems worked well on a static battlefield, but neither system seemed adequate for the advance of armored columns in Operation Cobra. General Quesada wanted both immediately responsive air support and close coordination. The solution was dedicated air power—armored column cover. Between four and eight P-47 Thunderbolts, armed with 500-pound bombs and .50-caliber machine guns, would fly in front of the armored columns of the 2d and 3d Armored Divisions, providing reconnaissance as well as attack support. The Thunderbolts would be replaced every 30 minutes by new aircraft, so that there would never be any gaps in the cover.

The idea of column cover was only feasible because of the innovation of putting VHF radios inside tanks in the armored column. Without direct radio contact between the planes and the tanks, commanders had had no effective means to ensure that planes did not attack friendly units or to prevent the aircraft from losing contact with the column. With the VHF radios, fighters would coordinate directly with the column through the air support party, an experienced pilot who rode with the lead tank and operated the VHF radio. Ground commanders could monitor the air radio channel to receive in-flight updates or send in requests to attack targets.

The Cobra air plan called for extensive use of close air support and column cover (74 percent of the planned missions). The 366th, 404th, and 368th Fighter Groups were tasked to fly column cover. The 70th Fighter Wing was assigned responsibility for scheduling and directing the flights. In addition to the column cover, additional fighter-bombers were kept on strip alert at the airfields ready to respond to requests from the air support parties.

In fact, even before General Watson launched his attack the air system had already proved its worth. CCB, 3rd Armored Division (supporting the 1st Infantry Division), had used the column cover technique to good affect, blocking the advance of counterattacks on the armored column as it advanced toward Marigny. Watson had every confidence that the air support would be just as effective during the 3rd Division's drive to Coutances.

Despite the addition of armored column cover and "rhino" hedge cutters, General Watson's predictions for his attack seemed pretty bold. Normandy was the 3d Armored Division's first campaign, and both General Watson and his command had yet to distinguish themselves. The 51-year-old graduate of West Point (class of 1915) had served in the American Expeditionary Force during World War I. Watson was one of the original cadre officers for the 3d Armored Division: he had first commanded the 40th Armored Regiment and later Combat Command A (CCA). In August 1942 he took over the division and began to prepare it for the invasion of Europe.

The division had landed in Normandy shortly after D-Day, and when General Watson sent his tankers into battle for the first time at the end of June, things did not go well. Watson had been "anxious to fight," but glad enough that the corps called off the attack when things turned sour.[9] In the division's second foray, supporting an attack by the 30th Infantry Division across the Vire River, the poorly coordinated operation bordered on farce. General Hobbs, the 30th Infantry Division commander, became so exasperated that he called VII Corps and pleaded, "Please get them out of our hair."[10] Operation Cobra gave Watson another chance to prove the power of U.S. armor.

So far Cobra had given the 3d Armored Division little opportunity to demonstrate tank speed. On the evening of 27 July the tankers were still tangled in the traffic jams around Marigny. The division needed to get moving, for the VII Corps's General Collins was beginning to have his doubts, thinking that he was beginning to see signs of "inept leadership" in the 3d Armored Division.[11]

Despite the pressure to push on, the 3d Armored Division was to see more difficulties ahead.[12] The division was headed toward some of the most easily defended ground in Normandy. Before Cobra had started, the ground chosen for the 3d Armored Division's outer ring had seemed ideal: Cerisy-la-Salle and Montpinchon sat on dominating ground over 400 feet high. The high ground overlooked a steep valley that covered the road west to Coutances. Tanks on that position would command the road like an iron fortress. In fact, the division's initial plan had been based on getting to this ground before the Germans and using Montpinchon/ Cerisy-la-Salle as the anchor of the VII Corps's outer ring. With the slow pace of the advance, however, getting to the high ground first was no longer a sure thing. (The attack by the 3d Armored Division is shown in Figure 10.1.)

As General Watson planned how to complete his drive toward Montpinchon on 28 July, he was hampered by a lack of clear intelligence on what was to his front. He was most worried about the 2d SS Panzer Division. German prisoners taken during the U.S. breakout had indicated that the division had only a few tanks left and was somewhere on LXXXIV Corps's west wing, but the U.S. 3d Armored Division G-2 did not have a good reading on where the elusive German armor might be. What the 3d Armored Division did know was that the Germans were capable of three courses of action. First, they could withdraw their left flank to the high ground north and east of Coutances with a secondary line south of the town extending to Montpinchon in the east. Second, they could counterattack to the east. Third, they could evacuate their forces throughout the area from Montpinchon to Coutances and set up a new defense line to the south.

The 3rd Armored Division G-2 concluded that the enemy was going to adopt the third course of action, moving through Montpinchon and Coutances in force. This analysis was based on an appreciation of the dominating terrain around Montpinchon and Cerisy-la-Salle, this ground guarding the fastest way for the U.S. divisions to turn west and controlling the best routes for the Germans' retreat to the south. In the division's plan for Cobra one of the key questions the G-2 had posed was, "Will Montpinchon–Cerisy-la-Salle be occupied?" Division suspected that when it finally got to the high ground the answer would be yes.

While the 3d Armored Division planned its offensive for 28 July what

Figure 10.1   Attack of the 3d Armored Division

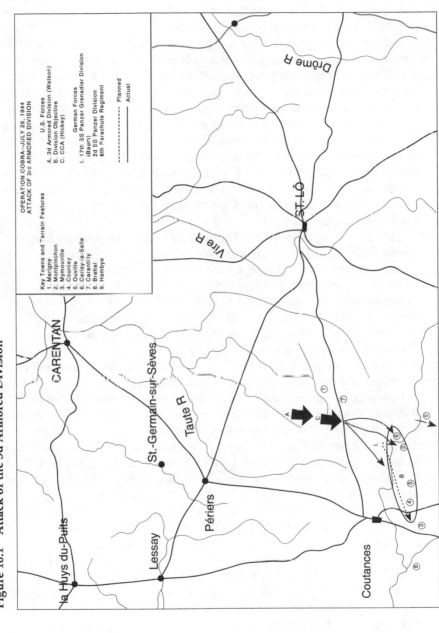

OPERATION COBRA—JULY 28, 1944
ATTACK OF 3rd ARMORED DIVISION

Key Towns and Terrain Features

1. Marigny
2. Montpinchon
3. Mymouville
4. Courcey
5. Ouville
6. Cerisy-la-Salle
7. Carantilly
8. Brehal
9. Hambye

U.S. Forces
A. 3d Armored Division (Watson)
B. Division Objective
C. CCA (Hickey)

German Forces
I. 17th SS Panzer Grenadier Division
   (Baun)
2d SS Panzer Division
6th Parachute Regiment

- - - - - Planned
———— Actual

was left of the 2d SS Panzer Division sat on the high ground at Montpinchon and Cerisy-la-Salle.[13] Authorized over 200 armored vehicles and 20,000 men on paper, the 2d SS Panzer Division, "Das Reich," was almost twice as large as the standard German tank division. Das Reich had fought with distinction on the Eastern Front, but 2 years of fighting and Russian winters had taken a heavy toll and the division had been sent to southern France for refitting. Then, only a week before the kickoff of Cobra, the reconstituted command was ordered to the Normandy front. Almost immediately the division had engaged in heavy fighting and taken serious losses. To add to the problems of Das Reich, its commander was wounded in the Cobra bombing. He was replaced by the commander of the panzergrenadier regiment, who was killed. When Cobra started, the depleted division (with the 6th Parachute Regiment attached) sat along the St-Lô–Périers road less than a mile west of where the U.S.VII Corps had broken through the German lines.

By 28 July battalions of the 6th Parachute Regiment, interspersed with armored units from Das Reich, had retreated into a series of stair-step positions from the eastern edge of Coutances to the bridge a mile and a half north of Courcy, and from there onto Belval, Ouville, Montpinchon, and Cerisy-la-Salla. To solidify the defense further, the 2d SS Panzer was consolidated with the 17th SS Panzergrenadier Division on its eastern flank.

The 17th SS Panzergrenadier Division was also in poor shape. The division was authorized two infantry regiments with organic tank battalions, but the unit had been deployed to Normandy with no tanks and only an improvised collection of transport and self-propelled guns. On 28 July the division was sandwiched into a narrow piece of ground between the 5th Parachute Division and the 2d SS Panzer Division. Lieutenant Colonel Otto Baum, the senior officer remaining, commanded the division. As the day dawned, Lieutenant Colonel Baum was gathering the forces that were left from his command (the 2d SS Panzer Division and the 6th Parachute Regiment) and preparing to execute a controlled withdrawal south guarding the flank of LXXXIV Corps.[14]

Unfortunately for Lieutenant Colonel Baum, he had to execute his orders with almost no knowledge of the tactical situation. He did not know the condition of the forces under his command or the actions of units on his flanks. Nor did he know what the Americans were up to. He had reports that U.S. forces (the VIII Corps) were pushing south along the Périers–Coutances road, but their attacks seemed tentative and cautious. What concerned him more were reports of U.S. armored attacks from the east (the VII Corps's advance east).

What Baum also did not know was that he was actually well positioned to block the U.S. advance (just as General Watson had feared). Baum's withdrawing forces had avoided the grasp of the VIII Corps, the 1st

Infantry Division, and CCB, 3d Armored Division, and most of his command was already behind the Soulles River. The remainder of his panzergrenadier units were covering the St-Lô–Coutances road. Farther east, Lieutenant Colonel Baum had a small force dominating the high ground near Montpinchon and Cerisy-la-Salle, guarding the main roads east into the flank of his makeshift force. All in all, if Baum had known anything about the tactical situation, he would have concluded that his forces were not in bad positions for covering a withdrawal.

Lieutenant Colonel Baum decided that his best course of action for 28 July was to conduct a fighting withdrawal south for 6 miles and take up positions behind the Bréhal–Hambye road where there was good ground for the defenders. Between his troops and the tanks of the 2d SS Panzer Division he had every hope of holding on. Based on the unclear picture he had of the enemy situation, the withdrawal plan was a safe decision and holding the high ground at Montpinchon and Cerisy-la-Salle seemed a prudent step.

When General Collins decided to continue to push the 3d Armored Division west toward Montpinchon and Cerisy-la-Salle on 28 July, he was sending the tanks straight into the German defenses. More important, Collins's decision appeared both to miss the intent behind the shift in the U.S. First Army plan and the changing character of the battle. Seizing Coutances no longer offered the potential of bagging German divisions by racing around their undefended rear. While some German units were fleeing the trap, others were turning east into the path of the armored spearhead to guard the withdrawal. Collins's decision to continue the drive could only expand the penetration by driving headfirst through the enemy.

Although General Watson did not know that he was about to commit his division to a frontal assault on a new German defense line, luckily he had already decided that for the attack on 28 July the 3d Armored Division would need the maximum amount of combat power at the front. Watson kept very few forces under his direct control: the 83d Armored Reconnaissance Battalion, 298th Combat Engineer Battalion; the 486th Antiaircraft Artillery Battalion (less A Battery); the division logistical support units; and the 3d Battalion, 33d Armored Regiment (division reserve).

Most of the division's combat power was assigned to Combat Command A (CCA). Brigadier General Doyle Hickey, the CCA commander, would lead the division's charge to Montpinchon. General Hickey was a veteran of the "old army." He had been studying for a legal career when World War I broke out, and after an officer training course, he had served as an artillery officer in France. In 1942, switching his allegiance to the fledgling armored force, he assumed command of CCA. The 54-year-old CCA commander, who habitually puffed on a battered briar pipe, had a reputation as a calm, soft-spoken, but determined leader.

General Hickey's CCA consisted of Lieutenant Colonel Leander L. Doane's 32d Armored Regiment; Colonel William W. Cornog Jr.'s 36th Armored Infantry Regiment (less one battalion); the 703d Tank Destroyer Battalion (less A company); 2d Battalion, 26th Infantry Regiment (detached from the 1st Infantry Division); A and B Company of the 413th Antiaircraft Artillery Battalion; a detachment from E Company of the 23d Engineer Combat Battalion; A Company, 45th Armored Medical Battalion; and A Company from the divisional maintenance battalion.

General Hickey divided the division's single spearhead into three task forces, designated task forces X, Y, and Z. Fire support for the task forces was to come from the 58th and 87th Armored Field Artillery Battalions. Colonel Frederic J. Brown, the 3d Armored Division artillery commander, organized the two artillery battalions into a "groupment" under the command of the armored regiment's direct-support artillery battalion commander.[15]

CCA to Montpinchon and Points West

At dawn on 28 July General Hickey found that CCA's fast war of movement had not gone very quickly. Task Force Y was more than 3 miles short of Cerisy-la-Salle. Task Force X was near Carantilly on the Terrette River, south of Marigny. The trailing Task Force Z was still struggling with traffic jams in Marigny.

For the day's advance, Hickey needed to speed up the operation. Until now CCA had advanced in column formation on a single axis. In this formation the command could move no faster than the lead tank, which meant, so far, not speedily at all. If the VII Corps hoped to cut off any of the German flank, Hickey needed to get his command moving much faster.

Hickey now decided to move on a broad front and send all his task forces racing straight toward their objectives, and the road network in CCA's zone seemed more than adequate to support this plan. There were a number of secondary roads; many of them appeared capable of supporting tanks. What was more important, a study of the roadwork clearly showed that most of the sideroads were oriented east to west in line with the CCA objectives. As the division's tactical study of the terrain reported, "All roads lead to Coutances." Within 2 miles of the city the CCA G-2 had counted ten different routes they could use.

General Hickey ordered Task Force Y to continue to push out from Canisy past the German positions at Cerisy-la-Salle and Pont-Brocard toward Montpinchon. Task Force X would seize the high ground at Cerisy-la-Salle. Task Force Z would turn west at Carantilly and head straight for Coutances.

Task Force Z for Coutances

As Task Force Z moved out on 28 July, the day saw another dramatic change in weather. The sun came out with a vengeance that dried the Normandy mud and produced clouds of white powder. "Clouds of dust cover the roads until we almost choke," a soldier recorded in his diary. "Still our attack continues without pause. The fine white dust covers everyone and everything . . . the goggles we are wearing, makes us look like aliens from another planet."[16]

Despite the clear weather Task Force Z had trouble even starting the attack. Even the Luftwaffe made a rare appearance over the battlefield. (Senior U.S. commanders knew through Ultra that the German commanders were screaming for air support to help stem the breakthrough, but they also knew that little was available.) This German air attack consisted of only a few planes. Their flares and bombs did little damage, but the disruption added to the chaos at the front. For example, when the Service Company from the 32d Armored Regiment fired on a circling enemy fighter, the plane circled backed and bombed the regiment's position, killing one man, wounding five, and scattering the vehicles in the column.

The effects of this brief air attack highlighted again the importance of Allied air supremacy to the Normandy breakout. If Germans had had more planes and free run of the skies, the U.S. armored columns would have offered very lucrative targets. Without the threat of any further German air attacks, however, the task force easily reorganized and got moving again.

In fact, it was traffic that was more of an obstacle than the Germans, and congestion prevented Task Force Z's column from moving before noon. The roads around Marigny were choked with U.S. troops, which was hardly the task force's fault. The traffic jams were the product of General Collins's decision to throw the 3d Armored Division in with the other forces already heading to Coutances and the 1st Infantry Division's unsatisfactory effort to squeeze a division and a half's worth of combat power onto the few, cratered roads leading to Marigny.

Once the Task Force Z column got under way, however, problems persisted. For instance, the 87th Armored Field Artillery Battalion supporting the task force was cut off by another column and lost contact; only with difficulty did the battalion get back on the road, and the gunners found a position southeast of Savigny from which they could fire. But all the effort seemed hardly worth it: once the artillery battalion got into position it found that since the task force was moving so slowly there was little to shoot at. The battalion fired only 254 rounds, mostly on interdiction and harassing missions. This lack of fire missions was clear evidence the task force was having trouble reaching the enemy.

Task Forces X and Y Move on
Montpinchon and Cerisy-la-Salle

While Task Force Z struggled to advance, CCA's Task Forces X and Y faced stiff opposition from the remnants of Lieutenant Colonel Baum's troops at Montpinchon and Cerisy-la-Salle. Aiding the Germans' defense, the slopes to the high ground were covered with hedgerows. Despite General Watson's assessment, the hedgerows proved to be much more than "psychological hazards." Neither task force had much luck in advancing to their objectives. Even with air power and rhinos, CCA found it tough going against the combined defenses of the 17th SS Panzergrenadier Division, the 2d SS Panzer Division, and the 6th Parachute Regiment.

As the attack progressed, General Watson found that there was no magic solution for fighting through the hedgerows. The tanks' rhino hedgerow cutters did not enable the armor to quickly cut down even hastily prepared defenses. One of the great myths of Operation Cobra, perpetuated by many historians (most recently Richard Overy), was that the rhino was responsible for the breakthrough. In fact, tank units on their own had improvised and used various types of hedgerow cutters during the campaign even before Cobra. But even when tanks ripped a clear path through the hedgerows, it still took the coordinated support of infantry and artillery to protect the tanks from antitank fire so they could move forward safely.

In addition, even with the rhinos it was difficult for the armor to traverse the Norman terrain: they could cut through hedgerows but they were no help in maneuvering down narrow roads, up steep banks, and across forested ravines. There were many instances during Cobra when the infantry had to advance alone, while the tanks muddled through in cratered fields, thick woods, and steep, uneven ground. U.S. Army combat engineers made a much more important contribution in clearing the obstacles and opening the roads for the Cobra advance than the hedgerow-cutting rhinos.

Attacks by fighter aircraft were no more successful in loosening up the enemy lines. Armored column cover was highly effective against moving enemy formations, but it was less useful against hedgerow defenses in which the Germans could find cover and concealment that made them difficult to find and attack. In short, even armed with constant air cover and rhino tanks, CCA's columns had a tough time fighting across the Normandy hills against even hastily prepared enemy positions.

All in all, it turned out to be a bad afternoon for CCA. The roads out of Carantilly toward Coutances proved far less usable than they appeared on the maps, and bad roads and pockets of enemy forces left CCA only 5 miles west of Carantilly by late afternoon. CCA also ran into more determined resistance near Ouville and Savigny, where the enemy held the high ground and had prepared hasty, but well-devised positions that could not be easily bypassed. The Americans quickly found that they would have to fight their way through. While keeping up the tempo of the attack was important, rushing headlong and unprepared at the enemy would most likely result only in high casualties and little progress. The tankers prepared for a major assault.

It was well after dark before the Task Forces X and Y were ready to attempt a coordinated advance against the enemy. They planned to precede the attack with a barrage from Colonel Brown's 3d Armored Division Artillery. On the night of 28 July the guns moved into position, and at dawn they fired a division massed fire mission on the German positions at Ouville. With the help of the artillery and support by elements of the 26th Infantry Regiment of the 1st Infantry Division, CCA cleared the enemy resistance near Savigny and moved on, but the 3d Armored Division was still some way from its final objective. Meanwhile, under the cover of darkness on 28 July the German forces at Montpinchon and Cerisy-la-Salle withdrew. When General Hickey's CCA finally reached the high ground it found a smoking, desolate landscape occupied only by a small enemy rearguard. The Germans had got away.

Results of the Fighting on 28 July

The result of fighting across the front on 28 July was another mixed bag for General Collins.[17] On the right flank, the Americans had split the boundary between the LXXXIV and II Parachute Corps so decisively that the U.S. First Army transferred control of the 30th Infantry Division and CCA, 2d Armored Division, to XIX Corps so that they could continue to push into the exposed flank of the II Parachute Corps. Meanwhile, the rest of the 2d Armored Division continued to attack south, CCB from General Brooks's 2d Armored Division reaching St-Denis-le-Gast; by dark on 28 July the division had reconnaissance elements as far south as Camery and Lengronne.

In the center of the VII Corps zone the 4th Infantry Division had virtually completed its mission. By the late afternoon of 28 July the majority of the division assembled near Notre Dame-de-Cenilly. Meanwhile, the division's 8th Infantry Regiment launched two battalions to eliminate the remaining German elements along the Montreuil–Carantilly road.

At the same time, General Eddy's 9th Infantry Division was enjoying a well-earned rest, passing into reserve. This division had been in the front lines for 19 days straight and 38 of the previous 45 days. For the first time in a long time no one would be fighting or dying in the 9th Infantry Division.

Meanwhile, on the critical right flank General Collins found nothing but disappointment. It was clear that the encirclement of the enemy had failed. General Huebner's 1st Infantry Division (with CCB, 3d Armored, still attached) continued its attack, but it found that most of the German resistance was now to the south, beyond the pocket created by VII Corps's encirclement. General Watson's 3d Armored Division attack had also shown meager results. In addition, the VII Corps had made contact with VIII Corps units near Coutances, another clear signal that it had missed encircling the bulk of the enemy force.

A Tank Attack, No Tank Speed

The 3d Armored Division's attack did not have much to show for a fast war of movement. The army's field manual on operations stated that the key to success in a war of movement was "to deprive the enemy of his freedom of action and prevent the coordinated employment of his forces."[18] In this respect General Watson's attack clearly fell short. The enemy defenses had recovered enough, at least temporarily, to hold off the U.S. armored spearhead.

The division's failure to close the ring around the Germans on 28 July could be attributed to a number of factors, including bad ground, bad luck, and a determined enemy. If the maneuver had succeeded, it would have been one of the most decisive moments of the campaign, yielding a wide open path to the Brittany ports. But the concept for the attack was clearly flawed from the start. The opportunity to envelop the enemy's flank had clearly passed. In addition, by remaining focused on trapping Germans, the attack lost sight of the primary objective for the offensive, breaching the enemy defenses in depth. In fact, Army Group B commander, General Kluge, had already given up any hope of holding Avranches, thus leaving the door to Brittany open. General Collins's choice for a decisive battle achieved little more than ensuring a meaningless engagement with the German rearguard, wasting lives and a day's use of a powerful armor force. In continuing to push west on 28 July, Collins had sent the 3d Armored Division off to fight the least productive kind of battle for an armored force, a frontal assault in the hedgerows.

In addition, General Watson's unbounded optimism for the potential of armor attacks in the hedgerows and his faith in quick-fix technical solutions was clearly misplaced. Facing prepared defenses, rhinos and armored column cover were useful, but proved not to be "silver bullets" for breaking hedgerow defenses, nor were they sufficient by themselves to change the course of the campaign. Tactical innovations only made significant contributions when they were thoroughly integrated with the U.S. Army's other capabilities so that they could be exploited to their fullest. To make the most of these "silver bullets," the Americans would first have had to force the Germans out of prepared defenses and into a fast war of movement—and these conditions were never achieved during the 3d Armored Division's drive toward Coutances.

On the other hand, as far as executing the tasks they had been assigned, there seemed to be little that General Hickey and the other CCA commanders could be faulted for. To fight their way west the task forces had aggressively searched out gaps and routes through the enemy defenses. When CCA encountered stiff resistance near Ouville and Savigny, commanders coordinated and massed combat power and then continued to attack. The field-grade leaders proved that they could plan and execute "on the fly." They could adapt; they could improvise; and they could overcome adversity and uncertainty and keep the offensive going. All in all, it was a creditable performance by a still fledgling armored force with little combat experience.

General Collins, however, thought differently. He felt "throughout the COBRA operation the 3d Armored Division was overcautious."[19] General Collins was not pleased with the results of the advance, but the outcome of the battle had resulted in large part because his VII Corps had not adjusted the division's objective to take into account the developing tactical situation on the battlefield. In other words, the division failed to conduct a decisive attack because it had been given the wrong mission. Rather than completing the envelopment, which no longer offered a distinct operational advantage, General Collins should have used the 3d Armored Division to push south and further expand the depth of the penetration. To achieve victory in battle, commanders must assign objectives that are not only definable and achievable but also relevant to the task at hand. In this respect, General Collins's use of the 3d Armored Division during Cobra was sorely wanting.

Collins's decisions about the employment of the 3d Armored Division dispute's Russell Weigley's claim that it was Collins rather than Bradley who was the driving force behind turning the breakthrough into a breakout. To the contrary, Collins clearly had remained focused on completing the envelopment (the original intent of the breakthrough attack). It was General Bradley, with his decisions on 27 July to follow up the possibilities created by Cobra, who recognized the potential to not only clear the way to the Brittany ports but also roll up the entire flank of the German Seventh Army. Given the goals of the campaign and the current situation in the British sector, Bradley's decision to explore vigorously and simultaneously both opportunities was a reasonable choice. In short, Bradley's decisions during, and in the aftermath, of Cobra reflected the character of a confident, competent operational commander.

Prelude to Disaster

On July 29 General Watson's 3d Armored Division finally accomplished its assigned task, but the enemy it was supposed to trap and destroy was nowhere to be seen. Where were the Germans and what were they doing?

The answer to this mystery had begun to take shape the previous evening as the Germans prepared for one big, last desperate effort to turn back the tide of Cobra. Late on 28 July Lieutenant Colonel Baum, the temporary commander of the 17th SS Panzergrenadier Division, the 2d SS Panzer Division, and the 6th Parachute Regiment, received a dispatch from General Choltitz, LXXXIV Corps commander. The message was not what Baum expected. Rather than directing him to continue his retreat south as the west wing's rearguard, General Choltitz ordered a counterattack from the west toward the southeast against the U.S. penetration! Baum was perplexed. This decision seemed hazardous in the extreme: an attack southeast into the U.S. advance risked the entire LXXXIV Corps flank. Once the Americans had pushed south out of Coutances, there would be no organized force in their path all the way to Avranches and the Brittany coast.

Lieutenant Colonel Baum would have been gratified to know that General Choltitz's superior, General Kluge, Army Group B commander, was worried about exactly the same problem. Kluge believed the U.S. attack had made a decisive penetration, threatening the entire wing of the army group's front, and he had already given up any thought of holding the Americans forward of Avranches. Still, he needed a quick counterattack to slow the Americans and gain time to reestablish the defensive line, so he decided to launch an armor strike from the east through the II Parachute Corps sector to close the gap. The news of another counterattack from the west by the left flank of LXXXIV Corps came as a complete surprise. General Hausser, Seventh Army commander, had come up with the idea of a strike out of the west on his own; he believed that if the German forces trapped along the coast pulled back straight south, the Seventh Army would be split in two—ensuring a U.S. breakthrough. Even if the troops could escape south, Hausser thought they were too weak to block the enemy, so it was better to risk all and close the breach. That, however, was not the way General Kluge, his superior, saw the situation. When Kluge found out about Hausser's initiative he became almost violent because it risked the entire left wing of the front. He ordered the attack canceled immediately.[20]

While the senior German commanders debated the form of the counterstroke against Operation Cobra, that evening Ultra decoders at Bletchley Park in England pieced together the rough intentions of the counterattack.[21] Before the night was over, senior commanders on both sides of the battlefield realized that another clash of armor was rapidly approaching on 29 July.

Notes

1. For a cogent summary of operations on July 28, see Blumenson, *Breakout and Pursuit,* pp. 256–266.

2. Eugen Koenig, "91st Airborne Division" (10 Jul–Aug 1944), MS B-010.

3. Hansen, War Diary, 27 July 1944, MHI.

4. Ibid.; Headquarters, First U.S. Army, U.S. Army, Field Order No. 2, 28 July 1944.

5. Sylvan, War Diary, 17 July 1944, MHI.

6. Hansen, War Diary, 18 June 1944, MHI.

7. Ibid., 21 June 1944. For a thorough treatment of General Quesada's role in the development of tactical air-ground support and useful overview operations in Normandy, see Hughes, *Overlord;* Sullivan, *Overlord's Eagles,* pp. 142–145. Information on IX TAC air support innovations is taken from Headquarters, IX TAC Operations Order for Operation Cobra, 19 July 1944, microfilm, Roll B5731, AFHSO; Robert H. George, Ninth Air Force, April to November 1944, microfilm, Roll K1005, AFHRA; AAF Evaluation Board, ETO, Tactics and Techniques Developed by U.S. Tactical Air Commands in the European Theater, MHI; Tactical Air Operations in Europe, 19 May 1945, MHI; Army Air Forces, ETO, U.S. Army Air Forces, The Effectiveness of Third Phase Tactical Air Operations in the European Theater, 5 May 1944–8 May 1945, August 1945; *Report of the General Board: The Control of Tactical Aircraft in the European Theater of Operations, Study No. 55,* CARL.

8. Richard H. Kohn and Joseph P. Harahan, eds., *Condensed Analysis of the Ninth Air Force in the European Theater of Operations,* pp. 25, 68.

9. Hansen, War Diary, 30 June 1944, MHI.

10. Blumenson, *Breakout and Pursuit,* p. 117.

11. Collins, *Lightning Joe,* p. 243.

12. Unless otherwise noted, plans and operations of the 3d Armored Division are taken from Headquarters, 3d Armored Division, U.S. Army, Field Order No. 4 (revised), 21 July 1944; *History of the 3d Armored Division, April 1941–July 1958,* p. 6; *Spearhead in the West,* pp. 196–198; Headquarters, 3d Armored Division, U.S. Army, Action Against Enemy, After Action Report, 19 August 1944; *History of the 87th Armored Field Artillery Battalion,* pp. 40–42.

13. Unless otherwise noted, information on the operations of the 2d SS Panzer Division in Normandy are summarized from James Lucas, *Das Reich,* pp. 134–140, and Max Hastings, *Das Reich: The March of the 2nd SS Panzer Division Through France.* Information on joint operations of the 6th Parachute Regiment with the 2d SS Panzer and 17th SS Panzergrenadier Divisions from 27–29 July is from Heydte, "A German Parachute Regiment in Normandy," pp. 35–44. There are official divisional records from this period extant, but they do not provide information on operations during the period of 27–29 July 1944. See also War Journal of Headquarters Army Group B, 1–31 July 1944, microfilm, T311, Roll 1; Eddy Florentin, *Stalingrad en Normandie: la destruction de la VIIe armée allemande dans la poche Argentan-Falaise, 31 juillet–22 août 1944.*

14. Blumenson, *Breakout and Pursuit,* p. 275.

15. Frederic J. Brown, "Spearhead Artillery," *The Field Artillery Journal* 36 (September 1946): 506.

16. Willis, *The Incredible Years,* p. 25.

17. For a summary of U.S. First Army operations on 28 July, see Blumenson, *Breakout and Pursuit,* pp. 266, 275–277, 290, 299–300, 305–306, 311–314.

18. FM 100-5, *Field Service Regulations: Operations,* p. 113.

19. Adjutant General's Office, World War II Operations Notes on Operation Cobra and Mortain, Box 24235, RG 94, NARA.

20. War Journal of Headquarters Army Group B, 1–31 July 1944, microfilm, T311, Roll 1, NARA; *Kriegstagebuch des Oberkommandos der Wehrmacht. Band IV. 1. Januar 1944–22. Mai 1945,* p. 327. See also General Speidel's recollection in Speidel, *We Defended Normandy,* pp. 136–137.

21. Bennett, *Ultra in the West,* p. 104.

11

A Battle Without Fronts

By dawn on 29 July all the senior Allied commanders had already concluded that Operation Cobra was a complete success. When General Eisenhower visited the U.S. First Army Headquarters that afternoon, he found General Bradley elated over the progress that had been made. Bradley's assessment left Eisenhower impressed and optimistic. General Bradley's enthusiasm was contagious. Eisenhower declared: "It would certainly please me if we were in Paris to celebrate my birthday (Oct. 14th). We'd take over the biggest hotel, close it off to everyone else and have the biggest party in the world until everyone got tight."[1]

Although the U.S. forces had not enveloped and annihilated the Germans' western flank, they had done something much more important. They had opened up room for the advance to Brittany and at the same time unhinged the enemy's defenses in the east. The gap in the German lines was already 21 miles wide.

The split between the German Seventh Army's forces created new operational opportunities for the Allied armies to take the offensive. Unless the Germans could launch some kind of "miracle" counterattack to threaten the U.S. salient, there seemed little that could stop the Allies' momentum. It had been an extraordinary few days for the U.S. Army, a real taste of operational maneuver, a modern war of movement. To General Bradley the previous few days were a vindication that he had been right all along about the potential of the army. When properly handled, it was a flexible instrument that could change the course of a campaign.

No command served to demonstrate what General Bradley meant more than the VII Corps's 2d Armored Division, the most successful of Cobra's exploitation forces. During Operation Cobra, Major General Edward H. Brooks, the 2d Armored Division commander, was still a rookie commander leading a combat-tested division. He had taken over the unit, nicknamed "Hell on Wheels," after it had completed the North Africa and Sicily campaigns, and Operation Cobra gave General Brooks his first lesson in fast-paced warfare.[2]

Entering battle on 26 July, the division experienced more than its fair share of slapdash, unexpected encounters with the enemy. On the first night of its attack, a halftrack pulling a trailer had sped past a CCA column north of Canisy, prompting the commander in CCA's lead tank to growl, "Hell, I'm supposed to be leading this column." Then he realized that the vehicle that had just raced by was a German armored car. A running firefight with the enemy vehicle ensued.

On 27 July the 188th Field Artillery Group had been supporting the division's attack from locations near Pont-Brocard when a bypassed German infantry force attacked the gunners. Colonel Thomas A. "Tory" Roberts, commander of the 2d Armored Division artillery, ordered his artillery battalions to each dispatch a fifty-man relief force. The artillery-men-turned-infantrymen subdued the Germans, capturing 175 prisoners.

On 28 July three German tanks had taken up a position at the La Denisière crossroads after CCA's lead elements had already passed. The tanks opened fire on the 14th Armored Field Artillery Battalion as it followed the U.S. armor toward the front, and soon the gunners found themselves in a pitched battle. One battery opened fire on the tanks at a range of less than 500 yards. The panzers held their ground and started firing at the supply vehicles following the column. Every vehicle that passed the intersection had to run the gauntlet of fire until the German tanks withdrew.

After 3 days in a battle that seemed to have no fronts General Brooks had had enough experience in a fast war of movement to last a lifetime. Mixed with the confusion and danger experienced by the 2d Armored Division, however, was a lot of tactical success. By the morning of 29 July the division was the only force to have achieved all the expectations laid out for it in the original Cobra plan, exploiting the breakthrough in depth and forming the outer ring of the envelopment.

In fact, the 2d Armored Division's advance was the most spectacular success of the VII Corps's attack. When General Collins initially launched the division on 26 July he saw their role, Martin Blumenson wrote, as a "a protective mission: guarding the COBRA flank on the south and southeast."[3] By the end of the operation, however, the 2d Armored Division had achieved much more than General Collins had ever expected.

The division's success was unanticipated because, before the offensive, U.S. intelligence had not figured that the route planned for the 2d Armored Division would split the German Seventh Army's two corps. In addition, the Americans did not know that the Germans had fewer reserves to block the 2d Armored's attack than suspected, and General Collins could not foresee that the division's advance would cut the Seventh Army's defensive line completely in two, exposing the enemy's flanks both to the east and the west, and opening up opportunities for the U.S. forces on either side of the 2d Armored Division's penetration to advance.

Unfortunately, General Collins never fully exploited the advantage provided by the division's unforeseen but remarkable achievement. By 27 July it was clear that Brooks's forces had thoroughly disrupted the German defenses in depth, but Collins remained focused on forming the outer ring of the envelopment, rather than exploiting success. Collins should have abandoned the encirclement of Coutances to the VIII Corps and concentrated on deepening the penetration. General Huebner's 1st Infantry Division and the 3d Armored Division under General Watson (wasted in a fruitless effort to trap the Germans at Coutances) could have continued the battle south, while the entire 2d Armored Division turned southeast, collapsing one wing of the German Seventh Army, spoiling the counterattacks that were forming to strike back against Cobra, and creating even more openings for rapid exploitation. General Collins, however, opted for a more conservative course and continued, by and large, to execute his original scheme of maneuver for Operation Cobra.

Throughout Cobra little of the 2d Armored Division's achievements were related to any decision made by General Collins. The division's accomplishments were due to the fact that it attacked through the area where the carpet bombing's effects had been the greatest. In addition, the division had the advantage of cracking the weakly held boundary between the LXXXIV and II Parachute Corps.[4] Finally, there was no question that the 2d Armored Division's leaders and soldiers had been aggressive and determined. The division had never lost the high tempo of its attack.

Holding Open the Breach—Planning on the Run

The "Hell on Wheels" advance was so successful that on 28 July the support of the 258th and 188th Field Artillery Groups was withdrawn and CCA, 2d Armored Division, was detached to the U.S. XIX Corps in order to continue the attack along the Vire River on 29 July.[5] Despite the division's progress, however, concerns remained. There was one decisive act left in the aftermath of Operation Cobra. Although General Bradley considered Cobra complete, the battles discussed in this chapter are still relevant to the story of the spearhead.[6] Although it was too late for the Germans to take back Cobra's gains, an audacious countermove at this point still held the potential of limiting the U.S. First Army's advance. Operation Cobra was predicated on speed, keeping up a tempo of operations so quick that the enemy could never recover. Beyond the range of the Americans there were still river lines, particularly on the Vire and Sienne, that, given time, could be used to set up new defense positions to keep the U.S. First Army from completely routing the German Seventh Army. A well-placed maneuver to counter the Americans and allow the Germans time to establish new defense lines along one of these rivers could still slow the advance of the breakthrough. As a result, U.S. forces had to be concerned about holding off any last-minute counterattacks that might impede operations just as the Allied armies were preparing to roar out of the lodgement area.

Indeed, before dawn on 29 July German activity picked up. The pressure of enemy units flooding toward Pont-Brocard had became so intense that General Brooks, the 2d Armored Division commander, committed his reserve. Ironically, this threat by the Germans had appeared by mistake. General Hausser, the Seventh Army commander, had originally ordered the 17th SS Panzergrenadier Division, the 2d SS Panzer Division, and the 6th Parachute Regiment to counterattack into the U.S. penetration. General Kluge, the Army Group B commander, after an acrimonious meeting had rejected the plan. Kluge ordered the attack canceled and directed the forces to fight a holding action and allow the LXXXIV Corps to establish a new defense line from Bréhal to St-Denis-le-Gast to Gavray (a line later moved south of the Sienne River). Unfortunately for General Hausser, the cancellation order did not reach all the commanders at the front.

Among the German forces mistakenly preparing to go on the offensive were the paratroopers of Lieutenant Colonel Freidrich-August Freiher von der Heydte's 6th Parachute Regiment. They had been steadily retreating for 2 days alongside troops of the 2d SS Panzer and 17th SS Panzergrenadier Divisions. The last order Lieutenant Colonel Heydte received from Lieutenant Colonel Baum, the ad hoc force's temporary commander, was to continue a fighting withdrawal south and set up a new main line of resistance. It seemed like a prudent course of action. But, when Heydte returned to his command post at 1:00 A.M. on 29 July, his staff informed him that he had received an urgent message—new orders. Unfortunately, the message was encrypted with the codes for 28 July, and, in accordance with standard procedures, his staff had destroyed the decoding charts at midnight. At 3:00 A.M. the order was repeated on the radio without encryption. It was not an order to continue the retreat, but to attack![7]

Lieutenant Colonel Heydte was used to tough fighting. A veteran of North Africa, Sicily, and the Eastern Front, he enjoyed a reputation as an independent and innovative commander. He had even been featured in German newsreels. His troops were tough as well. Even though the regiment had only been recently formed (consisting mostly of 17-year-old volunteers) and was critically short of equipment and replacements, it had an outstanding combat record. The ranks were sprinkled with veteran officers and NCOs who had fought in Crete, North Africa, and the Soviet Union. After weeks of hedgerow combat, the young troops that Heydte had left had hardened into a tough, determined force.

Despite Heydte's confidence in his soldiers, the new order came as an incredible shock, heaping disaster on adversity. The paratrooper force had been whittled to nothing. One of the battalion commanders had suffered a nervous breakdown. There were fewer than 3 hours of darkness left to prepare an attack that was supposed to carry them several kilometers from Roncey to Percy via St-Martin-de-Cenilly. It seemed an impossible task.

It took till dawn on 29 July to assemble the troops near Roncey and mount the tanks of the 2d SS Panzer Division. In addition to the tanks and Lieutenant Colonel Heydte's paratroopers, all the force that could be mustered were some assault guns from the 17th SS Panzergrenadier Division, the 17th SS Pioneer Battalion, and a few bits and pieces of other scattered units.

Even after the column was ready to attack, there were problems. Lieutenant Colonel Heydte had no contact with Lieutenant Colonel Baum, the temporary commander of the 17th SS Panzergrenadier Division. Unknown to Heydte Baum had already withdrawn the rest of his force to the south beyond the Sienne River. In fact, no one was in charge of the forces left behind. On the night of 28 July much of the Panzer Lehr and the 353d, 275th, and 17th SS Panzergrenadier Divisions had already retreated south past the U.S. lines. Heydte and his patchwork command were truly on their own, and they would be attacking blindly without knowing the enemy's size, location, or dispositions.

CCB and the Battle of All Directions

It would have given Lieutenant Colonel Heydte little comfort to know that his force was headed toward a U.S. unit commanded by a steady, tested combat leader, who also suspected that the Germans were up to something. Brigadier General Isaac D. White, commander of CCB, 2d Armored Division, had a reputation as a trailblazer in armored warfare. By the advent of Cobra he was already a veteran commander, having lead tank forces in North Africa and Sicily. From the enemy activity the previous day, General White concluded that the Germans were pressuring the corps's encirclement by pushing southeast. He expected more attacks and decided that the best course of action was to consolidate CCB's positions. It was a sound decision, but there were problems. The biggest was that consolidation would not be an easy task. After completing the Cobra envelopment, in accordance with the scheme of maneuver mapped out by the VII Corps's General Collins, on the morning of 29 July CCB's forces were strung out along the length of the division zone. (See Figure 11.1 for a picture of the 2d Armored Division's operations.)

Figure 11.1   Attack of the 2d Armored Division

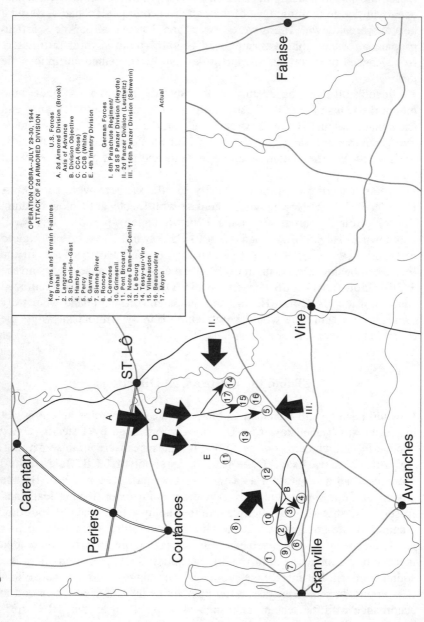

OPERATION COBRA--JULY 29-30, 1944
ATTACK OF 2d ARMORED DIVISION

Key Towns and Terrain Features
1. Brehal
2. Lengronne
3. St. Denis-le-Gast
4. Hambye
5. Percy
6. Gavray
7. Sienne River
8. Roncey
9. Cerences
10. Grimesnil
11. Pont Brocard
12. Notre Dame-de-Cenilly
13. Le Bourg
14. Tessy-sur-Vire
15. Villebaudon
16. Beaucoudray
17. Moyon

U.S. Forces
A. 2d Armored Division (Brook)
   Axis of Advance
B. Division Objective
C. CA (Rose)
D. CCB (White)
E. 4th Infantry Division

German Forces
I. 6th Parachute Regiment/
   2d SS Panzer Division (Heydte)
II. 2d Panzer Division (Leuttwitz)
III. 116th Panzer Division (Schwerin)

————— Actual

The 82d Reconnaissance Battalion
on the Banks of the Sienne

Lieutenant Colonel Wheeler G. Merriam commanded the CCB's western-most unit, the 82d Reconnaissance Battalion. Since the 1st Infantry Division had failed to push as far west as expected, General Collins had ordered the 2d Armored Division to move past Lengronne and secure Cérences and Bréhal, blocking the Germans' withdrawal south. In turn, General White had sent Lieutenant Colonel Merriam's 82d Reconnaissance Battalion ahead to secure an objective near Lengronne and take control of the Coutances–Gavray road, as well as the bridge crossings on the Sienne River. Lieutenant Colonel Merriam's battalion set up defensive positions covering all the bridges on the Sienne River east of Cérences, except for one near Gavray, which a determined German force refused to give up.[8]

The Task Force at Cambry

Not far from the 82d Reconnaissance Battalion, a task force of H Company, 3d Battalion, 67th Armored Regiment (less one platoon), and G Company, 3d Battalion, 41st Armored Infantry Regiment, with an engineer platoon of B Company, 17th Armored Engineer Battalion, a medical detachment, and an air-support party was sent out to secure the crossroads at Cambry on the Coutances–Gavray road. Driving off six enemy vehicles, the detachment had cut the highway, blocking the German withdrawal and providing flank security for the movement of the main body.

CCB's Main Body Moves Up

The rest of CCB was stretched out for 7 miles on either side of the road from Pont Brocard to St-Denis-le-Gast. The 1st Battalion, 67th Armored Battalion, and the 1st Battalion, 41st Armored Infantry Regiment, comprised the western part of the main body. The 1st Battalion, 67th Armored Regiment, commander had been killed the day before and he was replaced by Major Clifton Batchelder, who ordered the column to continue south-west toward Lengronne to link up with the 82d Reconnaissance Battalion. Meanwhile, Lieutenant Colonel Marty Morin's 1st Battalion, 41st Armored Infantry Regiment, followed at the rear of the column, well situated to guard against attacks from retreating Germans.

The eastern column of CCB's main body, led by Lieutenant Colonel John D. Wynne's 2d Battalion, 67th Armored Regiment, was near Le Bourg, a small village northeast of Notre Dame-de-Cenilly. This task force included the battalion's Headquarters Company, Company E, and a platoon from another company of the battalion. Also with Lieutenant Colonel Wynne's command were I Company, 3d Battalion, 41st Armored Infantry Regiment, and 1st Platoon, C Company, 238th Combat Engineer Battalion. Following was Lieutenant Colonel Marshall Crawley's 3d Battalion, 41st Armored Infantry Regiment, supported by F Company, 2d Battalion, 67th Armored Regiment. Unknown to the task force, as it advanced it had moved directly in the path of Lieutenant Colonel Heydte's makeshift force.

Behind CCB's main body was a rearguard of Lieutenant Colonel Harry L. Hillyard's 3d Battalion, 67th Armored Regiment (less one company), and Lieutenant Colonel Wilson D. Coleman's 2d Battalion, 41st Armored Infantry Regiment. The armor and infantrymen were defending the area around Notre Dame-de-Cenilly and Pont-Brocard. On 29 July they planned to continue to move south toward St-Denis-le-Gast.

Meanwhile, the 2d Armored Division's rear area was tenuously tied to the 8th Infantry Regiment, 4th Infantry Division, near Notre Dame-de-Cenilly. On 29 July Colonel Sidney R. Hinds, the 41st Armored Infantry Regiment and division reserve commander for the 2d Armored Division, was trying to tighten up the division's position by turning over the area from Pont-Brocard to Notre Dame-de-Cenilly to the 4th Infantry Division.

Both the CCB commander, General White, and General Brooks, the division commander, viewed the division's situation with some concern. Had General Collins's plan for forming Cobra's outer ring spread the division's forces too thin? The inner ring that was to be provided by elements of the 1st Infantry and 3rd Armored Divisions had been slow in forming. As a result the 2d Armored would have to face any enemy that had slipped past the other divisions, as well as being concerned about counterattacks from the south or east.

At least the two generals reassured themselves that there was some good news. Even though CCB's advance had stopped several miles from the coast and the enemy could still flee south down a narrow corridor, the Germans needed a bridge to cross the Sienne River—and the 2d Armored Division controlled all but one of the bridges. The odds were that if the Germans tried to retreat, they would find "Hell on Wheels" in their way. In short, the division had pretty much bottled up the last of the Germans left inside the VII Corps's envelopment.

Despite the fact that the 2d Armored Division had completed the envelopment, having its forces dispersed over a wide area was a serious concern. Unknown to the 2d Armored Division, however, it had another problem, one that its commanders knew nothing about. The CCB intelligence estimate for Operation Cobra had listed all the forces that would be capable of withdrawing through its area, but the list was incomplete. The division's estimate accounted for Lieutenant Colonel Heydte's 6th Parachute Regiment, but it did not include the 2d SS Panzer Division tanks that were accompanying the paratroopers.

The Enemy Attacks at Dawn

Before dawn on 29 July Lieutenant Colonel Heydte accompanied a column of about thirty vehicles with infantry and 2d SS Panzer Division tanks led by an 88mm self-propelled gun. At first, the weather appeared to be on their side. When dawn finally came it was masked by an early morning fog. Unfortunately, by 8:00 A.M. the fog was burned off and the skies were clear. Heydte expected at any minute that Allied fighters would come down on the column. None appeared, and unmolested, the Germans hit the U.S. lines at the crossroads southwest of Notre Dame-de-Cenilly and St-Martin-de-Cenilly and pushed northeast directly into the main body of CCB, 2d Armored Division.

Lieutenant Colonel Heydte's force ran straight into I Company from Lieutenant Colonel Crawley's 3d Battalion, 41st Armored Infantry Regiment, and a company of tanks from the 67th Armored Regiment near Notre Dame-de-Cenilly. Sergeant Robert Lotz of I Company watched as the gray German column emerged from the dissipating morning mist and turn directly toward him. The long row of vehicles snaked down the road toward the crossroads like a caravan on holiday. As the Germans approached his position, Sergeant Lotz's men opened fire on the lead vehicle, a self-propelled gun. The vehicle crashed just as it reached the crossroads, blocking the road and stalling the German column behind the disabled gun. Heydte's infantry dismounted and assaulted Sergeant Lotz's position, but they were stopped by machine gun fire.

Heydte tried to bypass I Company by sending a company of infantry on a wide flanking movement. The colonel led the advance himself, taking the men in single file through the hedgerows. They eventually reached Notre Dame-de-Cenilly, but saw that the Americans obviously held the town in force. Lieutenant Colonel Heydte decided to withdraw without attacking, and when he returned to the column he found his force still pinned down by fire from Sergeant Lotz's position.

The rest of Lieutenant Colonel Crawley's 3d Battalion, 41st Armored Infantry Regiment, task force had come to the sergeant's aid. Infantry and armor, joined by the 92d Armored Field Artillery Battalion, poured fire onto the enemy column. Faced with overwhelming enemy firepower, the Germans withdrew leaving behind seventeen dead and 150 wounded. The Americans lost a halftrack, a tank, and fifty casualties. Sergeant Lotz, who had initiated the firefight with the German column, moved forward to inspect the destroyed self-propelled gun that had blocked the crossroads and prevented the enemy advance. The driver and gunner were dead in their seats, but the engine was still running—and there was a round loaded in the gun's breech.

Lotz's unit was not the only U.S. force to have an anxious morning on 29 July. Nor was Lieutenant Colonel Heydte's command the only patch-work German unit trying to fight its way through the VII Corps's outer ring. The 78th Armored Field Artillery Battalion, supporting CCB, was in a position at the crossroads southwest of Notre Dame-de-Cenilly. Before 29 July the 78th's commander, Lieutenant Colonel H. M. Exton, had found Cobra to be mostly an exhausting grind that amounted to lots of moving and little firing. That dawn, however, he was to have more problems than just being tired.

Lieutenant Colonel Exton received reports of enemy tanks approaching from the southwest, followed shortly by the sound of machine gun and artillery. Then suddenly his firing batteries became the front. Between 8:30 and 9:00 A.M. German troops overran the covering force of the 8th Infantry Regiment, 4th Infantry Division, and stormed into the rear of CCB and the 78th Armored Field Artillery Battalion.

Even Lieutenant Colonel Exton's command post came under enemy machine gun fire. B and C Batteries held off the enemy ground assault, while A Battery lobbed shells onto the attacking Germans. Four tank destroyers from the 702d Tank Destroyer Battalion and antiaircraft weapons from nearby units took up positions behind the artillerymen and joined in the fight. The division artillery also provided support, firing three concentrations only 500 yards from the battalion's front. Eventually armor and infantry reinforcements from the division reserve arrived. At 10:20 A.M. the Germans withdrew. Exton's battalion reported 126 enemy dead, numerous wounded, and several destroyed Mark IV tanks.

By midmorning the German attacks had ended. Lieutenant Colonel Heydte of the 6th Parachute Regiment discovered that he had lost half his column in the morning fog and the battle outside Notre Dame-de-Cenilly. To add to his woes, Heydte and his counterpart, the acting regimental commander from the 2d SS Panzer Division, could not agree on who should be in charge. The panzer commander was only a major, but he declined to accept orders from Heydte, and Heydte was no more inclined to listen to the panzer officer. They agreed on a compromise. The road to St-Denis-le-Gast was reported to still be open, and they decided that the best course of action would be to withdraw quickly directly to the south through the town. The panzer major, however, withdrew his tanks without waiting for Heydte to collect his scattered command. Heydte assembled the remaining men and marched south; as far as he was concerned the counterattack was over.

CCB's Main Body Moves on
St-Denis-le-Gast and Lengronne

While the Germans withdrew, General Brooks's 2d Armored Division renewed its advance as General Barton's 4th Infantry Division took over the armored division's rear area near Notre Dame-de-Cenilly. Leading the way, Lieutenant Colonel Morin's 1st Battalion, 41st Armored Infantry Regiment, and the 1st Battalion, 67th Armored Regiment, commanded by

Major Batchelder, headed toward Hambye, St-Denis-le-Gast, and into Lengronne to help out Lieutenant Colonel Merriam's 82d Reconnaissance Battalion. En route, the Americans found Hambye still occupied by the Germans and bypassed the town. St-Denis-le-Gast, on the other hand, was unoccupied (part of Lieutenant Colonel Heydte's lost command and a handful of tanks from the 2d SS Panzer Division had already passed through and withdrawn south) and the U.S. forces moved into the town.

While the task force continued on to Lengronne, it left B Company from Lieutenant Colonel Morin's 1st Battalion, 41st Armored Infantry Regiment (with a platoon from the battalion's C Company), and 2d Platoon, A Company, from Major Batchelder's 1st Battalion, 67th Armored Regiment, to secure St-Denis-le-Gast. The division reserve under Colonel Hinds assumed command of the stay-behind force, ordering B Company to take up positions south and north of the town, while the tank platoon under the command of Lieutenant William H. Hough moved into the center of St-Denis-le-Gast to act as a reserve. The armored platoon had a section of tank destroyers attached, positioning one gun north of the town and one south. As the remainder of the division reserve moved up, Colonel Hinds also added a string of six outposts and roadblocks that stretched as far west as Grimesnil, northwest of St-Denis-le-Gast. In addition, the 67th Armored Regiment's Reconnaissance Company was also ordered to send a platoon to St-Denis-le-Gast and another to clean out the Germans in Hambye. Meanwhile, the rest of the reconnaissance company moved on to Lengronne to establish linkup points with the VIII Corps's 4th Armored Division. By the afternoon of 29 July General Brooks's tankers held St-Denis-le-Gast in force.

By 3:30 P.M. "Hell on Wheels" armor also closed on Lengronne, where they found Lieutenant Colonel Merrian's 82d Reconnaissance Battalion still anxiously holding on with C Company at Trelly, west of Cambry (on the Coutances–Gavray road), and B Company spread out in the St-Denis-le-Gast–Gavray sector, watching the bridges on the Sienne River. A Company, 82d Reconnaissance Battalion, covered the river crossings except for the bridge at Gavray still occupied by the Germans.

After joining up with Lieutenant Colonel Merriam's reconnaissance battalion, the task force consisting of Lieutenant Colonel Morin's 1st Battalion, 41st Armored Infantry Regiment, and Major Batchelder's 1st Battalion, 67th Armored Regiment, thickened the defenses in the area with a line of positions that covered Cérences and Lengronne.

Task Force Linkup at Cambry:
Overwatch at Bomber Paradise

While the main body of CCB moved near Lengronne, Lieutenant Colonel Wynne's 2d Battalion, 67th Armored Regiment, and Lieutenant Colonel

Crawley's 3d Battalion, 41st Armored Infantry, all under the command of Lieutenant Colonel Paul A. Disney, shifted west to secure the ridgeline on the main road from Cambry to Grimesnil, blocking all the north-to-south roads in the area. Lieutenant Colonel Disney's force linked up with another CCB task force consisting of H Company, 67th Armored Regiment, and G Company, 41st Armored Infantry Regiment. Together the units seized the crossroads on the Coutances–Gavray road at Cambry, south of Lengronne.

As General Brooks consolidated his forces, the tankers received almost no interference from withdrawing Germans. The afternoon skies had cleared, and any moving enemy from Roncy to St-Denis-le-Gast drew the punishing attention of air power and artillery. An air observer of the 92d Armored Field Artillery Battalion spotted Germans moving from Roncey toward St-Denis-le-Gast and directed fire in their path. Observers with Lieutenant Colonel Wynne's 2d Battalion, 67th Armored Regiment, also spotted the enemy and called for artillery fire from the 62d Armored Field Artillery Battalion.

Planes from the 405th Fighter Group were returning from a weathered-out bombing run over Villedieu when they spotted the withdrawing Germans harassed by U.S. artillery. The aircraft raked the columns from head to tail, calling back to the airfields for more planes. For the rest of the afternoon, sorties of fighter-bombers rotated over the pocket attacking targets at will. The retreating enemy withered under U.S. fire: the pilots called it "fighter bomber paradise."[9] The pressure on the enemy was terrifying and relentless. It was perhaps the single most devastating display of close air support in the young history of air power.

While the air forces stampeded across the Normandy skies in the days following the Cobra bombing, their task was far from effortless. Close air support was a difficult, dangerous business. One unit reported:

> The 10th Sqd. [Squadron] lost two good men [on 28 July]. Lt. Jacks was NYR [not yet returned] and Lt. Moore was seen to crash in flames. . . . On the 29th [of July] the 313th [Squadron] lost a plane, the pilot parachuting. Lt. [Philbin] is not yet reported. The 10th [Squadron] lost Lt. Cagny who crashed in flames. Lt. Charbenneau bailed out and turned up in a hospital the next day with both legs broken.[10]

Although the duty was hazardous, General Quesada proclaimed that "a real breakthrough has been accomplished and by gosh! By gum! You have all done more than your share."[11] The fighter-bombers had left their mark on the German LXXXIV Corps.

The last of Lieutenant Colonel Heydte's troops were attacked by fighters north of St-Denis-le-Gast, and when they got to the main roads near the town they found it choked with U.S. tanks. The paratroopers hid behind the hedgerows and waited for the tanks to pass and then darted across the road. Heydte spent the rest of the day infiltrating his troops south through the

U.S. lines to La Mancellière, a small village southwest of Percy. Linking up with the rest of his command, Heydte hid his force in nearby barns. He had less than a battalion of exhausted, dispirited men; he remained bitter about the order that had sent his command to virtual destruction. Later he recalled, "It still cannot be understood why we went southeast directly into the arms of the Americans. We were lucky to escape with as much of our hides as we did."

At least some of Lieutenant Colonel Heydte's troops had escaped. Others had not been so fortunate. The Americans counted over 350 assorted vehicles in various states of wreckage, some abandoned, some destroyed, the byproduct of 4 days of attacks, artillery, and aerial fire. Colonel Jesse Hawkins, the 2d Armored Division G-2, who personally inspected the devastation, claimed the early reports were "modest."[12] The landscape was covered with the skeleton of the LXXXIV Corps.

Night Attack on CCB

The artillery and air attacks devastated the retreating Germans, but there were still enemy troops and operational vehicles north of the Sienne River inside the VII Corps outer ring. The enemy hid by day and prepared to withdraw under darkness on 29 July. On a moonless night, illuminated only by the dim light of stars, the Germans resumed their frantic push to the south. At about 1:15 A.M., on 30 July, the outposts of Lieutenant Colonel Wynne's 2d Battalion, 67th Armored Regiment, reported the sound of armor moving in the dark. The road east of Cambry ran parallel past the town and then turned abruptly west for a few hundred yards, intersecting the Cambry–St-Denis-le-Gast road west of the tiny hamlet of Grimesnil. The road ran right through the U.S. positions—and there was something moving on it. The suspicious noise was coming right toward Lieutenant Colonel Wynne's 2d Battalion headquarters as well as nearby troops, including an infantry company, a tank company, and an engineer platoon.

A German force supported by a Mark IV tank and a self-propelled gun brushed past the 2d Battalion's northernmost outpost and headed down the road toward Grimesnil. The next roadblock held the Germans off with machine gun fire while the squad leader, Sergeant Hulon B. Whittington, ran for reinforcements. He returned in a short time crouched on the deck of a Sherman tank. The tank fired on the lead German vehicle, while the sergeant engaged the German infantry with small arms and hand grenades. Sergeant Whittington soon found his counterattack reinforced by mortar fire from the Headquarters Company, 2d Battalion, 67th Armored Regiment. The mortars raked the enemy column. Exploding white phosphorous shells illuminated the dark. The headquarters of the 2d Battalion, 67th Armored Regiment, jumped in to help fight off the attack, with even the commander, Lieutenant Colonel Wynne, his staff, drivers, and radio operators joining the battle.

Artillery support came from Lieutenant Colonel Exton's 78th Armored Field Artillery Battalion and the nearby 62d Armored Field Artillery Battalion. In the dark that was cut only by the flicker of burning vehicles and bursting shells, artillery observers adjusted rounds onto the enemy by the sound and flash of the exploding rounds.

Scattered by the artillery fire, the German infantry and vehicles of all descriptions fanned out into the darkness. As the roar of combat subsided, Colonel Wynne watched the flash of firing weapons, like evening summer lightning, drift off to the west toward the rest of CCB.

Next, the battle spread to Lieutenant Colonel Hillyard's 3d Armored Battalion, 67th Regiment. The battalion's command post had settled into an orchard only a few hundred yards from Colonel Wynne's positions. Hillyard's headquarters troops had been joined by the battalion's mortar and assault gun platoons. Lieutenant Colonel Hillyard was checking the outpost line when Warrant Officer Donald Manning at the battalion command post contacted the commander by radio and reported that they were under attack: a German tank had pushed its barrel through the hedgerow marking the command post's perimeter and systematically destroyed every vehicle in sight. The remnants of Hillyard's headquarters troops abandoned the position and fled to the west toward Lieutenant Colonel Coleman's 2d Battalion, 41st Armored Infantry Regiment, to take refuge.

The command post of the 2d Battalion, 41st Armored Infantry Regiment, quickly became embroiled in the night fighting, and the battalion commander, Lieutenant Colonel Colemen, was caught in the middle of the battle. Grabbing a bazooka, he incapacitated the enemy tank leading the attack and then jumped into his jeep to race back and alert the command. He was killed a short time later while organizing a counterattack (the second battalion commander in CCB to be killed during the operation). Meanwhile, the fighting grew increasingly desperate and confused. Many small groups fought alone in the dark against equally desperate remnants of German units, while other Americans ventured out to search for the wounded.

The attack also spread to Lieutenant Colonel Exton's 78th Armored Field Artillery Battalion, which had taken up positions between St-Denis-le-Gast and Lengronne, along the Bréhal–Lengronne road. B Battery was north of the road. Headquarters and A and C Batteries were lined up from east to west, south of the road. The German attack hit their positions from the north. For the second time in less than 24 hours the artillerymen found themselves in an infantryman's fight.

Only 300 yards away from the artillery positions, at Colonel Hinds's division rear command post, reports of the enemy advancing from the north were punctuated by the sound of battle. Hinds's men could see the effects of the enemy attack as vehicles burned from exploding ammunition, lighting up the sky. Adding to the glow, a nearby house caught fire and the night danced with the shadows of combat. The red glow and the din of battle marched toward them. Finally Colonel Hinds's command post came under attack.

Meanwhile, not far away, guarding the outposts in St-Denis-le-Gast, the 67th Regiment's reconnaissance company also found itself heavily engaged. A German column that had been hiding during the day after the abortive morning attack attempted to escape under the cover of darkness. About 1:00 A.M. it ran straight into the company's roadblock. Inside the town, Lieutenant Hough and his tank platoon from the 1st Battalion, 67th Armored Regiment, were resting after a hard day of fighting and moving. The lieutenant hoped that if they were lucky they would spend a quiet night in St-Denis-le-Gast, but then the German column crashed into the outposts of the reconnaissance company and headed toward Lieutenant Hough's small command. The tank destroyer positioned north of the town was hit and withdrew. B Company, 1st Battalion, 41st Armored Regiment, was also pushed back and withdrew under the protection of Lieutenant Hough's tank platoon. Guarded by the armor, the Americans headed to the high ground north of the town where they set up defenses for the night.

Colonel Hinds was unaware of all the battles going on around him; he had lost contact with just about everyone. The colonel, his executive officer, Lieutenant Colonel Robert B. Galloway, and a detail of eight men took the command truck to a position along the road to the cemetery on the north edge of the high ground near St-Denis-le-Gast to reestablish communications. From there the colonel had contact with the division command post and the division artillery, but no word from his own units. Two men from the command group volunteered to go forward and reconnoiter the situation in the town. Only 500 yards from their position, they saw the German column that had chased Lieutenant Hough's tank platoon out of the town.

Shocked by the sight of enemy in St-Denis-le-Gast, the scouts returned and reported that panzer units controlled the area. Colonel Hinds and Lieutenant Colonel Galloway, led by the soldiers, went back to look for themselves. A brief firefight with a German armored car convinced the colonel that the soldiers were right and they withdrew, followed by the entire enemy column. The German force, disoriented in the fighting, rather than heading east toward the objective of the counterattack or south to escape the Americans, headed west right past Colonel Hinds and down the road in the direction of Lengronne and the rest of CCB.

The VII Corps, alerted to the enemy attacks, directed the 4th Infantry Division to send reinforcements, but there was little likelihood the infantry could arrive in time to influence the battle.[13] CCB's commanders were on their own. Meanwhile, the Germans charging out of St-Denis-le-Gast headed straight for Lieutenant Colonel Exton's luckless 78th Armored Field

Artillery Battalion. The battalion's command post was 50 yards south of the main highway on a sunken path paralleling the road. At 2:15 A.M. an officer from the 67th Armored Regiment's reconnaissance company came to the command post, telling everyone that the regiment's outposts at St-Denis-le-Gast had been thrown back by the Germans. He was followed by an M10 tank destroyer and an armored car that happened into the battalion area. The tank destroyer had been damaged in the fighting at St-Denis-le-Gast, and the crew was looking for a safe place to work on their vehicle. The crippled vehicle joined the headquarters perimeter, taking up a position near the battalion command post. A short time later, an armored column appeared. At first the outposts believed that it was more U.S. tanks evacuating St-Denis-le-Gast; troops from the tank destroyer that had just pulled in went out to the main road to direct the column around their disabled gun. The vehicles rolled down the main road past the tank destroyer and the battalion's antitank outpost. Finally, two U.S. officers approached the column and when they challenged the lead vehicle, they were answered in German.

The night exploded in fire.

Not only the artillery headquarters came under attack. B Battery, which had already fought a battle for half an hour against German infantry on one flank, suddenly found itself engaged on a second front. The Germans, who thought they were on the road south to safety, were as surprised at the encounter as the Americans. Most of the combat took place at ranges of less than 50 yards. Fifty-caliber machine guns from Headquarters and B Battery halftracks parked on the roadside cut into the night drawing long lines of red tracers across the sky. A German personnel carrier exploded, turning the darkened battlefield briefly into day. The damaged U.S. tank destroyer and the battalion's antitank gun used the flickering light to find their targets.

The desperate battle lasted till dawn. By 7:30 A.M., on 30 July, all firing had stopped. The battalion headquarters counted twenty destroyed vehicles, fifty enemy dead and 200 prisoners. On the other flank, where B Battery had been attacked, another forty German dead and wounded were found. The artillerymen's losses amounted to five killed and six wounded, including the intrepid battalion commander Lieutenant Colonel Exton.

The battle had taken its toll of the Germans: two hundred of them staggered into the 62d Armored Field Artillery Battalion positions near Lengronne and surrendered. Even the 2d Armored Division Artillery got into the act. At 5:00 A.M. Colonel Roberts led a detail from the headquarters to relieve the 78th Armored Field Artillery Battalion. When the relief force arrived, it found the situation under control, but, still, Colonel Roberts's men managed to flush out ten prisoners.

General Brooks's 2d Armored Division had survived the night shaken, but only slightly bruised. Despite the battle in front of its headquarters, the 3d Battalion, 67th Armored Regiment, reported only seven dead, nine missing, and thirteen wounded. The 67th Armored Regiment's reconnaissance company reported over fifty men missing during the night from the fighting near St-Denis-le-Gast. Most showed up in the morning with enemy prisoners. The 82d Reconnaissance Battalion had survived the night without a loss and reported killing more than 100 Germans and taking 250 prisoners. In fact, 150 members of the 2d SS Panzer Division had walked right into the battalion's position and surrendered.

Finally the last of the threat was silenced—but suddenly, there were more reports of 2d Armored Division positions being fired on. The new threat turned out to be the 4th Armored Division of VIII Corps pushing south. Colonel Hinds contacted the division commander and got the firing stopped: his troops had had a tough enough time without being shot at by their own side.[14] The battles of the 2d Armored Division, however, were not over. On 30 July, on the other flank of the breakthrough, the Germans were making one last attempt to stop "Hell on Wheels."

The Situation at the End of the Operation

30 July was a Sunday, though General Bradley's aide recorded in his diary that it was not a day of rest. Bradley was preparing to activate the 12th Army Group headquarters and turn over command of the U.S. First Army to General Hodges. Meanwhile, Major Hansen was off reconnoitering the location for the new army group command post. They were busy, but their thoughts were not concerned with the situation on the front. The German Seventh Army defenses had been breached beyond any hope of recovery. Success seemed assured—or so they had thought.

While the Americans were basking in Cobra's success, General Eugen Meindl, the II Parachute Corps commander, whose units were on the east flank of the breakthrough, continued to try and save his own beleaguered force and the last Seventh Army defense line.[15] Without any reserves available, however, there seemed little he could do. He desperately wanted help, but when he was briefed on the plan to counterattack with the 2d and 116th Panzer Divisions from the east into the U.S. penetration he was totally dismayed. General Meindl did not like the looks of the plan at all. First of all, the attack was not to be under his control, but directed by General Hans Freiherr von Funck, the LXVII Panzer Corps commander. Next, General Meindl, fearing Allied air power, opposed the idea of a daylight attack. Finally, rather than an ambitious counterattack, General Meindl wanted a limited armor strike on a narrow axis to prevent the enemy from securing Percy and uncovering the II Parachute Corps's flank.

General Meindl went to General Hausser's Seventh Army headquarters to plead his case, but to no avail. Hausser stated that General Kluge, the Army Group B commander, had ordered the attack and wanted it done as quickly and aggressively as possible. On the way back to his own headquarters, Meindl's command car was strafed by U.S. planes, and the incident only reinforced his doubts. He could not imagine conducting a massed armor counterattack in broad daylight when the Americans had air supremacy. When General Funck came to Meindl's headquarters to coordinate the offensive, Meindl warned him that "any resistance put up by us would not only be pounced on gleefully by enemy planes, but would also be smashed by enemy tanks."

Ignoring Meindl's concerns, Funck's counterattack called for the II Parachute's 352d Division to secure the attack's staging area along the Vire River. In addition, the last of General Bayerlein's Panzer Lehr Division was to hold the area near Percy. Blocking the Americans at Percy would hold them in place to receive the counterstroke from the 2d and 116th Panzer Divisions across the Vire River.

While the Germans were preparing to attack, so were the Allies. General Montgomery had ordered the British Second Army to advance along the British-U.S. boundary to draw the Germans away from the Vire River. The British operation, code-named Bluecoat, was not scheduled to start until 30 July.[16] This was General Montgomery's third attempt to synchronize an attack with Operation Cobra. The Goodwood offensive had kicked off on 18 July, a week before Cobra, and fell well short of expectations. Montgomery then had General Dempsey launch the II Canadian Corps in Operation Spring, an attack on 25 July to coincide with Cobra. As John English has noted, "By any measure 'Spring' was an unmitigated tactical debacle."[17] Spring saw the Canadian army take its most brutal causalities in a single day since the raid on Dieppe, but the attack did nothing to advance the cause of Operation Cobra.

Montgomery had higher hopes for Operation Bluecoat. Once again, however, British help for Operation Cobra was less than it could have been. Operations Goodwood and Spring had not put enough pressure on the Germans to stop them from sending two armored divisions against the Americans. Operation Bluecoat would start too late to prevent Army Group B from attempting its last counterattack to block the breakthrough.

As the Second British Army was still preparing for Bluecoat, the U.S. First Army increased the tempo of its operations. General Bradley ordered the XIX Corps to push farther south. This move would not only protect the penetration, but open up the possibility of enveloping additional German forces. The XIX Corps commander selected the high ground that ran in a line west to east from Percy to Pont-Farcy (on the Villedieu-les-Poêles–Caen road) as the objective for the new attack.

As the XIX Corps planned its next move, it was well aware of the impending German counterattack. Thanks to Ultra General Bradley had adequate warning of the enemy strike, and he had every confidence that U.S. First Army could handle the threat without holding back the XIX Corps's exploitation of the Cobra breakthrough. The First Army warned the

XIX Corps of the Germans' intentions, but also ordered the corps to press on.

The XIX Corps, alerted to the 2d Panzer Division's movement west on 27 July, believed the panzers would try to cross the Vire River at Tessy-sur-Vire.[18] In response, corps had sent General Hobbs's 30th Infantry Division to take Tessy-sur-Vire and CCA, 2d Armored Division, to push through Villebaudon and on to Percy. From the high ground south of Tessy-sur-Vire, CCA could flank any enemy that tried to push east across the river, as well as control the last crossing on the Vire River that could be used by the panzers.

Preparing for the Last Battle

General Maurice Rose, the commander of CCA, 2d Armored Division, was the right commander to have at the point of the spear. He was a tested, veteran combat leader. A former division chief of staff, he had served stints with the 1st Armored and 3d Infantry Divisions before taking command of CCA in 1943.

For his latest mission, General Rose had reorganized his command into three columns. The first column had been sent southwest past Villebaudon to Percy and the crucial high ground around the town. It included a company of medium tanks from the 3d Battalion, 66th Armored Regiment; K Company, 22d Infantry Regiment; 3d Platoon, F Troop, 24th Cavalry Squadron (light tanks); a platoon from the 17th Engineer Combat Battalion; a platoon from the 66th Armored Regiment's Reconnaissance Company; an air support party; and the 702d Tank Destroyer Battalion (minus Company C). In addition, the XIX Corps attached the 113th Cavalry Group under Colonel William Shepard Biddle III to CCA, and General Rose ordered the cavalrymen to Villebaudon to help shore up the town's defenses.[19] Together, these forces had taken Villebaudon and fought their way to Percy, but had had a difficult time fighting their way into the town through the last remnants of Bayerlein's Panzer Lehr Division.

Meanwhile, Rose had dispatched a second column toward Moyon and then Beaucoudray to cover CCA's eastern flank and guard the command's tenuous supply lines. The task force contained a light-tank company and two medium-tank companies of the 2d Battalion, 66th Armored Regiment; C Company, 22d Infantry Regiment; 2d Platoon, Troop F, 26th Cavalry Squadron (light tanks); an assault gun platoon; a platoon of A Company, 17th Combat Engineer Battalion; maintenance and medical detachments; and a platoon from the 66th Armored Reconnaissance Company. The task force encountered stiff enemy opposition in its drive toward Moyon.

CCA's third force was headed southeast toward Tessy-sur-Vire to seal off the threat of counterattacks across the Vire River. This column consisted of a company of medium tanks; F Company, 22d Infantry Regiment; 1st Platoon, F Troop, 24th Cavalry Squadron (light tanks); an assault gun platoon; a platoon of C Company, 17th Engineer Combat Battalion; medical and maintenance detachments; and a platoon from the 66th Armored Reconnaissance Company. The task force withdrew after it encountered German tanks from the 2d Panzer Division near Tessy-sur-Vire.

All the U.S. attacks experienced difficulties, causing General Rose concern for CCA's operations on 30 July. The presence of German armor in Tessy-sur-Vire made CCA's continued attack south toward Percy problematic. If Rose ignored the threat from the east and continued south, he might expose his flank to an enemy counterattack. There were good routes to support an armor attack out of Tessy-sur-Vire heading west toward Villebaudon and into the U.S. positions. German forces were already pressing on the road from Villebaudon to Le Mesnil-Herman. In addition, enemy tanks and artillery from the area near Moyon threatened to cut supply lines through the intersection at La Denisière. A few German fighters had also made a rare appearance on the battlefield and bombed the U.S. columns. From the tip of the spear to the rear of the column no part of the command was free of enemy harassment.

To make matters worse, General Rose's command had to contend with the movement of the XIX Corps's 29th Infantry Division. The XIX Corps commander had ordered the division to push up behind CCA. As the two units became intermingled clearing fires became impossible, and instances of friendly fire were reported. Units had established no-fire lines to prevent other units from shooting into their area, but the rapid proliferation of control measures and constricted terrain exacerbated the problem. General Rose and Major General Charles H. Gerhardt, the 29th Infantry Division commander, got into a "big fight" over the issue. This prompted General Rose's relief from command, a decision made in the heat of battle and quickly reversed, however. Still, the issues were never satisfactorily worked out. As one commander recalled, "There used to be a saying in CCA that we had fought the 29th Division at the Battle of Tessy-sur-Vire, and that they were not bad fighters."[20]

The fact that most of CCA was utterly exhausted did not make things any easier. Commanders knew that after 48 hours without uninterrupted sleep a leader's capacity to make clear and coherent decisions began to diminish—the division had been on the move for twice that time. Days of nonstop moving and fighting had begun to show in the faces of CCA. One commander complained they were all "dog tired," with virtually no opportunity to sleep. Each day at midnight General Rose would call a meeting at the CCA command posts. The gatherings would not finish until 1:30 A.M., and then the leaders would have to get back on the road to their own commands to prepare new plans and issue orders. By the time they finished it was dawn and time for operations to begin again.

In the latest of the nightly meetings General Rose briefed the most recent changes in CCA's plan. The 29th Infantry Division would move up and take over the ground on CCA's flanks so that the armor could turn its full attention to the Vire River crossings. What the tankers of CCA did not know was that while they were turning to eliminate the threat of the 2d Panzer Division, the 116th Panzer Division was preparing to strike north aimed right at CCA.[21]

The Task Force at Tessy-sur-Vire

Waiting for the CCA Task Force on 30 July at Tessy-sur-Vire was the spearhead of the 2d Panzer Division, under the command of General Baron Diepold Georg Heinrich Luettwitz. The aristocratic General Luettwitz came from a long line of soldiers from as far back as the 14th century. He had volunteered to fight as a private on the Western Front during World War I and later received an officer's commission. He remained in the army after the war, and in 1931 transferred to work with Germany's fledgling armored forces. A series of successful commands on the Eastern Front, including a stint as an acting division commander, had brought him both experience and notoriety. In 1943 the 47-year-old Luettwitz assumed command of the 2d Panzer.[22] General Luettwitz had supervised the transfer of the remnants of the division from the Soviet Union to France, where he had rebuilt the command in less than 6 months.

The reconstituted 2d Panzer Division was a standard German armored division and did not have nearly the combat power of a U.S. heavy armored division. The German division had only one armored regiment with two battalions and two armored infantry regiments, each with two battalions. The division also included an armored artillery regiment with one light and two medium battalions, as well as reconnaissance and support units.

In the summer of 1944 the rebuilt 2d Panzer gained combat experience in battles against the British. Unfortunately, its lessons were gained at a pretty serious cost—heavy casualties. The lack of adequate replacements exacerbated the division's problems. Even before the counterattack, General Luettwitz's command was already a "worn out division."[23] Once they reached the front, rather than attacking, Luettwitz's troops moved into line with the 352d Division and tried to hold on, waiting for the commitment of the 116th Panzer Division on 30 July before resuming their offensive.

Meanwhile, on 30 July, CCA, 2d Armored Division, unaware of the impending commitment of the 116th Panzer, continued to push a task force toward Tessy-sur-Vire. Moving through Le Mesnil-Herman and Villebaudon toward Tessy-sur-Vire, the task force collided with Germans from the 2d Panzer attacking west. The Americans, later reinforced by guns from the 702d Tank Destroyer Battalion, took on the Germans in a 13-hour battle.

While combat raged outside Tessy-sur-Vire, an exhausted Lieutenant Colonel Carl Irven Hutton, commander of the 14th Armored Field Artillery Battalion, had his batteries back on the road again with new orders to march from Villebaudon to Percy. Since Cobra had started, his units had been shot at and cut off, and had moved and moved again more times than he cared to remember.[24] In addition to taking care of his own guns, Lieutenant Colonel Hutton had to control the fires of the 44th Field Artillery Battalion.

Pairing two artillery battalions (like the 14th and the 44th) in a "groupment" was a common practice for supporting armored columns. The extra artillery expanded the front that the artillerymen could cover, an important consideration in trying to support dispersed, fast-moving armored task forces. That the artillery could mix and match units with such relative ease was another reflection of the tremendous flexibility that the U.S. artillery demonstrated during the course of Operation Cobra. The skill Lieutenant Colonel Hutton had shown so far in supporting the tankers was, however, only a prelude to the unprecedented demands that would be made of him in the next 24 hours.

On 30 July Hutton's battalion was on the road again, this time moving toward Percy. Only a few hours later, however, the gunners were told to stop. At 11:30 A.M. the battalion received word of a strong German counterattack from the east by the 2d Panzer Division on the Villebaudon–Tessy-sur-Vire road. Hutton ordered the units to take up positions and start firing. Throughout the day artillery, mortars, and enemy direct fire harassed the gunners. Friendly infantry retreating through the battery positions and the decreasing range of the calls for fire alerted the gunners to the relentless approach of enemy armor. The 14th Armored Field Artillery Battalion stayed in position until enemy tanks were within 2,000 yards.

While the battalion repositioned, Hutton coordinated for fire from other units. Since there was no division artillery headquarters (the 2d Armored Division artillery headquarters was with CCB), the battalion became the de facto artillery headquarters. In addition to the 44th Field Artillery Battalion, the 18th and 65th Armored Field Artillery Battalions provided support. The XIX Corps Artillery also sent a liaison officer to coordinate requests for fire from the corps artillery.

The massive artillery support was only possible because of the coordination provided by Lieutenant Colonel Hutton's battalion fire direction center. The only limitation to the number of artillery tubes he could bring to bear on the problem was the range a piece could shoot. Hutton's achievement was another affirmation of the U.S. Army's fire direction system. It was battles like this that led General Patton to proclaim after the war, "You all know who won the war. The artillery did." While the acclamation may have been an overstatement, it underscored the unprecedented power that the U.S. artillery could put at the disposal of every battalion and regimental commander.

With crushing artillery support, the task force on the Villebaudon–Tessy-sur-Vire road fought the Germans to a standstill. The Germans, paralyzed by overwhelming artillery fire, became easy targets for the U.S. gunners. The tank destroyers of the 702d Tank Destroyer Battalion alone accounted for eleven German tanks. The U.S. task force held its ground, but the battle seemed like a defeat: the task force was still far short of controlling the river crossing and was worried that the Germans might try to renew their push on Villebaudon. In fact, the Americans had scored a clear victory. The 2d Panzer Division's tankers were thinking more about how they were going to retreat than continuing to attack.

CCA, the Air Force, and the Final Attack

Everything now fell on the shoulders of Major General Gerhard Graf von Schwerin and the 116th Panzer Division, the last unit that had a chance to slow the Cobra breakthrough.[25] This was the climactic moment. If the German attack succeeded, it might blunt the U.S. penetration; the Americans might even be forced to stop their attack and reorganize, giving the German commanders time to reestablish the Seventh Army's defenses. On the other hand, if the 116th Panzer Division failed there was nothing to stop the Americans.

The 116th Panzer was a veteran outfit. It had been reorganized as a standard tank division after withdrawing from the Eastern Front. Moving to France, it had been held in reserve and after reconstitution was almost at full strength and ready for combat in Normandy. The 116th Panzer Regiment had between 160 and 180 armored vehicles. The 60th and 156th Panzergrenadier Regiments were fully manned. The force was equivalent in size to the unit it was preparing to meet in battle, CCA, 2d Armored Division—and, unlike General Luettwitz's 2d Panzer Division, the 116th Panzer Division was fresh, at full strength, and ready for battle.

As his division prepared for combat, General Schwerin headed for the front to assess the situation. He assumed his division was going to be attached to the II Parachute Corps and went straight to General Meindl's headquarters to coordinate the attack. General Schwerin and his command group reached the corps command post in a village southeast of Percy, only to find that Meindl was not in charge. In fact, General Meindl's staff did not know much about the situation at all, other than that the Americans (one CCA task force and elements of Colonel Biddle's 113th Cavalry

Group) were pushing south toward Percy. This had been no great deduction, because from the command post they could hear machine gun fire coming from the town.

Wherever he went the news General Schwerin received was more and more ominous. From Meindl's headquarters, Schwerin made his way to General Funck's command post, where he found out that the 2d Panzer Division's attack had sputtered out against heavy resistance. Next, General Schwerin visited General Bayerlein's headquarters, where the last of the Panzer Lehr Division and other remnants of LXXXIV Corps were holding on at Percy. Bayerlein reported that the options for attack were few. The ground east of Percy was impossible for tanks, too hilly, and with too few roads. The only place for the 116th Panzer Division to start its advance from was the area north and northeast of Percy. The most promising direction for an attack was due west.

General Schwerin established his command post near Courson and began to plan his offensive. By the time the 116th Panzer was finally in position and ready to go, General Funck appeared at the division command post with new orders. The 2d Panzer was locked in a battle at Tessy-Sur-Vire and needed help. Schwerin's new mission was to go to their rescue. Rather than attacking west into the U.S. flank, the 116th Panzer would have to attack directly south and relieve the 2d Panzer. General Schwerin protested. As General Bayerlein had already pointed out, the area east of Percy was terrible for armor. General Funck brushed aside the division commander's concerns. General Schwerin found General Funck's attitude "cynical and disparaging," but he had no options, so the division would attack.

On the morning of 30 July, while CCA was preoccupied with the battle on the road from Tessy-Sur-Vire to Villebaudon against the 2d Panzer Division, the 116th Panzer Division launched its offensive. General Schwerin's armor crashed through a CCA position at Beaucoudray, north of Percy on the Bréhal–Tessy-sur-Vire road, but the attack made little progress after that. General Bayerlein had been right, the ground was too difficult to maneuver across country, so Schwerin's tanks had to move in single file down the roads. The Mark V tanks and assault guns proved too wide for the narrow side roads and had to move on the main thoroughfares. Diverting the tanks, and the resulting traffic jams, slowed the attack considerably.

Meanwhile, it turned out to be a bright, clear day with only scattered clouds and the U.S. planes out in force. As soon as the aircraft flying column cover spotted the German tanks, they radioed for reinforcements. Propellers at scattered airstrips across Normandy spun and planes raced into the sky hungry for targets. A swarm of U.S. fighter-bombers ruined General Schwerin's road-bound columns. These air attacks were the culmination of the 5,105 sorties by the IX TAC directed against the Germans between 27 and 30 July. It was an unbelievably powerful display of air power.

General Schwerin was awed by the air attack: anything that moved was straffed and bombed mercilessly. At midday he called off his offensive and ordered his troops to try and hold on until the 2d Panzer Division's forces withdrew east across the Vire River. The German counterattack had failed. Schwerin bitterly reported that repeated air strikes in depth prevented coherent counterattacks against the enveloping U.S. forces.

Winning the War Without Fronts

General Brooks's 2d Armored Division had fought some of the most chaotic and the most successful battles of Operation Cobra. More than any other division, it demonstrated that General Bradley's notions of a fast war of movement could be more than just the musings of generals. Weapons like artillery, armor, and airplanes under the right operational conditions had the potential to change the traditional notions of how battles were fought. The speed and range of modern weapons could erase the boundaries between the friendly rear area, the front lines, and the enemy's rear. In such battles forces found themselves in a war without fronts, where there was no clearly defined combat area and no sanctuary. A force that could fight in this environment had the potential to overwhelm its opponent, robbing the enemy of initiative and confronting him with too many problems and too many ways to die.

This was the kind of war that really empowered field-grade leaders and made them true instruments of operational warfare. It allowed them to exploit their initiative and aggressively employ all the assets at their disposal. It also put the enemy at maximum risk, getting him out in the open, making him move, and exposing him to the tremendous firepower of artillery, armor, and air attack.

The 2d Armored Division's operations demonstrated both the perils and possibilities of operations without fronts. Troops in rear areas, such as headquarters, support locations, and bivouac sites, which were normally safe from direct ground attack, now had the additional burden of providing security and, in some cases, fighting for their lives. The 78th Field Artillery Battalion and the 14th Armored Field Artillery Battalion, for example, were required to fight off multiple ground attacks and, all the while, continue to provide continuous artillery support. These were no easy tasks for exhausted men who had been moving and shooting nonstop for 4 or 5 days.

Command and control also became more complicated, as evidenced by the difficulties CCA experienced in clearing artillery fires and coordinating maneuvers with the 29th Infantry Division. The challenges were exacerbated by physical exhaustion, the distances between headquarters, the rapidly changing tactical situation, and the confusing intermingling of friendly and enemy forces.

On the positive side, all the combat commands demonstrated tremendous flexibility and endurance—planning, changing, reorganizing on the run, improvising all the way. Commanders conducted dispersed operations, gaining ground, making the most of opportunity, and yet keeping their operations coherent and focused on the overall objectives despite some of the most perilous and chaotic fighting of the campaign. The commanders proved more than ready for the clash of armor.

Equally important, the division's maneuvers demonstrated that deep air attacks orchestrated with land operations could disrupt and defeat enemy attacks before they even reached ground forces. Devastating air attacks allowed mechanized troops to swiftly bypass and unhinge enemy defenses without getting bogged down in costly battles of attrition.

While the results of the air attacks were particularly impressive, they have to be placed in context. The Americans had enjoyed air superiority since the first day of the campaign, but the fighter-bombers had never racked up kills on the scale they achieved during Cobra. The reason for this was that before Operation Cobra, the Germans had hidden from the Allies' aerial strength by digging in, camouflaging positions, and moving most of their forces at night. Cobra forced the enemy to move in daylight, which in turn exposed the Germans to Allied planes. It was the synergistic affect of working ground and air forces together that took away the enemy's options. Ground maneuver forced the enemy out into the open. Air power finished the job—and then the ground forces exploited the opportunity.

The air-ground team's success in fighting off German counterattacks also reinforces the conclusion that General Collins was overly cautious in his approach to Operation Cobra. Collins focused on ensuring a swift and secure envelopment. The ability of the air force to crush enemy units on the move and the armored divisions' ability to provide for their own security and defeat counterattacks demonstrated that the VII Corps could, and should have, been more aggressive and assumed more risk in penetrating the German defenses.

In fact, the performance of the 2d Armored Division demonstrated that the U.S. Army had achieved a far greater degree of operational flexibility than General Collins had realized. U.S. forces matured a good deal over the course of the campaign. They had shown that when the conditions of battle were properly set and commanders given the right mission, they could change the course of a campaign. The 2d Armored Division's actions had been critical to the success of the Cobra. In securing and holding its objectives, the division had achieved the ultimate objective of the operation, breaking through the German lines in depth and creating new opportunities for operational maneuver.

The Operation's End

While the operation had ended on 31 July, Walter Klein, the company medic from Battle Group Heintz, was still fighting on with the last eleven men of his unit. They had been fighting and fleeing from Americans since the first bombs had fallen on their positions on 25 July. Finally, Klein's little group had come under fire when it tried to withdraw across an open field. Klein attended to the wounded; he was wearing a red cross arm band and the Americans allowed him to move about unmolested. For the next 18 hours Klein helped evacuate both American and German casualties. When the work was finished, he was marched off to the POW collection point. For him the war was over.[26]

That same day the German high command concluded that there was no doubt that the Americans could not be stopped. Situation reports showed a "breakdown of the whole German front between the river Vire and the coast. . . . It was no longer possible to restore a continuous strong German defense front." For the Allies the way out of Normandy was open.

31 July was also General Bradley's last day as the First Army commander, and he busied himself in farewells to the staff. He planned to take Major Hansen and a few others in his personal entourage with him to the 12th Army Group headquarters. The other old Bradley hands, General Kean and Colonels Thorson, Dickson, and Hewitt, would stay behind and serve the new commander, General Hodges.

Bradley was also leaving an aspect of command behind. He would never again direct corps and divisions in battle or personally command men like Collins, Eddy, Hobbs, Barton, Huebner, Brooks, and Watson. Together, despite their mistakes and miscues, these commanders had demonstrated that the U.S. Army could become the flexible, operational instrument that Bradley believed it to be. When leaders set the operational conditions right, conditions that would allow the field commanders to exploit the tremendous strengths of the U.S. Army, then they could, as Bradley predicted, change the course of the campaign. But now Bradley was moving on to a different level of operational warfare, further removed from the immediacy of the battlefield. Others would have to carry the responsibility of bridging the span between the aspirations of the campaign plan and reality of the battleground. For Bradley, it was time to leave the triumphs and tragedies of Cobra behind and turn to the next mission: planning the liberation of France and the defeat of Nazi Germany.

Notes

1. Hansen, War Diary, 29 July 1944, MHI.
2. Vignettes of 2d Armored Division operations for 26–28 July are taken

from William C. Boice, ed., *History of the Twenty-Second United States Infantry Regiment in World War II*, p. 31; Donald E. Houston, *Hell on Wheels: The 2d Armored Division*, pp. 220, 230.

3. Blumenson, *Breakout and Pursuit*, p. 254.

4. Some equipment modifications also did not hurt. Three-quarters of the tanks had been equipped with bocage-busting rhinos. Ordnance teams also rearmed a handful of the Sherman tanks with new 76mm high-velocity guns, and the heavier guns enabled the division to take on the German Mark V tanks.

5. Unless cited otherwise, information on 2d Armored Division operations are from *History, 67th Armored Regiment*, pp. 26–27, 84–87, 246–248; Headquarters, 2d Armored Division, U.S. Army, After Action Report, pp. 39–40; Headquarters, 2d Armored Division Artillery, U.S. Army, After Action Report, pp. 2–3; Headquarters, 2d Armored Division, U.S. Army, G-2 Log, 28 and 29 July 1944; E. A. Trahan, ed., *A History of the 2d Armored Division;* Glenn T. Pillsbury et al., Employment of 2d Armored Division in Operation Cobra 25 July–1 Aug 44.

6. General Bradley wrote to General Eisenhower summing up the results of the attack; he concluded with "To say that the personnel of the First Army is riding high tonight is putting it mildly. Things on our front look really good." General Bradley finished by adding that he knew two German armored divisions were preparing to counterattack "to help save the situation," but "in any case we are feeling pretty cocky." Letter to General Eisenhower, 28 July 1944, Omar N. Bradley, Papers, Correspondence with Major Historical Figures, 1938–1960, MHI.

7. Unless cited otherwise, information on German operations on 28 and 29 July are from Heydte, "A German Parachute Regiment in Normandy," pp. 38–42. There are no extant operational unit records for this period.

8. Just getting to the Sienne River had been an adventure for the 82d Reconnaissance Battalion. During the advance, Lieutenant Morton Eustis of C Company had crossed paths with three enemy trucks loaded with Germans. The trucks chased his patrol. The Americans hid behind hedgerows and ambushed the German trucks as they raced by. This was only one incident. Lieutenant Eustis counted coming under fire ten times during the advance, and his experience was typical. At one point the battalion was cut off and had to be relieved by CCB tanks. See Morton Eustis, *The War Letters of Morton Eustis to His Mother, February 6, 1941, to August 10, 1944*, pp. 239–243.

9. Blumenson, *Breakout and Pursuit*, p. 278.

10. Historical Data, AAF Headquarters, Group Fighter, Fiftieth Fighter Group, 1 July to 1 August 1944, microfilm, Roll B0144, p. 4, AFHSO.

11. Headquarters, Fiftieth Fighter Group, Memorandum to All Officers and Enlisted Men of Site 10A, 29 July 1944, microfilm, Roll B0144, AFHSO.

12. Headquarters, VII Corps, U.S. Army, The History of VII Corps, p. 38.

13. Ibid., p. 39.

14. Houston, *Hell on Wheels*, pp. 226–227.

15. General Meindl's assessment of the Army Group B counterattack plan and the 2d Panzer Division's operation are from Meindl, "II Parachute Corps,"; Blauensteiner, "Commitment of the II Parachute Corps," pp. 2–3. See also War Journal of Headquarters Army Group B, 1–31 July 1944, microfilm, T311, Roll 1.

16. Blumenson, *Breakout and Pursuit*, pp. 289–290.

17. English, *The Canadian Army*, p. 249. See also Michael Reynolds, *Steel Inferno: I SS Panzer Corps in Normandy*, pp. 190–197.

18. Ultra did not identify the commitment of the 116th Panzer Division. See F. H. Hinsley et al., eds., *British Intelligence in the Second World War: Its Influence*

on Strategy and Operations, vol. 3, pt. 2, *Summer 1944 to the End of the War with Germany,* pp. 226, 233.

19. Ben L. Rose, *The Saga of the Red Horse,* p. 13.

20. Hutton, *An Armored Artillery Commander,* p. 113–114, USAFAS.

21. While 2d and 116th Panzer Divisions prepared the last counterattack of the campaign, some major changes were taking place. On 30 July General Choltitz, the LXXXIV Corps commander, was replaced by Lieutenant General Otto Elfeldt. This would have very little effect on the course of the day's battle, since there was very little of LXXXIV Corps left to command.

22. Mitcham and Mueller, *Hitler's Commanders,* pp. 147–156.

23. Bayerlein, "An Interview with GENLT Fritz Bayerlein: Critique of Normandy," p. 9.

24. The operations of the 14th Armored Field Artillery Battalion on 29 and 30 July 1944 are from Hutton, *An Armored Artillery Commander,* pp. 114–115, USAFAS; Headquarters, 14th Armored Field Artillery Battalion, U.S. Army, Operations Annex, 29 and 30 July 1944.

25. Information on the 116th Panzer Division's counterattack is from Gerhard Graf von Schwerin, "116th Panzer Division," ETHINT 17, pp. 1–11; Bennett, *Ultra in the West,* p. 105; See also War Journal of Headquarters Army Group B, 1–31 July 1944, microfilm, T311, Roll 1. There are no extant operational unit records.

26. Klein, "Bombing and Operation Cobra," pp. 8–9.

Epilogue:
The Aftermath

B y 1 August 1944 Operation Cobra had run its course. General Bradley moved up and took control of the newly operational 12th Army Group. General Hodges assumed command of the U.S. First Army. Meanwhile, General George S. Patton led the recently activated U.S. Third Army on the drive south into Brittany, exploiting the success of the Cobra breakthrough. Within the week the first U.S. troops marched past the Germans' crippled defenses into Rennes, Brittany's capital.

Cobra had achieved its purpose. At the same time, it had revealed operational opportunities far beyond the plan's original intent. While the Americans under General Patton raced south, the British and the Canadians finally pushed past the armor killing fields around Caen. The Normandy stalemate was over from one end of the coast to the other. Hitler had exacerbated the Germans' problem by ordering a less than clearly thought-through counterattack against the U.S. wing of the offensive. After a brief glimmer of success the German attack had sputtered to a stop outside the city of Mortain. The Allies renewed their assault, leaving the enemy defenses exposed on both flanks. As Normandy's summer of war came to an end the German army reeled back toward Paris.

In the end Cobra proved remarkable both for its contribution to breaking the stalemate on the Western Front and for its demonstration of the U.S. forces' operational flexibility. The battles of Operation Cobra revealed much about the origins of this illusive and essential skill. Cobra clearly showed that the success of the Americans in Normandy did not come from unique "hedgerow-busting" tactics or special equipment such as the rhino tanks. Innovative equipment and tactics did not play a significant role in any of the Cobra battles. Nor could individual weapons such as strategic air, armor, artillery, or tactical air power be credited independently with giving the Americans a decisive edge. The carpet bombing offered land forces the opportunity to break through by disrupting the commitment of reserves and delaying counterattacks, but the battle to pierce the Germans' front lines had to be fought and won on the ground. Armor was effective only after the infantry had broken through the prepared defenses and opened up routes for the tanks to maneuver. Artillery barrages, both before and during the operation, were often ineffective. Artillery was only used to good effect when the U.S. infantry and armor could advance and see the enemy and then direct cannon fire directly on the German positions. Likewise, tactical support was only potent when ground troops could get the enemy to move in the daylight where they could be spotted and attacked by the fighter-bombers. There was no magic bullet for Cobra's success. Independently, all the U.S. Army's capabilities had been used on the Normandy battlefields before and had never provided the Allies an overwhelming advantage. It was the manner in which the operation was executed, the ability of commanders to combine all their assets in support of Cobra that proved to be the real magic.

The ability to understand and exploit the full capabilities of the U.S. Army was something that evolved only gradually over the course of the campaign. When the U.S. Army landed at Normandy it was far from being a perfect instrument of war. Despite its preponderance of power, the army that fought on the sands of Omaha and Utah on 6 June 1944 could not have executed the maneuvers of Operation Cobra on 25 July 1944. The German tactical defensive scheme, the superiority in firepower that the enemy achieved in close-in engagements, and the difficult hedgerow terrain outmatched the Americans' infantry, armor, artillery, and air power.

It took time for the Americans to learn how to fight in Normandy. Time to unlearn the methodical and impractical tactics of fire and movement. Time to learn how to compensate for the dramatic losses in front-line infantry soldiers. Time to learn how to coordinate infantry with tanks, and tanks with air support. Time to learn how to bring all the power that the U.S. forces had to bear on the battlefield. And time to gain the space required to employ all the assets at the Americans' disposal to their best affect.

The Americans' overwhelming dominance in their ability to protect and sustain ground forces bought them the time they needed. The materiel advantages of the U.S. troops gave them more than just brute force. Logistical support and the U.S. Army's ability to protect its soldiers from the debilitating forces of war (from enemy fire to infectious diseases) allowed the Americans the luxury of surviving and learning from their mistakes, recovering to fight another day—and, more important, gaining experience and confidence in their combat capabilities and tactical judgement. Sustainment and protection provided commanders both the means to fight and the time to develop the skills to execute.

While the U.S. forces had significant material strengths, it was equally important that they did not squander their advantages. The ability to protect and sustain combat forces was only part of what gave the U.S. forces operational flexibility. The Americans' skill emerged in large part from the capacity of leaders to achieve the objectives laid out in the operational scheme—a combination of both knowing how to harness the combat power available and realistically understanding what that power could achieve.

The expertise of the senior U.S. commanders only partly explains how U.S. forces managed to focus their combat power and crack the German defenses. Unquestionably the leadership of the U.S. First Army commander, General Bradley, was an important factor. He selected the best course of action for the attack. In fact, most of the senior German commanders on the scene recognized that a sharp, focused assault by the Americans west of St-Lô was the most dangerous threat possible to the stability of the German Seventh Army's defenses. In addition to attacking at the right time and place, General Bradley saw the tremendous opportunities Cobra had created, not just for the advance into Brittany but also to unhinge the Germans' entire Normandy front. As the attack unfolded, Bradley rapidly redistributed forces and objectives to give commanders the opportunities to press their attacks both south toward the Brittany ports and east out of Normandy and on toward Paris.

General Bradley's generalship, however, was not flawless. His most serious error was in the safety precautions put in place before the carpet bombing on 25 July. All the Allies' operational experience with employing air power in proximity to ground troops suggested there was great danger in Bradley's scheme. The senior air commanders impressed upon him that his safety measures were inadequate. Even Bradley's desire to have the planes run a parallel course to the target area (if it had been executed as planned) would have been insufficient to preclude friendly causalities. General Bradley assumed an excessive risk and his soldiers paid the price.

Even though responsibility for the causalities from the short bombing must surely rest with General Bradley, the senior Allied air commanders can hardly be exonerated. The air war in Europe should never have become a debate between strategic bombing and tactical air support. The truth was that there were enough assets to do both. There were few instances when tactical conditions were appropriate for the use of bombers in direct support of ground operations. Taking a handful of days out of a multiyear air campaign to aid the ground battle hardly represented a serious strain to the overall strategic bombing plan. With some modest additional coordination, training, and a few technological innovations to improve air-ground coordination, the air commanders could have executed their strategic air campaign and still provided effective direct support to the ground forces in Normandy on the occasions where the tactical situation demanded a powerful and dramatic firepower strike. Nevertheless, although their cooperation and support was less than it could have been, the ultimate responsibility remained with General Bradley and he handled this aspect of the operation badly.

As for other key senior U.S. ground commanders, many of their decisions were even more faulty. In particular, General Collins's contributions
to Cobra have been overrated; none of the major revisions he recommended
to Bradley's plan significantly improved the execution of the operation. In
addition, several key decisions General Collins made during Cobra were
significantly flawed.

Collins's gravest error was insufficiently weighting the strength of the
attacking forces on the first day of the attack. Even with the addition of the
4th Infantry Division, Collins did not give sufficient consideration to the
difficulty of completing the penetration all the way to the key terrain at
Marigny. He did not provide General Eddy an appropriate mission. When
the understrength and inadequately supported 9th Infantry Division failed
to reach its objectives, sending in the 1st Infantry Division to complete the
penetration cost the VII Corps's attack an additional 24 to 48 hours—time
that could have been used to rapidly expand the split in the German
defenses.

The VII Corps commander's most aggressive decision during the operation was equally flawed. Having reports of U.S. troops in Marigny on 26
July, General Collins determined that conditions were right to launch the
last of his exploitation force, the 3d Armored Division. In fact his decision
was made on bad information. The Americans did not control the town. If
General Collins had had an accurate assessment of the situation (that
progress had, in fact, been much slower than reported), he might well have
become even more cautious in pressing the attack and slowed the breakthrough even further.

In addition, as the battle unfolded and new operational opportunities
opened up to widen and deepen the penetration, General Collins was slow
to exploit them. He had, for example, the 3rd Armored Division continue
on its original attack vector toward Coutances at least 24 hours after the
changing tactical situation had made that maneuver irrelevant. Each hour
that General Collins's decisions added to the breakthrough allowed the
Germans more time to recover from the affects of the attack and diminished
the Americans' advantage.

Finally, it must be noted that the real exploitation in the breakthrough
was achieved by the 2d Armored Division, whose advance cleaved the
Seventh Army defenses in two and handily defeated the only serious counterattacks against the VII Corps penetration. Ironically, when General
Collins committed the division on 26 July, he did not envision their attack
as a bold stroke of exploitation but as primarily a protective measure,
guarding the outer ring of the breakout. The extraordinary successes of the
2d Armored Division surprised General Collins as much as anyone.

In short, by focusing his efforts on Marigny and Coutances too much
Collins missed other opportunities to push the offensive even further. With
the tremendous forces at his disposal and the crippling situation facing the

German Seventh Army, Collins had the means and the opportunity to force the attack much deeper, much faster. If he had executed with greater skill the results of Cobra might possibly have been even more spectacular.

General Collins's failure to increase the tempo of the attack was exacerbated by the botched advance of the 1st Infantry Division on Marigny. Here responsibility falls largely on the shoulders of General Huebner, the 1st Infantry Division commander. Armed with more combat power than any other command on the battlefield, the general executed a cautious, tentative strike to clear the penetration. Poorly executed, his advance was mired in miscommunication, poor reporting, and atrocious management of the attacking forces. As a result, rather than swiftly advancing south the division spent much of its time bogged down in traffic, fighting with itself to clear the routes to Marigny.

Although there were significant errors by senior U.S. commanders that kept the operation from reaching its full potential, Cobra did achieve the key objectives set for it, and, in fact, in some respects exceeded the expectations of its commanders. This success can clearly be credited to the Americans' capacity to bring all their capabilities together at the point where the enemy was weak and vulnerable, an accomplishment largely achieved by the field-grade leaders—the combat command, regimental, and battalion commanders. It was these commanders who controlled the key combat assets (reserves, armor, air, and artillery support) that could be introduced quickly to shift the outcome of an engagement. They were also the commanders who had access to the fresh, relevant combat information from the front that was needed to make timely decisions on when to commit additional combat resources.

In some respects, the battalion and regimental commanders in Normandy were the equivalent of Napoleon's marshals. They were the "on-the-scene commanders" who had to make the independent decisions that translated the general's intent into reality on the ground. The skill and judgement of field-grade leaders empowered the U.S. Army's operational capabilities and turned the course of the war in Normandy. They demonstrated clearly that for success in battle, operational skill and tactical prowess had to go hand in hand. The leadership of field-grade commanders was essential for Cobra's success, even though their contributions have been perhaps the most neglected aspect of the operation.

As a final point, it is worth speculating why the conclusions of this study on Operation Cobra contrast significantly with previous assessments of the battle. The answer lies in the challenge of breaking through the tyranny of the traditional World War II narratives. Initially, a focus on generalship and the more dramatic aspects of Operation Cobra, such as the hedgerow-busting rhino tanks and the role of air power, dominated the story. In addition, sensitivities about the reputations of senior commanders as well as inter-Allied (British-American) and interservice (army–air force) rivalries have complicated approaching the subject. These factors significantly colored the first narrative histories of the operation, and historians have not been particularly successful at piercing the veil of these initial impressions, leaving unchallenged many of the assumptions for Cobra's successes and shortfalls.

Studies of Operation Cobra have been deficient in two respects. First, they failed to weave the strategic, operational, and tactical aspects of Cobra into a single, connected, cohesive, analytical narrative. Not linking a critique of the operational plans with a detailed study of the tactical battles, for example, explains the persistent overemphasis on the importance of General Collins's contributions to Cobra's success. In contrast, placing each action fully in the context of the strategic, operational, and tactical situations provides for a more accurate assessment on the role of senior and subordinate commanders.

The second shortcoming of historical accounts of Operation Cobra is that they do not analyze its battles fully and systematically. A complete recounting of an engagement must include all the relevant information describing what was supposed to happen (the plan) and what actually took place (the battle) from both the friendly and enemy perspective. Historians must look at all sides of the tactical problem to accurately measure influences on the engagement. The example of rhino tanks is a case in point. Many historians have noted the Americans' intent to use the devices to break through the hedgerows, but none have offered any comprehensive analysis of the battles to determine such devices' actual contributions to victory. Alternatively, accurately tracing the lines between conception and consequences offers far more engaging and satisfying opportunities to evaluate the performance of armies in battle.

A rigorous study of Operation Cobra demonstrates that we can do better. It argues that military history does have some very powerful tools to break down the traditional, unchallenged narratives of World War II and wring new insights from the wealth of available, albeit admittedly incomplete and imperfect, evidence that we have. New histories of the war can be far more than simply retelling tales and repeating wartime debates. Far from being a dead subject, there is still much that can be learned from a disciplined, systematic study of military operations during World War II.

Facing the Future

Cobra represented not only a significant turning point in the campaign, but it marked the beginning of the end of the battles of Normandy. Almost as soon as the soldiers moved out bucolic life began to creep back into the Norman countryside. Farmers pressed cider. Cows gave milk. Women turned the milk into fine Norman cheese. The dark of war passed again from the Normandy skies. The battlefields were turned over to the grass, and the deeds and misdeeds of soldiers who fought there were turned over to history.

Left behind among the Normandy hedgerows were the remembrances of the dark of war—the cemeteries. Today, there are cemeteries for all the casualties of Normandy. Each site reflects a mixture of the national culture and the war experience of its saddened nation. The British buried their dead in small cottage gardens laced with benches and flowers reminiscent of life in the English countryside. The Germans were laid in solemn reverence under close-clipped grass facing home. For the French, the wives, husbands, and children caught in the cross fire rest in their ancient village cemeteries. The Americans are mustered in long majestic rows aligned on the cliffs above the seas where the boys first came ashore at Omaha Beach—a symbol of the nation's powerful commitment to the liberation of Europe. Together, the silent ranks of crosses and Stars of David, the tall stones emblazoned with regimental symbols, the dark monoliths, and weathered family markers are grim reminders of war's terrible toll.

For the Americans the cost of the Normandy battles, the price of gaining operational flexibility, both in lives and national treasure, was great. The lesson of Operation Cobra was that operational flexibility was built on the back of skillfully led, trained and ready forces. Whether these skills are gained before the battle or on the fields of war, they are a prerequisite for stemming the multiplying fields of stone. There are no easy solutions in war. No magic weapon, tactic, or operational maneuver can guarantee swift and bloodless victory in a struggle between two determined foes. The cemeteries of Normandy should dispel any illusion that campaigns can be cheaply won.

Bibliography

What Happened and What Remains: Notes on Sources

We do not write the history of what happened but the history of the records that remain. This certainly is true for the story of Operation Cobra. As with any historical narrative, this study is the product of my own compromises and choices in attempting to piece together what remains and to get as close as possible to what happened.

Official records must be the backbone of any military history and I have made extensive use of the records available. Unless otherwise cited the official U.S. Army documents cited can be found at the National Archives and Records Administration (NARA), College Park, Maryland. These records are also available on microfilm, indexed by unit and date. Copies of German military records are in Records Group 242, NARA (available on microfilm). Relevant official Air Force documents, other than mission reports, are at the U.S. Air Force Historical Research Agency (AFHRA), Air War College, Maxwell Air Force Base, Alabama, and the Air Force History Support Office (AFHSO), Washington, D.C.

Official documents, however, rarely tell the whole story. Operations are never executed exactly as written in the orders. Logs, after-action reports, and operations summaries often include errors and omissions. To help fill out the picture there are a number of unofficial histories including combat journals, personal papers, unit histories, memoirs, and oral histories. Fortunately, for World War II a number of these sources are available. As a caution, it should be noted that while these sources can be interesting and informative they occasionally contain inaccuracies and embellishments. It is important, therefore, to cross-check the information with other sources. James T. Controvich, *United States Unit Histories: A Reference and Bibliography,* Manhattan: Kansas State University, 1983, offers a useful guide to published unit histories. The most extensive oral history collections on senior officers are at the Military History Institute

(MHI) at the U.S. Army War College, Carlisle Barracks, Pennsylvania, and AFHRA.

Another advantage in piecing together the World War II story is the access to the personal views of the enemy. After the war, a number of German officers were interviewed about their experiences by U.S. Army intelligence. For a guide to this material see Headquarters, United States Army, Europe, *Guide to Foreign Military Studies 1945–54, Catalog & Index*. An extensive collection of these studies (MS) can be found at the Combined Arms Research Library (CARL), U.S. Army Command and General Staff College, Fort Leavenworth, Kansas. On the whole I found these interviews honest and straight forward, but the German recollections are not always completely accurate or sincere and must be used with caution and checked against other sources. Where possible, I cross-checked the interviews with the German command war diaries and Allied intelligence documents.

In addition, the secondary literature on the campaign is useful for understanding the context of the battles of Operation Cobra. For an excellent recent guide to secondary works see Colin Baxter, *The Normandy Campaign, 1944: A Selected Bibliography*.

The most accurate and detailed campaign maps on Normandy operations can be found in Martin Blumenson's *Breakout and Pursuit* and *The West Point Atlas of American Wars*, vol. 2.

Finally, on the subject of Internet sources there are a number of pages on the World Wide Web with information relevant to U.S. operations in Normandy. I found the best technique to search for material is to do a subject word search on one of the Internet search engines (like Yahoo). In terms of searching for archival material on the Web, the Web sites of the U.S. Library of Congress, the U.S. National Archives, and the Military History Institute are indispensable. In particular, the Library of Congress site includes a search engine that you can use to conduct a subject search for selected archival collections throughout the United States. In terms of searching for secondary sources, particularly articles, I found ProQuest Direct, Nexus-Lexus, and JSTOR to be the most comprehensive and useful sites. For research inquiries, book reviews, Web links, bibliographies, and guides to sources, H-Net—Humanities & Social Sciences OnLine is a good place to start. In particular, H-Net includes H-War, a site dedicated to military history. In addition, the Military Education and Research Library Network (MERLIN) provides a searchable database of several important U.S. military libraries. I have not included URLs (internet addresses) for these Web sites because they change frequently. They all can be easily found, however, by conducting a simple subject search through any Internet search engine.

Even with all the sources available there are noticeable gaps in the record. I have tried to balance all the above sources to recreate the picture that commanders saw on the battlefield in 1944.

Abbreviations

AFHRA U.S. Air Force Historical Research Agency, Air University, Maxwell Air Force Base, Alabama

AFSHO Air Force History Support Office, Washington, D.C.

CARL Combined Arms Research Library, United States Army Command and General Staff College, Fort Leavenworth, Kansas

CMH U.S. Army Center of Military History, Washington, D.C.

CSI Combat Studies Institute, United States Army Command and General Staff College, Fort Leavenworth, Kansas

DDE Dwight David Eisenhower Library, Abilene, Kansas

HHI Herbert Hoover Institute, Stanford University, Palo Alto, California

LC Library of Congress, Washington, D.C.

NARA National Archives and Records Administration, College Park Maryland

MHI U.S. Army Military History Institute, Carlisle Barracks, Pennsylvania

USAAC United States Army Armor Center and Patton Museum of Calvary and Armor, Fort Knox, Kentucky

USAFAS Morris Swett Library, United States Army Field Artillery School, Fort Sill, Oklahoma

USAIM United States Army Infantry Museum, Fort Benning, Georgia

USMA Special Collections, United States Military Academy at West Point

Sources

AAF Evaluation Board, ETO, Tactics and Techniques Developed by U.S. Tactical Air Commands in the European Theater. MHI.

Ackerman, Robert W. The Employment of Strategic Bombers in the Tactical Role, 1941–1945. Microfilm K1010. 1953. AFHRA.

Activities of General Eddy, 24 March 1944 to 30 September 1944. War Diary of General Manton Sprague Eddy. USAIM.

Adair, M. C. Combat Diary, 2d Battalion, 8th Infantry Regiment, 4th Infantry Division. MIII, 25 July 1944.

Adjutant General's Office. World War II Operations. RG 94. NARA.

Adjutant General Section, General Correspondence 1940–47. RG 338. NARA.

AGF Immediate Report No. 16. CARL.

AGF Observation Board, ETO, Report No. 138, "Notes on Hedgerow Warfare in the Normandy Beachhead." CARL.

AGF Observation Board, ETO, Report No. 141, "German Defenses in the Hedgerow Terrain." CARL.

AGF Observer Immediate Report No. 5. CARL.

AGF Observer Immediate Report No. 1. CARL.

Allen, Max S., ed. *Medicine under Canvas*. Lawrence: University of Kansas School of Medicine, 1949.

Ambrose, Stephen E. *Citizen Soldiers: The U.S. Army from the Normandy Beaches to the Bulge to the Surrender of Germany*. New York: Simon and Schuster, 1997.

———. *Supreme Commander: War Years of General Dwight D. Eisenhower*. New York: Doubleday, 1970.

Anderson, Frederick Lewis. Papers. HHI.

Armeeoberkommando 7, K.T.B. Entwurf und OB Chef-IA-Gespräche, 6 Juni–16 August 1944. Microfilm. T312. Roll 1568. NARA.

Army Air Forces, ETO. U.S. Army Air Forces. The Effectiveness of Third Phase Tactical Air Operations in the European Theater, 5 May 1944–8 May 1945. August 1945.

Army and Navy Journal. 11 October 1941 and 5 August 1944.

Army and Navy Register. 12 August 1944.

Balkoski, Joseph. *Beyond the Beachhead: The 29th Infantry Division in Normandy*. New York: Dell, 1989.

Baldridge, Robert C. *Victory Road*. MHI.

The Battle for Normandy. File 8-3.1 AF. CMH.

Baxter, Colin. "Did Nazis Fight Better Than Democrats? Historical Writing on the Combat Performance of the Allied Soldier in Normandy." *Parameters* 25 (Autumn 1995): 113–118.

———. *The Normandy Campaign, 1944: A Selected Bibliography*. New York: Greenwood Press, 1992.

Bayerlein, Fritz. "An Interview with GENLT Fritz Bayerlein: Panzer Lehr Division Jan–28 Jul 44." ETHINT 66. CARL.

———. "An Interview with GENLT Fritz Bayerlein: Critique of Normandy Breakout Panzer Lehr Division from St. Lo to the Ruhr." ETHINT 67.

———. "An Interview with GENLT Fritz Bayerlein: Panzer Lehr Division at the Start of Operation COBRA." ETHINT 69.

Ben-Moshe, Tuvia. "Winston Churchill and the Second Front: A Reappraisal." *Journal of Modern History* 62 (September 1990): 503–537.

Bennett, Ralph. *Ultra in the West: The Normandy Campaign 1944–45*. New York: Charles Scribner's Sons, 1979.

Berlin, Robert H. *U.S. Army World War II Corps Commanders: A Composite Biography*. CSI, 1989.

Bérubé, Allan. *Coming Out Under Fire: History of Gay Men and Women in World War II*. New York: Free Press, 1990.

Biennial Reports of the Chief of Staff of the United States Army to the Secretary of War, 1 July 1939–30 June 1945. Reprint Edition. Washington, D.C.: Center of Military History, Reprint.

Blauensteiner, Ernst. "Commitment of the II Parachute Corps in Northern France." MS B-346. CARL.

Blumenson, Martin. *The Battle of the Generals*. New York: Morrow, 1993.

———. "A Deaf Ear to Clausewitz: Allied Operational Objectives in World War II." *Parameters* XXIII (Summer 1993): 16–27.

———. "Why Military History? To Analyze the Past, Discover the Present," *Army* 25 (January 1975): 33–38.

———. *The Patton Papers, 1940–45*. 2 vols. Boston: Houghton Mifflin, 1974.

———. "Some Reflections on the Immediate Post-Assault Strategy." In *D-Day: The Normandy Invasion in Retrospect*. Lawrence: Kansas University, 1971.

———. *Breakout and Pursuit.* Washington, D.C.: U.S. Government Printing Office, 1961.

Blumentritt, Günther. "Three Marshals, National Character, and the 20 July Complex." MS B-344. CARL.

———. "Defense." MS B-299. CARL.

Boice, William C., ed. *History of the Twenty-Second United States Infantry Regiment in World War II.* Phoenix: 1959.

Bonn, Keith E. *When the Odds Were Even: The Vosges Mountain Campaign, October 1944–January 1945.* Novato, Calif.: Presidio Press, 1994.

Bowdle, Paul H., and Edward R. Broadwell. *Combat History of the 391st Armored Artillery Battalion.* Frankfurt: Derndruck.

Bradley, Omar N. *A Soldier's Story.* New York: Henry Holt, 1951.

———. Oral History Interview, Revised Transcript. MHI.

——— and Clay Blair. *A General's Life.* New York: Simon and Schuster, 1983.

———. Papers. USMA.

———. Papers. MHI.

Brereton, Lewis Hyde. *The Brereton Diaries: The War in the Air in the Pacific, Middle East and Europe.* New York: William Morrow and Company, 1946.

Breuer, William B. *Hoodwinking Hitler: The Normandy Deception.* Westport, Conn.: Praeger, 1993.

Brown, John S. "Winning Teams: Mobilization-Related Correlatives of Success in American World War II Infantry Divisions." Thesis. U.S. Army Command and General Staff College. 1985.

Brown, Frederic J. "Spearhead Artillery." *The Field Artillery Journal* 36 (September 1946): 502–510.

Brownlee, R. L., and William J. Mullen III. *Changing an Army: An Oral History of General William E. Depuy, USA Retired.* MHI, 1987.

Butterton, Meredith L. *Metric 16.* Durham, N.C.: Moore Publishing Company, 1972.

Carell, Paul. *Invasion—They're Coming! The German Account of the Allied Landings and the 80-days Battle for France.* Trans. David Jonhston. New York: Dutton, 1963.

Cawthon, Charles R. *Other Clay: A Remembrance of the World War II Infantry.* Niwot: University Press of Colorado, 1990.

Chandler, Alfred D., Jr., ed. *The Papers of Dwight David Eisenhower: The War Years.* Vol. 3. Baltimore: The John Hopkins Press.

Choltitz, Dietrich. "LXXXIV Corps (18 Jun–15 Jul 1944)." MS B-418. CARL.

———. *Un Soldat Parmi des Soldats.* Avignon: Aubanel, 1964.

Clark, A. F., Jr. "History Through a Thousand Eyes." *Army Information Digest* 6 (June 1947): 51–55.

Coakley, Robert F. "Reflections on Writing the Green Books." *Army History* 25 (Summer 1993): 37–39.

Coates, Charles H. "Notes on Interviews with Various Infantry Commanders in Normandy, France, 6 June–8 July 1944." Report to War Department Observation Board (5 August 1944). CARL.

Cochran, A. S., Jr. "Magic, Ultra and the Second World War: Literature, Sources and Outlook." *The Journal of Military History* 46 (April 1982): 88–92.

Cockrell, Philip Carlton. "Brown Shoes and Mortar Boards: U.S. Army Professional Education at the Command and General Staff School Fort Leavenworth, Kansas, 1919–1940." Ph.D. Diss., University of South Carolina, 1987.

Colby, John. *War from the Ground Up: The 90th Division in WW II.* Austin, Tex.: Nortex, 1991.

Coll, Blanche D., Jean E. Keith, and Herbert H. Rosenthal. *The Corps of Engineers: Troops and Equipment.* Washington, D.C.: Office of the Chief of Military History, 1958.

Collins, J. Lawton. *Lightning Joe.* Baton Rouge: Louisiana State University, 1979.

———. "Answers to Generalship Study Questionnaire." A Study of Requirements of Senior Commanders for Command-Control Support. 16 November 1966. CARL.

———. *Reflections on General Courtney Hodges.* MHI.

———. Senior Officers' Oral History Program. MHI.

———. Papers. DDE.

Combat History of the 119th Infantry Regiment. MHI.

Combat History of the 120th Infantry Regiment. MHI.

Conn, Stetson, *Historical Works in the United States Army 1862–1954.* MHI, 1980.

Cooling, Benjamin Franklin, ed. *Case Studies in the Development of Close Air Support.* Washington, D.C.: Government Printing Office, Office of Air Force History, 1989.

Cooper, Belton Y. *Death Traps: The Survival of American Armored Division in World War II.* Novato, Calif.: Presidio Press, 1998.

Cosmas, Graham A., and Albert E. Cowdry. *Medical Service in the European Theater of Operations.* New York: Free Press, 1994.

Craven, Wesley Frank, and James Lea Cate, eds. *The Army Air Forces in World War II.* Vol. 3. *Europe: Argument to V-E Day, January 1944 to May 1945.* Chicago: University of Chicago Press, 1951.

Crosby, Donald F. *Battlefield Chaplains.* Lawrence: University Press of Kansas, 1994.

Crosswell, D. K. R. "Anglo-American Strategy and Command in Northwest Europe, 1944–1945." In Loyd E. Lee, *World War II in Europe, Africa and the Americas with General Sources: A Handbook for Literature and Research.* Westport, Conn.: Greenwood Press, 1997.

Crowley, Thomas T., and Gerald C. Burch. *Eight Stars to Victory: Operations of the First Engineer Combat Battalion in World War II.* Brussels: L'Imifi, 1947.

Dastrup, Boyd. *King of Battle.* Fort Monroe, La.: Office of the Command Historian, 1992.

Davis, Richard G. *Carl A. Spaatz and the Air War in Europe.* Washington, D.C.: Center for Air Force History, 1993.

D-Day: The Normandy Invasion in Retrospect. Lawrence: University Press of Kansas, 1971.

Deighton, Len. *Blood, Tears annd Folly: An Objective Look at World War II.* New York: Harper-Collins, 1993.

Denno, Bryce F. "Allen and Huebner: Contrast in Command." *Army* 34 (June 1984): 62–70.

D'Este, Carlo. *Decision in Normandy.* New York: Dutton, 1983.

———. *Patton: A Genius for War.* New York: Harper Collins, 1995.

Department of the Army Pamphlet. No. 20-233. *German Defensive Tactics Against Russian Break-Throughs.* October 1951.

Dickson, Benjamin A. "Algiers to the Elbe." Dickson Papers. MHI.

Dietrich, Steve E. "In-Theater Armored Force Modernization." *Military Review* 73 (October 1993): 34–45.

Dively, D. G. *End of Mission: 957th Field Artillery Battalion.* Heidelberg, 1945.

Dorst, Charles L. *My Times and Service in the Military.* MHI.

Doubler, Michael D. *Closing with the Enemy.* Lawrence: University of Kansas Press, 1994.

————. *Busting the Bocage: American Combined Arms Operations in France, 6 June–31 July 1944.* Fort Leavenworth, Kans.: Combat Studies Institute, 1988.

Dutour, Françoise. *The Liberation of Calvados 6th June 1944–31st December 1944.* Translated by Michel and Michele Morin. Caen: Calvados Départment Archives, 1994.

Eighth Air Force, History of Operations Analysis Section, October 1942–June 1945. AFHRA.

899th Tank Destroyer Battalion History. MHI.

Eisenhower, David. *Eisenhower at War.* New York: Random House, 1986.

Ellis, John. *Brute Force: Allied Strategy and Tactics in the Second World War.* New York: Viking, 1990.

————. *World War II: A Statistical Survey.* New York: Facts on File, 1995.

English, John A. *The Canadian Army and the Normandy Campaign: A Study in Failure.* New York: Praeger, 1991.

Esposito, Vincent J., ed. *The West Point Atlas of American Wars.* Vol. 2. New York: Praeger, 1959.

Eustis, Morton. *The War Letters of Morton Eustis to His Mother, February 6, 1941, to August 10, 1944.* New York: Spiral Press, 1945.

Farrell, Brian P. "Grand Strategy and the 'Second Front' Debate." In Loyd E. Lee, *World War II in Europe, Africa and the Americas with General Sources: A Handbook for Literature and Research.* Westport, Conn.: Greenwood Press, 1997.

Featherston, Alwyn. *Saving the Breakout: The 30th Division's Heroic Stand at Mortain.* Novato, Calif.: Presidio Press, 1993.

First United States Army, Report of Operations, 20 October 1943 to 1 August 1944. Printed in Europe, 1946.

Florentin, Eddy. *Stalingrad en Normandie: la destruction de la VIIe armée allemande dans la poche Argentan-Falaise, 31 juillet–22 août 1944.* Paris: Presse de la Cité, 1974.

FM 6-20. *Field Artillery Field Manual Tactics and Techniques.* Washington, D.C.: U.S. Government Printing Office, 1940.

FM 71-5. *Infantry Field Manual: Organization and Tactics of Infantry, the Rifle Battalion.* Washington, D.C.: U.S. Government Printing Office, 1940.

FM 71-10. *Infantry Field Manual: Rifle Company, Rifle Regiment.* Washington, D.C.: U.S. Government Printing Office, 1945.

FM 71-15. *Infantry Field Manual: Heavy Weapons Company, Rifle Regiment.* Washington, D.C.: U.S. Government Printing Office, May 19, 1942.

FM 100-5. *Field Service Regulations: Operations.* Washington, D.C.: Government Printing Office, 1941.

Fraser, David. *Knight's Cross: A Life of Field Marshall Erwin Rommel.* New York: Harper Collins, 1993.

Freeman, Roger A. *The Mighty Eighth: Units, Men and Machines.* Garden City: Doubleday and Company, 1970.

Fritz, Stephen G. *Frontsoldten: The German Soldier in World War II.* Lexington: University of Kentucky Press, 1995.

Folkestad, William B. *The View from the Turret: The 743d Tank Battalion During World War II.* Shipensburg, Pa.: Burd Street Press, 1996.

Fowle, Barry W., and Floyd D. Wright. *The 51st Again! An Engineer Combat Battalion in World War II.* Shipensburg, Pa.: White Mane Publishing, 1992.

Fussell, Paul. *Wartime: Understanding and Behavior in the Second World War.* New York: Oxford University Press, 1989.

G-2 Officer, Supreme Headquarters Allied Expeditionary Forces, files. MHI.

G-3 Section, Supreme Headquarters Allied Expeditionary Forces. "Employment of Tanks and Infantry in Normandy." *Military Review* XXIV (December 1944): 13–17.

Gabel, Christopher. *U.S. Army GHQ Maneuvers of 1941*. Washington, D.C.: Center of Military History, 1991.

———. "Seek, Strike and Destroy: U.S. Army Tank Destroyer Doctrine in World War II." *Leavenworth Papers No. 12*. Fort Leavenworth, Kans.: Combat Studies Institute, U.S. Army Command and General Staff College, 1985.

———. "Books on Overlord: A Select Bibliography and Research Agenda on the Normandy Campaign, 1944." *Military Affairs* 48 (July 1984).

Gajkowski, Matthew. *German Squad Infantry Tactics in World War II*. Privately Published, 1995.

Ganz, A. Harding. "Questionable Objective: The Brittany Ports, 1944." *Journal of Military History* 59 (1995): 77–95.

Gelb, Norman. *Ike & Monty: Generals at War*. New York: William Morrow and Company, 1994.

General Staff, G-2, Terrain Estimate of Nantes-Caen Line as a General Line of Defense. Intelligence Research Project 6183. April 1951. MHI.

George, Robert H. "Normandy." In Wesley Frank Craven and James Lea Cate, eds., *The Army Air Forces in World War II*. Vol. 3. *Europe: Argument to V-E Day, January 1944 to May 1945*. Chicago: University of Chicago Press, 1951.

George, Robert H. Ninth Air Force, April to November 1944. Microfilm. Roll K1005. AFHRA.

Gerald Astor Collection. MHI.

German Order of Battle. Reprint ed. Intro. I. V. Hogg. London: Greenhill Books, 1994.

Gersdorff, Rudolf. "Normandy and Mortain." MS A-893. CARL.

Geyr von Schweppenburg, Leo Freiherr. "Reflections on the Invasion." 2 parts, *Military Review* 41 (February 1961): 2–11, (March 1961): 12–21.

Gillespie, David, ed. *The 47th Infantry Regiment*. Munich: Bruckman, 1946.

Giles, Henry. *The G.I. Journal of Sergeant Giles*. Ed. Janice Holt Giles. Boston: Houghton Mifflin, 1965.

Gooderson, Ian. "Heavy and Medium Bombers: How Successful Were They in Tactical Close Air Support During World War II?" *The Journal of Strategic Studies* 15 (September 1992): 367–399.

Gorman, Paul F. *The Secret of Future Victories*. Reprint. Fort Leavenworth, Kans.: U.S. Army Command and General Staff College Press, 1994.

Greene, Joseph I., ed. *The Infantry Journal Reader*. Garden City, N.Y.: Doubleday, Doran and Company, 1943.

Greenfield, Kent Roberts. *American Strategy in World War II: A Reconsideration*. New York: Krieger, 1982.

Hale, Elmer. *History of the 18th Field Artillery Battalion, World War II*. Tulsa, 1946.

Hall, Chester B. *History of the 70th Tank Battalion*. MHI.

Hall, Tony. *D-Day: Operation Overlord from Its Planning to the Liberation of Paris*. London: Salamander, 1993.

Hallinan, Ulick Martin. "From Operation COBRA to the Liberation of Paris: American Offensive Operations in Northern France, 25 July–25 August, 1944." Ph.D. Diss., Temple University, 1988.

Hallion, Richard P. *Strike from the Sky: The History of Battlefield Air Attack 1911–1945*. Washington, D.C.: Smithsonian Institute Press, 1989.

————. *The U.S. Army Air Forces in World War II: D-Day 1944, Air Power over the Normandy Beaches and Beyond.* Washington, D.C.: U.S. Government Printing Office, 1994.

Hamilton, Nigel. *Master of the Battlefield: Monty's War Years, 1942–1944.* New York: McGraw-Hill.

————. *Monty: The Battles of Field Marshal Bernard Montgomery.* New York: Random House, 1994.

Hansen, Chester B. War Diary. Chester B. Hansen Papers. MHI.

————. Bradley's Commentary on World War II. Chester B. Hansen Papers. MHI.

Harrison, Gordon A. *Cross-Channel Attack.* Washington, D.C.: Office of the Chief of Military History, 1951.

Harrison, William K. Oral History. MHI.

Hart, Charles E. *Reflections on General Courtney Hodges.* MHI.

Hastings, Max. *Das Reich: The March of the 2nd SS Panzer Division Through France.* New York: Holt, Rinehart and Winston, 1982.

————. *OVERLORD: D-Day and the Battle for Normandy.* New York: Simon and Schuster, 1984.

Hausser, Paul. "Normandy Seventh Army." MS A-974. CARL.

Headquarters, Allied Expeditionary Force. Subject: Operation "Cobra," 20 July 1944. Microfilm. Roll A5129. AFHSO.

Headquarters, First U.S. Army. Outline Operations Plan "Cobra." 13 July 1944.

Headquarters, First U.S. Army. Air Support Report. 6 August 1944. Section V. Operation Cobra. Microfilm. Roll C5127.

Headquarters, First U.S. Army. U.S. Army. Field Order No. 2. 28 July 1944.

Headquarters, 1st Infantry Division. U.S. Army. After Action Report. July 1944.

Headquarters, 1st Infantry Division. U.S. Army, G-2 Journal. July 1944.

Headquarters, 1st Infantry Division Artillery. U.S. Army. Unit Report of Action 1 July to 31 July 1944. 5 August 1944.

Headquarters, 1st Infantry Division Artillery. U.S. Army. Unit Report of Action 1 July to 31 July 1944.

Headquarters, 2d Armored Division. U.S. Army. After Action Report. July 1944.

Headquarters, 2d Armored Division Artillery. U.S. Army. After Action Report. July 1944.

Headquarters, 2d Armored Division. U.S. Army. G-2 Log. July 1944.

Headquarters, 3d Armored Division. U.S. Army. Field Order No. 4 (revised), 21 July 1944.

Headquarters, 3d Armored Division. U.S. Army. Action Against Enemy, After Action Report. 19 August 1944.

Headquarters, Combat Command B. 3d Armored Division. U.S. Army. Report of Action C. COMD. B 3RD ARMD. DIV. for Period 25 July to 31 July 1944. 6 August 1944.

Headquarters, 4th Cavalry Group. U.S. Army. After Action Reports. 1944.

Headquarters, 4th Infantry Division. U.S. Army. Letter to G-3 Air, VII Corps "Air in Support of Infantry." 1 July 1944.

Headquarters, 4th Infantry Division. U.S. Army. Actions Against Enemy, After Action Reports. 10 August 1944.

Headquarters, 7th Armored Division. U.S. Army. Division Intelligence Summary No. 40. July 1944.

Headquarters, VII Corps. U.S. Army. The History of VII Corps, U.S. Army, Covering Operations in Normandy, France, from 1–31 July 1944. 6 August 1944.

Headquarters. VII Corps. U.S. Army. Operation "Cobra." Field Order No. 6 (revised copy). 20 July 1944.

Headquarters, VII Corps. U.S. Army. Operations Memos 44–52. July 1944.

Headquarters, VII Corps. U.S. Army. Administrative Orders. July 1944.

Headquarters, VII Corps. U.S. Army. G-2 Periodic Reports. 1 July to 30 July 1944.

Headquarters, 8th Infantry Regiment. U.S. Army Field Orders. July 1944.

Headquarters, 8th Infantry Regiment. U.S. Army. S-3 Journal. 25 July 1944.

Headquarters, Ninth Air Force. Air Force Logistical Data. 1946. CMH.

Headquarters, 9th Infantry Division Artillery. U.S. Army. Combat Log.

Headquarters, 9th Infantry Division. U.S. Army. G-3 Journal. July 1944.

Headquarters, 9th Infantry Division. U.S. Army. G-2 Reports. July 1944.

Headquarters, IX TAC Operations Order for Operation Cobra, 19 July 1944. Microfilm. Roll B5731. AFHSO.

Headquarters, IX TAC Air Command. 3 August 1944, Memorandum 20-2, Standard Operating Procedures for Air Support Parties. Microfilm. Roll C5127. AFSHO.

Headquarters, 14th Armored Field Artillery Battalion. U.S. Army. Operations Annex. 31 July 1944.

Headquarters, 26th Infantry Regiment. U.S. Army. Unit Journal. July 1944.

Headquarters, 30th Infantry Division Artillery. U.S. Army. *History of the Thirtieth Division Artillery.* 1945.

Headquarters, 30th Infantry Division. U.S. Army. After Action Report. 1944.

Headquarters, 30th Infantry Division Artillery. U.S. Army. After Action Report. 1944.

Headquarters, Fiftieth Fighter Group, Memorandum to All Officers and Enlisted Men of Site 10A, 29 July 1944. Microfilm. Roll B0144. AFHSO.

Headquarters, 97th Combat Bomb Wing. 25 July 1944. Field Order. No. 143-44. Microfilm. Roll B5788. AFHSO.

Headquarters, SHAEF. "Notes on German Booby Traps." October 1944. CARL.

Hechter, S. Notebook, Statistical Summary of the 4th Medical Battalion. MHI.

Hess, John D. *Move Out, Verify: The Combat Story of the 743rd Tank Battalion.* Frankfurt-on-Main: 1945.

Hewitt, Robert A. *Interviews with Major General Robert A. Hewitt.* MHI.

Hewitt, Robert L. *Workhorse of the Western Front: The Story of the 30th Infantry Division.* Washington, D.C.: Infantry Journal Press, 1946.

Heydte, Friedrich-August Freiherr von der. "A German Parachute Regiment in Normandy: Operations of the 6th Fallschirmjäger Regiment 6 June–15 August 1944." MS B-839. CARL.

Hill, Jim Dan. *The Minute Man in Peace and War: A History of The National Guard.* Harrisburg, Penn.: Stackpole, 1964.

Hillyard, H. L. "Employment of Tanks by the Infantry Division." *Military Review* XXVII (June 1947): 50–60.

Hinsley, F. H., et al., eds. *British Intelligence in the Second World War: Its Influence on Strategy and Operations.* Vol. 3. Part 2. *Summer 1944 to the End of the War with Germany.* London: Her Majesty's Stationer's Office, 1988.

———— and Alan Stripp, eds. *Codebreakers: The Inside Story of Bletchley Park.* Oxford: Oxford University Press, 1994.

Historical Data. AAF Headquarters, Group Fighter, Fiftieth Fighter Group, 1 July to 1 August 1944. Microfilm. Roll B0144. AFHSO.

History of the 489th Bomber Group.

History of the 3d Armored Division, April 1941–July 1958. Darmstadt: Stars and Stripes, 1958.

History of the Thirtieth Division Artillery. 1945.

History, 67th Armored Regiment. Brunswick: Westermann, 1945.

History of the 87th Armored Field Artillery Battalion. 1945.

History of the 120th Infantry Regiment. Washington, D.C.: Infantry Journal Press, 1947.

Hobbs, Leland Stanford. Papers. DDE.

Hobbs, Joseph Patrick, ed. *Dear General: Eisenhower's Wartime Letters to Marshall*. Baltimore: Johns Hopkins University Press, 1971.

Hodges, Courtney Hicks. Papers. DDE.

Hogan, David W., Jr. "The First U.S. Army Headquarters in the European Theater during World War II." Forthcoming, CMH.

Horne, Alistair, with David Montgomery. *Monty: The Lonely Leader, 1944–1945*. New York: Harper Collins, 1994.

House, Jonathan M. "Toward Combined Arms Warfare: A Survey of 20th Century Tactics, Doctrine and Organization." *Research Survey No. 2*. Fort Leavenworth, Kans.: Combat Studies Institute, U.S. Army Command and General Staff College, August 1984.

Houston, Donald E. *Hell on Wheels: The 2d Armored Division*. San Rafael, Calif.: Presidio Press, 1977.

Howard, Charles F. AGF Observer Report. CARL, 27 July 1944.

Howenstine, Harold D., and George E. Troll. *History of the 745 Tank Battalion, August 1942 to June 1945*. Nürnberg: Sebaldus-Verlag, 1945.

Hughes, Thomas Alexander. *Overlord: General Pete Quesada and the Triumph of Tactical Airpower in World War II*. New York: The Free Press, 1995.

Hurkala, John. *The Fighting First Division*. New York: Greenwich Books, 1957.

Hutton, Carl I. *An Armored Artillery Commander in the European Theater*. USAFAS.

Infantry in Battle. Washington, D.C.: The Infantry Journal Incorporated, 1939.

Intelligence Reports and Estimates of the Situation on the Front of Army Group B July 1–December 1, 1944. Microfilm. T311. Roll 1. NARA.

Jacobs, Bruce. "Tensions Between the Army National Guard and the Regular Army." *Military Review* LXXII (October 1993): 5–17.

Jacobs, W. A. "The Battle for France, 1944." In Benjamin Franklin Cooling, ed., *Case Studies in the Development of Close Air Support*. Washington, D.C.: Government Printing Office, Office of Air Force History, 1989.

Jeesup, John E., Jr., and Robert W. Coakley. *A Guide to the Study and Use of Military History*. Washington, D.C.: Center of Military History, 1979.

Johns, Glover S., Jr. *The Clay Pigeons of St. Lo*. New York: Bantam, 1985.

Johnson, David E. *Fast Tanks and Heavy Bombers. Innovations in the U.S. Army, 1917–1945*. Ithaca: Cornell University Press, 1998.

Jordan, Chester H. Bull Sessions: World War II Company K, 47th Infantry Regiment, 9th Infantry Division from Normandy to Remagen. MHI.

Kaplan, L. Martin. "Harnessing Indirect Fire, 1905–1941: A Study of Field Artillery Training, Readiness, and Signal Communications." Unpublished monograph. CMH.

Keegan, John. *Six Armies in Normandy from D-Day to the Liberation of Paris*. New York: Penguin Books, 1984.

———. *The Battle for History: Re-Fighting World War II*. New York: Vintage, 1996.

Kemp, Anthony. *D-Day: The Normandy Landings and the Liberation of Europe*. London: Thames & Hudson, 1994.

Kennett, Lee. *G.I.: The American Soldier in World War II*. New York: Charles Scribner's Sons, 1987.

Kilpatrick, Charles E. "Lesley J. McNair Training Philosophy for a New Army." *Army Historian* (Winter 1990): 11–15.

————. *Omar Nelson Bradley: The centennial.* Washington, D.C.: U.S. Army, 1992.

Kleber, Brooks E., and Dale Birdsell. *The Chemical Warfare Service: Chemicals in Combat.* Washington D.C.: U.S. Government Printing Office, 1966.

Klein, Walter. "Bombing and Operation Cobra." MS A-910. CARL.

Knickerbocker, H. R., et al. *Danger Forward: The Story of the First Division in World War II.* Nashville: Battery Press, 1947.

Koenig, Eugen. "91st Airborne Division (10 Jul–Aug 1944)." MS B-010. CARL.

Kohn, Richard H., ed. "The Scholarship on World War II: Its Present Condition and Future Possibilities." *The Journal of Military History* 55 (July 1991): 365–393.

———— and Joseph P. Harahan, eds. *Condensed Analysis of the Ninth Air Force in the European Theater of Operations.* Washington, D.C.: Office of Air Force History, 1984.

Kriegstagebuch des Oberkommandos der Wehrmacht. Band IV. 1. Januar 1944–22. Mai 1945. Frankfurt: Bernard & Graefe Verlag für Wehrwesen, 1961.

Kurowski, Frank. *Die Panzer-Lehr-Division bei grösse deutsche Panzer Division und ihre Ausgabe: die Invasion zerschlagen—die Ardennen Schlacht entscheiden.* Podzun: 1964.

Lada, John, and Frank A. Reister, eds. *Medical Statistics in World War II.* Washington, D.C.: U.S. Government Printing Office, 1975.

Lamb, Richard. *Churchill as War Leader.* New York: Carroll & Graf, 1991.

————. *Montgomery in Europe, 1943–1945: Success or Failure?* New York: Watts, 1984.

Lee, Bruce. *Marching Orders: The Untold Story of WW II.* New York: Crown, 1995.

Lee, Loyd E. *World War II in Europe, Africa and the Americas with General Sources: A Handbook for Literature and Research.* Westport, Conn.: Greenwood, 1997.

Lewin, Ronald. *Ultra Goes to War: The First Account of World War II's Greatest Secret Based on Official Documents.* New York: McGraw-Hill, 1978.

Liebling, A. J. "St. Lo and Morain." In H. R. Knickerbocker et al., *Danger Forward: The Story of the First Division in World War II.* Nashville: Battery Press, 1947.

Linderman, Gerald F. *The World Within War: America's Combat Experience in World War II.* New York: Free Press, 1997.

Little, D. C. "Artillery in Support of the Capture of Hill 192." *Military Review* XXVII (March 1948): 31–37.

Lucas, James. *Das Reich.* London: Arms and Armour, 1991.

————. *The Last Year of the German Army, May 1944–May 1945.* London: Sterling, 1996.

Lupfor, Timothy L. *The Dynamics of Doctrine: The Changes in German Tactical Doctrine During the First World War.* Fort Leavenworth, Kans.: Combat Studies Institute, 1981.

Luvaas, Jay. "Military History: Is It Still Practicable?" *Parameters* (Summer 1995): 82–97.

Mansoor, Peter R. "Building Blocks of Victory: American Infantry Divisions in the War Against Germany and Italy." Ph.D. Diss., Ohio State University, 1995.

————. *The G.I. Offensive in Europe: The Triumph of American Infantry Divisions, 1941–1945.* Lawrence: University of Kansas Press, 1998.

Marshall, John Douglas. *Reconciliation Road: A Family Odyssey of War and Honor.* Syracuse, N.Y.: Syracuse University Press, 1993.

Marshall, Samuel Lyman Atwood. *Men Against Fire: The Problem of Battle Command in Future War.* New York: Morrow, 1947.

Maule, Henry. *Caen: The Brutal Battle and Breakout from Normandy.* London: David & Charles, 1976.

Maurer, Maurer, ed. Air Force Combat Units of World War II. 1963. Microfilm 32311. AHRA.

Mayo, Lida. *The Ordnance Department on Beachhead and Battlefield.* Washington, D.C.: Center of Military History, 1968.

McArthur, Charles W. *Operations Analysis in the U.S. Army Eighth Air Force in World War II.* London: London Mathematical Society, 1990.

McKee, Alexander. *Caen: Anvil of Victory.* London: White Lion, 1976.

McManus, John C. *The Deadly Brotherhood: The American Combat Soldier in World War II.* Novato, Calif.: Presidio, 1998.

Meindl, Eugen. "II Parachute Corps." MS B-401. CARL.

———. ETHINT 78. CARL.

Melchior, Ib. *Case by Case.* Novato, Calif.: Presidio Press, 1993.

Messenger, Charles. *The Last Prussian: A Biography of Field Marshal Gerd Von Rundstedt 1875–1953.* London: Brassey, 1991.

Mildren, Frank T. "The Attack of Hill 192 by the 1st Battalion, 38th Infantry: Personal Experiences of a Battalion Commander." CGSC Student Monograph 1946–1947, CARL.

Mitcham, Samuel W., Jr. *The U.S. Army Air Forces in World War II: D-Day 1944, Air Power over the Normandy Beaches and Beyond.* Westport, Conn.: Praeger, 1997.

———. *The Desert Fox in Normandy: Rommel's Defense of Fortress Europe.* Westport, Conn.: Praeger, 1997.

———. *Rommel's Last Battle and the Normandy Campaign.* New York: Stein, 1983.

———. and Gene Mueller. *Hitler's Commanders.* Lanham, Md.: Scarborough House, 1992.

Mitchell, Reid. "The GI in Europe and the American Military Tradition." In Paul Addison and Angus Calder, eds., *Time to Kill: The Soldier's Experience of War in the West, 1939–1945.* London: Pimlico, 1997.

Mittelman, Joseph B. *Eight Stars to Victory: A History of the Veteran Ninth U.S. Infantry Division.* Washington, D.C.: Ninth Infantry Division Association, 1948.

Mortensen, Daniel R. *A Pattern for Joint Operations: World War II Close Air Support, North Africa.* Washington, D.C.: Office of Air Force History and U.S. Army Center of Military History, 1987.

Mulligan, Timothy. Intro. *Ultra, Magic, and the Allies.* New York: Garland, 1989.

Mullins, William S., ed. *Neuropsychiatry in World War II.* Vol. 2. Washington, D.C.: Office of the Surgeon General, 1973.

Murray, G. E. Patrick. *Eisenhower Versus Montgomery: The Continuing Debate.* Westport, Conn.: Praeger, 1996.

Murray, Williamson, and Allan R. Millett, eds. *Military Innovation in the Interwar Period.* Cambridge: Cambridge University Press, 1996.

Nenninger, Timothy K. *The Leavenworth Schools and the Old Army: Education, Professionalism, and the Officer Corps of the United States Army.* Westport, Conn.: Greenwood Press, 1978.

Nettling, Dan A., ed. Omar Nelson Bradley, 1893–1981: A Bibliography. 1993. MHI.

Newton, Steven H. *German Battle Tactics on the Russian Front.* New York: Shiffer, 1994.

Nofi, Albert A., ed. *The War Against Hitler: Military Strategy in the West.* New York: Stackpole, 1995.

Oberkommando der Wehrmacht. Fuhrerhauptquartier. Stenograpischer Dienst. 5 Vols. HHI.

Observer Board (ETO), U.S. Army, Army Ground Forces. *Reports of the AGF Observer Board, ETO.* 6 Vols. 1944–1945. CARL and MHI.

Odom, William. *After the Trenches: The Transformation of U.S. Army Doctrine 1918–1939.* College Station: Texas A&M University Press, 1998.

Office of the Infantry Board. Report. "Artillery-Infantry Test." January 1943. USAFAS.

Operation Cobra. VII Corps in Operation Cobra. File 8-3.1AK Pt. 2. CMH.

Operation RANKIN: Revision of the Spheres of Responsibility. Report by the JCS Planners. File 2025. MC.

Ose, Dieter. *Entscheidung im Westen 1944.* Stuttgart: Beiträge zur Militär und Kreigsgeschichte, 1985.

————. "Rommel and Rundstedt: The 1944 Panzer Controversy." *Military Affairs* 50 (January 1986): 7–11.

————. *Entscheidung im Westen 1944: Der Oberbefehlshaber West die Abwehr der aliierte.* Stuttgart: Deutsche Verlags-Anstalt, 1982.

Overy, Richard. *Why the Allies Won the War.* New York: W. W. Norton and Company, 1995.

Palmer, Robert R., Bell I. Wiley, and William R. Keast. *The Procurement and Training of Ground Combat Troops.* Washington, D.C.: Office of the Chief of Military History, 1948.

Palmer, Williston Birkhimer. Interview with Williston Brikhimer Palmer. MHI.

Panzer Lehr Meldungen, Befehle, Anordungen and Fernschreiben. Microfilm. T315. Roll 2292. NARA.

Paret, Peter. "The New Military History." *Parameters* (Autumn 1991): 10–18.

Parrish, Thomas. *The American Codebreakers: The U.S. Role in Ultra.* Chelsea, Mich.: Scarbourough, 1991.

————. *Roosevelt and Churchill: Partners in Politics and War.* New York: William Morrow and Company, 1989.

Patton, George S. Papers. LC.

Patterson, Charles G. Reflections on Courtney Hodges. MHI.

Pemsel, Max Joseph. "Comments on the Study: Dealing with the Battle on Normandy." MS C-056. CARL.

Persons, Howard P. "St. Lo Breakthrough." *Military Review* 27 (December 1948): 13–23.

Perret, Geoffrey. *There's a War to Be Won.* New York: Random House, 1991.

Piekalkiewicz, Janusz. *Die Invasion: Frankreich 1944.* Munich: Herbig, 1994.

Pillsbury, Glenn T., et al. Employment of 2d Armored Division in Operation Cobra 25 July–1 Aug 44. Research Report prepared by Committee 3, Officers Advanced Course, The Armored School. Fort Knox, May 1950. USAAC.

Powers, Stephen T. "The Battle of Normandy: The Lingering Controversy." *The Journal of Military History* 56 (July 1992): 455–471.

Quesada, Elwood R. Interview of Lt. Gen Elwood R. Quesada. Air Force Oral History Collection. AFHRA.

————. Papers. DDE.

Raines, Rebecca Robbins. *Getting the Message Through: A Branch History of the U.S. Signal Corps.* Washington, D.C.: Center of Military History, 1996.

Ratliff, Frank G. "The Field Artillery Battalion Fire Direction Center: Its Past, Present and Future." *The Field Artillery Journal* (May–June 1950): 116–119.

Records of the Strategic Bombing Survey. Box 71. RG 243. NARA.

René, Herval. *Bataille de Normandie: Récits de Témoins.* Paris: Editions de Notre Temps, 1947.

Renwick, Robin. *Fighting with Allies: America and Britain in Peace and War.* New York: Times Books, 1996.

Report of the General Board: Chemical Mortar Battalions, Study No. 70. CARL.

Report of the General Board: Organization, Equipment and Tactical Employment of the Infantry Division, Study No. 15. CARL.

Reports Received by U.S. War Department on Use of the Ultra in the European Theater, World War II. SRH-037. CARL.

Reynolds, Michael. *Steel Inferno: I SS Panzer Corps in Normandy.* New York: Sarpedon, 1997.

Rhoades, John F., and Dale E. Strick. *The History of the Fourth Cavalry Reconnaissance Squadron, European Theater of Operations.* Frankfurt: Gerhard Blumlein, n.d.

Ritgen, Helmut. *Die Geschichte der Panzer-Lehr-Division im Westen 1944–1945.* Stuttgart: Motorbuch-Verlag, 1979.

Roberts, A. Eaton. *Five Stars to Victory.* Birmingham, Ala.: Atlas Printing and Engraving, 1949.

Rose, Ben L. *The Saga of the Red Horse.* Nijmegen: N. V. Drukkerig, 1945.

Rossengarten, Adolph G., Jr. "With Ultra from Omaha Beach to Weimar, Germany: A Personal View." *The Journal of Military History* 42 (October 1978): 127–132.

Ruge, Friedrich. *Rommel in Normandy.* Trans. Ursula R. Moessner. San Rafael, Calif.: Presidio Press, 1976.

Russell, Henry D. *The Purge of the 30th Division.* Macon, Ga.: Lyon, Marshall and Brooks, 1948.

Rust, Kenn C. *The 9th Air Force in World War II.* Fallbrook: Aero Publishers, 1967.

Schmidt, Hans. "Battles in Northern France." MS A-973. CARL.

Schramm, Percy. "OKW War Diary 1 April to 18 December, 1944." MS B-034. CARL.

———. "Notes on the Execution of War Diaries in the German Forces." MS A-860. CARL.

Schwerin, Gerhard Graf von. "116th Panzer Division," ETHINT 17. CARL.

Schulz, John. *Unternehmen Overlord: Kampf und Untergang Der Nachtshattenflotte.* Balve: Zimmermann, 1961.

Scutts, Jerry. *Republic P-47 Thunderbolt: The Operational Record.* Osceola, Wis.: MBI Publishing, 1998.

Second Report of the Commanding General of the Army Air Forces to the Secretary of War. 27 February 1945.

Shepard, William Shepard Papers. MHI.

Shrader, Charles R. "World War II Logistics." *Parameters* 25 (Spring 1995): 133–138.

———. "Friendly Fire: The Inevitable Price." *Parameters* XXII (Autumn 1992): 29–44.

———. *Amicide: The Problem of Friendly Fire in Modern War.* Fort Leavenworth: Combat Studies Institute, 1982.

———. *A Comprehensive Bibliography of First Infantry Division Materials in the United States Military History Institute.* Carlisle, 1989.

SHAEF Diary. Book X. January 23, 1944. A-1007. File 2–3.7 CB 8. CMH.

Simon, Max. "Evaluation of Combat Infantry Experience." MS C-055.

Sligh, Robert Bruce. *The National Guard and the National Defense: The Mobilization of the Guard in World War II.* Westport, Conn.: Praeger, 1992.

Smoler, Fredric. "The Secret of the Soldiers Who Didn't Shoot." *American Heritage* 40 (March 1989): 37–45.

Snoke, Elizabeth R. *Dwight D. Eisenhower: A Centennial Biography.* Fort Leavenworth, Kans.: Command and General Staff College, Combat Studies Institute, 1990.

Spaatz, Carl A. *The Papers of Carl A. Spaatz.* Manuscript Collection. LC.

Spearhead in the West, 1941–1945, the Third Armored Division. Frankfurt-am-Main: Kunst and Wervedruck, 1945.

Speidel, Hans. "OB West: A Study in Command." MS B-718. CARL.

————. *We Defended Normandy.* Trans. Ian Colvin. London: Herbert Jenkins, 1951.

————. *Invasion 1944: Rommel and the Normandy Campaign.* Chicago: Henry Regnery, 1950.

Spiller, Roger J. "S. L. A. Marshall and the Ratio of Fire," *RUSI Journal* 133 (Winter 1988): 63–71.

St-Lo. Reprint. Washington, D.C.: Center of Military History, 1984.

Stanton, Shelby L. *World War II Order of Battle.* New York: Galahad, 1984.

Steadman, Kenneth A. "The Evolution of the Tank in the U.S. Army, 1919–1940." *Combat Studies Institute Report No. 1.* Fort Leavenworth, Kans.: Combat Studies Institute, U.S. Army Command and General Staff College, 21 April 1982.

————. "A Comparative Look at Air-Ground Support Doctrine and Practice in World War II." *Combat Studies Institute Report No. 2.* Fort Leavenworth, Kans.: Combat Studies Institute, U.S. Army Command and General Staff College, 1 September 1982.

Story of the 371st Fighter Group in the E.T.O.

Stussman, Morton J. *60th Follow Thru.* Stuttgart: Scheufele.

Sullivan, John J. "The Botched Air Support for Operation Cobra." *Parameters* XVIII (March 1988): 97–110.

————. *Overlord's Eagles: Operations of the United States Army Air Forces in the Invasion of Normandy in World War II.* Jefferson, N.C.: McFarland & Company, 1997.

Supply Situation of the Units Engaged on the Normandy Front, Army Group B, 1 July–31 July 1944. Microfilm. T311. Roll 1. NARA.

Sweet, John J. T. *Mounting the Threat: The Battle of Bourguébus Ridge, 18–23 July 1944.* San Rafael, Calif.: Presidio Press, 1977.

Sylvan, William C. War Diary. William C. Sylvan Papers. MHI.

Synthesis of Experiences in the Use of Ultra Intelligence by U.S. Army Field Commands in the European Theater of Operations. SRH-006. CARL.

Tactical Air Operations in Europe. 19 May 1945. MHI.

Taylor, Charles E. *Miss You: The World War II Letters of Barbara Wooddall Taylor and Charles E. Taylor.* Judy Barrett Litoff, David C. Smith, Barbara Wooddall Taylor, and Charles E. Taylor, eds. Athens: University of Georgia Press, 1990.

Toby, Nelson W. *History, 7th Field Artillery, World War II.* USAFAS.

Todd, Walter E. Report of Investigation of Bombing July 24–25. In U.S. Strategic Bombing Survey, Europe War, G-2 Target File. 2478. Box 71. RG 243. NARA.

Trahan, E. A., ed. *A History of the 2d Armored Division.* Atlanta: Albert Love Enterprises, 1946.

Triepel, Gerhard. "91st Airborne Division Artillery." MS B-469. CARL.

Troxel, Orlando Collette, Jr. *The Papers of Colonel Orlando Collette Troxel, Jr.* MHI.

Urban, Matt, and Charles Conrad. *The Hero We Nearly Forgot: The Matt Urban Story.* Holland, Mich.: The Matt Urban Story Incorporated, 1989.

U.S. Forces. European Theater. *Reports of the General Board.* 131 Vols. MHI. CARL.

U.S. Strategic Bombing Survey, Europe War, G-2 Target File 2478. NARA.

U.S. War Department, *Handbook on German Military Forces*. Reprint. Intro. Stephen E. Ambrose. Baton Rouge: Louisiana State University, 1990.

U.S. War Department. Reports Received by U.S. War Department on Use of the Ultra in the European Theater, World War II. SRH-037. CARL.

U.S. War Department. "Synthesis of Experiences in the Use of Ultra Intelligence by U.S. Army Field Commands in the European Theater of Operations." SRH-006. CARL.

Van Crevald, Martin. *Fighting Power: German and U.S. Army Performance, 1939–45*. Westport, Conn.: Greenwood, 1982.

Vandenberg, Hoyt S. *The Papers of Hoyt S. Vandenberg*. Manuscript Collections. LC.

Vannoy, Allyn R., and Jay Karamales. *Against the Panzers: United States Infantry versus German Tanks, 1944–1945*. Jefferson: McFarland & Company, Inc., 1996.

Waddell, Steve R. *United States Army Logistics: The Normandy Campaign, 1944*. Westport, Conn.: Greenwood Press, 1944.

Wade, Gary. Transcribed "Conversations with General J. Lawton Collins." *Combat Studies Institute Report No. 5*. Fort Leavenworth, Kans.: Combat Studies Institute, U.S. Army Command and General Staff College.

Waitt, Alden, H. "Gas on a Hostile Shore." In Joseph I. Greene, ed., *The Infantry Journal Reader*. Garden City, N.Y.: Doubleday, Doran, 1943.

Walsh, John J. Papers. DDE.

Wanke, Paul. "American Military Psychiatry and Its Role among Ground Forces in World War II." *Journal of Military History* 63 (January 1999): 127–146.

War Journal of Headquarters Army Group B. 1–31 July 1944. Microfilm. T311. Roll 1. NARA.

Ware, Francis L. Family Doctor to 2nd Battalion, 12th Infantry Regiment, 4th Infantry Division. MHI.

Weigley, Russell F. *Eisenhower's Lieutenants*. Bloomington: Indiana University Press, 1981.

———. "From the Normandy Beaches to the Falaise-Argentan Pocket: A Critique of Allied Operational Planning." *Military Review* 70 (September 1990): 45–64.

Weinberg, Gerhard L. *Germany, Hitler and World War II*. Cambridge: Cambridge University Press, 1995.

Wells, Mark K. *Courage and Air Warfare: The Allied Aircrew Experience in the Second World War*. London: Frank Cass, 1995.

Whitlow, Robert S. Ultra Intelligence Procedures - IX Air Force, 24 July 1944–1 June 1945. MHI.

Wilke, Gustav. "5th Parachute Division (6 June–24 July 1944)." MS B-820. CARL.

Williams, F. D. G. *SLAM: The Influence of S. L. A. Marshall on the United States Army*. Fort Monroe, La.: Office of the Command Historian, United States Army Training and Doctrine Command, 1990.

Willis, Donald J. *The Incredible Years*. Ames: Iowa State University Press, 1988.

Wilson, John B. *Maneuver and Firepower: The Evolution of Divisions and Brigades*. Washington, D.C.: Center of Military History, 1998.

Wilson, Theodore A. "Who Fought and Why? The Assignment of American Soldiers to Combat." In Paul Addison and Angus Calder, eds., *Time to Kill: The Soldier's Experience of War in the West, 1939–1945*. London: Pimlico, 1997.

Wilt, Alan F. *War from the Top: German and British Military Decision Making during World War II*. Bloomington: Indiana University Press, 1990.

———. *The Atlantic Wall: Hitler's Defense in the West, 1941–1945*. Ames: Iowa State University Press, 1975.

Winterbotham, F. W. *The Ultra Secret*. New York: Dell, 1979.

Wolfert, Thomas O. *From Acts to Cobra: Evolution of Close Air Support Doctrine in World War II*. Maxwell Air Force Base, Ala.: Air Command and Staff College and University, 1988.

World War II Survey. MHI.

Wray, Timothy A. *Standing Fast: German Defensive Doctrine on the Russian Front during World War II*. Fort Leavenworth, Kans.: Combat Studies Institute, 1986.

Ziegelmann, Fritz. "The Battle for St. Lo." MS B-464, CARL.

———. "History of the 352d Infantry Division." MS B-432, CARL.

———. "Operations from 25 July until 30 July." MS B-489, CARL.

Zijlstra, Gerrit. *Diary of an Air War*. New York: Vantage Press, 1977.

Zimmermann, Bodo. OB WEST, Command Relationships (1943–1945). MS B-308, CARL.

Zuckerman, Solly. *From Apes to Warlords: The Autobiography of Solly Zuckerman*. London: Hamilton, 1978.

Index

About the Book

In Operation Cobra, six U.S. divisions during 6 dramatic days in Normandy ended the stalemate on the Western Front, breaking through German defenses after 7 weeks of grueling attrition warfare. *After D-Day* examines the experiences of U.S. soldiers in the July 25–30, 1944, Normandy campaign: their mistakes, hardships, and fears, as well as their leadership, courage, and determination.

Drawing on original archival sources, Carafano argues that previous accounts of Operation Cobra are flawed. Standard explanations of its success—the force of air power, innovative tactics, superior logistics, the inestimable value of "citizen-soldiers," hedgerow-busting "rhino" tanks—are in fact myths. And serious mistakes were made: one of the most famous U.S. generals, Omar Bradley, ordered strategic bombing close to U.S. lines, a decision that led to the killing and maiming of hundreds of U.S. soldiers by "friendly fire." Nonetheless, Carafano demonstrates, "operational flexibility"—the ability of commanders to exercise effective combat leadership and take advantage of troop strengths and material advantages—resulted in Allied victory.

Lt. Col. James Jay Carafano has held a variety of command and staff positions in tactical, operational, and strategic assignments with the U.S. Army. He has taught European and military history at Mount St. Mary College, U.S. Army Field Artillery School, and the U.S. Military Academy at West Point.